Digging

Second Edition

Deeper

A Canadian Reporter's Research Guide

Robert Cribb
Dean Jobb
David McKie
Fred Vallance-Jones

OXFORD
UNIVERSITY PRESS

OXFORD
UNIVERSITY PRESS

8 Sampson Mews, Suite 204, Don Mills, Ontario M3C 0H5
www.oupcanada.com

Oxford University Press is a department of the University of Oxford.
It furthers the University's objective of excellence in research, scholarship,
and education by publishing worldwide in

Oxford   New York

Auckland   Cape Town   Dar es Salaam   Hong Kong   Karachi
Kuala Lumpur   Madrid   Melbourne   Mexico City   Nairobi
New Delhi   Shanghai   Taipei   Toronto

With offices in

Argentina   Austria   Brazil   Chile   Czech Republic   France   Greece
Guatemala   Hungary   Italy   Japan   Poland   Portugal   Singapore
South Korea   Switzerland   Thailand   Turkey   Ukraine   Vietnam
Oxford is a trade mark of Oxford University Press
in the UK and in certain other countries

Published in Canada by Oxford University Press

Library and Archives Canada Cataloguing in Publication

Digging deeper : a Canadian reporter's research guide / Robert Cribb ... [et al.]. – 2nd ed.

Includes index.

ISBN 978-0-19-543230-5

1. Investigative reporting—Canada—Handbooks, manuals, etc. 2. Reporters and reporting—Canada.
3. Research—Canada—Handbooks, manuals, etc. I. Cribb, Robert M. (Robert Miles), 1967–

PN4914.I58D53 2010   070.4'30971   C2010-901561-4

Cover image: Edvanderhoek/Gettyimages

Oxford University Press is committed to our environment. This book is printed on
Forest Stewardship Council certified paper, harvested from a responsibly managed forest.

Printed and bound in Canada.

3 4 5 – 15 14 13

Contents

Acknowledgements

To my family, Louise, Laura, Anna, Kathleen, and Caroline who endure my near obsession for journalism and journalism education and have always been there for me.

—*Fred Vallance-Jones*

I would like to thank my employer, the Canadian Broadcasting Corporation, the Canadian Association of Journalists, and the American organization Investigative Reporters and Editors for inspiring me to become a better investigative journalist and teacher. My ultimate thanks goes to Deirdre for her love and patience as I continue to learn my craft.

—*David McKie*

For Ally in gracious thanks for showing me the real rewards of digging deep.

—*Robert Cribb*

I would like to thank Cliff Newman for making this book a reality, and Kerry Oliver for her support as it was being written. I am also grateful to my colleagues at the University of King's College School of Journalism—Stephen Kimber, Kim Kierans, Tim Currie, Sue Newhook, Kelly Toughill, Fred Vallance-Jones, Doug Kirkaldy and Kelly Porter—for their advice and encouragement.

—*Dean Jobb*

Part I

Getting Started

1

An Introduction to Investigative Journalism

Investigative journalism is not a career path for the faint of heart.

When the first edition of *Digging Deeper* appeared in 2006, we wrote of the deep satisfaction that can come from 'seeing your hard-hitting, impeccably researched story roll off the presses or hit the airwaves.'

The words seem almost quaint now.

At the time, Facebook was in its infancy, cell phones were still mostly for making phone calls, and most investigative journalism was done by traditional media organizations. Now, Facebook is a reporting tool, reporters write and file on cell phones, and foundations and non-profit organizations are taking an increasing role in funding investigative work. And while plenty of investigative stories still roll off the presses or hit the airwaves, many others debut online.

The times are changing, and the change is affecting investigative journalism as much as any other field. The online explosion has created new ways to dig up information and present it. And new sources of information appear every day.

In this context, a revision of *Digging Deeper* is not just a good idea, but pretty much essential.

The one thing that hasn't changed, though, is the hard work that goes into investigative work.

Getting to the publication, web-post or broadcast takes hard work, perseverance, and creativity. There are often long hours, elusive sources, and legal ramifications to consider. Get it wrong, and you can do severe damage to your credibility.

Our desire to help journalists get it right was the main reason we wrote *Digging Deeper* in the first place. There just wasn't a good investigative manual written from a Canadian point of view. Now, the time has come to take it to the next level.

We have been gratified by the overwhelmingly positive response to the first edition and by the fact it has found a home on the bookshelves of many journalists and researchers, and on the curriculum of quite a number of university and college journalism programs across the country. We certainly hope this second edition will prove to be as valuable as the craft of investigative writing continues to redefine itself.

But What Is Investigative Journalism?

One of the most useful definitions comes from the US organization, Investigative Reporters and Editors (IRE), which used a poll of its members to choose the following: investigative journalism is 'in-depth reporting that discloses something that someone wants to keep secret, and is largely the reporter's own work.' Later, the organization expanded the definition to include 'uncovering systemic failures and misguided policies.'[1]

For this book, we broaden the definition further to include short-term investigative work done by daily journalists, bloggers and citizen journalists, and investigations by non-journalists. However, the core principle is the same for all: investigators seek the truth. By that, we mean the facts, as best as they can be determined, laid out fairly and comprehensively.

At their best, investigative stories reveal injustice and misery, expose wrongdoing, force accountability, uncover wasteful spending, and point out the failures of public officials or public systems. Ideally, the stories move people in authority to fix the problems.

Investigative journalists play a critical role in our democratic society, acting as a counterweight to the many forces that seek to control the flow of information and obscure the truth.

As you proceed through this book, you will be introduced to some of the best examples of Canadian investigative work in recent years—work that has ranged from probing Taser use by police officers, to uncovering long-hidden details of an environmental fiasco in Nova Scotia, to helping find a serial killer on the mean streets of Vancouver's Downtown Eastside.

The material here is structured to take you from the general to the specific. You'll read first about the philosophy of investigation, and how it differs from everyday journalism. From there, you'll learn about the basic building blocks of investigations, and the wide array of public records available to investigators. We'll talk about the investigative interview, about specialized skills such as computer-assisted reporting, and about special situations, such as going undercover. Finally, we'll talk about organizing the material and writing the story.

We start with philosophy.

Where Daily Journalism Ends and the Investigation Begins

When Clifton Richards accused the Toronto Police of arresting him merely because he is black, it was a sensational but short-lived story. Richards, an immigrant from Jamaica, was stopped by Constable Scott Aikman, who had become suspicious about him driving a van with three passengers. A struggle ensued between the two men, and Richards was charged with resisting arrest and trying to choke the officer. He was convicted in the lower courts, and he appealed.

During the 1999 appeal, he raised the spectre of what has become known as *racial profiling*, saying he had really been stopped for 'driving while black'. Complaints about such discrimination had long circulated in the city's black community, whose leaders felt blacks faced systemic discrimination at the hands of the city's mostly white police force. The issue had gained little traction outside of the black community, however, and the Richards case did little to change that.

After a flurry of coverage in the Toronto newspapers, the Richards story died. The appeal court later quashed his conviction, although for reasons not directly connected to his claim of racial profiling.[2]

The coverage of the Richards case was typical of daily news reporting of such contentious issues: honest accounts of what two opposing sides said and what took place in a public venue (in this case, the courts). This kind of routine journalism is very important. It constitutes most of the news coverage you see in daily and weekly newspapers, on television and radio, and on the Internet. It drives public debate on a day-to-day basis, contributes to our understanding of complex issues, and routinely delivers information that would otherwise have been kept secret. It is the life's work of thousands upon thousands of journalists and bloggers. But, as any general assignment or beat reporter knows, it has limitations. In their effort to produce carefully balanced stories, writers typically don't attempt to determine which side is right. Without the time and other resources to delve more deeply into the facts, this is the only fair way to proceed. The audience is left to decide which side to believe.

Even print reporters, who typically have more time than their broadcast or Internet cousins, must often take a story from idea to finished copy within one day and often have to file for online editions as soon as they get the bare facts. Increasingly, they also have to carry audio recorders and video cameras to collect multimedia content for news websites. All this means the quest is limited to those sources a journalist can reach on that day, and to those documents that are easily obtained. Even reporters who have developed impressive networks of sources and become skilled at gathering the necessary elements in a few hours may still lack the time to verify facts, probe statements made by sources, or explore the broader context. Without a doubt, continued daily reporting on a subject can dramatically improve the depth of a reporter's writing, but most staffers find themselves pushed relentlessly from story to story.

The treadmill speeds along even faster for broadcast and online reporters. They may be expected to file several stories on several different subjects on the same day, and these writers must cope with the additional technological constraints. For many television reporters, this means all of the research and interviewing for a story must be completed by early to mid-afternoon. This allows time for reviewing shots, writing and recording scripts, and editing the final product for the broadcast. This leaves even less time for anything beyond the most basic coverage. Online reporters may have to file a story every time there is a new development. So, no matter how good the journalist, the finished product may be just one slice of the bigger story.

One consequence of so many early deadlines is that the news cycle often becomes the spin cycle. Armies of media-relations officers are deployed by governments, corporations, and interest groups. These professional information managers offer invaluable help to reporters who need a quick comment, position, or fact, but these people also act as a filter, ensuring that the carefully crafted message of their employers gets through to the public. Access to key players is restricted, and the media-relations people become conduits for whatever information is to be released. Reporters have little choice but to co-operate because they need someone by their deadline.

It becomes a symbiotic relationship. The reporter gets a comment; the media-relations person makes sure the comment is 'on message'. But it is often an unequal battle. The media-relations community has made a careful study of the media's methods and knows how to exploit weaknesses. In his book, *In The News: The Practice of Media Relations in Canada*, William Wray Carney devotes an entire chapter to the mechanics of the news cycle and succinctly captures the challenges faced by journalists at daily news outlets:

> Generally speaking, day-to-day reporters are rushed, inexpert, trying to get to the heart of the matter as quickly as possible and working under career-ending deadline pressure.... The journalist relies on the communicator for basic information and access to expert authorities, while the communicator relies on the journalist to disseminate information and reach key audiences.[3]

A good example of this symbiotic relationship is the close partnership between Canadian media and Statistics Canada, the national data agency.

Studies from StatsCan, as reporters call it, get widespread coverage in Canadian news media, not only because taking the pulse of the nation is important work, but because of the agency's well-oiled media-relations machine. StatsCan distributes information to media outlets about significant new studies, as well as routine releases such as the change in the inflation rate, early every weekday morning. Media-savvy officials write news releases and other accompanying materials in an easily accessible style, so all a reporter has to do is call the necessary human sources before writing the story. Contacts are typically provided to ease that part of the job.

Take, for example, a release on Canadians' charitable donations and volunteerism that was put out on the morning of 8 June 2009. It was promoted not only by StatsCan itself, but also, in a separate release, by a national volunteer advocacy group.

StatsCan's release helpfully summarized a much larger document that the agency had published on its website. With regional breakdowns of the data, the statistics agency ensured there would be interest in all parts of the country. The result was coverage by the Canadian Press wire service, *The Globe and Mail*, the *Calgary Herald*, the *Winnipeg Free Press*, CBC.ca, CTV, and others.

It was an easy story to get and to write. Little, if any, investigation was needed to land it. Everyone got something. The media got a story and Statistics Canada got publicity for its work.

Manipulation of the daily media goes well beyond the relatively simple mechanism of the handout. Journalists conducting interviews often encounter people who have been specially schooled in how to disarm and use members of the media to deliver a canned message to the public. Former CBS executive producer cum media trainer George Merlis counsels those facing interviews to craft 'intentional message statements', which can be deftly dropped into responses to reporters' questions.[4]

'I tell my clients to never go into an interview without at least five IMSs [intentional message statements],' he writes. Later, he explains how an interviewee can easily shift from the reporter's question to an IMS by paying 'factual lip service' to the question, then using a verbal bridge to move on to the prepared message.[5]

Canadian media trainer Barry McLoughlin also counsels clients to use the bridging technique before 'driv[ing] your message back onto your message track.' His firm, McLoughlin Media, suggests using the McLoughlin Wedge®, a technique to insert a pre-planned message into an interview in short chunks, beginning with an opening statement. 'Front-end-load your message,' his firm's *Encountering the Media* guide counsels, 'so if you get interrupted, you've already got your message out.'

One of the best ways to overcome such manipulation is investigation.

The trainers know this.

Carney and Merlis counsel great caution when dealing with the threat of investigative journalists. Reporters who have mastered investigative techniques will detour around intentional message statements, taking the time to find reluctant or elusive sources, turn up documents, file freedom-of-information requests, and wait out media-relations people who so often use delay as a tactic to frustrate the conventional journalist's search for the facts.

In the fall of 2002, when Jim Rankin and a team of *Toronto Star* journalists published their investigative series on racial profiling in the Toronto Police Service (entitled Race and Crime),[6] they provoked a more substantial response than the Clifton Richards stories had done several years earlier. The advance of time and the growing sensitivity to minority concerns was certainly a factor, but more important was the tremendous depth of the *Star* series. The reporters analyzed the Police Service's own electronic database of arrests, and made a compelling case for the allegation that the police were pulling over black people more often than people of other colours for certain motor vehicle offences, such as driving without registration papers, that could not have been observed from outside the vehicle.

The *Star* series rocked the city. Even though the police and the police union denied the allegations as forcefully as ever, this time the newspaper offered compelling evidence, sparking a thorough public debate. It displayed the power of investigative journalism to foster change.

More than seven years after the original series, Rankin and the *Star* published a February 2010 follow-up based on additional data obtained through a freedom-of-information request that wound up requiring seven years of appeals, court cases, and intense negotiations. But while the police fought release of the data, once the story came out that officers stopped and questioned black people three times as often as whites, the police chief—not the same chief as in 2002—didn't dispute the findings, and he sat down with the *Star* to explore the problem and search for solutions.[7]

The sea change had much to do with Rankin's methodical and careful approach, his commitment to getting it right. This highlights the responsibilities borne by the investigative reporter.

An investigative journalist aims to tell it as it is, not as people say it is. The expectations for thoroughness, accuracy, and authority are much greater than with daily journalism. Also, the editor or news director is going to expect something extraordinary for the effort and time poured into the story, and the reporter had better do everything possible to deliver or risk getting reassigned to more conventional duties.

Investigative journalism is not a career path for the faint of heart. At many times from the beginning to the end of an investigative project, reporters will experience the terror that their story might not come together at all. But some fundamentals to the craft can help allay those moments of terror and encourage the success of even a novice reporter. We'll call them the 'twelve keys' to successful investigations.

The Twelve Keys

1. Curiosity
Curiosity may have killed the cat but it has given many an investigative story life. It gives rise to the most important questions: *I wonder what happened? I wonder why? Who was responsible? How much money was involved? What happens next? How is it supposed to work? How does it really work?*

The investigative journalist must viscerally want the answers to questions such as these. Curiosity is the engine that powers many other crucial parts of the investigation. It also keeps you going when obstacles and frustrations impede you along the way.

2. Preparation
This one can't be overemphasized. Being prepared will always, *always* pay off for the investigative reporter. Consider interviews: in daily journalism, they are often conducted on the fly with little time to get to know much about the interviewee, or sometimes even the subject. Investigative interviews, however, are conducted only after careful preparation. You will want to research prospective interviewees, find out not only what they do and what they should know, but also what they are like and how they may react in an interview. You will also examine

documents, notes from previous interviews, and electronic data, drawing up a list of questions or talking points before you come close to doing an interview. Preparation is the key to other parts of the investigative process as well, especially writing. You will spend as much or more time on organizing material as on writing the story.

3. Organization

There are probably as many systems for staying organized as there are investigative reporters. The trick is to find one that works for you.

Cecil Rosner, a Winnipeg-based journalist with CBC Television, learned this lesson when he interviewed a heart researcher who was involved in a professional dispute. 'Every time [the researcher] spoke with someone, there would be a separate entry, dated and timed, in his binder,' explains Rosner. 'It was all there. And it allowed him to prove a case forcefully.'[8]

Rosner went on to co-author a book on David Milgaard, who spent 23 years in jail after being wrongfully convicted of murder. Milgaard always said he was innocent, and Rosner's book helped prove it. While writing the Milgaard book, Rosner applied what he had learned from the heart researcher: 'I organized material in file folders and binders, each devoted to a separate topic or chapter in Milgaard's life. All the material within each binder was chronologically arranged.' Rosner swears by the chronology as a way to make sense of material—one of the biggest challenges faced by investigative writers.

On any project, more and more information accumulates as the researcher digs deeper into the subject. There will be interview notes and transcripts, electronic files, links to websites and printouts, notations, databases and spreadsheet files, and any number of other paper documents. You'll know what each one is for when you obtain it, but weeks or months later, you can become overwhelmed by it all. Some reporters use manila file folders to stay organized, others keep spreadsheets, and still others use small file cards. Some make 'to do' and 'to interview' lists; others keep all of the phone numbers they come across on a single sheet or in a single file. The key is to be able to quickly find any document or interview you need and understand its significance, as well as to come to understand the bigger picture and develop a list of key points. If you stay organized throughout, you will save hours, or days, of work when you reach the writing stage of your project.

4. Patience

It takes patience to research and write an investigative story. You are always waiting for something, whether it be a reluctant source to return your calls, public officials to respond to freedom-of-information requests, or inspiration to hit.

For those accustomed to the faster pace of daily reporting, all of this waiting can be frustrating. But it is often the difference between getting most of the story and getting all of it. Some projects can take months to go from idea to publication or broadcast, and you will face many pressures along the way to speed that process up. Of course, you need to know when you have done enough research, when that last document isn't worth waiting for. But rushing can lead to incomplete, and inaccurate, stories that will fade away as quickly as yesterday's headlines.

5. Tenacity

This is one of the most important qualities for the investigative journalist. Many times, you will face obstacles that will tempt you to give up or give in. Bureaucrats will fight to stop you from obtaining public documents. Key sources will be difficult to find or reluctant to speak to you. Databases will seem impenetrable and unintelligible. Sometimes, you just won't have a clue how to nail a crucial piece of information. The key is sticking with it.

Persistence paid off for Lindsay Kines, the *Vancouver Sun* police reporter who first told the stories of women who had vanished from the city's Downtown Eastside. The drug users and prostitutes were part of society's lowest stratum living in what is perceived to be, by far, Canada's poorest and most dangerous neighbourhood. The Downtown Eastside comprises a few bleak blocks of rundown hotels, unsavoury criminals, and a massive drug trade. Kines started with a single story in 1997 about a woman looking for her missing sister. Over time, more cases came to light, and Kines stuck with the story, developing contacts on the street and trust within the police department.

He faced resistance in his own newsroom and other media outlets mostly ignored the story. But, in time, Kines would help uncover what became the largest serial murder case in Canadian history. His work, and that of fellow reporters Kim Bolan and Lori Culbert, helped reveal not only the extent of the slaughter, but also the sorely deficient initial investigation by the Vancouver Police. 'The longer I stayed on the story, the more people felt comfortable with me and trusted me,' Kines said. 'In the end, it helped me get crucial interviews with disgruntled cops who had worked on the investigation. They trusted me because they said my reporting on the case had been fair, and when it came time to blow the lid off all the problems with the initial investigation, they trusted me to tell it.'[9]

Kines and Bolan went on to break the story of Robert William Pickton, the Port Coquitlam pig farmer, who later was convicted of second-degree murder in the deaths of six women: Sereena Abotsway, Mona Wilson, Andrea Joesbury, Marnie Frey, Brenda Wolfe, and Georgina Papin. The two journalists won a National Newspaper Award for that story, and, along with Culbert, were runners up for the Michener Award for their series.

Persistence and tenacity over many years allowed Kines and his colleagues to overcome monumental community indifference and tell important stories.

6. Resourcefulness

Not everything will be obvious or easy when you are pursuing an investigative story; you will need to use your initiative in deciding where to look. Information about people can be harvested from unlikely places on the Internet. Online records of a person's political contributions or property-tax assessments can reveal his or her home address. Documents obtained through freedom-of-information requests yield leads that take you to new and unexpected facts. While daily reporters generally use their sources directly—describing, for example, what a new StatsCan study reports or what a politician said—investigative reporters often use sources as means to an end. A report or study might offer you a name that leads to an interview with someone who can put you in touch with the person you really want to talk to, and so on. The creative use of the available resources, which is the subject of much of this book, can help you to assemble your information successfully.

7. Thoroughness and completeness

Investigative reporting differs from the daily variety in that you have the time, and the obligation, to be thorough and complete. While a daily story remains tightly focused, an investigation follows up numerous leads and goes down many roads, not all of them productive. You want to know that you have exhausted, or very nearly exhausted, the possibilities before you state something to be true. The need to be thorough applies to every aspect of an investigation. When you are engaged in the early prospecting stage, you want to *thoroughly* canvass existing information on a subject. This will help you *thoroughly* plan your research. Once into the research stage, you must *thoroughly* investigate leads. You should *thoroughly* prepare to write, and the writing itself needs to be *thorough* and complete. The result is authority and the potential to make a real difference.

'The need to file for deadline should never override the need to do exhaustive research,' says Rosner, regarding his Milgaard book. 'But at a certain point the journalist must ask: has enough work been done to validate my original hypothesis? If the answer is yes, then the story can be written or broadcast.'[10]

The last thing you want to do is go to press or to air and discover you left out a couple of important details or you made a statement unaware of a crucial mitigating fact. As it is, you will worry enough even if you have everything right, so you don't want to add to your anxiety.

8. Attention and observation

Investigators need to be assiduous observers, always on the lookout for the unexpected and, just as importantly, for any facts that contradict their hypothesis. Investigators read documents with extra attention, listen just a little more carefully during interviews, and constantly assess the progress of their projects. While interviewing in the field, the investigative journalist pays special attention to the surroundings. Are there family pictures or other objects that will provide an easy entrance into a discussion of the subject's personal life? Are there objects in the office that provide other insights into the character of the person?

The same principle applies when visiting the scene of a crime or an accident. What can you learn about the events simply by observing?

9. Open-mindedness

You want to be accurate and right. You don't want to dissect a government program only to have the media-relations department successfully discredit your story. You certainly don't want to accuse someone of wrongdoing and then find out that mistakes have left you open to a million-dollar libel suit.

Another undesirable outcome could go as such: Imagine publishing an exposé only to discover that some aspect of the story you ignored along the way is more important than what you published, and will now be scooped up by competing media. This suggests that it will behoove you to keep an open mind. No matter what your hypothesis is, and no matter what pressure you may be under to deliver the story you originally conceived, you have to be ready to change course. Reporters working on investigative stories often become deeply involved in the work and find themselves contained in a narrow silo of facts and evidence that can blind them to what else may be going on. Constantly challenge your assumptions. Try just as hard to disprove your hypothesis as to prove it.

10. Care, caution, and discretion

Those doing investigations often have the reputations of others in their hands. With this power comes great responsibility.

Perhaps even more so than in daily reporting, discretion is king. If you promise confidentiality to a source, for example, you must adhere to that promise not only for ethical reasons, but also because your own reputation is your most valuable asset. It will not remain intact for long if you are untrustworthy.

Livelihoods, even lives, can be on the line, as in the *Star's* aforementioned Race and Crime series. 'One component of the reporting involved interviews with black Toronto police officers, both active and retired,' remembers reporter Jim Rankin. 'If it became known at police headquarters that certain officers had talked to us, it would have surely meant big-time grief, and possibly the end of careers. While some of the interviews became part of the story, with identities protected in the case of active officers, one active black officer painted such a detailed picture of what he had personally encountered that he couldn't be used at all. Bits and pieces of his story, if read by fellow officers, would have identified him in an instant.'

11. Skepticism

Paired with the need to keep an open mind is the equally important need to maintain a healthy skepticism. This shouldn't be confused with cynicism, which the *Canadian Oxford Dictionary* defines as 'doubting or despising sincerity and merit'.[11] A skeptic doesn't dismiss merit, but instead tests every fact or statement that comes his or her way. Facts stated in press releases, for example, are checked with original sources rather than just repeated. The same goes for statements made by sources. They need to be verified by other sources or in documents. The better the information seems for your story, the more you need to be skeptical until you are certain that you have solid facts. Skepticism is at the heart of developing an investigative frame of mind.

12. Time

Buttressing the 11 key elements mentioned above is the one that makes them all possible. Whether an investigation takes two weeks, two months, or two years, it is the luxury of time that allows the extensive research, backgrounding, and thinking to unfold. Time is the elixir that allows ideas to percolate and evolve, and allows the reporter to build the patchwork and connect the dots to bring the investigative story alive.

Of course, this doesn't mean that you can't do investigative journalism if you are also doing daily assignments. You will simply have to fit the work in between other responsibilities. This is not impossible, but requires organization and discipline. If you squeeze in a phone call here and read a document there, you'll be amazed how much work you can get done in the time you didn't know you had.

Conclusion

Many investigative journalists are motivated by something—a sense of outrage, curiosity, call it what you want—that prompts them to continually ask deeper questions. When attempting to peel back the layers that separate truth from folly, Harvey Cashore, an award-winning CBC journalist and author, likes to ask the question, 'How did we get here?'[12] More often that not, such a question can be answered only after rigorous research, which requires time, discipline, and a zeal to uncover details that will prompt citizens to demand action. As such, an investigative journalist's quest for truth has a moral dimension. For their book *Custodians of Conscience: Investigative Journalism and Public Virtue*, James Ettema and Theodore Glasser interviewed some of the top journalists in the United States about their work, and this topic of morality came up:

> Their particular sort of reporting yields stories that are carefully verified and skillfully narrated accounts of specific injury and injustice but stories with a meaning that transcends the facts of the particular case. Their stories call attention to the breakdown of social systems and the disorder within public institutions that cause injury and injustice; in turn, their stories implicitly demand [the] response of public officials—and the public itself— to that breakdown and disorder. Thus the work of these reporters calls us, as a society, to decide what is, and what is not, an outrage to our sense of moral order and to consider our expectations for our officials, our institutions, and ultimately ourselves.
>
> *In this way, investigative journalists are custodians of public conscience.*[13]
> [Emphasis added.]

As we see from this observation, the result of an investigation may be *subjective,* in that a journalist achieves his or her desire to prompt discussion and action. However, the methodology is painstakingly *objective.* Media scholar Philip Meyer likes to talk about 'objectivity of method' and 'subjectivity of purpose'. We explore the implications of this distinction in the rest of this book.

Suggestions for Further Reading

Rosner, Cecil. *Behind the Headlines: A History of Investigative Journalism in Canada.* Don Mills, ON: Oxford University Press, 2008.

Ruvinsky, Maxine. *Investigative Reporting in Canada.* Don Mills, ON: Oxford University Press, 2008.

2 The Nuts and Bolts of Investigations

Researching an investigative story is like assembling a jigsaw puzzle—a very hard one.

Think investigations, and you may recall the famed *Washington Post* duo, Bob Woodward and Carl Bernstein, working 18-hour days pursuing the Watergate story until they helped bring down a president in 1974. Anyone who has read their book, *All the President's Men*,[1] or seen the movie with Dustin Hoffman and Robert Redford, will have some idea of the rigour, and the tedium, involved in an investigation, the hours spent on the telephone, the reams of documents to read, and the moments of both good and bad luck.

Researching an investigative story is like assembling a jigsaw puzzle—a very hard one. Most of the pieces (the facts, people, and events) are missing and, to make the task harder, the cover of the puzzle box is gone. The journalist must look high and low to find the bits, and may have little sense of where they go and what the picture should look like once the puzzle is completed. Many people have seen all or parts of the picture—these are the journalist's sources—but they cannot agree on what it looks like. A few people will refuse to disclose what they saw, while others will be deliberately misleading.

To find the pieces of your particular puzzle and to fit them together correctly, you must have a research plan that sets out the work to be done. Often, a single fact gleaned from one source or document will be the key to finding other records or sources that may have been overlooked. You must have the flexibility to alter the plan as you go, but a systematic approach ensures that time is not wasted.

Each investigation is unique, but most will follow a well-worn path from finding the idea to doing preliminary research using secondary sources and interviews, moving on to detailed research using documents and interviews, before culminating in the collation and writing of the material. Each step builds on the last, and doing each one well helps build a strong foundation for the story you will ultimately publish or broadcast.

The first step is finding something to write about.

What Makes a Good Investigative Story?

Investigative stories can be on almost any topic imaginable and may take many approaches. They can be multi-part series in major metropolitan newspapers, revealing unsafe products or secret political deals. They can be segments on television shows such as the CBC's *the fifth estate*. They can be one-off websites probing deeply into a problem or issue. They can be well-researched stories in the daily section of the paper or in TV newscasts, stories that go beyond the daily handout cycle.

All this said, some stories work better than others. There are certain qualities that are more likely to lead to a successful investigation.

The under-reported story

When *The Hamilton Spectator* investigated the ongoing problem of deliberately set car fires in the vast rural reaches of the southern Ontario city, one of the things that made the story compelling was that it was so under-reported. Even though the fires happened month after month, and the calls often crackled across the emergency scanners in the newsroom, the *Spectator* had written almost nothing about the subject. No special-interest groups had taken up the case, and the topic was virtually ignored by the police and fire departments, despite the fact that car fires are dangerous for those who fight them and amounted to a third of all fire calls in Hamilton in 2002 and 2003. Each fire was so small, it didn't attract much attention. But, put together, property losses from all of the fires were impressive— about $2 million each year. It was the classic under-reported story.[2]

An injustice

Investigations that uncover real injustice will always be well read. The reason the David Milgaard story, discussed in the previous chapter, was such compelling reading is because what happened to this young man was so unjust. Not out of his teens when he was sent to jail, Milgaard was imprisoned for more than two decades before the calm determination of his mother prompted another look at the case—and her son's eventual exoneration by way of DNA evidence.[3]

Corruption or crime

Corruption and/or crime will always make for good investigations, although they will also be some of the most difficult. The stories offer compelling reading and have great potential to make a difference. The Vancouver Police might have cracked the case of the missing women from the Downtown Eastside without the work of Lindsay Kines and his colleagues, but it would have taken them much longer.

A faulty system or process

When *Toronto Star* reporter Robert Cribb fell ill after eating in one of that city's restaurants, he set out to investigate the state of Toronto's eateries, and the food-handling practices that take place out of sight in the kitchen. After a long battle to obtain a city food inspection database, Cribb wrote a blockbuster series of stories revealing not only the poor conditions in many of the city's eateries, but showing that city inspectors, who were supposed to be keeping the food safe, were failing to do the required checks.[4] It was a classic story about a system that was supposed to work one way, but really worked another. The stories prompted the city to crack down on bad eateries and introduce a posting system to alert diners to problems found by inspectors.

A human element

The best stories, including the best investigative stories, have people at their core. Whether the people are those affected by a government process gone wrong, or they are characters central to the story, without a human element nobody will read your ambitious six-part series.

Something new

Any investigative story worthy of the term puts something on the record that wasn't known publicly before. This can take the form of something completely unknown (such as a public figure's involvement in a financial scandal); something widely believed but never proven (e.g., revelations about dirty restaurants); or a previously unrecognized pattern, perhaps drawn from disparate public sources.

A story appropriate for your audience

No matter how good your research, how extensive your interviews, how brilliant your synthesis of the facts, all that work is wasted if nobody watches, listens to, or reads your story. This isn't to say that your audience has to be universal—far from it. But you do need to report for the audience that will see or hear your story. That means if you are writing for a broad, general-interest publication such as a metropolitan daily newspaper, you may not want to launch into an investigation of the mating habits of chimpanzees, but such a story could be perfectly appropriate for a wildlife magazine.

Where Good Ideas Come From

There is no magic to finding ideas. They can come from just about anywhere. Still, some sources are more fruitful than others.

The beat

If you cover a beat, you are already connected to one of the best sources for investigative story ideas. Beat reporters tend to develop significant expertise in their assigned areas, and develop numerous sources. Inevitably, they will come across stories that merit deeper investigation. If you are not on a beat yourself, talk to other reporters who are; they may offer their ideas, or help you develop your own. *The Vancouver Sun*'s missing-women investigation is a perfect example of a story that began on the beat.

Clippings

Daily news stories are often a fruitful source. Sometimes a brief clip will hint at a much bigger story that hasn't received much attention. A story about a disaster may prompt you to begin an investigation of the circumstances that made the disaster possible. On other occasions, an investigation begins because a reporter wants to follow up on promises of action made by officials after previous stories on a subject. *The Hamilton Spectator*'s investigation into Ontario's Drive Clean program[5] began with brief news stories about alleged unfairness and ineptitude in the mandatory emissions testing. That prompted the newspaper to file a freedom-of-information request for data, which the provincial government didn't release for three years (and then only when ordered to do so), eventually resulting in stories that uncovered fraud at testing sites and showed how the science behind claims of air-quality improvements was unreliable. The government moved quickly to make changes to the program.

As you develop as an investigator, you will start to notice stories where you know there is more to be told. It is a good idea to keep a file of such clippings.

Websites

The Internet is filled with good investigative story ideas. Many news outlets archive their more ambitious series online, so you can see the kinds of stories that have been done by reporters in other geographic areas. A problem—be it racial profiling, dirty restaurants, or elder abuse—uncovered in one city may well exist in yours, too.

The Web is also filled with forums and discussion groups where people go to share information about unscrupulous businesses, health issues, and airline safety. Trolling through groups and subscribing to mailing lists can provide a rich harvest of story ideas.

Tipsters

Sometimes, a story will land in your lap by way of a phone call, email, or letter. A lot of other people out there are frustrated that something they feel is important is not getting the coverage it deserves. Much of the time, these calls will not lead to viable investigative projects, but on occasion, they will. Be careful not to immediately dismiss people who seem to be obsessed with a perceived wrong-doing. Sometimes, these people are right, such as the excitable Winnipeg war veteran who kept calling the CBC in the mid-1990s to talk about the chemical warfare experiments he had undergone at Camp Suffield. That tip led to a CBC Manitoba investigation that revealed the harrowing personal stories of veterans who had been used as guinea pigs in Second World War experiments with blistering mustard gas.[6] As part of the probe, the CBC obtained long-classified documents from the Department of National Defence, including photographs; these portrayed the tests in stomach-turning detail. The surviving veterans were eventually compensated by the federal government.

The key to assessing tips is to check them out. Question the tipster to see if the story makes sense and is internally consistent. Once off the phone, do some basic online research. If the tip still seems credible, start digging deeper.

A hunch

Sometimes, a question or detail will just be bugging you, and you'll wonder why something happened or how something works. Following these instincts can lead to top-rate investigative ideas. In the late 1990s, reporters with CBC Radio were concerned about Zyban, a stop-smoking drug that had been the subject of safety concerns. The reporters felt there was more to this story than just one questionable product. They spent five years obtaining a database of adverse drug reactions, and eventually broadcast a series that raised compelling questions about the drug-approval system in Canada, and about the fact that drugs not approved for those under 18 years of age were being administered to children.[7]

Documents

Documents are not only crucial to the investigative process, but they can also be its genesis. The good investigative reporter takes the time to peruse the public accounts, government gazettes, city council agendas, company annual reports, and so on in search of ideas. Watch for unusually large payments, expenditures, and other red flags.

Databases

You will at times discover stories by trolling through a government or other database that you have obtained or built. Reporters usually have something specific in mind when they obtain data, but analysis can reveal unexpected facts. The series on car fires conducted by *The Hamilton Spectator* is a case in point. Trolling through a database of fire calls alerted the newspaper to the frequency and timing of deliberately set vehicle fires.

Friends and neighbours

The investigative reporter is never really off duty. Ideas can come from casual comments uttered by a neighbour, an interviewee, or a friend at a party—even though these people may not be trying to tip you off. You never really know when an idea will jump out. Make a habit of carrying a small notebook or recording device to get the idea down before you forget it.

Direct observation

Just as you should keep your ears open when talking to people casually, you should keep your eyes open when you are out and about in the community. Sludge floating down a creek could tip you off to an environmental problem. An accident on a busy expressway may get you thinking about highway safety. A panhandler on a street corner may prompt you to investigate homelessness in your community. Potential investigations are everywhere.

Advocacy organizations

There are hundreds of organizations that exist solely to lobby or advocate for a single issue, whether it be pollution, rights of welfare recipients, or mental health. Their newsletters, websites, and even press releases can be sources for investigative ideas. Of course, these organizations will have their own take on an issue—and their own biases—but they have often amassed impressive collections of valid background information.

Reviewing and Auditing the Idea

A great many factors have to be considered before you devote substantial energy and time to an investigation.

Think about the final product, as much as you can imagine it at this stage. Do you think it is something that will be of interest to your readers, listeners, or viewers? Is it the kind of story your news outlet would tell? What impact might the story have? Is there an injustice to correct or a faulty system that could be changed? Is there a strong people element?

Ask yourself how you feel about the idea. Are you passionate about it? Do you care enough to devote days, weeks, or even months to it?

Ideally, can you reduce your inquiry to a simple question such as, 'How many people are dying from this drug?' or 'Why isn't this program working, and what must be done to fix it?'

Finally, for better or worse, can you bring your editors or producers on board? It doesn't matter how good the idea is if you don't have support from your managers. You must make the case to them.

If the answers to these kinds of questions are promising, you are ready to move to the next stage: developing a plan. Remember, this plan is not static, but a living document that you will amend as new information comes to light. Remember also that while we present these steps in an order here, not every investigation follows the same path. You are very likely, however, to include most of these steps at some point in the project.

Developing a plan

Dean Tudor, who has taught research techniques at Ryerson University's School of Journalism, advises journalists to look before they leap into an investigation. They should know what they are looking for, what kind of information is available, and where it can be found. 'Success depends entirely on how well researchers are prepared, and such preparation can save much wasted time and unnecessary work.'[8]

As a result of reviewing and auditing the idea, you should have a simple question that captures what the investigation is about. For instance, 'What is wrong with the government's tendering policies or the ethical rules governing doctors, and what should be done about it?' Or perhaps, 'What facts are needed to substantiate the conflict-of-interest allegations against the cabinet minister or the accusations of unsafe working conditions at the factory?'

'Define your problem', advises Robert Berkman, a writer and editor based in Washington, DC. 'Break it down into its component parts. Determine *why* you need this information and *what* you plan to do with it.'[9] Write down the major points or issues to be addressed, then start making a checklist of what you will need.

Mapping out each step in advance gives the journalist a clear sense of the sources of information to be checked, as well as other tasks. If you need to file requests under access-to-information statutes, you'll have to get this done as early as possible—it can take weeks or months to have the records released.

You must also understand the context of the story. Who are the key players and how are they connected? What are the laws or rules that apply to the activity at the heart of the story, and which agency or government department enforces them? Steve Weinberg, a former executive director of the group, Investigative Reporters and Editors, suggests some basic questions that should be posed at the outset of any investigation: 'How is something supposed to work, and how well is it actually working? Who wins and who loses? Why? How?'[10]

Many investigators also follow an approach similar to that used by scientists. They devise a hypothesis. In journalism, this is a statement of the essence of your story, which one subsequently sets out to prove or disprove. (Remember that good journalists always try as hard to disprove their hypothesis as to prove it.)

In the *Spectator's* Drive Clean investigation, the working hypothesis was that the government-sponsored program forced people to take emissions tests they didn't need, that some people were using fraudulent means to avoid testing, and that the program had a shaky scientific foundation. That hypothesis was based on initial results from querying the database of Drive Clean results as well as from online and other secondary source materials such as research papers in scientific journals.

Typically, researchers work from the general to the specific, from those most peripherally involved to those at the centre of the investigation.

Consulting secondary sources

The most general picture is in secondary sources—i.e., materials already published or broadcast. With these, somebody has already done the reporting and synthesis, which means the sources contain a layer of interpretation and the potential for mistakes. However, as you will read in the next chapter, secondary sources are invaluable during the early research stages of a project when you need to know what has already been said on a subject. You don't want to re-till old ground when you should be breaking virgin turf. Secondary sources will also point you to human sources and reveal the existence of primary documents.

Honing the research plan

The secondary materials will bring new public records to your attention, as well as a better sense of the key people in the field. You may add some of these to your interview list. And you'll probably know better what questions you need answered after you've consulted secondary materials.

At this point, you should revise your plan, and perhaps reorder some of your priorities. (You also have an opportunity here to end your investigation if it is no longer showing promise.) You need to create a *to-do list*, typically with target dates. As tasks accumulate—and they will accumulate—you add them to the list. When they are completed, you check them off.

For the Drive Clean investigation, here are just some of the things the *Spectator* reporters had on their list:

Key questions
- Why do such a large percentage of vehicles pass their Drive Clean tests?
- Is there good reason to test the vehicles despite this high pass rate?
- What scientific basis is there for requiring cars to be tested for emissions every two years?
- Is there fraud?
- If there is fraud, who is responsible?
- Why is it possible to defraud the program?
- What is it about the program design that makes fraud possible and allows it to continue?
- Is the fraud being effectively countered?
- What could be done to stop it?

Primary records to pursue
- Records of disciplinary actions taken against Drive Clean facilities (N.B.: this eventually required a freedom-of-information (FOI) request)
- Internal reviews of the program's effectiveness and operation (also requested under FOI)

- Pollution reduction estimates (done by Drive Clean)
- Reports on the effectiveness of other emissions-testing programs in British Columbia and the United States

Interviews
- Scientific experts on emissions-testing programs
- Critics and supporters of emissions testing
- Garage owners and employees
- Drive Clean spokesperson and top bureaucrats
- Consumers whose vehicles have undergone Drive Clean tests

The Heart of the Investigation

Armed with your research plan, your question list and your to-do list, you are ready to move into the heart of the research. Much of the rest of this book goes into detail on the different kinds of primary sources, from public and justice records to archival and historical materials, computerized databases, and—of course—people. For now, note that as you progress, you will answer some of your questions, and those answers will raise fresh questions. You must keep track of the different resources and records you have consulted, the main points they raise, and the information they provide. Many investigators prefer to store as much as possible electronically, using a word processor or spreadsheet to create large searchable files. Some even develop websites with links to online documents.

One tool that can prove invaluable is a chronology. Whether maintained electronically or on a long piece of paper taped to the wall, a chronology allows you to see how events uncovered in your investigation relate to each other in time. A chronology should include all dates unearthed in primary documents, secondary sources, or interviews. Not only will a chronology help keep time lines straight, it can reveal inconsistencies in what interviewees say—people may not remember correctly when things happened, or they may actually lie.

Each time you review a record or complete an interview, assess what questions have been answered, what new pieces of the puzzle have been revealed and how they relate, what new questions are raised, and how close you are to your goal of proving or disproving your hypothesis.

Even when the hypothesis stays much the same, an investigator must usually proceed through several stages—and a variety of sources—before finding the heart of the story. Returning to the Drive Clean investigation in Ontario, we can see how reporter Fred Vallance-Jones steadily built up information in this way:

- He suspected fraud after he analyzed emissions-testing data and discovered something strange. Two tests would sometimes be conducted, within minutes of each other, on the same car. The first test would result in a fail; the second, a pass.

- He requested official records of the Ministry of the Environment's disciplinary actions against garages. These revealed specific garage names, and Vallance-Jones set out to interview garage owners to hear their stories.
- One of the garage owners mentioned he had heard that an employee of a garage in Kitchener had been involved in a large emissions-testing fraud. He recalled a name, which he gave to the reporter. It turned out that the Ministry of the Environment had suppressed details about this particular fraud when it released its disciplinary records, on the basis that publishing details of it could interfere with an ongoing investigation.
- Vallance-Jones confirmed the information about the garage employee by calling the courthouse, and went to the court to obtain the official account of the charges laid.
- Vallance-Jones went back to the courthouse on the next court date, found the accused, and obtained his story. He also spoke to the owner of the garage, who turned out to be an innocent victim. The owner filled in further details, including the fact that the Ministry of the Environment had done nothing about the fraud for a year and a half, despite a computer system that was supposed to detect suspicious testing.
- The reporter eventually questioned the ministry.

The resulting story was so significant that it prompted quick change, including new measures to combat emissions-testing fraud.

> Adam Mahn turned his employer's Drive Clean machine into a personal money-spinner, producing as many as 654 phony certificates for at least $100 each.
>
> He got away with it for 16 months.
>
> It's the largest scam against Drive Clean yet revealed, but Mahn—who worked for a Kitchener used car dealer—was discovered by accident. This raises troubling questions about the effectiveness of Drive Clean's surveillance system and about how many other cars are being illegally passed in other garages.
>
> 'The way it looked on their computer, there was nothing to go *wham, look at that!*' Mahn said. 'It's not rocket science . . . you could sit there and make it look good on paper. As long as it looks good on paper they don't give a shit.'
>
> Mahn, 25, made as much as $100,000 by issuing fake certificates for cars that were never tested. That's more than many facilities have made doing legitimate tests.[11]

The point here is that information tends to build on information. By following up on leads, the names of individuals, recollections, and details in documents, a reporter will build up facts, connect dots, and even stumble upon surprises such as the Mahn fraud.

Because you are searching for the truth, you need to triangulate information. This means that if somebody asserts something to be true, you must seek out others who can confirm the information, as well as public documents and other primary sources that can corroborate what the source has said. Likewise, if you find a reference in a public document, you will likely want to speak to the people involved to hear their story, and put a human face on the information.

Some journalists like to write rolling drafts as they investigate, because this helps them to identify what information they have, and what they still need to obtain. This can also guard against over-investigation, the gathering of material that goes beyond what is necessary.

If you stay focused, your to-do list will eventually get shorter, and you will fill in enough pieces of the puzzle that you finally understand what the picture on the front of the puzzle box would have been. This is the point at which you are ready to begin assembling your story.

The key is to be able to say, assuredly, 'This is what happened' or 'This is who did it.'

Special Situations

Cutting your losses

No matter how hard the journalist tries, some investigations are doomed to failure. The tip that launched the investigation turns out to have been wrong, or leads that at first seemed promising fail to pan out. There may be a lack of the hard evidence needed to back up allegations or assertions. The people needed to verify the story may refuse to co-operate. Crucial information may not be accessible through public records or by way of a leak from a friendly source. While it is hard to admit defeat, you must recognize that in some cases, further investigation is futile. Sometimes, the reason is simple: there was no story to find in the first place. But this does not mean your efforts have been wasted. Every investigation introduces you to new sources of information or new ways to use those consulted in the past. What you amassed before the project was abandoned may be of use in a future investigation. At the very least, you will have a better sense of when to cut your losses and move on to more promising investigations.

Surveillance and undercover techniques

Journalists strive to gather information in an open, transparent manner. It is standard practice for reporters to identify themselves as media representatives when they speak to potential sources. They keep their tape recorders and cameras in clear view, making sure that the subject knows his or her words or actions are being recorded and may be publicized. But some stories cannot be verified using conventional research methods, such as when no documents exist and sources refuse to provide the evidence. If you suspect that some activity is undermining the public interest, putting public safety at risk, or squandering public money, you may have no alternative but to go undercover in order to witness first-hand what is happening.

Going undercover demands careful strategy, specialized technology, and a strong ethical compass. Most ethical codes for journalists recognize that the public interest may justify using covert means in rare circumstances. The Canadian Association of Journalists' *Statement of Principles on Investigative Journalism*, for example, says that misrepresentation is justified

> only in cases where illegal or fraudulent activity is strongly suspected to have taken place, the public trust is abused or public safety is at risk. Documentary evidence of problems may not exist and officials may fail to respond to inquiries. Sources may not exist, or refuse to speak for fear of retribution. For example, when investigating controversial activities ([e.g.,] illegal purchases over the web, or the dissemination of hate speech), we may find it necessary to cloak our identity.[12]

The decision to go undercover or to use hidden microphones or cameras is a tough one. Most stories simply don't justify the ethical complexities of misrepresenting yourself. More conventional methods of getting access to documents or insiders may offer the same information for far less time, energy, and risk. Reporters and their editors or producers must ask themselves two questions before pursuing any undercover investigation:

- *Is there an overwhelming public interest involved?*
- *Is going undercover the only way to get the information?*

Only after other efforts to obtain witnesses and documents have failed should a journalist consider using deception. As Nick Russell puts it in a Canadian textbook on media ethics, 'The journalist must first exhaust all traditional, socially acceptable methods of investigation before resorting to the clandestine.'[13] Making up a false name, lying about credentials, secretly recording what people say or do—such conduct has the potential to undermine public trust in the journalist or the media as a whole. When journalists misrepresent themselves while gathering information, their stories should explain the methods used and why they were considered necessary. By coming clean, journalists allow readers, listeners, or viewers to judge whether the ends justified the means.

There are also legal and privacy considerations when working undercover. In Canada, unlike in some US jurisdictions, it is legal to record a conversation with other persons without their knowledge. The consent of one of the people taking part in the conversation is all that is required, and this can be the consent of the journalist who is asking the questions.[14] Print reporters are free to record an interview and publish what has been said. Radio and television journalists face greater restriction if a conversation takes place over the phone—a regulation of the Canadian Radio-television and Telecommunications Commission forbids media outlets from broadcasting a telephone interview or conversation without the consent of the person on the other end of the line.[15] A journalist cannot record a private conversation between other people without the consent of at least one of those people. It is a criminal offence, for instance, to publish or broadcast information picked up by a tape recorder secretly left running in a room where a private meeting is taking place.[16] Journalists planning to make secret recordings should consult with an editor or the news organization's legal advisors before proceeding.

Having decided to cloak your identity, you must consider a number of logistical issues. Beyond the ethical pitfalls, going undercover can be both difficult and even dangerous.

First off, never go it alone. If you're entering into a situation undercover, recruit a partner and rehearse your cover story until you get it straight—your names and relationship to each other, where you live, your phone number, why you are there, and how you heard about the location. Two sets of eyes and ears make it far easier to witness and record what's happening in an undercover situation. In teams of at least two, reporters can divide responsibilities, speak to more people, gather more documents or observations, and increase the credibility of their information. It can also be valuable to have more than one witness if the resulting story leads to litigation in which reporters are called to account for what they saw. Even more important, however, is personal safety. Walking into potentially dangerous situations comes with a high degree of unpredictability. A partner provides a measure of protection in case your cover is blown and the subjects of an investigation become verbally or physically threatening. Have a plan to make a hasty exit in case things go awry or the subject of the story becomes suspicious.

Another major consideration is equipment. There are several ways to document what you see and hear undercover.

Audio recorders
If you're a print reporter and only need audio, this is far simpler than using a hidden camera. Make sure you load up on new batteries and set the machine to record a sufficient length of time.

Hidden cameras
For this approach, plan some serious preparation time. You'll need a tiny camera (they come as buttons, in eyeglasses, etc.) and a microphone (they come hidden in the caps of pens, etc.) which both plug into a digital video camera. The most difficult part to hide is a video camera because of its size. If it's winter, you can likely use oversized jackets with inside pockets for the job. Another option is a so-called fanny bag. None of these options are terribly elegant. So you'll want to find the smallest possible machine and spend time with it, understanding how it works.

Wire yourself up with the video camera and microphone beneath your clothes and practise shooting to get a sense of what you're capturing, the proper angles, etc. Load up on extra batteries (especially if it's cold outside), digital videotape, and electrical tape (to secure connections).

Going undercover can open up new storytelling possibilities for journalists. A *Toronto Star* investigation into fraudulent telemarketing operations relied on hidden audio and video devices to document false claims being made about goods sold to unsuspecting US citizens. The newspaper discovered that Toronto was a haven for companies that were using the border as protection against tougher US anti-fraud laws. In Canada, they were safely and cheaply targeting a massive US market while staying clear of the tougher laws stateside.

To expose the industry and its practices, two reporters applied for jobs at about a dozen telemarketing operations in the city that advertised in free employment publications. They showed up separately at the so-called 'boiler rooms' within a few minutes of each other, went through the brief interview process and were then individually assigned to be 'trained' for a day or two with experienced telemarketers on staff. They spent days watching, listening, and recording as telemarketing agents made call after call to places such as Houston, Kansas City, and Montana, calling the homes of people whose names and numbers were listed on small pieces of paper purchased by the companies. Those potential customers were people with credit problems, whose names and contact information were listed in databases shared by telemarketing operations. People desperate to fix their credit ratings forked out money for credit cards that never arrived or for bonus gifts worth far less than promised.

Being inside allowed the reporters to witness the deceptive pitches and gather documents and recordings of the telemarketers' pressure tactics—evidence that formed the basis for a series of stories that led to the closure of dozens of telemarketing boiler rooms within days.

Original evidence gathered this way can often prompt police investigations, charges, and convictions. In another case, the *Star* documented deplorable conditions inside an illegal slaughterhouse north of Toronto that produced meat destined for the city's restaurants and butcher shops. In this case, journalists decided there was no way to prove allegations of illegal slaughter without witnessing it.

For weeks, they monitored the broken-down barn and witnessed the steady traffic of customers driving in and out of the front gates with animal meat in the back. Eventually, they used a hidden camera to document the process of entering the farm, picking out an animal, watching it being inhumanely killed, bled, and slaughtered in a filthy barn under conditions that included bloody counters, unsanitized knives and saws, dogs roaming about, and no running water. Publication of the story prompted police and government officials to investigate, leading to charges and a conviction against the offender.[17]

These stories, like some undercover investigative pieces, prompted anonymous threats of violence against the reporters; on the other hand, stories like this often generate huge public response, vigorous debate, and meaningful public policy changes. Going undercover can be messy, time-consuming, and risky. But used carefully, it can also be powerful.

Getting Help When You're Stuck

Everyone will hit a brick wall at some point, and the wonderful thing about the investigative journalism community is that you can reach out to other journalists to help. The Canadian Association of Journalists maintains an Internet mailing list where you can pose questions to other journalists. Instructions for signing on are at *www.caj.ca*.

Investigative Reporters and Editors, a US organization, maintains a listserv specifically devoted to investigative reporting. Instructions to sign up are at *www. ire.org*.

Membership in one or both of these organizations is an excellent investment and their annual meetings offer an opportunity to network with other investigative reporters.

The Canadian Journalism Project, *www.j-source.ca*, has sections on investigative and computer-assisted reporting.

A Note on Ethics

Investigative reporting demands strict adherence to ethical codes. The rules are simple:

- Don't lie.
- Don't steal (e.g., documents from somebody's desk).
- Don't misrepresent yourself.

Conclusion

Conducting a journalistic investigation is a major undertaking, and there is no absolute prescription on how to do it. The methods included in this chapter are, however, typical of the work you will do. We now begin to examine some of the specific types of records you will use, beginning with secondary sources.

Suggestions for Further Reading

Berry, Stephen J. *Watchdog Journalism: The Art of Investigative Reporting.* New York: Oxford University Press, 2009.

CASE STUDY: Part I—Colin Parrott

Colin Parrott is a graduate of the University of King's College School of Journalism (Halifax). He was editor-in-chief on the Boat Harbour project. Located near the Pictou Landing First Nation Reserve, Boat Harbour has been used as a treatment pond for pulp-and-paper industrial waste for more than 40 years.

Q   What was the name of your story/project?

A   The investigative project was called Toxic Legacy: The Story of Boat Harbour (see boatharbour.kingsjournalism.com).

Q   Where was it published/broadcast?

A   Online and in *the Coast*, a Halifax weekly.

Q   How did you get the idea for the project?

A   It was decided upon by the investigative workshop team (2009) of students along with the instructor who led the workshop, Fred Vallance-Jones.

Q   What initial research did you do to confirm that the story was valid?

A   The idea for the story came from a chat one of the students had with an Aboriginal band member who told him about Boat Harbour. The student assistant (Kathleen Hunter) who helped with the workshop, along with the instructor, did initial research into the story for some weeks, unearthing a large number of public documents, such as previous environmental studies and assessments, long-forgotten news releases promising cleanups, and orders-in-council at the provincial and federal levels. By the time the actual investigative workshop began, there was a solid body of evidence to prove Boat Harbour was still a festering problem both literally and figuratively.

Q   Did you have an initial theory as to what the story would be?

A   That, despite a huge federal payout to the Native band at Pictou Landing in 1993, and various schemes advanced to clean up the pulp-mill waste-treatment pond at Boat Harbour, the pond was still a toxic mess.

Q   Once you had confirmed that you had a story, how did you plan out your research?

A   Through various group meetings.
      Because the class had a dozen or so students, it was possible to divide up the work of digesting all of the documents that had been gathered prior to the outset of the workshop. From there, the class developed an initial storyboard for the series of articles that would eventually run, came up with lists of initial interview candidates, identified further document research that was needed and created a list of initial research questions.

We requested Federal Court documents for information on the band's lawsuit against the federal government. We searched provincial archives to find information (letters and contracts) on the initial deal struck between the company and the band, the one allowing the mill to be set up in the first place. We used Factiva to research previous news stories and went to the library to request all articles related to Boat Harbour.

Q   What primary sources (documents, public records) did you use? How did they contribute to the story?

A   One of the outstanding features of this project was the wide array of public documents and records that we used. Provincial land-title records allowed us to identify landowners surrounding Boat Harbour affected by the waste-treatment lagoon. Minutes of town and county councils allowed us to reconstruct what municipal officials had done (or not done) at the time the lagoon was established. We scoured the debates of the House of Commons, the Nova Scotia House of Assembly, and committees at both levels of government to find public debate (or the lack thereof) that had occurred on the issue. Orders-in-council at the federal and provincial levels were a rich source of information on how key changes to the law were made that allowed the lagoon to be established and to continue operations. Many documents related to the issue were found in libraries in New Glasgow, Dartmouth (Environment Canada), and Halifax. We also consulted Federal Court documents for information on the band's lawsuit against the federal government. We searched provincial archives to find minutes of the administrative body that set up the lagoon for the paper company and the personal papers of then premier Robert Stanfield. These provided important background on how the decision to use Boat Harbour for waste disposal was made and what officials were saying privately before and after a pristine body of water was converted to a waste-treatment facility. Much of this material had never seen the light of day before.

Q   What were the most important interviews for the story? Why?

A   As is often the case, some of the most important interviews came near the end of the research. Among these were an interview with the lawyer for the Pictou Landing band, who provided us with information about the most recent developments on the issue and an interview with the lone provincial official tasked with finding a way to clean up Boat Harbour. Assumed power players in the story—such as then premier Rodney MacDonald and the Pictou Landing band chief—turned out to be very minor characters in the overall big picture; the former spoke briefly on the situation and the latter refused to comment when a group of three reporters approached her after a meeting with the band councillors.

Q   What methods did you use to organize your research? The material you found?

A   On such a big project, we needed to find a way to make the information unearthed by a group of reporters available to others, and to keep track of key points as they came up. Our answer was to use the Google Groups and Docs services. We created a private Google Group, into which were posted the transcripts of all important interviews. And using Google Docs spreadsheets, we maintained a list of key facts, a chronology (which had been begun by the student assistant), a list of contacts, an evolving to-do list, and a list of contacts. We also used the Google Group as a way to communicate with one another. Senior student editors met with the instructor every day to steer the research.

Q   Did you use any computerized techniques to do or organize research? If so, what were these, and how did you use them?

A   We used Excel® to build a chronology, which was later transferred to Google Docs. We also used mapping software to create maps of the area surrounding Boat Harbour. We plugged in property values and assigned those various colours to show how property values surrounding Boat Harbour were lower than the next adjacent area. The mapping program was also useful in pinpointing property owners close to the lagoon.

Q   Did you use any undercover reporting for the story? If so, what did you do?

A   No.

Q   Did you use freedom-of-information requests for the story? If so, what requests did you make, and how many?

A   A number of requests were made, but none yielded any records.

Q   How important were these requests for the story?

A   In the end, not important at all. Everything we needed was public information available to anyone.

Q   Many projects have a turning point when it all seems to fall into place. Was there such a point for this story/project? If so, please describe in detail that turning point.

A   The first breakthrough was when we were provided with a letter sent by the provincial government to the Pictou Landing band promising a cleanup, and an internal band newsletter indicating the band was contemplating refusing to allow the mill to use Boat Harbour any further. This led us on the trail of several interviews and documents.

I think another turning point was when we found out fairly near the end of the project that the band was having secret meetings to work out a new deal with the pulp mill. When we heard this, we tried to get a comment from the band chief (on this and on the other material we had unearthed) but she did not return calls and did not respond to a letter sent by registered mail. Eventually, several students staked out a band council meeting at which she would still not comment. But some other band members did go on the record that day, leading eventually to the pivotal interview with the band's lawyer.

Q   Did your story change from your first theory? If so, how?

A   We had no inkling of the money that had been paid to the band by the mill owners, nor about the secret talks that were ongoing when we began. We also knew little of the historical background with regard to the establishment of the pulp mill, as that story—at least the real story—had never been told. It emerged only after we'd done extensive archive research.

Q   How many stories did you write?

A   Three online, plus sidebars, and a main story in *the Coast*.

Q   What was the most challenging part about writing these stories?

A   Pulling all of the information from disparate sources together.

Q   Over how many days/broadcasts did the stories run?

A   It's an online project, so the stories are still running, and will run until some distant time when they are removed from the server. The article in *the Coast* was a one-day piece.

Q   Did your project include Internet elements? If so, what were these and how did they fit into the overall presentation?

A   It was mostly an Internet story but also ran in *the Coast* one day (and on their homepage). Elements unique to online presentation included actual historical and background documents (converted to PDF and posted on the site), maps, a chronology, and much more.

Q   On what dates did the stories run?

A   The series was launched 23 April 2009.

Q   What was the most difficult thing about doing this project?

A   The challenge was to organize such a vast amount of information and determine what would be needed for the story and what we could just ignore.

Q   What was the most satisfying part of the project?

A   Holding the government accountable for past mistakes and showing the people of the area and the rest of Nova Scotia that somebody still cares and the government can't just let this problem go away. Although not necessarily the most newsworthy story, our opportunity to tell the history of the mill was quite rewarding and interesting.

Q   What other comments would you make about this project?

A   It was the first such collaboration we know of between a journalism school and a local media outlet to research and produce an investigative project.

Q   How long did the project take to research and write?

A   Four months, including the time spent by the student assistant and instructor.

Part II

The Key Primary Resources

3 Building a Foundation:
Gathering Information Already Published or Broadcast

Locating and reviewing background information is an essential step in any investigation.

There is no single starting point that works for all investigations. Every story or problem is different and each investigation leads to its own array of human sources and paper records. You may go directly to the courthouse in search of files involving the target of the investigation, or immediately pick up the phone to find out what trusted contacts already know about the matter. But the most logical and the least time-consuming starting point is often a review of material already published about the person or subject: the secondary sources. Locating and reviewing background information is an essential step in any investigation. 'The goal,' says author Jessica Mitford, whose books have probed the funeral industry and the treatment of inmates in US prisons, among other issues, 'is to know, if possible, more about your subject than the target of the investigation does.'[1]

Media reports can be retrieved easily using online databases or libraries; even a query on Google, Bing, or another Internet search engine is bound to turn up a few news stories. Media coverage provides a fast and usually reliable source of background information, while alerting you to what has already been reported. This is particularly helpful in working out whether a tip or disclosure is, in fact, news. If it turns out that the issue or controversy has already received press attention, you may find there are still fresh angles to be explored. Best of all, media coverage offers information that has been packaged for a general audience and is not weighted down with jargon or technical detail. Think of media stories as briefing notes that help you grasp the complexities of a subject as you dig deeper into the story and prepare to interview experts.

The job may encompass a couple of hours of Internet searches or days of trolling through written material in a library, but the goal is always the same: to learn what has already been said so you don't have to 'investigate' what is already known.

Here are some secondary sources you might consult, with tips on how to use them.

Traditional Sources

Newspapers

Hardly a topic exists that hasn't been written about in a newspaper, so archived stories are a logical place to start an investigation.

Newspapers famously provide the 'first draft of history'. Created on the run by harried reporters and editors, they are a basic record of the public life and public conversation of our society. These days, archives of many of the largest newspapers can be accessed online with services such as LexisNexis, Newscan, FPinfomart, and Factiva. These can be quite costly, but your local public or university library may provide free access.

Smaller papers, especially weeklies, are less likely to be archived this way but you may sometimes need to consult them. The early days of a business person's career may have been chronicled only in a weekly local paper; a hometown paper may carry a politician's damaging comments that were never uttered to the big dailies. You may even need to find something obscure such as a revealing advertisement or notice.

When *The Hamilton Spectator* was investigating food poisonings in that city in 2001, documents obtained under a freedom-of-information (FOI) request made reference to a wedding at which the bride had become ill, along with dozens of guests. Names were removed, as the law requires, but the records included the date of the banquet, and a reference to the town of Grimsby, Ontario. Taking those two pieces of information, the reporter looked through a year's worth of issues of the local weekly paper on microfilm at a library in Grimsby. He eventually found a wedding announcement for a ceremony matching the date of the banquet, tracked down the couple, and confirmed that he had identified the correct wedding.

As the *Spectator* reporter did, you may need to consult small papers directly on microfilm or in hard copy. Some papers will sell you back issues by mail. These small papers are unlikely to be indexed, so you will need to know when your subject may have been in the news, and then search manually. More and more small papers have online editions, however, and these sometimes feature free or paid archives.

Magazines

Magazines are published on just about any topic imaginable, and tend to print material that is of greater depth and research than that found in newspapers. One or two definitive magazine articles can save a great deal of basic research time. Don't forget to look for regional magazines, too, which often run pieces on local high-profile people.

Finding articles is infinitely easier if you use an index. Traditionally, these were bound, annual volumes, but now they have migrated online and can be accessed through academic and public libraries. CPI.Q, the online version of the Canadian

Periodical Index, indexes more than 1200 Canadian periodicals, with full-text articles from more than 500. For US articles, *The Readers' Guide to Periodical Literature* is the standard hard-copy resource and is also available online through libraries with full-text articles.

Most libraries will have the print versions of these indexes if they are still issued that way. These can prove invaluable because they bring together a large number of publications in one place, and use standardized subject headings, which can make searches more precise than using key words.

Journals and other specialty publications

One step up the reliability ladder from magazines are academic journals, in which researchers at universities, at other institutions, and in companies and government showcase their latest work. Prestigious journals such as the *New England Journal of Medicine* or the *Canadian Medical Association Journal* frequently create breaking news. Increasingly, they are putting their most newsworthy studies online, well before the hard copy of the edition is released. Some also have their own alert systems, which send you tables of contents days before the issue is published.

There are hundreds and hundreds of other journals, many of which are available online. Specialized indexes such as the Social Sciences Index simplify searching. Internet services such as MedLine and PubMed, both in the medical field, allow easy keyword searching through millions of journal articles. You often have to pay to see the whole article, although if you contact the public-relations representative of the publisher, he or she might send it to you free of charge. Again, public and academic libraries may provide free access to cardholders or students.

Unlike general-interest publications, journals are written for narrower audiences. In the case of business journals, the audience could be investors looking for safe bets for their money; in the case of medical journals, it could be researchers and health-care providers seeking information on the latest treatment for cancer. The specialized audience means that a journal's language tends to be less accessible than that of a general-interest publication. Journals do, however, offer a forum in which issues are discussed that fall below the radar of mainstream-media outlets.

Theses

An easily overlooked source of secondary material is the university thesis. Published theses are valuable not only for the information they contain (and their bibliographies), but also for the insights they can provide into the writer. A thesis prepared by someone who has since become a prominent figure, or the target of your investigation, can show you a side of that person's character you might not get anywhere else. Often, these papers were written before their authors started to manicure their image or control access to information about themselves. Theses are typically maintained by the library at the institution the author attended. You can also search for them online at *www.collectionscanada.ca/thesescanada*.

Books

Many journalists and newsworthy individuals save important information for a book-length treatment. These books tend to slip under the radar and fail to benefit from wide publicity, except, of course, within the readerships to which they are geared. Books of this sort can be like 'trade magazines', in that they are designed to be read by a select audience. Most don't become best-sellers; they are especially likely to disappear quickly from the public eye when published by a regional or small press.

Bibliographies

Another gem of the research library is the bibliography—not just the list of references printed at the end of a book or essay, but the separate lists of published materials relating to a given topic. It's often worth enlisting the help of the reference librarian in navigating the available resources. One of the most useful aspects of bibliographies is that, although they are intended to guide you to texts, they can inadvertently offer leads to human sources.

Radio and television transcripts

While most radio and television programs disappear into the ether as soon as they are broadcast, some of them make transcripts or recordings available, which can be obtained for a fee or, sometimes, at no charge on the Internet. Increasingly, archived radio or television broadcasts can be downloaded, especially from larger broadcasters. The CBC's digital archives at *archives.cbc.ca* provide thousands of radio and television clips about notable Canadian events and people. Also, CBC Radio makes many of its programs available as podcasts that you can play on your computer or MP3 player.

Electronic Sources

The search for secondary sources used to be labour-intensive. You had to physically go to a library and wade through stacks of clippings, periodicals, and magazines. It was also necessary to formally request background information from advocacy groups, government institutions, or lawyers. The Internet has made the search for secondary sources much faster.

Websites

Most institutions and businesses have websites that advertise their wares or publicize their point of view. As such, the sites function as expanded news releases, in some cases disguised as real news. That said, some sites can be useful repositories of valuable information, posting news articles and lists of links to other relevant websites. For instance, a law firm's website may link to articles or documents related to its current legal battles, thereby providing a handy reference library for journalists just getting up to speed on an issue.

Social-networking sites

The explosion of Facebook, Twitter, and other social-networking sites has created yet another place investigators can go to find information, track unfolding issues and locate people. When pop music icon Michael Jackson died in June 2009, it was Facebook and Twitter that broke the story first. Fans flocked to both services to share information and memories of Jackson. It's now common practice for reporters to go to Facebook after local young people die accidentally. Friends often set up memorial sites with information about the deceased within hours of the accidents. As with any information of this type, careful checking is required before it is used in a broadcast or write-up, but there is no question that online social networks have become important resources for journalists, especially for issues and events involving younger people.

Mailing lists

Mailing lists—or listservs—are discussions to which you must formally subscribe. Think of the specialty publications discussed earlier. If you were to take all of the professionals who subscribe to the publications, gather them in a room, then be a fly on the wall, you would be able to glean a great deal from the conversations. With a listserv, instead of gathering such people in a physical space, their discussion is in cyberspace. The participants converse in emails, which are sent out to all members of the listserv. Just as there are specialty publications for many professions, so, too, are there listservs for every conceivable group. The listservs allow health-care advocates, lawyers, victims of crime, and—yes—journalists, to dispense advice, dispel rumours, and debate the hot issues.

As with many a group conversation, there tend to be people who dominate the proceedings while the others simply listen. But you don't have to be a member of the trade or occupation in question to join the mailing list. On many occasions, you can convince someone in the group to sign you up—let you into the club, so to speak. Listservs are also valuable because you can go beyond monitoring to asking questions or requesting interviews. However, David Akin of CanWest News cautions that there is an etiquette dictating when questions may be asked:

> Many reporters who are unfamiliar with listserv etiquette often will find that they get no response or a hostile response if they just show up the first day they subscribe to a new listserv and start asking questions. Listservs are like walking into a parlour, let's say, where there's a certain etiquette. Are people comfortable having a reporter in? Can you ask these kinds of questions? And does the community trust you enough to volunteer information?[2]

Discussion groups

Discussion groups, or newsgroups, are similar to listservs in that they consist of people who share similar passions, whether it be cars, politics, or rare fish. Some groups serve local communities and post news about upcoming events that, while of little interest to the mainstream media, may help with a particular investigation. Unlike listservs, discussion groups are more lax about membership. The groups can be found using the regular search engines, and you can join them more or less immediately.

Easy membership has its advantages and disadvantages. Reporters hunting for information or people for their stories can usually dip in and out of the discussion groups without having to submit to the potentially time-consuming process of obtaining approval from a moderator, as is the case with listservs. Say you were looking for someone who was still smarting from being victimized by an unscrupulous car dealer. You could easily find discussion groups consisting of car enthusiasts who regularly swap war stories about good deals and bad deals. And if you're really interested in having a particular person in your story, or in using him or her as a potential contact, you can post a question, requesting that the person respond directly to your email address. It can be that easy.

The downside is that the discussion can easily veer off topic, or it can be dominated by people who have little positive or interesting to say, forcing the rest of the people in the group into a stony, self-imposed silence. An additional and growing problem is the amount of unsolicited advertising messages in many newsgroups. The way to make the discussion groups work for you is to spend a bit of time looking for the ones that meet your needs.

Blogs

A blog is short for *weblog*, which is an online diary that can be kept by anyone. The diary can be full of personal details of little relevance to many people, or it can be replete with useful background information and names of people who could become sources for future stories. There are two basic ways blogs can be used: either as passive tools that dispense information or as active tools that blog owners can use to solicit information.

First, the passive tool: Just like a website, listserv, or discussion group, a blog is a place on the Internet that contains information the owner finds relevant. Search engines such as Technorati (*www.technorati.com*) allow you to search for blogs by subject. For instance, many columnists now have blogs that allow them to write in much more detail than they could ever dream of printing in their newpaper or even posting on the paper's website. This value-added information can range from personal opinion to views of experts in a particular topic.

Second, the active tool: A growing number of journalists maintain blogs that serve as more than vanity projects. Because an increasing number of people are visiting blogs and sticking around to read the content, these visitors constitute a ready supply of possible sources. David Akin, who maintains *davidakin.blogware.com*, recalls a time when, after reading the website of *The Atlanta Journal-Constitution*, he came across an idea to do a story on pre-teen magazines and the questionable content they were peddling to girls aged 10 to 12. Akin thought the idea would travel well south of the border. But there was only one problem: how would he find a pre-teen and a parent who would agree to go on camera for his story? He explains:

> At my blog, I put out the call, and asked some people to respond to me. And sure enough, I got quite a few responses and through that was able to find some sources that were perfectly suitable, had something interesting to say and away we went and did the television story. So there's a case where the Internet was where I found the inspiration for the story, then my blog became a helpful tool in finding a source.[3]

The key concept in Akin's explanation is the word *tool*. Like many of these Web resources, once you figure out the strengths and weaknesses, then you can use them to the maximum benefit.

Alerts

In addition to helping you find news stories, search engines such as Google allow you to create your own news alerts. With an alert, you specify keywords for stories you are interested in. Whenever a new article containing those words is posted somewhere in the world, an email is sent to your inbox with a short summary and a link. For example, while working on a series about drugs that kill, members of the CBC's investigative reporting team went to Google's news-alert page, specified that they wanted to receive articles and news releases having to do with clinical trials, pharmaceutical companies, and adverse drug reactions.

A host of search engines offer a similar service, as do major news organizations, albeit sometimes for a fee. The key here is convenience. With little effort, you can begin building a reference library that can be reviewed during the time you've set aside before or after work, between assignments, or just before rushing off to that news conference.

Internet news sites

Media outlets use the Internet to varying degrees of success, and you can use the news sections of search engines to find out which outlets provide the most information free of charge or offer the most extensive archives. Many media websites offer value-added information such as stories not included in the paper edition or the broadcast, extra charts and graphs, and transcribed or recorded interviews. An increasing number of media outlets are forcing people to pay for content, although that model has been controversial and, as of 2010, largely unsuccessful in attracting willing customers.

Conclusion

Secondary sources allow you to determine what has been said on the record. However, all such material, even from usually reliable sources, must be checked and double-checked for accuracy. This can be done in interviews, or by cross-referencing with official sources or public records.

When using a website, you must be able to determine which group the site truly represents. For instance, a site might have a name that suggests it is run by an independent group with a genuine interest in an issue. A bit of legwork might reveal, however, that the site is really a front for a company that makes the very product that the supposed group is championing.

Steve Weinberg, author of *The Reporter's Handbook: An Investigator's Guide to Documents and Techniques*, provides the following useful caution:

> All secondary-source information should be independently verified. An investigator must check later issues of the publication for corrections, dissenting letters to the editor and clarifying follow-up articles, then nail down accuracy by talking to the original sources. But secondary sources can provide an invaluable starting point.[4]

4

Using Public Records

Public records are the backbone of good investigative research.

Introduction

There was no tip.

No deep throat.

The biggest story of Andrew McIntosh's life started with an innocuous, three-sentence news brief in the French-language newspaper, *La Presse*.

It was August 1995 when McIntosh, a veteran investigative reporter working for the *National Post*, casually stumbled over a small news item about Delta Hotels buying former prime minister Jean Chrétien's 25 per cent stake in a Quebec golf course.

'I wondered what it was all about,' he recalls.

The story actually turned out to be false. But McIntosh's curiosity about the prime minister's golf course would remain buried in the back of his mind for nearly three years. Then, in 1998, he started digging. The result was a sweeping investigative series documenting Chrétien's troubled ownership of shares in the Grand-Mère Golf Club and the controversial payments he received for those shares while he was still in office. The series also revealed how, in Chrétien's St Maurice riding, businessmen with questionable professional qualifications, criminal records, and other problems with the law received more than $4 million in federal government job-creation grants and loans after doing business with the golf course.[1]

It was all news to Canadians. The series triggered hundreds of headlines, vigorous public debate, government and police investigations, and public-policy changes. And it was information that McIntosh pieced together largely by using documents and records available in the public domain.

For McIntosh, the path toward the now infamously dubbed 'Shawinigate' saga—a reference to Chrétien's hometown of Shawinigan, Quebec—was guided by a series of records available to anyone. Through the course of his research, he conducted hundreds of land title, corporate, and courthouse document searches in Quebec, Ontario, and even Belgium.

For example, land title records showed how, in 1993, Chrétien had sold the Grand-Mère Inn (which neighboured the golf course) to Quebec businessman Yvon Duhaime. The records also showed that Duhaime received more than

$600,000 in mortgage loans in 1997 from the Business Development Bank of Canada (BDC).[2] The circumstances around those loans raised questions in McIntosh's mind. Chrétien turned out to have retained a strong personal interest in the Grand-Mère. Although he had signed a deal in 1993 to sell his 25 per cent stake in the golf club, this deal fell through in 1996, leaving Chrétien to look for a new buyer at the very time federal grant money began flowing liberally to Shawinigan innkeepers.[3]

'Having searched the history of the inn property, I saw right away that Duhaime obtained the loan at a time his business was in economic distress,' McIntosh says. 'The documents left financial footprints that were very telling.'

So McIntosh began to look closely at how public money was being directed at rescuing the failing inn. Gradually, the records revealed to him how a small-town businessman short on cash attracted the lobbying power of a prime minister.

In a front-page story in November 2000, McIntosh used public records to report that Chrétien had called the head of the Business Development Bank 'repeatedly in 1996 and 1997 to urge him to grant a big mortgage loan to the near-bankrupt Grand-Mère Inn in his St Maurice riding.'[4] Duhaime needed Chrétien's political influence to land his hefty loan, McIntosh learned, because the innkeeper couldn't get it himself. Again, documents provided the reasons: The innkeeper had a lengthy criminal record for assault, forcible confinement, death threats, drunk driving, and income tax offences, all uncovered by McIntosh using extensive searches of Quebec court records in Shawinigan. The journalist also reported that Duhaime had not declared his criminal convictions on his loan application as required by the BDC.[5] A bank manager refused to approve the loan because, as documents showed, it 'did not meet normal policies and criteria of the bank' and 'the global risk for the bank was very high.'[6]

Opposition MPs seized on the stunning revelations, suggesting Chrétien was in a clear conflict of interest lobbying on behalf of a hotel adjacent to a golf club in which he had an ongoing financial interest.[7]

Records also showed McIntosh that Shawinigan hotelier Pierre Thibault received $1.5 million in government grants and loans despite being under criminal investigation in Belgium for defrauding his business partners and admitting in writing that he misappropriated close to $1 million.[8]

'I spent a week investigating across Belgium and obtained a copy of the forensic audit and actually obtained Thibault's signed confession,' McIntosh recalls.

Beyond documenting important facts in a story, public records also provide the essential ingredient of chronology. 'As I worked, I gathered and collected facts from interviews, court documents, land registry documents, government documents, and banking records, and drafted a detailed chronology.'

It paid off. In one story, McIntosh showed that Chrétien awarded Thibault's hotel a grant before Thibault had even filed a business plan with federal officials.[9]

'Bureaucrats rushed approvals because the PM had already announced it,' McIntosh says. 'What struck me was how public money was spread around the Prime Minister's riding without the minimum of financial background checks or credit checks. Sometimes actions make a story. Sometimes omissions by government officials are as telling and embarrassing. Reporters should look for both.'

Public records are the backbone of good investigative research. From court documents to government funding databases to motor vehicle records, they document human activity in the public sphere. They record how we are governed, how elected officials make decisions, and how these affect our lives. They show us how we treat our most vulnerable, identify where public money goes, explain threats against our health or our lives, and bring context and detail to matters of public debate.

Governments run on paperwork, producing an endless stream of information. Some of it is available online, free of charge. Much of it is not, including an array of information and data of particular interest to researchers and journalists. From daycare inspection reports to environmental studies to internal audits, governments monitor their own activities closely. But they aren't always open to outside scrutiny and accessing public records locked inside government filing cabinets isn't always easy.

Predictably, the more potentially damaging a record, the more prickly governments tend to be about releasing it. The corollary rule is that the more difficult a record is to obtain, the greater the likelihood it contains information of genuine interest and concern. There can exist a culture of secrecy in Canadian bureaucracies; it isn't uncommon for officials to avoid criticism of themselves or their superiors by withholding information that could prove damaging or embarrassing. The principle of self-protection is entirely understandable, of course. But when it comes to the operation of public institutions such as governments, it becomes problematic. Democratic institutions must be open and transparent. Governments may be the custodians of public information, but they are also accountable to the public, which means they must provide reasonable public access to the records that document the conduct of public business.

Levels of government openness vary from municipality to municipality and between federal and provincial departments. The Internet age has opened up unprecedented possibilities for governments to share storehouses of information with citizens. Records that once sat in dusty rooms can now be placed online for fast, widespread, and cheap public access. Some government departments and agencies in Canada have seized that opportunity. All federal and provincial departments, and the vast majority of municipalities, have websites that contain stock information about their activities. Some, which we will explore in this chapter, have gone beyond promotional material and press releases to provide information of real use to researchers and journalists.

For example, the now infamous federal sponsorship scandal (a.k.a. AdScam), in which millions in public money went to pay extravagant advertising agency commissions, first hit the public radar screen in 2000 when an internal audit was released on a government website. That audit became the basis for investigation by journalists, researchers, and federal officials. Their research has pointed to widespread misspending of extraordinary scope and breadth.

While the Internet hasn't triggered a revolution in government transparency, it has caused a steady trickle of information. For researchers, that's good news. The days of doing the doublespeak tango with bureaucrats in order to get a basic public report aren't over—not nearly—but, at least for some basic information, you no longer have to pick up the phone.

You do, however, still have to know where to find what you want. That means answering the following:

1. What level of government has jurisdiction over the issue you're researching—federal, provincial, or municipal?
2. What specific department would have the information? Would more than one department potentially maintain records on your research subject?
3. How are the records maintained and released to the public?

In this chapter, we will outline what information is available from governments at the federal, provincial, and municipal levels.

Where They Are

The most basic part of the research process entails knowing where to go to find answers. In this section, we present resources for all three levels of government in Canada.

The federal level

The government of Canada
The first online stop for any federal government research is the official website at *canada.gc.ca*. The offerings here explain federal structure, organizations, acts, and publications. There are also a number of practical and useful resources here (listed on the left sidebar of the site or within one of those sidebar hyperlinks), including

- *Departments and Agencies.* A listing of URLs for every federal department and agency.
- *Contact Your Government.* If you know the name of the government employee you need to contact, this database will turn up a title and contact information. If you don't have a name, you can also search by job title, telephone number, or organization.
- *Contact Your MP.* A searchable database of members of Parliament by name or postal code.
- *Senators.* A listing of current senators with biographies and links to their personal websites.
- *Embassies and Consulates.* A complete listing of all Canadian embassies and consulates with contact information.

There is also a series of extremely useful tools that let you search the online records of a particular department without the anguish of having to navigate through a complex and confusing set of aimless links.

Narrowing your search on the Government of Canada site, start by choosing the 'Departments and Agencies' link. This comprehensive listing of federal institutions is a good starting place. Consider which ministries and agencies might have jurisdiction over the issue you're researching. Dig into each site and you'll find the usual array of press releases and publications. But it's also a central resource for such important information as public opinion research, acts and regulations, and programs and services—all essential elements you'll likely need to consult for in-depth stories.

Use the A–Z Subject Index as a starting point. You'll find a list of topics under which a department's documents are organized. In the Agriculture and Agri-Food Canada index, choose 'Beef' as a topic and you'll find dozens of documents ranging from the self-promotional to the comprehensive.

Go to the Parks Canada homepage and type 'Waterton Lakes National Park' into the search field—thousands of pages emerge on issues ranging from water quality to environmental assessments to conservation plans in the southern Alberta park. The utility here is obvious. If you're researching problems with Canadian submarines, a check with the Department of National Defence search tool using 'submarines' as a keyword produces a long list of documents that provide background on the federal government's submarine contracts, purchases, and activities. As with any online search tool, the more specific you can be, using several keywords that gradually narrow your search, the more useful the results.

There is a sanitized quality to all of these records. The language is generally bureaucratic and the content has been thoroughly vetted by officials before ending up here. But as official government documents, they provide reporters with a solid grounding in the key issues, ideas for further inquiry, and a starting point for asking specific questions.

Also listed on each federal department site is a link called 'proactive disclosure'. Listed there will be travel and hospitality expenses for selected government officials and most contracts over $10,000, along with other interesting spending data. The records have prompted some intriguing public interest stories.

In 2008, the *Toronto Star* analyzed about 60,000 travel expenses from federal ministers, political staff, and senior public servants. Among the notable findings were $6000 flights to London, $18,000 flights to Australia, $7000 flights to Paris, and $11,000 flights to Indonesia.

Another useful site for researching federal government records is Info Source (*www.infosource.gc.ca*). It lists all records, including databases, held by government departments. Choose 'Sources of Federal Government Information', then go to 'List of Institutions'. Choose the relevant ministry or ministries and the 'Institution-Specific Classes of Records'. Then behold what amounts to a card catalogue of the department's record-keeping system and the specific records it maintains. Among the lengthy list of resources maintained by Environment Canada, for example, are records titled 'Toxicology Network', which document the work of Canadian university scientists conducting research 'in response to Canadians' concerns about toxic substances and risks posed to human health and the environment.' Make note of the record number (in this case, ENV STB 100) in order to make further inquiries with the department. Ask to see a sample of the records. Another useful record listed is titled 'Strategic Policy' (record number ENV SPB 510) defined as 'information on departmental directions and policies.'

A simple scanning of 'program records' for the most appropriate ministries or agencies will likely turn up a number of named records that could prove useful. Once you've identified records you're interested in, it's a good idea to get more detailed information from officials about exactly what's contained in the records and how you can obtain them.

You should also consult the 'Standard Classes of Records' link for a more general look at how federal government departments and agencies document their duties. Learning the bookkeeping practices will go a long way toward helping you conduct productive conversations with ministry officials. Learn to call records by the names they use. Speak their language. Just perusing the list of standard records will give you ideas. There are 'audits', 'disclosure to investigative bodies', 'access to information and privacy requests', 'procurement and contracting', and 'furniture and furnishings'.

Another resource of meaningful value to federal government researchers is the Treasury Board of Canada Secretariat's departmental performance reports (available at *www.tbs-sct.gc.ca*; look under 'Reports'). This section of the Treasury Board's site provides a central listing of federal department performance reports, internal audits, and other documents.

There are also some helpful tools for tracking the interests of politicians and bureaucrats. Most federal departments conduct public opinion polling, for example. The general intent is to gauge the mindset of the Canadian public on a particular policy direction, how best to frame an issue or direct an advertising campaign, and whether a particular initiative will fly at all with voters.

Public opinion research reports contracted after 1 August 2006 are collected here: *http://www.porr-rrop.gc.ca/index-e.html*. Look inside and you'll find reports searchable by ministry, keyword, contractor, or year. A 2009 report from the Department of National Defence, for example, documents a contract with a polling firm that conducted research evaluating TV and print 'advertising concepts promoting benefits of a career with the Canadian Forces among people involved in or interested in skilled trades.'

If there's a specific government bureaucrat you'd like to contact about any of the information you gather, you might try looking up their contact information, titles, and locations here: *http://sage-geds.tpsgc-pwgsc.gc.ca/cgi-bin/direct500/eng/ TE?FN=index.htm*.

An online collection of federal databases listed by department is available here: *http://dsp-psd.communication.gc.ca/Checklist/s01-01-e.html*. An invaluable resource, you'll find a comprehensive repository of public data sources maintained by the federal government—both a tool for accessing authoritative information and a place to go for new ideas on issues you might not have even considered before.

Non-governmental groups are also doing good work to help promote greater transparency for government information. *Visiblegovernment.ca* collects and publishes information from governments including contracts.

The non-partisan *Howdtheyvote.ca* is a handy tool for checking your local MP's voting record and utterances in Parliament. The collection of records, broken down by member, brings together a complete historical voting record (yeah, nay, absent, or abstained) and transcripts of the words they spoke while holding the floor.

Remember that you'll need to independently verify any information you collect from such sites since they're not official federal government sources.

The parliament of Canada

The main site at *www.parl.gc.ca* documents the workings of government—the players, the committees, the meetings, and the decisions. If your research has to do with federal government policy and procedure, this is the most authoritative online source for backgrounding the issues and the government's handling of them.

Among the tools here are

- *Senate and House of Commons debates.* Complete debate transcripts can be found here.
- *House of Commons committees.* You can get here a list of federal committees and subcommittees ranging from Aboriginal Affairs to Transport.
- *Committee records.* Much of the heavy lifting when it comes to public policy work is done by government committees. This resource lets you search the issues studied, the research collected, and the experts they've consulted. Detailed information is listed for each committee including a schedule of all meetings with date, time and location, the committee's studies and activities, reports, membership, and news releases. Also, see 'Substantive Reports of Committees'.
- *Parliamentary secretaries.* Here, you'll find a list of ministers' secretaries, including backgrounds and contact information. Secretaries to ministers are often good contacts for further information on a particular minister's portfolio.
- *Bills.* This includes a list of Senate and House of Commons bills up for debate, along with their text, status, and further background.

Searching by Subject

Sometimes, you don't know exactly what you're looking for or where it might be located. Rather than searching for the source, there are ways you can search by general subject areas for federal government information.

The federal government's official site contains a search-by-topic resource (*www.servicecanada.gc.ca*) with subject categories including health, seniors, consumer information, public safety, and youth.

Another way of finding the specific needles in the haystack for federal government information is the 'Search Engines by Departments and Agencies' page (*http://canada.gc.ca/depts/major/depind-eng.html*). It provides links to search engines for each of the federal ministries and agencies. Assuming you know which federal body has jurisdiction for the issue you're researching, this resource will take you directly to a search tool for that agency or ministry, and allow you to use keywords to track down the specific information you're after. This should prove much faster than fishing aimlessly through the seemingly endless links on the federal government site.

Library and Archives Canada, or the LAC (*www.collectionscanada.gc.ca/caninfo/ecaninfo.htm*), also provides a subject-based resource called 'Canadian Information by Subject', which catalogues information on such topics as Aboriginal peoples, sports, literature, black history, and labour. Of particular note for many journalistic researchers is the political science section, which has a list of archived material.

Political parties
Based on the research tools above, a researcher should be able to determine where a government of the day stands on a particular matter of public interest (although the power of political prevarication can never be underestimated). Researchers are often just as interested, however, in knowing the positions of opposition parties.

At both the federal and provincial levels, opposition parties are obviously good sources for views that challenge government positions. Opposition critics specialize in particular areas of public policy, such as agriculture, the economy, the military, and foreign affairs. They tend to do a great deal of independent research themselves on matters of public importance. Staff members collect documents, file access-to-information requests, and consult experts on a wide array of subjects. If the critics are willing to share those insights (and they often are in the interests of spurring debate), they can provide access to records that you might never otherwise know about, or to documents that could take months to obtain independently. Further, opposition parties and their staff members tend to have a strong grasp of the political machinations or hidden agendas that might be driving a particular government policy. All of that makes them valuable research sources.

Of course, their interests are firmly vested. But that doesn't mean their information doesn't have value; the more information you collect as a researcher, the better.

Here are the URLs for Canada's major federal political parties:

- The Liberal Party of Canada: *www.liberal.ca*
- The Conservative Party of Canada: *www.conservative.ca*
- The Bloc Québecois (French-language site only): *www.blocquebecois.org*
- The New Democratic Party of Canada: *www.ndp.ca*
- The Green Party of Canada: *www.green.ca*

The provincial/territorial level

Provincial and territorial governments are responsible for some of the most vital public services Canadians receive, from education to health care to public safety. That makes their work a matter of profound interest to researchers and journalists. In many cases, however, provincial governments are less approachable than their federal counterpart. They tend to have fewer staff people dealing with research requests from the public. And provincial ministries are less likely to make 'routine disclosures' of basic records to the same extent as federal departments. Still, there are vast amounts of material inside provincial offices that should be made public.

The first step in researching an issue of provincial jurisdiction is finding out which department or ministry is responsible. Some issues, of course, are obvious. If your research has to do with environmental spills, every province has some form of an environment ministry. If the work involves provincial finances, you'll be heading for the finance or revenue ministry. While the ministerial divisions and titles differ from province to province, there are general areas of public policy such as health, education, children's services, science, and economic development that are common across the country.

Some issues overlap ministries. Air pollution, for example, may be of interest to both the health and environment ministries. You will want to know what research and information is held by each. Studies, statistics, and reports should all be available for the asking or on the ministries' websites.

Every provincial government has a website outlining its ministries, ministers, programs, and policies. Generally speaking, these are brochure-like sites providing basic information distinctly from a government-policy perspective. You won't ever find open disclosure of records or data that contradict or challenge government policy or highlight problems. Instead, sites such as these reflect the agenda of the governing party, and are more often filled with carefully worded press releases, lists of government services, greetings from politicians, and thoroughly vetted government documents.

Still, those materials can be extremely useful. A central repository of government press releases, for example, provides a quick, easy way of accessing the governing party's position on any matter of public debate. And many provincial sites have search tools that let you dig up public statements on specific issues. Reading statements that were made some time ago can help you chart a government's evolving position, bringing you far greater understanding of public-policy decisions and their implications. Provincial budget documents, studies, water-quality advisories, committee reports, and texts of speeches are all valuable research resources.

Another handy tool is government directories, which provide contact information for all the various ministries and departments along with all elected representatives. Ontario's website (*www.gov.on.ca*), for example, has a directory that allows you to search by name, department, job title, or even phone number to track down the appropriate person in the maze of bureaucracy. Spend time digging into your provincial government's website and you're bound to discover interesting areas of inquiry you may well never have considered. Take, for example, the Crane Operators Appeal Board listed in the online government directory on Nova Scotia's site—the tribunal regulates the seemingly niche crane-operating industry.

There are also rare databases available on some provincial sites. For example, several provinces allow the public to conduct lien searches on their sites for a fee (discussed below). Many provinces also provide online databases listing public contracts up for bid and recently awarded. We'll deal more with these records below.

For quick reference, here are the main provincial and territorial websites:

- Government of Alberta: *www.alberta.ca*
- Legislative Assembly of Alberta: *www.assembly.ab.ca*
- Government of British Columbia: *www.gov.bc.ca*
- Legislative Assembly of British Columbia: *www.leg.bc.ca*
- Government of Manitoba: *www.gov.mb.ca*
- Legislative Assembly of Manitoba: *www.gov.mb.ca/legislature*
- Government of New Brunswick: *www.gnb.ca*
- Legislative Assembly of New Brunswick: *www.gnb.ca/legis*
- Government of Newfoundland and Labrador: *www.gov.nf.ca*
- House of Assembly of Newfoundland and Labrador: *www.assembly.nl.ca*
- Government of the Northwest Territories: *www.gov.nt.ca*
- Legislative Assembly of the Northwest Territories: *www.assembly.gov.nt.ca*
- Government of Nova Scotia: *www.gov.ns.ca*
- Nova Scotia Legislature: *www.gov.ns.ca/legislature*
- Government of Nunavut: *www.gov.nu.ca*
- Legislative Assembly of Nunavut: *www.assembly.nu.ca*
- Government of Ontario: *www.gov.on.ca*
- Legislative Assembly of Ontario: *www.ontla.on.ca*
- Government of Prince Edward Island: *www.gov.pe.ca*
- Legislative Assembly of Prince Edward Island: *www.assembly.pe.ca*
- Government of Quebec: *www.gouv.qc.ca*
- National Assembly of Quebec: *www.assnat.qc.ca*
- Government of Saskatchewan: *www.gov.sk.ca*
- Legislative Assembly of Saskatchewan: *www.legassembly.sk.ca*
- Yukon: *www.gov.yk.ca*
- Yukon Legislative Assembly: *www.legassembly.gov.yk.ca*

The municipal level

In many ways for citizens, municipalities are the most direct and accessible level of government. From traffic congestion to apartment-building inspections to parking, the issues dealt with by city and town bureaucracies have an immediacy in our daily lives in a way that foreign aid or national defence often do not. The practicality of municipal issues can make such research both approachable and it can also be fuelled by public interest. But cities and towns do a poorer job at opening up their records. Local governments generally have fewer resources than provincial or federal departments for communications, and public disclosure is frequently not a priority in the day-to-day workings of municipal staff.

The Federation of Canadian Municipalities provides links to all provincial and territorial municipal associations (*www.fcm.ca*). Read through some of these and you'll quickly discover that too few contain the in-depth information researchers might want—city contract details, council meeting minutes and reports, and inspection databases. The smaller the municipality, the greater the likelihood its website will simply be an online promotional publication. Larger centres—such as Vancouver (*vancouver.ca*) and Halifax (*halifax.ca*)—tend to provide more useful information.

Toronto (*www.toronto.ca*) has a very useful website which contains a vast array of information of interest to journalists and researchers. All of the city's food-establishment inspections are posted on the city's popular DineSafe site (*http://app.toronto.ca/food2/index.jsp*). The city's auditor general posts reports on the site, some of which make for interesting reading into the conduct of bureaucrats or politicians. The city's integrity commissioner, whose job it is to resolve complaints and dispense advice to councillors on issues related to the city's code of conduct, also posts complaints and reports on the site. They often deal with allegations against specific councillors and whether their conduct breached rules around issues such as conflict of interest. Toronto also has an ombudsman (responsible for investigating complaints of administrative unfairness) and a lobbyist registrar (who monitors lobbyist activities and conduct), both of whom detail their findings and reports on the site. Even if your municipality doesn't have such automatic disclo-sures, you might want to inquire about such records from the equivalent account-ability officers.

The patchiness of municipal online resources means that much of your research and record gathering may need to be done in person at city hall. A host of documents contained there deserve scrutiny, from budget and audit records to council and committee meeting minutes to public health documents.

Non-governmental sources

While governments are primary sources for the operation of public policy, plenty of other organizations follow the work of government and do their own public-interest research, providing important perspectives on matters of importance. They study everything from economics to culture to sports. And they generally cite or conduct research and studies—of varying quality—to back up their mes-sages. Those messages fall all across the political spectrum.

The Taxpayers Federation, for example, is a conservative, fiscally minded inter-est group concerned with government spending and taxation levels in Canada.[10] On the other side of the ideological fence are groups such as the Canadian Centre for Policy Alternatives, a left-leaning public-policy group that, among other things, has crafted alternative budgets recommending government spending increases and 'social reinvestment' to fund better services and public infrastructure.[11] Other non-governmental groups include the more centrist Canadian Policy Research Networks (*http://cprn.org*) which provides research on a range of topics from workplace safety to daycare.

It's important to understand the background of such organizations to recognize their ideological predispositions. Unlike opposition parties, the biases of special-interest groups and think tanks are not immediately obvious without some prior research. But those biases are inevitably there.

Studies on poverty or hospital wait times published by the Vancouver-based Fraser Institute, for example, must be considered in light of the think tank's right-leaning stance. Similarly, research from the Canadian Auto Workers Union is likely to reflect a left-of-centre vision. Those biases don't mean the research isn't valuable; the studies can contain important, often unique original research that sheds light on public-policy issues. But it needs to be considered in context.

What They Say

The political process is said to be conducted in public. Public-policy decisions are often the result of contentious debate, political grandstanding, and compromise. What politicians say in Parliament, provincial legislatures, or city council meetings is on the record and immensely valuable in terms of understanding how public policy is made. Debate transcripts in Canada are generally published in the *Hansard*, named after a family that served as official printers to the British House of Commons roughly two centuries ago. Today, a *Hansard* transcript is a substantially verbatim report, although repetitions and redundancies are often removed.

The federal level

As we mentioned earlier, House of Commons debates are available online with full transcripts updated daily (*www.parl.gc.ca*). You can search by date and subject of the debate. The site also includes Senate debates, journals, and details on legislation. The online transcripts date back to the mid-1990s; debate records prior to that are maintained by the federal archives.

Transcript records frame the general public debate on a particular issue, and help journalists and researchers hold officials to account over time. Promises and positions are committed to the public record. Studying a politician's views from several months ago, or even years ago, could bear some interesting fruit when you look at what that person is saying or doing today.

The provincial/territorial level

Legislative debates are also recorded and transcribed for public review. They are generally based on a similar structure that allows researchers the ability to search by date or subject.

Here are the online provincial sites for legislative debate transcripts:

- Alberta: *www.assembly.ab.ca* (look for *Assembly Documents and Records*)
- British Columbia: *www.leg.bc.ca/hansard*
- Manitoba: *www.gov.mb.ca/legislature/hansard*
- New Brunswick: *www.gnb.ca/legis* (look for *House Business*)
- Newfoundland and Labrador: *www.assembly.nl.ca* (look for *Proceedings*)
- Nova Scotia: *www.gov.ns.ca/legislature/house_business/hansard.html*
- Northwest Territories: *www.assembly.gov.nt.ca* (look for *Hansard*)
- Nunavut: *www.assembly.nu.ca/english/debates/index.html*
- Ontario: *www.ontla.on.ca* (look for *Debates and Proceedings*)
- Prince Edward Island: *www.assembly.pe.ca/hansard*
- Quebec: *http://www.assnat.qc.ca/en/travaux-parlementaires/assemblee-nationale/39-1/index.html*
- Saskatchewan: *www.legassembly.sk.ca/hansard*
- Yukon: *www.hansard.gov.yk.ca*

Newspaper databases and archives

There are other sources for documenting the words and arguments of elected officials. Reporters are usually present during political debates recording and transcribing debates and their work shows up in newspapers and broadcast outlets every day. They may quote only a few lines from an entire day of debate. But those quotations are generally designed to summarize the central debate and reflect the most important comments.

Most newspapers have online editions that allow you to read up-to-the-minute reports and articles. Some allow you to research articles dating back a few days. But only newspaper archive databases such as Factiva or LexisNexis will allow you to conduct detailed research on what has been said on the public record—in news stories, broadcast news transcripts, and press releases along with numerous news sources. Such subscription news databases can be extremely expensive. But many university, public libraries, and news organizations have subscriptions with news archive services.

What They Get

One ever-present consideration for journalists who research public-interest issues is the hidden influences on political decisions. Why, for example, did a particular elected official lobby on behalf of a particular firm for a government contract? Why does a certain politician vote consistently against environmental-protection measures?

As much as we might hope political decisions are made in the public interest, a heart-sinking array of evidence exists to the contrary. Sometimes, the motivations behind political actions can be traced to financial support for politicians. Political contribution data is one of the most basic tools for examining political motivations. Elected officials who receive financial support from corporations, unions, and other organizations may be seen to be influenced by the political or social aims of those donors.

A mining company that lavishes a local politician with financial support needed to get elected might expect its interests to be protected when industry-unfriendly legislation is proposed and voted on in Parliament. Political contribution records are one way of studying the underlying forces behind the conduct of elected representatives. Political contribution data can sometimes show links between elected officials and people in the community which can help shed light on the hidden reasons shaping political decision-making.

The federal level

As of January 2007, only Canadian citizens and permanent residents can make political donations to registered parties and candidates. Companies, unions, and unincorporated associations are banned from making donations. But that doesn't mean the practice doesn't happen through less official avenues. The challenge for researchers interested in political influence is connecting the names of individual donors with the corporate, union, or association interests they represent.

At the federal level, Elections Canada (*www.elections.ca*) collects and manages political contribution data. It is public and complete, and is easily searched by location, donor, candidate, or party. Search for the election financing section and the searchable database on contributions and expenses.

Most researchers will be interested in searching by candidate and donor for detailed summaries of what a particular MP received from whom. For example, the data shows Prime Minister Stephen Harper received nearly $16,000 from 24 contributors during the 2008 general election. Names of contributors who give more than $200 are listed in the records. In Harper's case, the 24 individuals, mainly from Alberta, gave amounts ranging from $250 to $1100 (the federal contribution limit) each. Their names, cities, provinces, and postal codes are listed in the records. Further research on those individuals would provide details on their professional affiliations.

The provincial/territorial level

Provincial governments generally provide similar disclosure around political contributions, although specific rules can vary. British Columbia (*www.elections.bc.ca*), Ontario (*www.electionsontario.on.ca*), Quebec (*www.electionsquebec.qc.ca*), and Newfoundland and Labrador (*www.elections.gov.nl.ca/elections/finance.asp*), for example, all have online databases detailing campaign contributions.

Donations by corporations and unions are illegal in Manitoba and Quebec.

The municipal level

Municipal political contribution records are also considered public across Canada. Most often, researchers have to visit the specific city or town hall to obtain the records.

Challenges interpreting campaign contributions

You need to be careful about researching political contribution records. There are caps on how much money companies and individuals can contribute to politicians each year (depending on whether the politician is running at the federal, provincial, or municipal level). The caps, which vary from province to province, are designed to eliminate undue political influence by unions and corporations. Those with deep pockets who are willing to contribute significant amounts of money to political parties might well expect something in return—this often results in perception problems with which governments across the country are wrestling.

But in most of the country, motivated donors—those with an interest in supporting a particular candidate beyond those caps—can donate well beyond stated caps by splitting up their contributions several ways. For example, they might contribute under the name of their company, contribute again under their own name, and perhaps even more under the names of family members or colleagues. Splitting contributions under different names gives an individual the opportunity to more than quadruple his or her contributions and donate well beyond the legal limit for an individual.

A joint analysis of political contribution records conducted by *The Hamilton Spectator* and the *Toronto Star* in 2003 found political contribution limits frequently broken with questionable results. One group of at least 24 Toronto-area companies donated more than $600,000 to Ontario's provincial Tories between 1995 and 2001, the newspapers reported. The same family of companies was involved in a controversial land deal in which, opposition politicians alleged, the government was planning to sell 800 hectares of Crown land at below-market rates without public notice.[12]

Understanding the true extent of the financial generosity of donors may take some diligence and investigative research. Generally speaking, journalists and other researchers are not merely interested in who donates to politicians and political parties. They're also interested in whether those donations represent a relationship that goes beyond general political sympathies. One of the classic methods of tracking those relationships is simply 'backgrounding' (i.e., doing detailed research on) people and companies involved, all the while looking for other names—of colleagues, relatives, or companies—that could appear on political contribution lists. Those names may be found using corporate searches, personal property searches, Web resources, and court records (all addressed elsewhere in this book). The goal here is to get a good sense of the universe of people surrounding the central figure. Those people or corporate identities may well share an interest in offering financial support to a particular politician or government. Find out who they are and then run their names through the same donation records.

'The people behind the companies involved in this kind of political largesse always say they have done nothing wrong and say they donate to support the democratic process,' says reporter Laurie Monsebraaten, one of the journalists who worked on the *Spectator–Star* joint project. 'While it's difficult to prove political favours were granted to political donors, the exercise of listing the government contracts or appointments of a particularly generous giver can certainly raise a red flag.'[13]

What They Do

The actions of governments are generally well documented. Public records document how officials conduct themselves in our name and the impact their actions have on the public interest. It's the role of journalists and other researchers to study public records in an effort to understand and publicize matters of importance. It would be impossible to produce a comprehensive list of specific Canadian public records here. But below is a sampling of documents and data that researchers often use to investigate public issues that matter to a wide array of people.

Government records

Meeting minutes
At all levels of government, people hold meetings, many of which are on the record, with published minutes kept that indicate who was there, what they said, any motions, and resulting votes and resolutions. Such records are maintained by the specific department, ministry, council, or agency.

Many federal departments produce minutes of committee meetings that don't provide the kind of detail journalists and researchers require. It's also important to note that meeting minutes will not contain record of any discussions held *in camera* (i.e., behind closed doors). These meetings present a serious problem for journalists in many Canadian municipalities. There are perfectly justifiable reasons for going in camera: councillors may need to discuss sensitive legal matters or personnel issues, for instance. But often, their deliberations deserve more public scrutiny, so you may need a strategy for getting past the closed-door treatment. One way is to find someone inside the room who is uncomfortable with secrecy and feels deliberations should be open to the public. A politician or bureaucrat prepared to break ranks and share information about the hidden proceedings is an invaluable source for circumventing unreasonable secrecy.

For any in-depth research, you should go beyond minutes and request access to the briefing documents that were prepared for officials who attended. In some cases, these can be obtained informally; other times, you may need to submit a formal request under the appropriate access legislation.

Auditor's reports

Auditors have emerged as powerful watchdogs over the financial workings of government. They have unmatched access to government records, the ability to analyze the stewardship of public funds, and the power to hold governments to account for their shortcomings. Auditor's reports often criticize governments for their misdeeds and point to general problem areas worthy of further investigation.

A report by Sheila Fraser, the auditor general, caused the now-infamous AdScam, or federal sponsorship scandal, in 2003: 'Rules were broken or ignored at every stage of the process for more than four years,' Fraser said in a statement featuring remarkably strong language. 'And there was little evidence of value received for the money spent.'[14]

Those revelations—and others that followed in months of intense media coverage—combined to paint an increasingly troubling portrait of government waste. It triggered a controversial federal government inquiry that reached ever upward to the top levels of power in Ottawa. Such insights into the operation of bureaucracies are rare, but auditor general's reports are among the fleeting opportunities we have to peek behind the curtain.

Auditors operate at all levels of government, from the municipal to the federal. Their audits are limited by the time and resources of the auditor's office, but a close read often points researchers in the direction of areas worthy of a much closer look. The reports tend to speak in general terms using cumulative data to draw attention to points of interest. They might mention $5 million in payments to six companies, for instance, without detailing the payments or naming the companies. Those figures are based on analysis of records that are not generally included with the public release of the report, raising interesting questions about who got the money and why. A detail like this offers a launching pad for investigations; it could prove extremely enlightening to know the names of individuals behind those companies who received the suspect government payouts.

The Federal Treasury Board maintains a handy 'Audit and Evaluations Database' (*www.tbs-sct.gc.ca/aedb-bdve/home-accueil-eng.aspx*) that lets you search by keyword, organizations, or simply by latest reports. If you click on a federal department, for example, a comprehensive listing of all audits and evaluations appear with links to the actual reports.

In July 2001, a city auditor's report in Toronto found that, in a random review of 90 payments to consultants, 71 per cent were processed without purchase orders as required. But while the report outlined numerous 'questionable' payments, it didn't name names. It wasn't until reporter Robert Cribb obtained the background records detailing those payments that the real story began to take shape.

The records revealed the names of the firms and individuals that had received millions in undocumented payments. Among them was a Rhode Island–based computer consultant whose firm billed $535,807, plus $8000 in hotel bills, for consulting work with the city even though only $180,000 of that was supported by purchase orders.[15] It raised more questions about why the operator of a small consulting firm from the United States was given a major consulting project with the City of Toronto. The consultant, as was heard later in a public inquiry, had an 'intimate sexual relationship' with the city's former treasurer, a woman who hired him to develop a tax-management system for the city.[16]

Municipal audit reports should be available from all municipalities. Below are the relevant links to the provincial and territorial offices:

- Alberta: *www.oag.ab.ca*
- British Columbia: *www.bcauditor.com*
- Manitoba: *www.oag.mb.ca*
- New Brunswick: *www.gnb.ca/OAG-BVG*
- Newfoundland and Labrador: *www.ag.gov.nl.ca/ag*
- Northwest Territories: *www.fin.gov.nt.ca*
- Nova Scotia: *www.gov.ns.ca/audg*
- Nunavut: *www.gov.nu.ca/finance/public.shtml*
- Ontario: *www.auditor.on.ca*
- Prince Edward Island: *www.assembly.pe.ca/auditorgeneral*
- Quebec: *www.vgq.gouv.qc.ca*
- Saskatchewan: *www.auditor.sk.ca*
- Yukon: *www.yukonenergy.ca/about/business/auditor_reports*

Public accounts and budget documents

Following the path of public money or the process behind important public-policy decisions inside a government bureaucracy isn't always easy, but it is one of the fundamental preoccupations of public-policy researchers and journalists. Elected officials are morally bound to be open and accountable with how they spend taxpayer dollars. When faced with officials who seek to avoid this obligation, you must find ways to access records that show where the money is going and why.

Budget records detail how governments spend. The federal receiver general prepares the public document each year covering the government's financial transactions over the previous 12 months. Surpluses or deficits, debt, gross domestic product trends, assets, and expenses are all detailed. The document is posted online at *www.tpsgc-pwgsc.gc.ca.*

Federal budget documents (*www.fin.gc.ca/pub/index-eng.asp*) provide valuable insights into finances and priorities that, with close review, can raise interesting questions or point to more specific areas of inquiry. The documents typically also have 'themed' sections that outline the government's plans in particular areas. For example, the 2007/08 federal budget contains sections on the government's statements on projected debt and overall economic health. It can be helpful to review these documents, even years after they are released, as a way of gauging how well a particular government met its stated fiscal goals.

As we discussed earlier, the federal government has adopted a so-called 'pro-active disclosure' policy compelling departments to publish travel and hospitality expenses for 'selected government officials', and details of contracts worth more than $10,000. Those statements are posted on individual federal ministry websites.

But the Treasury Board of Canada Secretariat maintains a centralized accounting of all those disclosures at *www.tbs-sct.gc.ca*.

Provincial and municipal governments also make budget documents open to the public either in hard copy or via their websites.

Here are the provincial and territorial online finance/budgetary resources:

- Alberta: *www.finance.gov.ab.ca*
- British Columbia: *www.gov.bc.ca/fin*
- Manitoba: *www.gov.mb.ca/finance*
- New Brunswick: *www.gnb.ca/0024/index-e.asp*
- Newfoundland and Labrador: *www.fin.gov.nl.ca/fin*
- Northwest Territories: *www.fin.gov.nt.ca*
- Nova Scotia: *www.gov.ns.ca/finance*
- Nunavut: *www.gov.nu.ca/finance*
- Ontario: *www.fin.gov.on.ca*
- Prince Edward Island: *www.gov.pe.ca/pt/index.php3*
- Quebec: *www.finances.gouv.qc.ca*
- Saskatchewan: *www.gov.sk.ca/finance*
- Yukon: *www.finance.gov.yk.ca*

Tender contracts

Governments do a great deal of business with the private sector. Each year, governments at all levels purchase goods and services from companies that bid for the contracts through a public tendering process. That process is designed to be open and subject to public scrutiny.

The federal government provides public access to its contracts and services through an online database called Contracts Canada (*contractscanada.gc.ca*). The information dates back to October 2004. (Accessing records prior to that date will likely require a formal access-to-information request, although it's always worth trying to get the records informally.) For example, go to the 'Contract History' tab at the top of the site and search for 'Bombardier', the Quebec-based aerospace giant, hitting the 'Vendor' option. The database turns up a list of federal contracts involving Bombardier. You can then view details of each contract.

Several provinces also have public tendering sites, including British Columbia (*www.bcbid.gov.bc.ca*), Alberta (*http://vendor.purchasingconnection.ca*), Saskatchewan (*www.sasktenders.gov.sk.ca*), and Quebec (*www.seao.ca/index.aspx*). But provincial and municipal contracts are not always online. It may well take some digging and phone calling to track down the amount of money that has gone to a particular company. But, however reluctant bureaucrats may be to help, the information should be public—it is, after all, public money.

Statistics

Canada is blessed with one of the best data-gathering agencies in the world: Statistics Canada (or StatsCan). The federal agency is an invaluable source of reliable data on everything from population to the environment to science and human behaviour. Much of it is posted online at *www.statcan.gc.ca.*

Census information—from community profiles that provide average income and population data to air-quality data—is available without charge. But the free material may not be as detailed as you would like. Delving more deeply into the data comes at a price.

CANSIM II (*cansim2.statcan.ca*) is a searchable Statistics Canada database containing more than 13 million socio-economic records. It's a remarkably useful site that allows you to customize requests for data on subjects as varied as the environment, labour, and 'social conditions'. For example, you can request the number of annual 'dangerous goods accidents recorded'. You can effectively create your own data chart, including the information you're most interested in, drawing from any of hundreds of different data sets. The charge for this service ranges from a few to hundreds of dollars.

It's important to contact Statistics Canada officials when you run up against data fees and to let them know why you want the records. The agency generally provides non-customized data for free to journalists, students, and researchers. Unfortunately, if you need customized material (requiring work by StatsCan staff), fees will likely be unavoidable.[17]

Canadian statistics are gathered and published by a number of government departments and agencies beyond Statistics Canada. They document everything from housing prices to Canadian incomes. Here is a sampling:

- Bank of Canada: *www.bankofcanada.ca*
- Canada Mortgage and Housing Corporation: *www.cmhc-schl.gc.ca*
- Canada Revenue Agency: *www.cra-arc.gc.ca*
- Department of Finance Canada: *www.fin.gc.ca*
- Industry Canada: *www.ic.gc.ca*

Provincial and territorial governments also maintain statistics on topics such as population, labour, and economics. Those records are maintained by provincial/territorial statistics agencies or within the various finance departments:

- Alberta: *www.finance.gov.ab.ca*
- British Columbia: *www.bcstats.gov.bc.ca*
- Manitoba: *www.gov.mb.ca/mbs*
- New Brunswick: *www.gnb.ca/0024/economics/index.asp*
- Newfoundland and Labrador: *www.stats.gov.nl.ca/Statistics*
- Northwest Territories: *www.stats.gov.nt.ca*
- Nova Scotia: *www.gov.ns.ca/finance/statistics/agency/index.asp*
- Nunavut: *www.gov.nu.ca/finance*
- Ontario: *www.gov.on.ca*
- Prince Edward Island: *www.gov.pe.ca/infopei*
- Quebec: *www.stat.gouv.qc.ca/publications*
- Saskatchewan: *www.gov.sk.ca/bureau.stats*
- Yukon: *www.eco.gov.yk.ca/stats*

There are also many statistical-gathering agencies in Canada outside of government, including

- Statistical Society of Canada: *www.ssc.ca*
- Canadian Institute for Health Information: *www.cihi.ca*
- First Nations Statistical Institute: *www.firststats.ca*
- Vital Statistics Council of Canada: *www.vscouncil.ca*
- Canadian Journal of Statistics: *www.mat.ulaval.ca/rcs*

Charity records

Charities are required to file annual statements with the federal government outlining their structure, directors, and financial information—how much money they've received, the sources of that income, and what they've done with it. It isn't exactly exhaustive public scrutiny, but it can provide an insight into organizations that vow to do public interest work with money from well-meaning donors.

There's no shortage of sobering stories contained in returns filed by Canada's 85,000 registered charities. The most exhaustive journalistic look into the charitable sector was a 2002 series in the *Toronto Star* by investigative reporter Kevin Donovan. He found nearly one in six charities spends more money on fundraising and administration than it does on charitable work. In the worst case, one charity received $651,823 from the public between 1997 and 1999, and devoted only $61,983 of that to charitable works—just 10 cents on the dollar.[18]

Charities submit an annual document called an 'information return' to the federal Charities Directorate (*www.ccra.gc.ca/charities*). In these records, charity directors are asked to '[describe] how the charity carried out its charitable purposes during the fiscal period,' including 'detailed information so a reader can clearly understand what the charity actually did to fulfill its mandate.' They are also asked to disclose any political activity, compensation to staff, revenues and expenses, along with how these were obtained or used.

Lobbyists

There are thousands of people in Canada employed to influence public policy by lobbying governments on behalf of corporations or organizations. Such arm twisting once occurred in private, but disclosure rules in Canada have now put lobbying on the public record federally and in some provinces.

There is nothing illegal or inappropriate about the act of lobbying decision-makers; the rules just require that lobbyists provide information about themselves and the subjects on which they are attempting to influence politicians. The *Lobbyists Registration Act* covers only people who are paid to lobby, including company employees for whom lobbying government represents 'a significant part of their duties' (20 per cent of their time or more). It also covers employees of not-for-profit organizations in which one or more workers lobby and the 'collective time devoted to lobbying for all those employees works out to be the same as a significant part of one employee's duties (20 per cent or more).' Lobbyists must now update their filings every six months. Volunteer lobbyists are not required to register federally.

Andrew McIntosh relied upon lobby registration records in his Shawinigate series. A federal register of lobbyists revealed that a Chrétien aide who lobbied local federal officials on behalf of Shawinigan hotelier Pierre Thibault wasn't registered as required by law. That revelation triggered the federal ethics counsellor's call for an RCMP investigation.[19]

Confusion exists around when lobbying is actually lobbying. The federal government has ruled that making simple inquiries or requests for information from government officials does not count. And calculating the percentage of time an individual within a company or organization devotes to lobbying opens up plenty of wiggle room.

Lobbyist records are available online through a public registry at *www.ocl-cal. gc.ca*, which you can search in a number of ways. You can find, for example, which lobbyists work on behalf of a particular company, or search by a lobbyist's name to determine if he or she is registered. The results will provide a detailed record of the lobbyist's registration, business address, and phone number. You will also find the subject matter on which they lobby (environment, industry, etc.); the government departments they lobby (e.g., National Defence, Industry Canada, etc.); and even communication techniques, such as 'informal communications', meetings, or telephone calls. The database can also generate a simple list of all active and terminated lobbyists according to criteria such as location and government institution. Search the corporate name Maple Leaf Foods, for example, and a long list of lobbyist names appear, some of which have an active registration to lobby government on behalf of the company and several more with inactive registrations.

There may be value in running the names of lobbyists, their partners, spouses, etc., through the election contribution database (discussed above) to see if they support specific politicians or parties.

Four provinces have also passed lobbyist disclosure laws: Ontario, Quebec, British Columbia, and Nova Scotia. Quebec's law is the most stringent, compelling all lobbyists—whether paid or not—to register. Following the federal model, all four of the provinces publish a registry of lobbyists that is open to public scrutiny. Here they are:

- British Columbia: *www.ag.gov.bc.ca/lra*
- Nova Scotia: *www.gov.ns.ca/snsmr/lobbyist*
- Ontario: *https://lobbyist.oico.on.ca*
- Quebec: *http://si2.commissairelobby.qc.ca/en/commissioner*

Environmental records
Environmental issues yield a whole host of public records and data. The sources range from government agencies to private companies and university researchers.

The National Pollutant Release Inventory (*www.ec.gc.ca*) is among the most high-profile environmental databases, giving data on annual pollution releases into the air, water, and land from more than 2500 facilities across Canada. Environment Canada also publishes greenhouse-gas emission data that's searchable online or downloadable to your computer for more precise analysis (*www. ec.gc.ca*). In addition to providing information and data on weather and climate, Environment Canada also publishes information about prosecutions under the *Canadian Environmental Protection Act* and *Fisheries Act* (*www.ec.gc.ca*). The records show the charges laid against companies and individuals, locations and dates, and their status before the courts. Many provinces have similar databases.

Also, check the Canadian Environmental Assessment Registry (*www.ceaa-acee. gc.ca*), which catalogues projects undergoing environmental assessment across Canada. It provides summaries of each project.

Food safety

When Canadians began dying from listeria-tainted cold cuts in the summer of 2008, the CBC and the *Toronto Star* conducted a joint investigation into what happened. The series of stories revealed there were no requirements for listeria testing in meat plants, that companies conducting tests detecting listeria did not have to warn federal inspectors, and that inspectors spent as little as 15 minutes a day ensuring food safety in large, complex meat plants. The investigation also revealed that meat produced at a Maple Leaf Foods plant in Toronto and served to elderly Canadians in nursing homes contained levels of the deadly bacteria that scientists hadn't detected beforehand. The result was 22 dead and hundreds—perhaps thousands—more struck ill.

The stories relied on federal food regulations and protocols, food pathogen test results, internal reports and studies and a range of other records that document how the country's food-safety system works. Many of those documents were difficult to obtain. It took access-to-information requests, leaks, and close work with sources. But the steady flow of troubling reports focused the minds of Canadians and government officials.

Within weeks, Canadian Food Inspection Agency (CFIA) officials announced new, tougher rules for listeria testing and mandatory reporting of positive test results to inspectors. It also triggered two federal investigations, which themselves created thousands of pages of insightful and revelatory records such as internal memos and reviews.

Food safety is among the top priorities of government and a foundational expectation of citizens. Among the basic published records from the CFIA are food recalls and allergy alerts (*www.inspection.gc.ca*). Whenever you learn of a recall from a specific company, it's worth checking the CFIA's site to see if the food producer has a history of similar recalls that point to a larger concern or pattern.

The CFIA also publishes audits, reviews, and evaluations (*www.inspection.gc.ca/ english/agen/eval/evale.shtml*), which contain potentially invaluable information about resource issues, 'lessons learned' from food-safety incidents, and proposed policy changes to food-safety oversight protocols.

Watching over the food safety watchdog is the Office of the Auditor General of Canada, which conducts regular reports on the CFIA to gauge how well it is meeting its mandate (*www.oag-bvg.gc.ca/internet/English/parl_lpf_e_1228.html*).

Also, keep in mind that Canada exports food to other countries that have an abiding interest in its safety. The United States, for example, sends inspectors to Canada each year to look inside our food-production facilities. The resulting reports are published by the US Department of Agriculture's Food Safety and Inspection Service (*www.fsis.usda.gov/regulations_&_policies/Foreign_Audit_Reports/index.asp*).

Health Canada, which also has federal jurisdiction covering food safety, publishes food-safety assessment reports online (*www.hc-sc.gc.ca/fn-an/securit/eval/reports-rapports/index-eng.php*)—useful records that evaluate current and proposed policies for protecting Canadians from food-borne illnesses.

While food-production oversight is generally a federal responsibility, provincial and municipal governments also play an important role. Many provincial health or agriculture ministries have oversight over smaller food-production and -processing facilities and conduct investigations into food-safety concerns. Municipal governments are generally responsible for inspecting restaurants and other food establishments—inspections which generate reports that should be made public on websites or upon request.

Transportation

For the first time in 2006, a Canadian news organization undertook a comprehensive analysis of aviation incident and accident data, revealing that Canadian passengers were at risk on nearly a daily basis. Three reporters from *The Hamilton Spectator*, the *Toronto Star*, and *The Record of Waterloo Region* teamed to analyze more than 50,000 aviation incidents that revealed troubling safety patterns and harrowing individual incidents. Among them were hundreds of potentially fatal mistakes by pilots and air-traffic controllers that brought planes too close together in the sky and on runways.

As a result of the *Spectator*'s four-year pursuit of the incident data, Transport Canada changed its policies to allow for the public release of the incident records.

Journalists and researchers can dig into aviation incidents contained in Transport Canada's Civil Aviation Daily Occurrence Reporting System (CADORS), which is now published online and through daily email updates (*www.tc.gc.ca*).

Transport Canada's website also contains a wealth of information on rules and procedures, laws and regulations, service difficulty advisories, airworthiness directives, and recent enforcement actions. Of particular note for researchers is the listing of service difficulty reports, a monthly summary of corporate offenders found to have breached aviation regulations (*www.tc.gc.ca/civilaviation/standards/enforcement/publications/corporate/menu.htm*) and the agency's annual reports (*www.tc.gc.ca/pol/en/anre/menu.htm*).

StatsCan publishes useful aviation service bulletins that include aviation trends, air-carrier statistics, and details such as the number of passengers carried and kilometres travelled (*www.statcan.ca/english/freepub/51-004-XIE/51-004-XIE2008001.htm*).

If you need to make contact with pilots, work through their professional organizations. For starters, try the Air Line Pilots Association, International (*http://alpa.org*).

The Transportation Safety Board of Canada (*www.tsb.gc.ca*) publishes an archive of all TSB accident investigation reports, summary statistics on accidents and incidents, TSB procedures, rules and regulations, and all TSB press releases.

Nav Canada (*www.navcanada.ca*), the non-profit operator of air-traffic-control services in Canada, publishes an invaluable glossary of aviation terms for decrypting acronyms that constantly crop up in accident-investigation reports. The site also provides basic information on Nav Canada's operations, including media releases and annual reports.

For ground transportation research, Transport Canada publishes motor vehicle collision statistics (*www.tc.gc.ca/roadsafety/resources/researchstats/menu.htm#collision stats*). Several provinces also publish their own collision data, including British Columbia (*www.icbc.com/road-safety/safety-research/collision-statistics*), Saskatchewan (*www.sgi.sk.ca/sgi_pub/road_safety/trafficcollisionstats/index.htm*), and Newfoundland and Labrador (*www.roads.gov.nl.ca/collisionstats/default.html*). Ontario publishes a comprehensive annual road-safety report that summarizes fatalities, injuries, and collisions (*www.mto.gov.on.ca/english/safety/orsar*).

Finally, Transport Canada's Road Safety Recall Database (*http://wwwapps.tc.gc.ca/saf-sec-sur/7/vrdb-bdrv/search/Search.aspx?lang=eng*) details vehicle recalls and safety issues.

Health

Some of the most important in-depth reporting in Canada surrounds health issues. It's an area of intense public interest and a matter of heated debate and concern among Canadians.

The prevailing challenges here are the complexity of the subject matter and the traditional secrecy of the medical profession. There are, however, some important points of entry where reporters can dig into the data in order to begin forming good questions.

The Canadian Institute for Health Information (CIHI) is the most authoritative national source of health data (*http://secure.cihi.ca*). In addition to publishing annual reports on the state of Canada's health-care services and health spending, the independent, non-profit organization collects information directly from hospitals, regional health authorities, medical practitioners, and governments. Look under 'Data Collection' for a sampling of the range of data available. If the provided data isn't exactly what you're after, you can file a customized request. But expect delays and fees.

StatsCan is also a tremendous resource for health data including statistics on deaths from infectious and parasitic diseases, health indicators, pregnancy outcomes, cancer rates, and many other health issues.

Of course, Health Canada is a vast repository of health information as well. It publishes Advisories, Warnings and Recalls by subject (*www.hc-sc.gc.ca/ahc-asc/media/advisories-avis/alpha-eng.php*), which serves as a handy tool to periodically check for concerns that may not be widely known, or for ties to local stories. Also, check Health Canada's Consumer Product Recalls (*http://209.217.71.106/PR/home-accueil-e.jsp*)

Health Canada's Drug Product Database (*www.hc-sc.gc.ca*) provides a comprehensive look at the 24,000 pharmaceutical and biological drugs, veterinary drugs, and disinfectant products approved for use in Canada. Among other information, the database contains records organized by brand name, drug identification number (DIN), company, and ingredients.

The Health Canada site also provides notice of compliance listings, which show details of any new human or veterinary drug product approved for use in Canada, and of any changes made to the approval of an existing product. After the CBC and the *Toronto Star* investigated an increase in people's adverse drug reactions in 2004, the health agency was pressured into posting additional information, including its national Adverse Reaction Database.

If it's experts you need to help walk you through the often intimidating language and data, try your local university or college.

Science and research funding

The Social Sciences and Humanities Research Council of Canada (SSHRC; *www.sshrc.ca*) is a federal agency that funds university-based research and training in the social sciences and humanities. It has a search engine that allows you to find out more about who gets the money, and the amount of funding provided.

The Canadian Research Information System (*http://webapps.cihr-irsc.gc.ca/cris/Search?p_language=E&p_version=CRIS*) is another federal granting body for scientific research. Its database shows where the grant money is going. Search the term 'Alzheimer's' and you'll get a list of researchers who have been federally funded for their research on the disease, their affiliation, and the amount of money they received.

Other searchable databases are available at the Canadian Foundation for Innovation (*www.innovation.ca/en/projects-funded*), which funded $5.2 billion in funding for health research between 1997 and 2009, and Canada Research Chairs (*www.chairs-chaires.gc.ca*), which funds research professorships at Canadian universities.

Personal records

The vast majority of government records related to individuals in Canada are protected by privacy legislation. Health information or bank account details are not a matter of public record. There are, however, open records that contain information about the public dealings of individuals or companies—the property they own, professional designations, accomplishments, and so on. Some are held by governments; others by regulatory bodies; still others are simply published independently.

Land titles, assessments, deeds, and mortgages

Andrew McIntosh relied heavily on property records in researching the Shawinigate story in the 1990s. Land-registry records, in combination with civil-court records, helped him confirm that Yvon Duhaime had accumulated massive unpaid debts at the time he applied for and received the BDC mortgage loan—a key fact in building the story. The same records proved that Duhaime had failed to pay the builders who completed the expansion of his inn.[20] Using land-registry records and corporate searches, McIntosh also revealed how Claude Gauthier, a millionaire businessman in St Maurice, bought a parcel of land for $525,000 from the Grand-Mère Golf Club just days after one of his companies, Transelec Inc., received a $6.3 million contract from the Canadian International Development Agency. The auditor general later said Gauthier's company ought to have been disqualified from the tendering process for that contract.[21]

Land-title, assessment, deed, and mortgage records detail property ownership. Land-title records provide an ownership history of a property, the financial details of the various sales and purchases, the size of mortgage, charges against the property, and other details. Access to these records varies across the country; in many places, they are available in electronic databases at land-title offices, or online by subscription. In some cases, you can search these records online after setting up an account with the appropriate government department (this usually costs money).

A whole array of assessments, deeds, and mortgages, which are often accessible through land-title offices or through provincial databases, will help you delve into the financial details of ownership. Local assessment rolls are a complete list of all assessed property in a community—they generally list a ratepayer's name and address, a legal description of the property, assessed value of the property, improvements, and administrative details such as property classification and taxable status. Property records can also provide details such as the terms and interest rates of mortgages and any special terms or conditions around the property ownership.

Here is a listing of online land-title, deed, and assessment information, where available, at the provincial and territorial levels. The sites contain information about whether records can be searched remotely (and whether there are fees for accessing the records), plus a list of land-title and assessment offices for in-person searches.

- Alberta Land Titles: *www.servicealberta.gov.ab.ca/LandTitles.cfm*
- British Columbia Land Titles: *www.ltsa.ca* (or *www.bconline.gov.bc.ca/land_titles. html*); assessments: *www.bcassessment.bc.ca*
- Manitoba Land Titles: *www.gov.mb.ca/tpr/agency/contacts.html*; assessments: *http://web5.gov.mb.ca/public/default.aspx*; City of Winnipeg Assessments: *www. winnipegassessment.com*
- New Brunswick Land Titles and Assessments: *www.snb.ca*

- Newfoundland and Labrador Deeds: *www.gs.gov.nl.ca/registries/deeds.html*
- Northwest Territories Land Titles: *www.justice.gov.nt.ca/LandTitles*; assessments: *www.maca.gov.nt.ca/lands/Property/index.html*
- Nova Scotia Deeds: *www.gov.ns.ca/snsmr/property*; assessments: *www.pvsc.ca*
- Ontario Land Titles: *www.ontario.ca/en/information_bundle/land_registration/ STEL01_130081;* assessments: *www.assessmentontario.com*
- Prince Edward Island Deed Registry: *www.gov.pe.ca/infopei*; assessments: *www. gov.pe.ca/envengfor/index.php3?number=1024443&lang=E*
- Quebec Land Titles: *www.mrn.gouv.qc.ca/english/land/register/index.jsp*
- Saskatchewan Land Registry: *www.isc.ca*
- Yukon Land Titles: *www.justice.gov.yk.ca/prog/ls/lto*

Lien records

These documents, available through provincial and territorial government offices across the country, are a record of consumer and business loans to individuals who use their own property as collateral. Ministries that deal with corporate and consumer issues, such as Ontario's Ministry of Consumer and Business Services, generally keep them. The documents are often called 'personal property security registration' (PPSR) or 'personal property registry' (PPR) records.

Lenders, such as car dealerships or banks, register a 'notice' of a lien by filing a statement with the appropriate provincial ministry. The statement details the size and conditions of the loan. The lenders or sellers stake their claim against the personal property of a debtor, so such notices are recorded publicly as a way of serving notice that a debt is owed. Cars, boats, furniture, or other big-ticket items for which an individual has secured loans tend to show up here. The records themselves generally show the name and address of the individual or company that has made the loan, the name and address of the debtor, the specific collateral, the serial number of the property in question, and a registration number.

You can search the registry using the debtor's name. You'll often also need a date of birth. The following is a list of provincial and territorial sites that offer personal-property registry search services:

- Alberta: *www.servicealberta.gov.ab.ca/8.cfm*
- British Columbia: *www.bconline.gov.bc.ca*
- Manitoba: *https://direct.gov.mb.ca/pprhtml/html/internet/en/ppr.html*
- New Brunswick: *www.acol.ca* or *http://app.infoaa.7700.gnb.ca/gnb/Pub/EServices/ ListServiceDetails.asp?ServiceID1=12875&ReportType1=All*
- Newfoundland and Labrador: *www.acol.ca* or *www.gov.nf.ca/gs/cca/cr/prop-lien-check.stm*
- Northwest Territories: *www.acol.ca* or *www.justice.gov.nt.ca/PropertyRegistry/ property.htm*
- Nova Scotia: *www.acol.ca* or *www.gov.ns.ca/snsmr/property/default.asp?mn= 282.46.82*
- Nunavut: *www.acol.ca*

- Ontario: *www.ontario.ca/en/services_for_business/access_now/stel01_086165*
- Prince Edward Island: *www.acol.ca*
- Quebec: *www.mrn.gouv.qc.ca*
- Saskatchewan: *www.isc.ca*
- Yukon: *https://ppsr.gov.yk.ca*

Motor vehicle records

Driving is one form of public involvement many of us engage in every day. And, predictably, that activity produces a paper trail. Driving records are generally available through provincial motor vehicle departments. In Ontario, for example, a three-year driving record abstract, searched for by driver's licence number, is available at government offices or online (*www.mto.gov.on.ca*) for $12. The information includes *Highway Traffic Act* and *Criminal Code* convictions.

The public can also search for the registered driver of a vehicle based on the licence plate number and a vehicle's ownership history, which lists the names of owners but no private address information. Also available to the public in Ontario are records—searchable by licence number—on a particular commercial carrier's safety ratings, from 'excellent' to 'unsatisfactory', a list of carriers in these categories, a synopsis of each carrier's performance over a 24-month period, and a five-year driving record for commercial vehicle drivers.

Deaths

There are a number of public records that document deaths in Canada. Autopsy reports may be made public and, in some provinces, they are filed with the courts. Coroner's reports, which detail the investigation of sudden or suspicious deaths, are generally covered by privacy legislation in Canada and not released to the public. They do become public in some cases, however, particularly when they are used as exhibits in a court case.

Journalists sometimes access coroner's reports in other ways. A coroner's office, while not releasing the full reports, will often comment on the basic findings, especially in high-profile cases. It's worth asking about such things as cause of death, for instance. As well, next of kin can generally request copies of the reports for themselves or advise a coroner's office to release the records to a third party such as a journalist. That opens the possibility that a family might be willing to share a copy of the records or provide written permission for the records to be obtained directly from the coroner.

'We've released coroner's reports in cases where families have asked for the report and once we give it to them, they're free to give it to whomever they like,' says Jim Cairns, former deputy chief coroner for Ontario. 'And we've had families write us and ask us to release the reports to a particular reporter. We've complied with that.'[22]

Provincial archives often hold historical records on deaths, including coroners' reports. A complete listing of provincial archive resources is available through Library and Archives Canada at *www.genealogy.gc.ca*.

For research on Canadians who died in the United States, the US Social Security Death Index (*www.familysearch.org*) lets you search by name, year or year range, social security number, and state.

Wills and estate records detail the division of a deceased person's assets among family, friends, and others. They generally include the will itself along with court records, affidavits, a listing of assets, and how they are divided. These documents fall under the jurisdiction of provinces and territories, but a complete resource list for wills and estate records is available through the LAC at *www.genealogy.gc.ca*.

For privacy reasons, current vital-statistics records regarding such things as birth and marriage are not generally accessible in Canada without written permission from the individuals involved. But historical records can be accessed through provincial and territorial archives and vital statistics offices. Again, a complete listing is available from Library and Archives Canada.

Here are the links to provincial coroners:

- Directory of Chief Coroners: *http://ccinfoweb.ccohs.ca/help/fatality/coroners.html*
- Alberta: *www.justice.gov.ab.ca/ocme*
- British Columbia: *www.pssg.gov.bc.ca/coroners*
- Manitoba: *www.gov.mb.ca/justice/about/chief.html*
- New Brunswick: *www.gnb.ca/0276/Coroner/index-e.asp*
- Newfoundland and Labrador: *www.justice.gov.nl.ca/just/department/branches/division/division_ocme.html*
- Northwest Territories: *www.justice.gov.nt.ca/Coroner/coroner.htm*
- Nova Scotia: *www.gov.ns.ca/just/CME.asp*
- Ontario: *www.mcscs.jus.gov.on.ca/english/office_coroner/about_coroner/about_coroner.html*
- Prince Edward Island: *www.gov.pe.ca/infopei/index.php3?number=52651*
- Quebec: *www.msp.gouv.qc.ca/coroner/coroner.asp?txtSection=bureau_coroner*
- Saskatchewan: *www.justice.gov.sk.ca/officeofthechiefcoroner*
- Yukon: *www.justice.gov.yk.ca/prog/cjps/crnr*

Fire reports

Fires that are considered suspicious, or that cause deaths, extensive damage, or explosions are generally investigated by a fire marshal. The resulting reports, which document the cause and circumstances of a fire, aren't generally available to the public unless a freedom-of-information request is made. They are usually available, however, to anyone who was directly involved, such as a homeowner, business owner, or neighbour. If any of those people are willing to provide a copy, that may be the fastest and easiest way of obtaining what could be a vital record of public interest. If you successfully file a freedom-of-information request, all personal information will be removed from the document before it is released.

Provincial and territorial fire investigation departments or offices have online presences at the following sites and pages:

- Alberta: *www.municipalaffairs.alberta.ca/cp_fire.cfm*
- British Columbia: *www.pssg.gov.bc.ca/firecom/info/index.htm*
- Manitoba: *www.firecomm.gov.mb.ca*
- New Brunswick: *www.gnb.ca/0276/fire*
- Newfoundland and Labrador: *www.ma.gov.nl.ca/ma/fes/ofc/firesafety*
- Northwest Territories: *http://forestmanagement.enr.gov.nt.ca/fire_management*
- Nova Scotia: *www.gov.ns.ca/EMO*
- Ontario: *www.ofm.gov.on.ca*
- Prince Edward Island: *www.gov.pe.ca/cca*
- Quebec: *www.msp.gouv.qc.ca/incendie*
- Saskatchewan: *www.cpsp.gov.sk.ca/OFC*
- Yukon: *www.community.gov.yk.ca/fireprotection*

Bankruptcy

The federal government makes bankruptcy records publicly available online through its Industry Canada website (*www.ic.gc.ca/eic/site/bsf-osb.nsf/eng/home*). The database contains records of all bankruptcies and proposals filed in Canada from 1978 to present and can be searched by an individual name for $8. The records also include all private and court-appointed receiverships filed between 1993 and now. To view the actual files, you'll likely need to visit a local office of the superintendent of bankruptcy.

Civil, criminal, and small-claims court proceedings

Some of the most valuable and credible records journalists rely on for research are contained in court files, which document public disputes, detail their circumstances, most often name all involved, and reveal how the justice system handled the matter. We address court records separately in Chapter 5.

Professional licensing and disciplinary records

Many trades are represented by organizations that could prove useful in helping you find a member and learn more about them. For example, the Canadian Home Builders' Association, which claims nearly 7000 members across the country, has an online directory of members, searchable by province, city, or name (*www.chba. ca*). Real estate agents in Nova Scotia are licensed by the province's Real Estate Commission, which also provides an online database of members (*www.nsrec. ns.ca/findlicensee*) that is searchable by name.

Most professions also face some form of regulation. Many are self-regulated by the profession itself, but those bodies generally hold open disciplinary meetings and make a number of records available to the public. Below are examples of resources that can help you in researching people's professional activities:

- Archeologists (*www.rpanet.org*): A directory of professional archaeologists in Canada and the United States.

- Dentists (*www.webdentistry.com*): A searchable directory of dentists in Canada and the United States. Be sure to also consult the provincial dental college in each province. These are self-regulatory bodies that oversee the registration and conduct of dentists in Canada.
- Lawyers: Canadian Law List (*www.canadianlawlist.com*)
- Medical Professionals: These are governed by self-regulatory bodies in each province. The Ontario College of Physicians and Surgeons, for example, regulates the province's doctors, investigates public complaints, holds disciplinary hearings, and issues public decisions. Similar colleges exist for medical professionals ranging from chiropractors to podiatrists. For backgrounding medical professionals, direct your attention to the relevant college in the province where your subject works.

Access rules vary, but many bodies have opened up their disciplinary hearings; in other cases, the member being disciplined may have the right to request a public hearing. Law societies in every province except New Brunswick permit public access to formal discipline hearings, but the investigative stages of the process remain private in all provinces. The disciplinary panel may have the power to ban publication of complainants' names and the disclosure of sensitive or confidential information.

Disciplinary hearings for Ontario doctors are held in public, but the panel has the power to close hearings or ban publication of sensitive evidence.[23] Provincial and municipal laws govern access to disciplinary hearings for police officers. In Ontario, hearings are open to the public unless security concerns or sensitive financial or personal information justify excluding the public. Prince Edward Island's Supreme Court has struck down a municipal regulation that required private discipline hearings for officers.[24]

Judicial councils—panels of senior judges—investigate complaints about the behaviour of other judges and hold disciplinary hearings when there is evidence of serious misconduct. If the Canadian Judicial Council holds an inquiry into whether a superior court judge should be removed from office, the hearing may be conducted in public. If it is, the council can ban publication of any information or document used as evidence if, in the council's opinion, it would not be in the public interest to reveal the information. The federal minister of justice can order a public hearing.[25]

The rules for inquiries involving provincially appointed judges vary. In Alberta, they are conducted in private but the report is a public document. The judges conducting the inquiry can, however, ban publication of information or documents relating to their work. An Ontario hearing can be closed only in 'exceptional circumstances'; if it is, the name of the judge under scrutiny must not be disclosed. Ontario's judicial council has the power to ban publication of the name of a judge accused of sexual misconduct or sexual harassment.[26]

While most professional regulatory bodies have online directories listing members, those sites rarely include disciplinary records. You have to request records, and may come up against restrictions on what can be published. Note that disciplinary hearings and decisions represent only the tip of the iceberg in terms of complaints by clients, patients, and so on. Complaints against medical professionals, for instance, are shrouded in secrecy with the result that patients cannot know whether the medical professional they rely on has been the subject of dozens of complaints or none.

In 2001, a series of articles in the *Toronto Star* entitled 'Medical Secrets' found that, of the 13,000 complaints about doctors received by the College of Physicians and Surgeons of Ontario (CPSO) over the previous six years, '99 per cent were either dismissed outright or handled internally and in secret.' Only 1 per cent actually reached a disciplinary hearing at which complaints are made public.[27] Following the investigation, the CPSO began posting disciplinary decisions online. A search of the college's website (*www.cpso.on.ca*) will list any disciplinary actions taken by the college against its members over the past five years. But that kind of disclosure is limited and unique. Patients across the country who bring complaints of medical incompetence forward are often never told the result of a college's investigation into their concerns.

The level of disclosure surrounding municipally licensed businesses or tradespeople is considerably better. Formal charges under municipal bylaws are a matter of public record, along with the resulting court decisions. The list of businesses and individuals licensed by municipalities varies across the country, but there are more licensed trades than many researchers consider. Here's a partial list of the ones that are often licensed:

- taxicab owners and drivers
- limousine owners and drivers
- driving-school owners and instructors
- tow-truck owners and drivers
- adult-entertainment parlours and dancers
- holistic centres and practitioners
- massage parlours
- public bath houses
- body rub parlours and attendants
- delicatessens, restaurants, butcher shops, coffee shops, grocery, fruit or fish markets, bake shops, hot dog carts, convenience and variety stores, pizza parlours
- bowling alleys
- coin-operated laundries
- parking lots
- salvage yards
- barber and hairdressing shops
- carnivals and circuses
- drug stores
- pet shops
- public garages and gas stations

- car washes
- automobile body repairs
- second-hand shops
- pawnbrokers and old gold dealers
- wine and liquor stores
- accident report centres
- plumbers, heating and electrical contractors
- auctioneers
- building renovators
- drain contractors
- insulation installers
- scrap collectors

Corporate records

For federally registered associations and companies, Industry Canada maintains an online database (*www.ic.gc.ca/eic/site/cd-dgc.nsf/eng/h_cs03750.html*) that is searchable by keyword. A company name alone will turn up a list of records including formal name, corporation number, address, incorporation date, status, and a list of directors. Unlike many provincial registries, the federal one doesn't provide the addresses of directors, but you can file a written request for that information.

Information on corporations registered provincially is public and generally accessible at provincial ministries that handle corporate affairs. Some provinces, such as Ontario, have contracts with private firms that charge the public for conducting searches of the database.

Companies that do business across the country or across borders tend to be registered federally while smaller firms that operate within a city or a province are more likely to turn up in provincial registries. In some provinces, corporate search records also indicate any documents filed by the corporation, which could detail anything from changes in directors to articles of incorporation. This is useful because a corporate record otherwise lists only the current makeup of a corporation's directors and officers. Just because a particular name doesn't show up on a current list of officers and directors doesn't mean it was never there. You may be interested in knowing whether someone was involved with the company in the past and subsequently resigned, or you may simply wish to know the names of previous officers and directors. If details or these changes have not been filed by the corporation, you will need a so-called 'point-in-time' report. By choosing a past date, you can, in some provinces, search a historical record of a corporation's officers and directors. A point-in-time search lists directors and officers at the time along with historical information including amalgamations and name changes.

It's also important to note that the names of those on corporate filings aren't always the people running the company. Those who wish to remain anonymous can list colleagues, partners, and others in corporate filings while continuing to exercise control from behind the scenes. Getting at the real influence behind a company doesn't always end with a corporate search.

Here is a listing of provincial or territorial government departments handling company incorporation and registries:

- Alberta: *www3.gov.ab.ca/gs/information/clctc*
- British Columbia: *www.bconline.gov.bc.ca/corp_reg.html*
- Manitoba: *www.companiesoffice.gov.mb.ca*
- New Brunswick: *www.snb.ca*
- Newfoundland and Labrador: *www.gov.nf.ca/gs/cca*
- Nova Scotia: *www.gov.ns.ca/snsmr/rjsc*
- Northwest Territories: *www.justice.gov.nt.ca*
- Nunavut: *www.gov.nu.ca/Nunavut/English/departments/JUS*
- Ontario: *www.cbs.gov.on.ca/mcbs*
- Prince Edward Island: *www.gov.pe.ca/corporations*
- Quebec: *https://ssl.req.gouv.qc.ca/slc0110_eng.html*
- Saskatchewan: *www.corporations.justice.gov.sk.ca*
- Yukon: *www.community.gov.yk.ca/corp*

Conclusion

The intent here is not to present an exhaustive list of public records, which would consume volumes, but to illustrate the wide array of resources available to researchers and to foster a 'document state of mind' which will help you imagine the records that might be out there. That process is all about asking good questions and learning how systems operate. It isn't until you understand how the paper trail works in a particular public agency or department that you can understand the kinds of records that might exist and what they can potentially tell you.

The process of researching public records may seem complicated and time-consuming. It is. It takes patience, attention to detail, and lots of coffee. But it's important work that can bring unique rewards. In-depth research of this type can empower your writing, helping you get at that most important journalistic objective: the truth.

5

Accessing Laws and Justice System Records

Before heading to the courthouse . . . the investigative journalist needs to have a basic understanding of laws and regulations and where to find them.

After the Ontario Provincial Police raided Aylmer Meat Packers in August 2003, during an investigation into allegations that dead cattle were being processed and sold, plant owner Richard Clare was in no mood to speak to reporters. But this wall of silence did not stop *The Globe and Mail*'s Paul Waldie from filing a detailed story that delved into Clare's background and business dealings. Just before the raid, Waldie discovered, Clare was boasting that his company was worth more than $1 million. Waldie's research also revealed that Aylmer faced pollution charges and that Clare was behind in his dues to the provincial cattlemen's association. He found a ruling in which a judge observed that Clare was 'not a "detail" person.' Waldie even got quotes from one of Clare's former lawyers and the owner of a truck-repair company who sued Clare for failing to pay his bills. The result was a profile of a businessman who, as one source put it, 'doesn't like to follow rules.'[1]

Waldie found much of his information and many of his sources by scouring court records for cases involving Clare and his businesses. People can wind up before the courts for a variety of reasons and many companies become embroiled in a legal dispute at some point. People break the law, get divorced, or get hurt in a car accident and sue the other driver for damages. Companies take customers to court to collect unpaid bills or file lawsuits against suppliers who fail to honour contracts. These disputes, and countless others, generate a paper trail that offers the investigative journalist a wealth of information about people, businesses, events, and issues. 'Court files provide a mountain of documents to use in stories that have nothing to do with the court system,' says Steve Weinberg, former executive director of Missouri-based Investigative Reporters and Editors.[2] A Canadian research guide agrees, noting that court records may reveal 'confidential information on individuals or businesses that is not available anywhere else.'[3]

In this chapter, we will introduce the records available in the Canadian justice system, show how and where to find them, and examine the laws that limit access or restrict their use. Before heading to the courthouse, though, the investigative journalist needs to have a basic understanding of laws and regulations and where to find them.

Researching Laws and Regulations

To get to the heart of a story—the causes of a disaster, the impact of a policy initiative, or a controversy over public spending—journalists must understand the rules that apply and the government agencies that monitor and enforce these rules. 'Bureaucracies can be a curse,' a veteran US reporter has noted, 'but also a blessing.'[4] The blessing, for journalists, is that a web of rules and regulations enable them to hold government agencies accountable, unearth inside information, and identify individuals and companies that are flouting the law. What regulations are in force to control the disposal of toxic waste? Which agency inspects slaughterhouses and what are the standards for cleanliness? What are the laws that ensure companies provide a safe workplace for their employees? Who enforces them? Which companies are the worst offenders? When Nova Scotia's Westray coal mine exploded in 1992, killing 26 miners, inspectors with the province's Department of Labour were criticized for failing to ensure the mine was safe. The department, as the lead agency responsible for workplace safety, was a lightning rod for controversy—and rightly so. But Nova Scotia's Department of Natural Resources also had a safety mandate; it issued the permits and licences Westray needed to begin operations and approved design changes that compromised the mine's safety. An investigation by *The Halifax Chronicle Herald* brought to the public's attention the wider failure of government regulators to avert the mine disaster.

Mine safety, toxic waste disposal, food processing, and a host of other activities are regulated by statutes. New statutes, and amendments to existing ones, are introduced in Parliament or provincial and territorial legislatures as bills. This draft legislation is debated and changes may be made to address the concerns of opposition parties and interest groups. Once passed by the majority vote of elected representatives (and after the formality of royal assent from the governor general or a provincial lieutenant governor) bills become law and are transformed into acts.

Statutes express the law in broad strokes, setting out the principles, goals, and how it applies. For instance, the *Access to Information Act*, which we discuss in Chapter 10, establishes how journalists and members of the public make an application for access to records, and how federal agencies should handle these requests. The act authorizes the government to levy an application fee and recover the cost of photocopying records, but makes no mention of how much money can be charged for these services. These nuts-and-bolts issues are dealt with in another form of legislation known as regulations, which are created under the authority of an act. The *Access to Information Regulations* stipulate that everyone who files an access request must pay a $5 application fee. As well, agencies are authorized to charge 20 cents per page to cover the cost of photocopying any records that are released. Regulations spell out precisely how the provisions of an act will be implemented and enforced. Cabinet has the power to create and change regulations by issuing orders-in-council, giving governments the flexibility to make minor changes—to increase the fee for photocopying documents to 25 cents per page, for instance—without going through the time-consuming process of seeking legislative approval.

Canada has three levels of government—federal, provincial/territorial, and municipal—and each is responsible for devising and enforcing laws within its jurisdiction. Sometimes, it is clear which level of government is responsible. Defence and foreign policy, for instance, are national concerns and logic dictates they are the responsibility of the federal government. Public education and land ownership have an impact at the local level and fall within the bailiwick of provincial and territorial governments. Jurisdiction is often split; the federal government and its provincial and territorial counterparts each have agencies responsible for fisheries, health, and the environment.

Finding federal legislation

Under our constitution, the federal government regulates matters of national scope and importance. Besides national defence and foreign policy, these include the criminal law, the safety of food and drugs, interprovincial and international trade, federal prisons, banking, communications, transportation, and border security. Ottawa also oversees national programs such as medicare, employment insurance, and the Canada Pension Plan. These are only a few examples; consult the federal government's website (*www.canada.gc.ca*) for a complete picture of its activities and agencies.

All federal laws and regulations can be searched online through the Justice Canada website at *http://laws.justice.gc.ca*, and through the Canadian Legal Information Institute's online database (*www.canlii.org*). To find bills, including private members' bills and proposed legislation that was withdrawn or never implemented, log on to the website of the House of Commons and Senate (*www.parl.gc.ca*).

Finding provincial and territorial legislation

Provinces and territories control matters of local and regional concern such as public education and the ownership of land. The list also includes hospitals, colleges, highways, workplace safety, food inspection, the administration of the justice system, provincial jails, and control of natural resources such as timber, minerals, and petroleum. The website of each province or territory provides information on its departments and agencies, as well as links to statutes, regulations, and bills. They are also accessible through the Canadian Legal Information Institute's website, *www.canlii.org*.

Orders-in-council

The federal cabinet (known as the Privy Council) and provincial cabinets have the power to implement day-to-day government decisions authorized by statutes. These orders-in-council are used to implement and change regulations, appoint people to public offices, and to make loans or grants to businesses. Orders-in-council are public documents and are kept on file at the cabinet office or, increasingly, in searchable databases available online. Federal orders-in-council are accessible at *www.pco-bcp.gc.ca/premier.asp*.

Municipal bylaws and ordinances

Cities, towns, villages, counties, and districts regulate activities within their borders. Municipal laws, known as bylaws and ordinances, control such matters as the zoning and development of land, garbage disposal, animal control, and building and rooming house standards. Bylaws and ordinances are published in hard copy and also available online through municipal government websites.

Finding and Using Court Records

It is the job of the courts to interpret federal, provincial, and municipal laws. Every prosecution of a crime or regulatory offence and every civil dispute between people or companies produces a file that, with few exceptions, is open to public scrutiny. An understanding of where to find these files and what they contain is essential for every journalist, not just those assigned to cover a specific case or legal issue. Indictments, pleadings, affidavits, transcripts, and court rulings are a treasure trove of information for the investigative reporter. 'Court records,' says Josh Meyer, a reporter for the *Los Angeles Times*, 'perhaps as much as any other kind of document, can make a great story—or break one, if you don't know where to look, or when to look, or how to look.'[5]

The structure of the courts

To know where to look for files, journalists need to understand the basic structure of the courts and the kinds of cases they hear.[6]

The highest echelons of the courts are known as superior courts. These include the Supreme Court of Canada (the country's highest court), the court of appeal of each province, and the top level of trial court in each province—which is known as the Superior Court, the Supreme Court, or the Court of Queen's Bench, depending on the province. A judge or a judge and jury preside over trials at this level. All serious crimes, major civil cases, divorces, and legal challenges are heard in the superior courts. Ottawa also maintains the federal court system, which consists of a trial and appeal court, and deals with cases that involve federal legislation. Income-tax disputes, immigration appeals, and the seizure of ships are examples of cases heard in the Federal Court of Canada.

The provinces and territories are responsible for the lower rungs of the court hierarchy, which are known collectively as the inferior courts. These courts have limited powers and jurisdiction, and generally deal with less-serious crimes and regulatory offences. Provincial court (or territorial court in the territories) is where everyone accused of a crime makes an initial appearance and is arraigned on charges. Persons accused of minor crimes usually stand trial in this court, while those facing serious charges can choose to be tried in superior court. In murder cases, defendants are arraigned in provincial court but the trial must be held in superior court. Youth courts follow procedures set out in the *Youth Criminal Justice Act* to deal with young people who are charged with crimes. Small-claims courts hold informal hearings to settle civil disputes involving modest amounts of money. In some provinces, family courts address access and custody issues when couples separate.

Court websites

Most courts maintain their own websites. The information offered varies, but the typical site provides access to dockets, news releases, a searchable database of rulings, and links to laws and background information about the justice system. The documents in a court file are rarely available in electronic format, although this is changing as courts move to allow the filing of electronic versions of documents. In the meantime, journalists can visit the court registry where the file is held to view and copy documents.

* Supreme Court of Canada: *www.scc-csc.gc.ca* This site provides access to news releases and weekly bulletins that track the status of hearings, rulings, and applications for leave to appeal. There is also a full-text archive of all rulings made since 1983.
* Federal Court of Canada: *www.fct-cf.gc.ca* Here, you can review an online database of rulings dating back to 1992.

Courts in the following provinces and territories maintain websites, and most offer electronic access to recent and archived rulings. They also provide the locations of registry offices, contact information for court staff, links to statutes and regulations, and other legal resources:

* Alberta: *www.albertacourts.ab.ca*
* British Columbia: *www.courts.gov.bc.ca*
* Manitoba: *www.manitobacourts.mb.ca*
* New Brunswick: *www.gnb.ca/cour*
* Newfoundland and Labrador: *www.court.nl.ca*
* Northwest Territories: *www.nwtcourts.ca*
* Nova Scotia: *www.courts.ns.ca*
* Nunavut: *www.nucj.ca/unifiedcourt.htm*
* Ontario: *www.ontariocourts.on.ca*
* Prince Edward Island: *www.gov.pe.ca/courts*
* Quebec: *www.justice.gouv.qc.ca/english/accueil.asp*
* Saskatchewan: *www.sasklawcourts.ca*
* Yukon: *www.justice.gov.yk.ca/prog/cs/courts.html*

The media's right of access

With few exceptions, the business of the courts is open to public scrutiny, ensuring that justice is done—and is seen to be done.[7] *The Charter of Rights and Freedoms* guarantees freedom of the press as well as a fair and public hearing for everyone accused of a crime. The Ontario Court of Appeal has described the openness of the courts as 'one of the hallmarks of a democratic society . . . a restraint on arbitrary action by those who govern and by the powerful.'[8] But few people have the time or inclination to attend court in order to keep the system honest; they rely on media reports to tell them what's happening in the justice system. Journalists are the watchdogs. A Supreme Court of Canada decision has observed the following: 'Openness permits public access to information about the courts, which in turn permits the public to discuss and put forward opinions and criticisms of court practices and proceedings. As a vehicle through which information pertaining to these courts is transmitted, the press must be guaranteed access to the courts in order to gather information.'[9]

In Canada's justice system, sealed files, secrecy, and closed hearings are the exceptions; public access and accountability are the rule. In the late 1970s, a Nova Scotia court official refused to release search warrants that the Royal Canadian Mounted Police used to seize political fundraising records during an influence-peddling investigation. Journalist Linden MacIntyre, along with the CBC, fought for access and, in 1982, the Supreme Court of Canada ruled that search warrants and other documents filed in criminal cases are public documents. Access can be denied only when it is vital to safeguard other important interests, 'to protect social values of superordinate importance,' as the court put it.[10] An example is the need to protect the identity of an innocent person whose home or office has been searched during an investigation; if no evidence is found, records of such a search will not be released.

This tug-of-war between openness and secrecy is played out on many fronts. Access is restricted to some court documents and, in rare cases, all or part of a court record may be sealed to protect someone's privacy, to ensure justice is done, or to protect the rights of those who face charges or seek justice. Justice would not be done, for instance, if a company declined to pursue a lawsuit for fear of exposing financial or sales information that could help its competitors. A similar rationale is behind *Criminal Code* bans on publishing information that could identify victims of sexual offences; there is a concern that victims may not report what has happened to them, for fear of having their names splashed across the media. The *Criminal Code* also gives judges the power to delay publication of evidence presented in the pre-trial phase of criminal cases, to prevent jurors from making up their minds that someone is guilty before a trial is even held.

Courts in some provinces have policies that set out which documents in a court file are freely available to journalists and members of the public and which ones may require a more formal request or the permission of a judge. Nova Scotia was among the first to formulate access guidelines (*www.courts.ns.ca/media_access/ access_media.htm*) and the access policy of the Court Services Division of Ontario's Ministry of the Attorney General is also available on the Internet (*www.attorney-general.jus.gov.on.ca/english/courts/policies_and_procedures/public_access*).[11]

The media has a constitutional right to challenge many restrictions on access to justice records and court hearings. In 1994, the Supreme Court made a landmark ruling which stated that competing rights such as privacy and the right to a fair trial do not automatically trump the media's Charter right to freedom of expression. In *Dagenais v. Canadian Broadcasting Corporation*, the court said judges faced with applications to ban publication of evidence must consider the impact on free expression. Orders restricting access to information should only be imposed when there is 'a real and substantial risk' to the fairness of the trial, and judges must consider alternatives such as partial or temporary bans.[12] The *Dagenais* test does not apply to all publication bans, only those that are imposed at a judge's discretion. But *Dagenais* is a watershed, a fundamental rethinking of how freedom of expression applies to publication bans as well as restrictions on access to court records.[13] In follow-up rulings to *Dagenais*, the Supreme Court has said that when a judge is faced with demands to restrict access to evidence, the impact on freedom of expression must be considered even if the media chooses not to challenge the ban.[14] And when considering a motion to seal documents presented as evidence in a court case, a judge must weigh the right of free expression and the principle of openness against demands to protect other important interests, such as confidential information about businesses.[15]

Qualified privilege and court documents

A legal principle known as 'qualified privilege' applies to all information discussed openly in the courtroom or revealed in documents filed with the court. This privilege, which also exists for the debates of Parliament and legislatures, ensures that parties and witnesses can speak freely and frankly—and the media can report what is said—without fear of being sued for libel. Journalists must bear in mind that it is the forum in which the information is made public that determines whether it is privileged, not the nature of the information itself. The protection of privilege stops at the courtroom door; if allegations made outside the protected forum are reported, both the source and the media outlet can be sued.

The immunity from lawsuits is described as 'qualified'; in other words, the privilege comes with strings attached. A news report of what is said in the courtroom must be a 'fair and accurate' representation of what happened. The media is not expected to produce verbatim accounts, but reports must be factually correct and reflect any contradictory information that is presented. 'The report,' one media law textbook advises, 'must be substantially correct and carry the same meaning as a word-for-word account.'[16] There must be no suggestion that the journalist published the information out of spite or for other improper motives.

Conduct seen by the courts as evidence of malice includes omitting key facts and publishing information the journalist knows to be false.[17] Qualified privilege also applies to news and investigative reports based on documents filed with the courts. The rulings of courts, tribunals, and official inquiries are covered, as are the contents of documents produced or discussed in open court or before a tribunal or inquiry. The Supreme Court of Canada has extended qualified privilege to fair and accurate news reports of pleadings—the plaintiff's statement of claim and the defendant's written response—filed with the courts in civil actions.[18] When reporting on pleadings, journalists should point out that none of the allegations has been proven in court and must make an effort to contact the target of the allegations for a response. These steps add balance to the story and fulfil the legal requirement for a news report to be fair and accurate.

This protection from libel lawsuits makes court documents of particular interest to investigative reporters. They are the building blocks for producing hard-hitting stories that are solid, factual, and libel-proof.

Electronic access to court documents

Canada's courts are in the midst of a transition from paper records to computerized systems to file-and-store documents. Most rulings are available in electronic format and can be accessed online. Many courts post dockets and case summaries on their websites and procedures to permit the electronic filing of documents in criminal and civil cases are in the works. But the ease of electronic access creates privacy concerns that have prompted courts in some provinces to restrict Internet access to rulings in family law cases. A divorce ruling, for instance, may reveal personal and financial information that would embarrass the people involved or leave them vulnerable to identity theft. A 2003 discussion paper on the issue called for policies to govern electronic access and to ensure courts across the country adopt consistent practices. According to the paper's authors, the starting point must be 'that the right to open courts generally outweighs the right to privacy.'[19] If so, court records will become more accessible—and even more valuable—to journalists. In 2005, the Judges' Technology Advisory Committee of the Canadian Judicial Council released a model access policy that emphasizes openness but advised court officials to remove 'personal data identifiers'—including birthdates, street addresses, email accounts, phone numbers, social insurance numbers, and bank account information—before posting court records online. While this strips online records of valuable leads for an investigative journalist trying to track down a source, this kind of information may still be available in the original case file kept at the courthouse. British Columbia has taken the lead in providing Internet access to court records, for a modest fee. Court Services Online (*https://eservice.ag.gov.bc.ca/cso/index.do*), a database that in the summer of 2008 contained electronic versions of documents filed in more than 200,000 civil cases, and there were plans to add some information about criminal cases.[20]

Criminal Case Documents

When criminal charges are laid, court staffers open a file and assign a number to the case. Journalists have the same right as any other citizen to inspect files at the court's registry during office hours. Each file is identified by number and indexed by the surname of the defendant or the name of the company being prosecuted. Newer files can be searched at registries on a computer database, but journalists may find that a card index is used to keep track of older files. (Note as well that older files are put into long-term storage at a separate location, or transferred to the provincial archives for preservation and cataloguing, and may take longer to retrieve.) There is generally a fee to retrieve each file and to photocopy documents.

The Supreme Court of Canada, based in Ottawa, offers online access to its docket, rulings, legal briefs and other information about cases on its website. Provinces are divided into judicial districts, with a superior court registry usually housed in each district's main courthouse. There is only one court of appeal for each jurisdiction, so all files are housed in a central registry office located in the provincial capital. Provincial court offices are usually found in every major city and town. Consult the court's website or the phonebook for the location of court offices and registries. If the court office is located in another city or province, a journalist may be able to make arrangements with court staff to photocopy or fax documents. This usually involves a fee.

Search warrants

Under the landmark *MacIntyre* ruling on access to court files, once police complete a search, seize evidence, and report what they found to the courts, journalists have a right to see three documents:

- The search warrant, which reveals the place that was searched and the kinds of evidence the police expected to find;
- The information to obtain the warrant, a key document that sets out the names of suspects, the exact offences being alleged against them, and details of the evidence gathered to date. Think of it as a roadmap of the investigation that describes the sources of the allegations and the facts the police have gleaned from witnesses and documents;
- The return, which provides a brief description of all the items and documents seized.

A judge or justice of the peace reviews and approves each application for a search warrant, to ensure police have established that there is enough evidence of wrongdoing to justify the search. The file is then stored in a centralized registry or may be kept at the office of the judge or justice of the peace who issued the warrant. Filing practices vary from province to province and sometimes within a jurisdiction, making search warrants difficult to track down. Police investigators sometimes apply for search warrants in a neighbouring city or town to make it even harder for journalists to locate the file. If the search turns up no evidence, the warrant and information to obtain are not made public.

Journalists can be forgiven for thinking they are not entitled to view search-warrant documents unless someone involved in the investigation has been charged. A check of the *Criminal Code* will turn up section 487.2(1), a publication ban created in 1985 to restrict the scope of the *MacIntyre* ruling. If a search did not lead to criminal charges, this section barred the media from identifying locations searched, the persons who occupied or controlled those premises, and anyone named in a search warrant as a suspect. An exception was made if the persons searched or named as suspects consented to being identified; but since the targets of investigations are unlikely to grant such permission, the ban effectively blocked access to any warrant until charges were laid. Courts in Ontario, Manitoba, and Quebec soon struck down the ban as a violation of the guarantee of freedom of expression under the Charter.[21] The provision remains in the Code but, in light of these rulings, media law experts consider the ban to be a dead letter.[22] Journalists can identify those searched or named in a search warrant before charges are laid, and even in cases where no one is ever charged.

A journalist seeking the records of a search may discover that the file has been sealed. Section 487.3(1) of the Code gives judges the power to block public access to search-warrant documents. The most common justification for sealing a warrant is to protect an ongoing investigation or the identity of a confidential informant. If an innocent person will be harmed, or someone engaged in an undercover operation will be endangered, the documents can be sealed. Judges can seal warrants 'for any other sufficient reason' but the need to suppress the information must outweigh the importance of granting access to the court process.[23]

A sealing order can be challenged. Journalists and other interested parties have the right to bring a motion before the judge who sealed the documents, asking that the order be rescinded and all or part of the file be made public.[24] Ontario's Court of Appeal has described orders sealing a search warrant or other document as a 'significant intrusion' on freedom of expression. Applying the *Dagenais* test, the court ruled in 2003 that warrants should be sealed only when there is a serious risk to someone's right to a fair trial or the administration of justice. The police claimed that publicity would hinder their efforts to question witnesses, but the court said these concerns were too vague and freedom of expression should not be sacrificed 'to give police a "leg up" on an investigation.' The ruling, later upheld by the Supreme Court of Canada, unsealed warrants used to search the Aylmer Meat Packers plant under suspicion for processing tainted meat, with minor editing to shield the identity of a confidential informant. Just as significantly, the court said the media has a right to intervene on motions to seal search warrants and to make the case for keeping all or part of a file in the public domain.[25] The message for journalists is, do not take 'no' for an answer; if the search warrant file of a major investigation has been sealed, a challenge is likely to bring at least some of the information to light.

A few words of caution when reporting information found in search warrants: since they are documents filed with the courts, logic dictates they should be subject to qualified privilege under defamation law. Media outlets that publish fair and accurate reports of their contents, in other words, should be safe if anyone named or accused in the warrant tried to sue for libel. But no court has explicitly stated that search-warrant files are covered by qualified privilege, and journalists and editors should seek legal advice before publication or broadcast. The allegations contained in a search warrant are just that—allegations. They have not been proven in court and no charges have been laid, so any media report on their contents should make this clear to the public. Once charges have been filed and the case is before the courts, a new factor comes into play. If a media outlet reported the contents of a search warrant file in the midst of a prosecution or trial, it could be seen as a violation of the accused person's right to a fair trial, and the outlet and journalist risk being charged with contempt of court. Again, it is prudent to seek legal advice if the legal implications of publishing or broadcasting the information are unclear.

Informations and indictments

The document setting out the criminal charges against a person or company is known as *an information*. It reveals the name, address, age, and sometimes the occupation of the person accused of the offence. The exact wording of the charge, the date, the place of the offence, and the victim's name are also disclosed. Informations are filed with the provincial court and become a running record of the case as motions and hearings are held. The judge or court clerk uses it to note the defendant's plea, any conditions of release pending trial, whether bans on publication apply to the case, and the date of the next hearing. If the case remains in provincial court for trial, or the accused person pleads guilty, the date of conviction and the sentence imposed will also be recorded. If the accused person chooses to be tried in superior court, the charges are restated in a new document known as an *indictment*.

Arrest warrants, undertakings, subpoenas, and court orders

These documents do the grunt work of the criminal courts. They summon the defendant to appear in court, authorize police to arrest those who fail to appear, and set the terms for release on bail. Subpoenas require witnesses to testify. Judges use court orders to control the prosecution, order the production of evidence, and to impose publication bans. For the investigative reporter, a subpoena or arrest warrant may contain the address of a potential source, while a court order may flag a publication ban that is still in effect or disclose the existence of documents relevant to a story.

Exhibits

As a trial unfolds, the prosecution and defence produce the physical evidence related to the crime. These exhibits, as they are known, include anything the police have seized at the crime scene or during a search—weapons, narcotics, financial records, documents, even the clothing a suspect or victim wore. Experts' reports, crime-scene and autopsy photos, a suspect's videotaped statement to police, maps, and diagrams may also be tendered as evidence. Once a witness has verified that each item is genuine, it is given an exhibit number and becomes part of the case before the court. The media often seek the right to examine or copy exhibits to ensure accuracy, to convey the reality of the crime, or to expose improper police conduct. The exhibits enable the investigative reporter to reconstruct a crime or trial, and to uncover information about the people or companies involved in the case. Financial records used in a court case, for example, may not otherwise be open to public scrutiny.

Judges have the power to deny access to exhibits in order to protect other interests. Exhibits that belong to a defendant or someone else connected to the case may be returned to their owner after the courts have made a final ruling.[26] Privacy concerns may also surface. In one case, a CBC Television producer sought access to a videotape in which a suspect confessed to a murder and re-enacted the crime. The Nova Scotia Court of Appeal overturned the man's conviction, ruling the confession could not be used as evidence because the police denied the man his right to speak to a lawyer. After the appeal was decided, the journalist sought a copy of the confession as part of an investigation into why a confessed murderer had been freed. Court officials refused to hand over the tape and the CBC fought for access all the way to the Supreme Court of Canada, but lost. In its 1991 ruling, the Court reiterated the media's right of access to court hearings and documents. But a majority of judges said the suspect's privacy interests should prevail. The suspect had been acquitted and must be treated as innocent; the confession had been improperly obtained, and the public's right of access was fulfilled when the tape was presented at the man's trial. The Supreme Court's decision set out rules for access to exhibits. A judge should take into account the type of evidence, privacy interests, and whether the exhibit has been produced in a courtroom. As well, judges reserve the right to ask how the exhibit will be used and to impose conditions on access.[27]

While these restrictions remain the basis for how most courts handle media requests for access to exhibits, the media have been successful in using the Charter right of freedom of expression to press for access to exhibits. The CBC and the *Edmonton Journal* were permitted to copy and publish photographs, hundreds of pages of transcribed interviews, and the videotaped confession of a man convicted of planting a bomb that killed nine Yellowknife miners in 1992. A Nova Scotia judge released a murderer's videotaped confession for copying and broadcast in 1999, noting that the man had pleaded guilty and could no longer claim his privacy interests would be harmed.[28] Courts have also allowed the media to broadcast a murder victim's calls to 9-1-1 dispatchers and a videotape of a police officer carrying a corpse into a police station.[29] Calgary newspapers were authorized to make copies of photos, a 9-1-1 tape, letters, X-rays, and hospital records used as evidence in a high-profile attempted-murder trial.[30] And, in 2008, an Ontario judge authorized the media to broadcast, and post on news websites, a videotape of police questioning convicted murderer Paul Bernardo.[31] But access is not guaranteed. A *National Post* columnist was denied access to autopsy photographs showing injuries to the victim of a violent swarming. Even though the columnist wanted only to see and describe the photos, the judge ruled the potential anguish to the girl's parents outweighed any right of access.[32]

Transcripts of trials and hearings

Every word said in the courtroom is recorded, in the event a ruling or the verdict is appealed. Transcripts are expensive to produce but if the prosecution or defence requires one to be made, it likely will be included in the court file. If no transcript has been made, courts in many provinces will provide recordings for a fee (but be prepared to wait—it may take weeks). The contents of the tapes are not intended for broadcast and there may be specific laws or court rules restricting such use.[33] Some courts also allow journalists to listen to recordings of hearings that have not been transcribed. An investigative reporter who needs a complete and accurate picture of what happened in the courtroom may find it is worth the time and expense to obtain a tape or transcript.

Note that publication bans usually apply to bail hearings, preliminary inquiries, and other pre-trial hearings. If a ban has been imposed, the transcript can be ordered or examined but the contents cannot be published until the prosecution ends and the ban expires.

Rulings

The verdict, the sentence imposed on a convicted offender, and other major decisions a judge makes during a criminal case are usually produced in writing and a copy is added to the court file. Rulings provide a snapshot of the evidence presented in a case and how the judge interpreted the law. They also provide the names of the lawyers for each party, who may be willing to help the journalist track down more information about the case or set up interviews with their clients. The Canadian Law List offers an online database of contact information for lawyers across Canada (*www.canadianlawlist.com*), which can be searched by name, location, or legal speciality.

Since precedents form the basis for our common-law system of justice, significant decisions are published in bound volumes, known as case-law reports, for future reference. Commercial publishers like QuickLaw offer searchable databases of rulings dating back many decades, but the Supreme Court of Canada and courts in many provinces offer online access to their recent rulings. The Canadian

Legal Information Institute (*www. canlii.org*) offers free online access to the full text of rulings of courts in all provinces. Access varies but the collection includes decisions dating back to the early 1990s, with older rulings being scanned into the system and new ones being posted as they are released. In the middle of 2008, the database contained more than 500,000 rulings.[34]

The Supreme Court of Canada and other courts have a practice of notifying the media of the release of decisions in high-profile cases, and procedures may be in place to make other rulings public soon after the parties involved have been notified.

Pre-sentence reports

These reports are prepared to give the judge as complete a picture as possible about an offender and whether he or she is a good candidate for rehabilitation. Probation officers interview relatives, former employers, and police officers in order to compile reports that explore, in detail, the offender's family background, work history, criminal record, and past behaviour. Pre-sentence reports are usually public but some courts reserve the right to seal all or part of a report if it invades another person's privacy or includes sensitive medical or psychological assessments. A journalist investigating the background of a repeat offender or a criminal killed in a shootout with police will find invaluable information in the person's latest pre-sentence report.

Appeal-court files

If a verdict or sentence is appealed, a new file is opened at the appeal-court level. Each case is indexed by the name of the appellant and the respondent. A notice of appeal is filed, listing the grounds for the appeal; also filed are transcripts of hearings and copies of all documents submitted before and during the trial. As the date for a hearing approaches, lawyers for each side file a document known as a *factum*, in which they review the evidence and set out their legal arguments.

Parole hearings and records

Parole hearings for federal inmates (those sentenced to two years or more in prison) are open to any journalist or other member of the public. A written request for observer status must be submitted in advance of the hearing. Since most hearings are conducted inside prisons, the National Parole Board may require up to 30 days to run a security check on the applicant. The board can deny access to anyone whose presence might disrupt the hearing or upset the victim of the crime, the victim's family, or the relatives of the offender. If these concerns arise during a hearing, the board can exclude an observer from part of the hearing.

Records of all parole applications dealt with after 1 November 1992 are accessible to the media and members of the public. The National Parole Board's decisions to grant or deny parole typically discuss the offender's upbringing, employment history, criminal record, and behaviour in prison. Even though the decisions are edited to remove information that might jeopardize someone's safety, identify a confidential informant, or hinder efforts to rehabilitate the inmate, these texts offer unsurpassed insights into an offender's background and motives and provide leads for further research.[35] A written application for access to the Parole Board's registry of decisions must state the reason for the request. The form is available online at *www.npb-cnlc.gc.ca*.

Civil Case Documents

Files of civil cases are generally housed in the same registry as criminal files and can be inspected during office hours. Lawsuits are assigned a number as they are filed, and indexed by the name of the plaintiff (the person or company that launched the lawsuit) and the defendant. If there are a number of plaintiffs or defendants, each name will be indexed. Journalists may be able to arrange for documents to be faxed from registries in other cities or provinces. There will likely be a fee for retrieving files and photocopying.

Pleadings, motions, and other filings

In the Hollywood movie *A Civil Action*, a personal-injury lawyer likens the filing of a lawsuit to a declaration of war. Courtrooms sometime resemble battlegrounds but the weapons of choice are documents known as pleadings. The pleading that launches a lawsuit is called a *statement of claim and originating notice*—it identifies the plaintiff and defendant, setting out the plaintiff's version of events and the allegations against the defendant. The document also states what the court is being asked to do to set matters right, which is usually to order the defendant to pay monetary damages to the plaintiff. The defendant has a deadline to respond with a statement of defence, a document that refutes some or all of the allegations and sets out the defendant's version of events. Defendants may turn the tables and file a counterclaim accusing the plaintiffs of wrongdoing and seeking damages.

Pleadings are one-sided, setting out what a plaintiff or defendant believes—or hopes—to be true. None of the allegations have been proven in court and the process of gathering evidence and questioning witnesses only begins after statements of claim and defence have been filed. Since pleadings are privileged documents, media reports on their contents are protected from libel actions; journalists do not have to prove the allegations are true but they must produce a balanced report and make clear that the allegations are unproven.

Investigative reporters consult pleadings in search of connections between people and businesses. Owners and officials may be named in a lawsuit along with their company, revealing an unknown link that could be crucial to a story. The lawyers who filed the documents on behalf of the parties are potential sources. Pleadings reveal events, business practices, financial transactions, and a host of other information that might otherwise remain hidden.

Other documents filed at the pleading stage may be of assistance to journalists. In a demand for particulars, a defendant asks for more detail about the plaintiff's allegations. Motions may be filed asking a judge to resolve a dispute during the pre-trial stage of the case. Each side must disclose all documents in its possession that are relevant to the lawsuit; lists of these documents are usually filed with the court. While the documents themselves remain private until produced at trial, these lists may reveal unknown information or suggest new avenues of investigation.

Civil disputes involve smaller amounts of money; typically, cases that cost roughly less than $10,000–$15,000 (the cut-off varies from province to province) are heard in small-claims court. The files are also modest, containing a form outlining the plaintiff's claim and, once the case is completed, the ruling of the adjudicator. Records of small-claims courts are usually filed with the provincial court registry.

Affidavits

There are two ways to present evidence in civil cases. Witnesses testify in court, of course, but they can also submit written evidence in an *affidavit*, swearing that the information is true, just as they would do in court. Affidavits are a valuable resource for investigative reporters, helping to identify people, their associates, and the businesses and properties they own. An affidavit filed in a civil case gave *The Globe and Mail*'s Paul Waldie direct quotes from a source (the owner of the Aylmer meat-packing plant) who refused to be interviewed. And these documents are sometimes the source of politically explosive allegations. In January 2005, a reporter for the *Toronto Star* tracked down an affidavit filed with the Federal Court of Canada by pizzeria owner Harjit Singh, accusing Toronto-area MP and cabinet minister Judy Sgro of promising to halt his deportation to India if he provided free food and volunteers during an election campaign. The document gave the newspaper the legal ability to report the sensational allegation, prompting the minister's resignation.[36] (Sgro was later cleared, and Singh issued a public apology.)

Discovery transcripts and documents produced in civil cases

In the pre-trial phase of a civil case, evidence is gathered through the exchange of documents and the questioning of witnesses at private hearings called examinations for discovery. If these documents or the transcripts of discovery hearings are filed with the courts, they become public documents and journalists have the right to publish the contents. Otherwise, discovery transcripts and documents produced as evidence are considered private and can be used only for purposes related to the court action. A lawyer or client who leaked information to the media can face punishment for contempt of court.[37] If documents or discovery transcripts are leaked, however, the law does not prevent journalists and media outlets from publishing the information.

Exhibits and rulings

The rules for gaining access to exhibits in criminal cases hold true for civil cases. And as in criminal cases, judges hand down all significant rulings in writing. Copies are available in the court file, online, or in law reports.

Files in family-law cases

Divorce files

Divorce files often contain private information that is otherwise off limits to journalists. Income-tax returns, personal financial records, and confidential information about businesses, properties, and investments may be disclosed as the courts decide how to divide up marital assets. In general, divorce- and family-law hearings are open to the public unless a judge decides a private session is justified. Likewise, the court file is open to public scrutiny unless a statutory provision, a court rule, or a judge's order requires that all or some of the documents be sealed.

Several provinces have enacted laws that restrict access to hearings and files in family-law cases. In British Columbia, a Supreme Court judge must approve requests to review the court file in a divorce or child-custody case. Judges in New Brunswick and Prince Edward Island can restrict access to financial and income statements filed in divorce cases. Supreme Court rules in Newfoundland and Labrador prevent anyone other than lawyers, judges, and the parties involved from viewing the court file in a family-law case.

In Quebec, financial information and details of support payments are kept confidential. In Saskatchewan, journalists and other members of the public must apply to a judge of the Court of Queen's Bench for an order granting access to all or part of a file.[38]

Child-protection cases

For the most part, journalists are able to attend and cover the court proceedings held after an abused or neglected child is taken into foster care. But access to the court file varies. Court rules in British Columbia, for instance, prevent anyone from viewing the file of a child-protection case without the authorization of the judge or a party or lawyer involved in the case. In Nova Scotia, access to the case file is restricted, but journalists and other persons can apply to a judge for an order granting access.[39] Laws in all provinces forbid publication of any information that could disclose the identity of a child or parent involved in these cases.

Adoption applications

Provincial legislation restricts access to adoption applications that come before the courts. Judges have the power to hold hearings in private, and access to adoption files is either prohibited or permitted only by court order.[40]

Restricted records

Certain records, while filed with the courts, are routinely sealed. These include contingency-fee agreements between lawyers and clients, applications to register an offender as a child abuser, victim-impact statements in written form, and records of private conferences designed to settle cases before trial.

Appeal-court files

As in criminal cases, an appeal triggers the creation of a new file that contains hearing transcripts, copies of all documents before the court at trial, and the lawyers' factums. Files are accessible through the registry office of the provincial appeal court and, for the few cases that make it that far, the Supreme Court of Canada. Each case is indexed by the name of the appellant and the respondent.

Probate files

Probate is a special court in each province that reviews wills and oversees the transfer of money or property from an estate to the people designated to receive it. Once a will is *probated*, it becomes public and journalists can find out what the deceased person owned and who has been named as a beneficiary. A journalist investigating rumours that a public official appears to be living beyond her means would be advised to check probate records; the official's new-found wealth may have come from an inheritance, not kickbacks or other illegal benefits.

Publication Bans and Other Restrictions on Court Documents

Sealing orders

Superior court judges have the power to seal documents presented as evidence or filed with the court. While such orders are more common in civil actions, they have been imposed in criminal cases. Three provinces—Ontario, Manitoba, and Prince Edward Island—give judges sweeping powers to seal any document filed in a civil case.[41] Under the rules of the Federal Court of Canada, a party can apply to a judge for an order to keep any document confidential.[42]

In the wake of the *Dagenais* ruling, judges must balance the right of access against privacy concerns or commercial interests when deciding whether to seal documents. In reviewing a sealing order sought under the Federal Court's rules, the Supreme Court of Canada ruled in 2002 that confidentiality should be granted only to prevent 'a serious risk to an important interest.' The federal government wanted to prevent an environmental group from seeing information about the sale of nuclear reactors to China. The Chinese government claimed it owned the information and the contract required Atomic Energy of Canada to keep it confidential. The Supreme Court ruled the information should be sealed because a commercial interest, one with wide implications for the public interest, was at stake: a confidentiality agreement under a business contract.[43]

Most confidentiality concerns arise in civil cases that attract little or no media attention, and sealing orders have been sought and imposed with little regard to the public interest. A Saskatchewan judge sealed the entire file of a civil case in order to protect the contents of a few documents. The order stood for nine years, until a second judge opened the file and ruled that court files should not be sealed 'other than in exceptional circumstances.'[44] Such reasoning not only bodes well for journalists' attempts to overturn sealing orders, but it should mean fewer documents will be sealed in the first place.

Criminal Code of Canada publication bans

Journalists using a court document must be certain that no court order restricts their right to publish its contents. The *Criminal Code* allows defendants, victims of crime, and witnesses to apply for bans that delay or permanently restrict publication of information. Judges have the power to bar the media from reporting any information that could identify complainants and witnesses under the age of 18 involved in prosecutions of sexual offences, or charges of extortion or loan-sharking.[45] The ban is permanent and has been expanded to allow victims and witnesses involved in any other crime to ask the court for an order banning publication of any information that could reveal their identities. An array of justice officials—politicians, judges, lawyers, jurors, court administrators, police officers, prison guards, parole officials, and customs officers—can also ask to have their identities protected in cases involving intimidation or offences relating to organized crime.[46] There is also a provision, in sexual assault cases, to ban publication of the details of a defence application to delve into the sexual history of a complainant.[47] Similar provisions apply to applications for access to the private records of a complainant or witness, including medical, psychiatric, counselling, education, employment records, adoption records, and personal journals and diaries. The media can report that an application has been made for access to such records, but all other details are subject to a publication ban.[48] Some jurisdictions flag files that are subject to publication bans, but journalists must also use common sense: for instance, if a case involves sexual allegations, it is likely there will be a ban on identifying the victim.

Journalists must also take care when reporting on the transcripts of pre-trial hearings in criminal cases, as temporary publication bans apply. Defendants can apply for a ban on all information presented at a bail hearing (also known as a *show-cause hearing*).The ban is broad in scope and covers the evidence presented, arguments advanced by lawyers, even the judge's reasons for granting or denying bail.[49] Judges can also ban publication of all evidence taken at a preliminary hearing.[50] There is an automatic ban on publishing details of any statement or confession from the defendant that is produced at the preliminary hearing; you cannot even report that such a statement or confession exists.[51] Each of these bans expires if the defendant pleads guilty, if the charges are withdrawn, or once the trial is over.

Judges have the power to devise further bans to restrict publication of other information that could jeopardize the right to a fair trial.The problem commonly arises when persons accused of the same crime are prosecuted separately, prompting judges to ban publication of evidence that incriminates those who have yet to stand trial.[52] Courts also have temporarily banned media coverage of a change-of-venue hearing.[53] The Supreme Court of Canada's *Dagenais* test applies to applications for these so-called discretionary bans.Any ban imposed must be limited in scope and strike a balance between the media's right to freedom of expression and the defendant's right to a fair trial.

Bans in terrorism and national-security cases

The federal government can invoke special measures to prevent the disclosure in court of information relating to cabinet secrets, terrorist acts, or national security. Once the government makes its objection, the court or tribunal has a duty to ensure 'that the information is not disclosed other than in accordance with this act.' Judges must hold a private session to determine whether the objection is valid.An appeal of an order to disclose or withhold the information also must be held in private.[54] The judge may order disclosure of 'all of the information, a part or summary of the information, or a written admission of facts relating to the information.' If the information is withheld, the judge must impose an order prohibiting its disclosure.[55]

Even if a judge orders that sensitive information should be disclosed, the federal justice minister can override an order to disclose information by issuing a certificate.The minister can intervene to protect national defence, national security, or information obtained in confidence from a foreign government or agency. The certificate is valid for 15 years and renewable, but it can be appealed to a judge of the Federal Court of Appeal for review.The process is dealt with at a private hearing and the court file can be sealed to ensure confidentiality. The certificate itself and any court order to cancel it or vary its terms, however, must be made public.[56]

After the 11 September 2001 terrorist attacks in the United States, the *Criminal Code of Canada* was amended to allow judges to hear certain terrorism-related cases in private. If an organization or group on the government's list of terrorist organizations applies to have the designation rescinded, the judge must examine the relevant security or criminal intelligence reports in private. An edited summary of the case against the organization may be released after removing information that might harm national security or endanger someone's safety. The government can apply to a judge of the Federal Court of Appeal for an order to seize or freeze assets or property belonging to an organization accused of supporting terrorism. Again, these hearings are private.

The amendments also created investigative hearings in cases of suspected terrorism. If the authorities have reason to believe a person has information about a terrorist act or plans to commit one, the person can be forced to appear before a judge to answer questions and produce evidence. The judge has the power to take steps to protect the interests of the witness, other persons, and any ongoing investigations.[57] When the first investigative hearing was sought in connection with the 1985 bombing of Air India Flight 182, which killed 329 people, the witness involved challenged the law as a violation of Charter rights. A judge of the British Columbia Supreme Court heard the challenge in private, released a brief synopsis of her decision, and sealed the complete ruling and details of the case. The Supreme Court of Canada ruled in 2004 that this secrecy was excessive; in future, hearings and rulings in such cases must be open to the public, subject to any publication ban the judge may consider necessary to protect a person or an ongoing investigation.[58]

Youth-court restrictions

Access to youth-court files
Criminal offenders between the ages of 12 and 18 are dealt with under the *Youth Criminal Justice Act*, which imposes strict controls on access to files. While youth-court hearings are open to journalists and members of the public, written or electronic records relating to cases are accessible only to court and jail officials, lawyers, judges, and the police. Journalists and researchers must apply to a youth-court judge, who has the power to grant access if the person has 'a valid interest in the record.' The judge must be satisfied that disclosing the record is 'desirable in the interest of the proper administration of justice.'[59]

The act imposes strict time limits on applications for access. Deadlines range from two months to five years after the completion of the case, depending on the outcome and the sentence imposed. An exception is made for youths convicted of serious crimes and sentenced to the same punishment as an adult. Once all avenues of appeal have been exhausted, records of these cases are open to public scrutiny like any other criminal file. After a Nova Scotia youth was convicted of criminal negligence causing death in 2006, a judge ruled the media had the right to see pre-sentence reports, psychological reports, and correctional services' reports prepared for the court on a youth's behaviour while in custody.[60]

Youth-court publication bans

The *Youth Criminal Justice Act* shields the identities of most of the persons involved—the young person charged as well as children and young persons who are victims of crime or appear as witnesses. It is an offence to publish the name of a young person or 'any other information related to a young person' charged with a crime if the information 'would identify' that person. An exception is made for offenders convicted of a serious offence such as homicide, attempted murder, or aggravated sexual assault, or if it is the youth's third conviction for a violent offence.[61] Once offenders reach the age of 18, they can authorize the media to reveal their identities if they are no longer in custody for a youth crime. Younger offenders and those still in jail can apply to a judge to have the ban lifted.[62]

There is an identical ban on identifying young victims and witnesses and similar procedures for waiving or lifting the ban. The parents of a young homicide victim also have the right to authorize the media to identify their child. Once one media outlet has been authorized to identify a young person involved in a youth court case, other media can publish or broadcast the name without seeking further permission or court approval.[63] Unless the ban is waived or lifted, it is permanent and continues even after the person reaches adulthood. Journalists who discover that an adult offender was convicted of crimes as a youth are barred from reporting that this criminal record exists, even if it is revealed in court.[64]

Bans in civil cases

Judges presiding over civil cases have the power to ban publication of information that is considered private, sensitive, or confidential. While the civil courts are as open to public scrutiny as the criminal courts, some of the information presented during a dispute between private litigants may be seen as having little or no public interest. Laws in Ontario, Manitoba, and Prince Edward Island permit judges to exclude the public from a courtroom to prevent serious harm or injustice to any person. If a hearing is closed, judges have the power to issue an order prohibiting the disclosure of the information presented.[65] But in the words of one judge, publication bans in civil cases should 'only be granted in a narrow range of circumstances.'[66] Courts have banned publication of the names of people involved in lawsuits which allege sexual abuse, because there is a real risk of causing humiliation or serious damage to reputations. But embarrassment alone is not grounds for shielding the identity of the parties involved in lawsuits. As the Supreme Court of Canada has said, 'the sensibilities of the individuals involved' in a case is no basis for deviating from the principle of openness.[67]

Publication restrictions have also been put in place to protect a child, the safety of a witness, details of patents, or a company's trade secrets, and have been used when 'the administration of justice would be rendered impracticable by the presence of the public.'[68] The whole point of an action claiming damages for theft of confidential business information, for instance, would be defeated if the plaintiff had to reveal the information in court.

Accessing Other Justice Records

Boards, commissions, and tribunals

The federal, provincial, and territorial governments have created a system of administrative tribunals that complements the work of the courts. Tribunals operate like courts—they hear witnesses, review evidence and legal arguments, and make rulings—but their hearings tend to be less formal than trials. Federal tribunals settle disputes over such matters as employment insurance benefits and human-rights violations. Provincial and territorial tribunals deal with workplace standards, claims for workers' compensation, disputes between landlords and tenants, power-rate increases, and many other issues. Tribunal hearings and their records are usually open to the public. The legislation establishing the particular tribunal and setting out its procedures will indicate whether it has the power to restrict access to records or ban the publication of evidence.[69] The Canadian Legal Information Institute's website (*www. canlii.org*) includes the rulings of many federal, provincial, and territorial tribunals.

Extradition, immigration, and refugee cases

The *Extradition Act* allows a judge to ban publication or broadcast of the evidence presented at a bail hearing for a person facing extradition to stand trial in a foreign state. Publication of evidence presented at the extradition hearing itself can also be banned. Both bans remain in place until the defendant is discharged by the Canadian courts or the trial in the foreign country is completed.[70] All hearings of the Immigration and Refugee Board are open to the public. This includes sessions of the Refugee Protection Division, Refugee Appeal Division, the Immigration Division, and the Immigration Appeal Division. But any hearing can be closed if publicity would threaten 'the life, liberty or security of a person,' undermine the fairness of the proceeding or disclose 'matters involving public security.' Hearings into claims for refugee protection are to be held in private unless those presiding are satisfied it would be appropriate to conduct an open hearing.[71]

The federal immigration minister and solicitor general can issue a certificate to expel a permanent resident or foreign citizen who is considered undesirable or a security threat. The list includes persons accused of terrorism and the violation of human rights as well as those with a serious criminal record or links to organized crime. A judge of the Federal Court of Canada must review the certificate and decide whether it is lawful and reasonable. During these reviews, judges must protect information gathered by police and spy agencies, confidential information obtained from Canadian sources or foreign governments, and information that could jeopardize someone's safety.[72] If such concerns exist, the judge must review the information in private and exclude it from the case summary released to persons facing expulsion and their lawyers. Similar precautions must be taken with security and intelligence information presented at immigration hearings, detention reviews, appeals before the Immigration Appeal Division, and court reviews of immigration panel rulings.[73]

Courts martial

Military trials are held in public but all or part of a hearing can be closed to prevent the disclosure of information that could jeopardize public safety or national defence. Other grounds for closing a hearing include protecting international relations, public morals, and the administration of justice. The Court Martial Appeals Court has the option of sitting in private when hearing evidence (including new evidence).[74] The judge advocate presiding at a court martial also has the power to impose a publication ban on all or part of the evidence.[75]

Public inquiries

When disaster strikes or a political scandal unfolds, governments often set up a public inquiry or royal commission to investigate. Public hearings are conducted to find out what happened and to recommend measures to prevent future disasters or scandals. Commissioners have broad investigative powers and can force witnesses to testify and produce documents. They also have the power to impose publication bans and can convene private hearings to protect confidential information or other important interests. It has become routine for inquiries and royal commissions to allow their hearings to be televised.[76]

Discipline hearings for judges

Judicial councils—panels of senior judges—investigate complaints about the behaviour of judges and hold disciplinary hearings when there is evidence of serious misconduct. Complaints are considered confidential at the investigation stage and these bodies will only confirm the existence of a complaint against a specific judge if a hearing is ordered. The Canadian Judicial Council, which deals with complaints against superior court judges, has the power to decide whether its hearings will be closed or held in public. Even if it is public, the council can ban publication of any information or document used as evidence if, in the council's opinion, it would not be in the public interest to reveal the information. The federal minister of justice can, however, order a public hearing.[77] The rules for inquiries involving provincially appointed judges vary. Alberta inquiries, for instance, are conducted in private but the inquiry report is a public document. The judges conducting the inquiry can ban publication of information or documents relating to their work. An Ontario hearing can be closed only in 'exceptional circumstances' and, if it is, the name of the judge under scrutiny must not be disclosed. Ontario's judicial council has the power to ban publication of the name of a judge accused of sexual misconduct or sexual harassment.[78]

Putting Justice Records to Work

Finding and backgrounding people

Most people can be tracked down through phone listings or a city directory. If a person has an unlisted number, has moved away, or is simply proving to be elusive, court records may offer new leads. Criminal and civil files usually reveal where people were living when the case was before the courts, and the old neighbours may know where they are now. Court documents may include contact information for the person, including a phone number; at the very least, they will reveal the name of the person's lawyer and other people involved in the case who may be willing to point a reporter in the right direction.

Court records are an unsurpassed resource for compiling background information about a person. Has the person sued or been sued? Has he or she broken the law and, if so, what was the outcome? Who are the person's associates and business partners, past and present? Does the person own property or operate a business that has become mired in a legal dispute? Check out court files wherever the person has lived. To get started, do a keyword search for the person's name in the Canadian Legal Information Institute's online database of court rulings in all provinces and territories (*www.canlii.org*). The results will not be definitive—as noted, the database does not include many older rulings, and only a small percentage of court cases culminate in written rulings—but may turn up a case or two to kick-start an investigation.

Finding criminal records

There are several ways to use justice records to find out whether someone has a criminal record. Check the criminal index at the local courthouse and in other cities where the person has lived to locate the details of individual cases; the pre-sentence report in the most recent file will list all criminal convictions and the sentences imposed. If the person served time in a federal prison after 1992, his or her parole file will disclose any previous criminal offences. And don't forget to search the Canadian Legal Information Institute's online database for recent rulings in criminal cases involving the person.

Backgrounding businesses

Does a company have a reputation for financial mismanagement, questionable business or labour practices, polluting the environment, or ignoring government regulators? Searching criminal- and civil-court indexes and tribunal records for cases involving the company and its top officials may turn up pollution charges, safety violations, disputes with unions, and lawsuits launched by competitors, as well as a host of other information about the company and the people behind it. A keyword search of the company's name in the *www.canlii.org* database may be the first step in pinpointing significant prosecutions or lawsuits.

Monitoring the regulators

Are government agencies and inspectors doing their jobs? To find out, dig into the files of prosecutions for violations of the laws and regulations that govern workplace and consumer safety, the environment, labour standards, and other activities. They will disclose if people and business are being held accountable and whether regulators are being vigilant in protecting the public interest.

Investigating the justice system

In the spring of 1992, a team of *Montreal Gazette* reporters spent three months monitoring sessions of the city's municipal court, which handles minor crimes and traffic offences. They discovered that judges earning salaries of $110,000 were working half-days, despite demands for the construction of a new courthouse to deal with a backlog of thousands of cases.[79] The paper's exposé is just one example of the media's role as a watchdog of the justice system. Are our courts being run efficiently? Are judges handing down sentences that are too lenient or too harsh? Are prosecutors going easy on offenders who are wealthy or powerful? Do the authorities deal differently with members of visible minorities? The paperwork of the justice system is the key to compiling the evidence, statistics, sources, and case studies the investigative reporter needs to answer these and other important questions, and to help ensure justice is done.

Suggestions for Further Reading

Canadian Journalism Project (J-Source). 'Reporting on the Justice System: Access to Hearings and Records', 'Contempt of Court', and 'Bans on Publication', law section, *www.j-source.ca.*

Jobb, Dean. *Media Law for Canadian Journalists*, 2nd ed. Toronto: Emond Montgomery Publications, 2010, Chapters 1, 2, 5–8.

Martin, Robert. *Media Law.* Toronto: Irwin Law, 2003, Chapter 3.

6

Digging into the Past:
Using Historical Resources

It is often easier to obtain historical records than more recent ones,
which may be in private hands or subject to access restrictions.

When calls to reinstate capital punishment surfaced in the mid-1980s, the controversy prompted a question for one Nova Scotia journalist: When was that province's last execution? Capital punishment was abolished in 1976 and the date of the last hanging in Canada was well known—two men were hanged in Toronto's Don Jail in 1962 for a double murder. But in other provinces, it had been decades since a condemned murderer was sent to the gallows.

The date of Nova Scotia's last hanging proved elusive. History books were silent on the subject. The question drew a blank when posed to historians. Lawyers and judges, some of them grey-haired veterans of the criminal courts, could only shake their heads. The answer lay in an obscure 1950s parliamentary report on capital punishment, which identified the last man hanged in Nova Scotia as Everett Farmer, executed in the seaside community of Shelburne in December 1937. Newspaper coverage of the man's trial and court records held in archives in Halifax and Ottawa supplied a wealth of details. The paper trail led the journalist to the doorstep of a man who covered the case as a young reporter and was among the handful of people who witnessed the execution.[1]

There is usually an historical component to an investigation regardless of the subject. How has the provincial welfare system evolved over time? What was a town or city like a half-century ago, when the person being profiled was growing up there? When was the city's last major flood or fire? Who was the cabinet minister responsible for jails in the 1950s, when allegations first surfaced that guards were abusing prisoners? To answer such questions, journalists need to apply their research skills to historical records. For the definitive book on Ontario teenager Steven Truscott's wrongful conviction for murder in 1959, Julian Sher and his associate Theresa Burke sought out old newspaper accounts and dusted off neglected trial transcripts and police records. Sher reminds journalists that it is often easier to obtain historical records than more recent ones, which may be in private hands or subject to access restrictions. He managed to unearth everything from old photographs tucked away in small-town museums to the private papers of key figures involved in the case. 'The advantages, if you're doing historical things, is that, inevitably, there'll be (information on) paper and it's going to be more accessible because the principals are dead or the government is less worried' about what will be found.[2] In this chapter, we explore the library, archival, and online resources available to journalists who need to travel back in time.

Historical Reference Tools

The Canadian Encyclopedia

The Canadian Encyclopedia is the best starting point for any foray into Canadian history, whether you are in search of an elusive fact or date needed to complete a story, or you need to find background information during the initial stages of an investigation. With some 14,000 entries, the *Encyclopedia* is a comprehensive guide to Canada's history, geography, political events, social trends, and economic and cultural development. Short biographies of important people and sketches of cities and towns are also included. The entry on the history of capital punishment reveals that members of Parliament passed by just six votes the 1976 motion to end the practice. The encyclopedia's most recent edition, published in one large volume by McClelland & Stewart in 2000, can be found in most libraries. An up-to-date version, with the full text of all articles, is available on the Internet (*www.canadianencyclopedia.ca*). The online encyclopedia Wikipedia (*en.wikipedia.org*) is a useful starting point for historical information on Canada, but it is neither complete nor authoritative.

Dictionary of Canadian Biography

The *Dictionary of Canadian Biography* is a great source of detailed information about the people who built Canada. Prime ministers and business tycoons rub shoulders with soldiers, First Nations leaders, artists, lawyers, clerics, and ordinary people who made their mark on Canada's history. The *Dictionary* contains more than 7700 biographies of men and women who died before 1930. Each entry is rich in anecdotes and the contributors—most of them professional historians—have consulted scholarly works and archival records to bring people and events to life. The full text of the *Dictionary's* 15 printed volumes is available online (*www.biographi.ca*) and can be searched by name or keyword. Each entry provides a detailed list of sources and a link to a contributors' page, making it easy to track down the author and more information about the person profiled.

The book is a work in progress and entries for people who died between 1930 and 1980 are being added to the database as they are completed. In the meantime, for brief biographies of Canadians who were prominent in the early- to mid-twentieth century, consult W. Stewart Wallace's *The Macmillan Dictionary of Canadian Biography*.[3]

Canadian Parliamentary Guide

Published annually since 1901 (and from 1862 to 1900 as the *Canadian Parliamentary Companion*), this is an excellent source of basic information on federal and provincial politicians. Each volume contains biographical sketches of every member of Parliament, senator, and provincial politician who was in office that year, making it easy to determine, for instance, who was in cabinet when a controversial decision was made. The *Guide* includes the biographies of the judges of the Supreme Court of Canada and the Federal Court of Canada, as well as a phone directory for politicians and Canada's embassies. Biographical information about prime ministers, cabinet ministers, MPs and senators (past and present) is also available through the Parliament of Canada website (*www.parl.gc.ca*). Click on the 'Senators and Members' link near the top of the homepage to find the menu of historical information. The site includes features such as a list of politicians who have switched parties, statistical tables on women who have stood for federal office, and a rundown of the previous occupations of MPs and senators.

Each volume of the *Guide* provides a riding-by-riding tally of votes cast in the most recent federal and provincial elections, enabling a researcher to confirm the party affiliation of those who have lost bids for elected office. This information for all elections since Confederation has been consolidated into a searchable database titled History of Federal Ridings since 1867, which is accessible through the Parliament of Canada website (*www2.parl.gc.ca/sites/lop/HFER/HFER.asp*).

The Canadian Annual Review of Politics and Public Affairs

For much of the twentieth century, this publication revisited the major events and the political, economic, and social issues of the year. It draws on government reports, newspaper accounts, and other contemporary records to provide an overview of what happened and why. There are sections on federal politics, economic development, trade, industry, finance, labour, and foreign affairs, plus detailed examinations of trends and events in each province. Most volumes provide a chronology of significant events and brief obituaries of prominent individuals who died that year. It's the fastest way to find arcane information like the price of oil in the mid-1980s, the New Brunswick government's budget estimates for 1928, or how the Ontario government combatted unemployment during the Great Depression of the 1930s. Available at most libraries, it was published as *The Canadian Annual Review of Public Affairs* from 1901 to 1938. Publication was suspended until 1960, when it reappeared as *The Canadian Annual Review*. The title was changed in 1970 to *The Canadian Annual Review of Politics and Public Affairs* and new volumes take a few years to compile. The latest edition, covering the year 2007, was published in December 2009.

Historical Statistics of Canada

This Statistics Canada online publication could be subtitled 'Canada by the Numbers'. It's a collection of more than 1000 tables documenting the changing face of Canadian life and society from the early 1800s to the mid-1970s. Subjects include population growth, immigration trends, family structure, education, personal incomes, industrial production, employment levels, wholesale and retail prices, and crime and policing. One table tracks the number of parole violations between 1957 and 1975; another shows the number of men and women who earned a university or college degree in selected years between 1831 and 1973; a third compares the size of families at 5- or 10-year intervals between 1881 and 1976; yet another documents the number of forest fires and the acreage burned each year between 1908 and 1975. The tables are available as downloadable files (to find the main product page, go to the StatCan website, *www.statcan.gc.ca*, and enter 'Historical Statistics of Canada' as a search term). Each table is prefaced with an explanation of the terms used and how the data was collected and compiled.

Library Resources

Vertical files

Most public libraries maintain vertical files—a collection of file folders containing material on a wide range of subjects. They are a key source of information about local history, prominent people who have lived or made their mark in the area, and local, regional, or national issues of importance to the community. The public library in Penticton, British Columbia, for instance, maintains a large vertical file collection that includes subjects such as acid rain, medical care, forests and forestry, dude ranches, and the Yukon. The main branch of the Halifax Regional Library, meanwhile, has files on the city's history, local businesses, and civic issues like downtown development and the sewage treatment project for Halifax Harbour. A typical vertical file contains a hodgepodge of information: newspaper clippings, magazine articles, pamphlets, and reports, all of it compiled over the years and much of it difficult, if not impossible, to find anywhere else. Files may contain obscure material like old restaurant menus, railway tickets, and transit schedules. Vertical files are not comprehensive but they are readily accessible, easy to use, and a good starting point for an investigation with a local or historical angle. Vertical files are usually accessible through the library's reference desk.

Newspapers

Earthquakes are rare in Atlantic Canada. When one rattles the region, journalists will scramble to find out when the last one occurred and whether there was any damage done or lives lost. Few sources can match the immediacy and colour of a contemporary newspaper account. When the 'smart shock' of an earthquake jolted Bathurst, New Brunswick, on the night of 5 August 1852, a writer for Fredericton's *Daily Gleaner* recorded in vivid detail how it felt: 'The motion of the earth seemed a rocking one, and then followed several (perhaps eight or ten) lift-ings or vibrations of the ground. It was accompanied by a heavy rolling sound. . . . The whole lasted at least five to six minutes.' The only damage, fortunately, was cracked plaster, a few broken panes of glass, and some frayed nerves.[4]

Hundreds of newspapers have been published in Canada since the first, the *Halifax Gazette*, appeared in 1752. The late author and journalist Pierre Berton, a master of recreating historical events and characters, considered newspapers an essential resource for capturing the look and feel of the past.[5] 'Journalism is all about creating time and place,' notes Julian Sher, who pored over newspapers to soak up details of small-town life at the time of the Steven Truscott trial. Among his unexpected discoveries was that *The Hanging Tree*, a 1959 movie starring Gary Cooper, was playing at the cinema across the street from the courthouse in Gode-rich, Ontario, when a judge sentenced the teenager to be hanged for murder.[6]

Archives and libraries have extensive collections of daily and weekly news-papers on microfilm. The challenge is finding a shortcut to locate the information you want without scanning page by page, issue by issue. An index of *The Globe and Mail* and major dailies published in Vancouver, Montreal, Winnipeg, and Hali-fax is available in print form in the reference sections of most libraries, covering the years 1977 to 1998. It was published under various titles, as the *Canadian Newspaper Index* in the late 1970s, as the *Canadian News Index* from 1980 to 1992, and as the *Canadian Index* from 1993 to 1998. Indexes exist for some older news-papers but coverage is spotty. Nova Scotia's provincial archives has a card index that lists hundreds of obscure newspaper articles by subject, and a similar resource may be available at other archives and at libraries and museums. If no index is available, you will have to search based on knowing the approximate date a story appeared or an event occurred. To locate newspaper stories about an old murder case, for example, look up the court file at the archives, find out when each hear-ing was held, and then consult the following day's newspapers to see what was reported.

Newspaper archives are moving online, making it possible to search for articles using a name or other keyword. Most newspapers offer online access to the elec-tronic archives of previously published articles for a fee, and selected newspapers can be searched through commercial databases like Newscan (*newscan.com*), FPinfomart (*fpinfomart.ca*), and Factiva (*factiva.com*). Newscan, for instance, offers access to the archives of more than 150 Canadian newspapers, from big-city dai-lies like the *Winnipeg Free Press* and the *Montreal Gazette* to small community papers like Victoria's *Oak Bay News* and St Anthony's *Northern Pen*, based in northern Newfoundland. Articles may be accessible for only the past few years for some titles, but others have extensive archives; Newscan's *Montreal Gazette* hold-ings, for instance, date to 1985. Many news organizations and most libraries sub-scribe to these and similar databases, allowing journalists to find and copy articles at no cost. JournalismNet, a website of research resources, provides links to newspaper archives in Canada and abroad, as well as a brief introduction to each resource (*www.peoplesearchpro.com/journalism*).

Back issues of Canada's two major newspapers have been scanned, making it easier and faster to track down contemporary accounts of people, places, and events. *The Globe and Mail* has compiled Canada's Heritage since 1844, a database of searchable full-page images of all editions published since the paper's founding in Toronto as *The Globe*. Not to be outdone, the *Toronto Star* offers Pages from the Past, with digitized versions of its back issues since 1892. Both databases can be accessed at no charge through many libraries, either by using the library's computers or by logging into your library account from your home or office. More newspaper archives are certain to be scanned and made available online in the future. The most ambitious undertaking is the Alberta Heritage Digitization Project (*www.ourfutureourpast.ca/newspapr*), which is scanning every Alberta newspaper published before 1950. The University of Victoria has digitized *The British Colonist*, British Columbia's leading newspaper of the late nineteenth century, for the period 1858–1910 (*britishcolonist.ca*). And check library and newspaper websites for digitized collections of selected back issues and articles. The Saskatchewan News Index (*library2.usask.ca/sni*), for instance, provides access to stories on agriculture, politics, and other subjects that were published in the province's newspapers since 1884.

Electronic versions of older US newspapers are more common. More than 15 million articles published in *The New York Times* since 1851, including many reports on Canadian issues and events, can be searched and retrieved for free on the paper's website (*query.nytimes.com/search*). Clicking on the advanced search function near the top of the screen gives users the option of searching for articles published between 1851 and 1980 and for articles that have appeared since 1981. Back issues of hundreds of other US newspapers are accessible for a fee through the newspaper's own website or using commercial sites such as *ancestry.ca* and *newspaperarchive.com*. If these services prove too costly for your search, use the archive's index as a shortcut to identify dates of articles, then look up and copy the article at a library that has the paper's back issues on microfilm.

Magazines

The most comprehensive printed resource for finding magazine articles is the *Canadian Periodical Index*, published annually from 1920 to 2000. It lists, by author and subject, all articles that appeared in major magazines like *Maclean's*, *Canadian Business*, *Saturday Night*, *Chatelaine*, and *Canadian Geographic*, to name just a few. An online version, known as 'CPI.Q', is available through libraries; it includes indexes to major US magazines and some titles can be searched for articles that appeared as far back as the 1970s.

Electronic versions of magazine articles published after 1990 may be available. Newscan offers electronic access to back issues of some business-oriented magazines, including *Marketing Magazine*, *Manitoba Business*, and *Alberta Report* (now published as *Report NewsMagazine, Alberta Edition*). FPinfomart subscribers can tap into the archives of *Maclean's, Canadian Business, Toronto Life, Financial Post Business*, and other magazines. Some magazines offer free but limited access to archived articles on their websites: *Canadian Business* (*canadianbusiness.com*), for example, allows users to search a large selection of articles published since 2001.

Access to older Canadian magazines will improve as more titles are digitized. The website of *Canada's History* (the country's second-oldest magazine and, until March 2010, known as *The Beaver: Canada's History Magazine*), features a searchable index of articles on historical subjects published since 1920 (*historysociety.ca/beaver/index/index.cfm*). Links to the full text of articles are being added as the magazine digitizes its archives. *TIME* provides free access to articles published since the magazine's founding in 1923 at *www.time.com/time/archive*, which includes coverage of significant Canadian events. Library and Archives Canada (LAC) maintains a database containing hundreds of photographs and engravings that appeared in the *Canadian Illustrated News* between 1869 and 1883, a collection that includes the full text of articles on significant events, such as the Red River Rebellion of 1870 (*collectionscanada.gc.ca/databases/cin*).

Books and journals

Many public and university libraries offer searchable online catalogues, making it easy to locate books on historical subjects available in your area. Google is in the midst of a massive project to digitize books and Google Books (*books.google.ca*), a vast and expanding full-text online database that includes numerous Canadian titles, can be searched by keyword. Older works that are in the public domain can be downloaded for free and books subject to copyright will be available for a fee under an agreement reached with publishers and authors in 2009. All books in the database can be searched for free regardless of copyright, so it can be used to identify books worth purchasing or borrowing from a library. Some of these books may not have an index, making this a valuable tool for finding references that would otherwise remain hidden or require extensive research to locate.

Scholarly journals publish shorter studies that examine the country's political, economic, and social history. The leading journal is the *Canadian Historical Review*, which is published four times a year and first appeared in 1919. As an example, the June 2004 issue includes articles on the reform of women's prisons in Canada in the 1970s, the plight of unwed mothers in Victorian-era Toronto, and the Social Credit Party's breakthrough win in the 1952 British Columbia election.[7] A database of all review articles is accessible online through public and university libraries; for those without access to a user account, the *Canadian Historical Review*'s main site (*utpjournals.metapress.com/content/120322*) offers a search function that can be used to identify articles.

America: History and Life, a database available through many libraries, offers another searchable index of articles published in the *Canadian Historical Review* and also in dozens of other journals that explore Canadian history. Individual journals may offer online access to articles or an index. For instance, the website for *Acadiensis* (a journal of Atlantic Canadian regional history) includes an index of articles published in the journal since 1971, searchable by author and subject (*www.lib.unb.ca/Texts/Acadiensis*). In addition, local historical societies publish collections of articles aimed at a general audience, including some with online access.

Theses and dissertations

An unpublished thesis or dissertation can be a source of historical information or offer insights into the author, who may have gone on to a prominent career. University libraries keep copies of theses written by their graduates, but theses written since 1965 are also available through Library and Archives Canada (search the index at *www.collectionscanada.gc.ca/thesescanada*). The LAC preserved them on microfilm or microfiche until 1998, and these can be obtained on loan. Theses written since 1998 have been digitized or were collected in electronic format. Of the 300,000 theses in the library's collection, some 50,000 are available in electronic format and can be downloaded through LAC's website.

Specialized Tools

Online discussion groups

Internet chat and information-exchange groups accessible though sites such as Google Groups (*groups.google.ca*) can be searched for obscure information and to contact history buffs, reunion groups, collectors, and hobbyists with specialized knowledge. While researching his book on the Steven Truscott case, Julian Sher tapped this resource to find someone who knew the colours of the licence plates of every province in a given year. He used a chat group for children who grew up on Canadian military bases to track down people who had grown up with Truscott or lived on a nearby base in the late 1950s, when the youth was wrongly convicted of murder.[8]

Weather data

Back issues of a local newspaper have on record whether it was sunny, raining, or foggy on the day an event occurred. The issue published the day before the event should have the forecast and the one that appeared the following day should provide a recap of conditions. Two online tools are worth checking as well: Environment Canada's Climate Data Online (*climate.weatheroffice.ec.gc.ca*) offers weather data dating back to the 1930s for some areas, and daily and hourly conditions are available for more recent dates. The Old Farmer's Almanac (*almanac.com/weather-history*) provides weather information since 1946 for selected Canadian cities and towns, but access to older information is spotty.

Inter-library loan

In the wake of the 1992 explosion that killed 26 men at Nova Scotia's Westray coal mine, sources advised reporters for *The Halifax Chronicle Herald* to check into the safety record of the mine's top manager. The manager, they suggested, had been criticized during an inquiry into the deaths of four men at an Alberta mine a decade earlier. But hard evidence proved elusive: The manager was not mentioned in newspaper accounts of the earlier disaster or in the inquiry's final report. Further inquiries turned up an eight-volume transcript of the inquiry's hearings, which was tucked away in the library of the Alberta Department of Labour in Edmonton. Ordering a photocopy of the huge document would have been expensive but the department's librarian suggested an inter-library loan, using the newspaper's in-house library as the destination. Within days, the reporters were thumbing through the transcripts, which were peppered with criticism of the manager and his hard-nosed management style. The borrowed transcripts became the basis of a front-page exposé that was nominated for the National Newspaper Award for enterprise reporting.[9]

Inter-library loan may be the best option for tracking down books and government documents that are not available through local libraries or on the Internet. Anyone with a library card can borrow materials from any library in Canada, the United States, or other countries. There will likely be a small fee for each request and an additional fee to obtain photocopies of shorter items, such as articles from magazines and journals. Books, government reports, newspapers on microfilm, dissertations and some microfilmed archival materials can be borrowed, but reference works and rare books are excluded. Library staff will locate the material and make the application on your behalf. Libraries that have a copy of the book, article, or report you are seeking can be identified through LAC's online catalogue (*collectionscanada.gc.ca/amicus*). Search the site by title, author, or subject, then click the locations tab. The WorldCat database (*www.worldcat.org*) provides access to the electronic holdings of libraries around the world and can locate more than a billion books, journals, CDs, DVDs, and videos.

The drawback to using an inter-library loan is time: it could be two to four weeks before the material arrives but you may be able to arrange for faster delivery by paying an additional fee.

Using Archives

Archival resources

Think of archives as the attics of the nation. They preserve government documents, yellowed newspapers, court files, deeds, photos, maps, film and sound recordings, genealogical records, and the diaries and personal papers of famous and ordinary Canadians alike. They offer tangible links to the nation's past.

The LAC collection in Ottawa is vast—it has millions of pages, plus tens of thousands of hours of film and sound recordings. The collection of architectural plans and drawings alone comprises 2.5 million items dating to the sixteenth century. In addition, each province has its own archives, housing local records and personal papers. Libraries, museums, and some institutions and corporations maintain archives, too. Many of these holdings, as noted below, can be searched on the archive's website and, in some cases, the records and images themselves have been digitized and posted online.

Most records, however, still must be searched on-site, so a research trip will likely be required. Most archives offer lists of researchers who will do the work on your behalf, for a fee. If the search is specific and can be conducted without too much effort, archives staff will field written or emailed requests for information on their holdings. Staff at LAC field almost 4000 written requests each month and aim to reply within 30 days. There is no fee for this service and requests can be submitted by letter, fax, or by using an electronic form available at the Library and Archives Canada website. The mailing address for submitting a written request is

Client Services Division
Library and Archives Canada
395 Wellington Street
Ottawa, Ontario
K1A 0N4

Journalists may find allies among archives staff as they try to hunt down information. While researching his book on the Steven Truscott case, Julian Sher recalls, he gave up on efforts to locate the military's personnel file on a suspect the police overlooked in the rush to convict Truscott. But one archivist refused to accept defeat and eventually found the file, which contained hundreds of pages of material and provided details of the man's mental health and his whereabouts at the time of the murder.

Keep in mind that many people have a personal archive of old letters, newspaper clippings, family photos, and other keepsakes. 'I ask people if they have anything—letters, papers, photographs—that might shed light on the story I'm working on or might corroborate things they're telling me,' says author and journalist Stephen Kimber, who teaches journalism at the University of King's College in Halifax and wrote a book recreating life in the city during the Second World War. 'It sometimes amazes me what people keep. Photographs can be especially useful, providing not only material for contemporary physical description of people and places but often also . . . invaluable leads to other sources.'[10]

Online access

The Canadian Council of Archives maintains a website (*www.archivescanada.ca*) that makes it possible to do a keyword search of the holdings of more than 800 archives across the country. A search by subject or name provides detailed information about each collection of material, including a link to the relevant archive's website. If you type in the name 'Steven Truscott', for instance, the database will turn up three items: A recording of an interview with Truscott that aired decades ago on an Ottawa radio station and documents in the personal papers of parliamentarian Stanley Knowles, who lobbied for Truscott's release in the 1960s, are housed at LAC. The third reference is to a law professor's research notes on the life of Justice Emmett Hall, a Supreme Court of Canada judge who heard one of Truscott's appeals, which are housed at the University of Saskatchewan Archives. This site has a link to the Archival Community Digitization Program and its array of virtual exhibits and archival records in electronic format. Subjects include a history of the Saskatchewan Wheat Pool in pictures; an illustrated history of the *Bluenose*, the famous Nova Scotia racing schooner of the 1920s depicted on Canada's ten-cent piece; an exhibit chronicling 150 years of Ottawa history; and an overview of politics in Montreal since 1830.

A more extensive collection of archival and historical material digitized between 1996 and 2004 is available at *collections.ic.gc.ca*. There are more than 60 entries under the letter *S* alone, including material on Sable Island, Canadian satellites, Prince Edward Island shipwrecks, the history of the Snuneymuxw First Nation of Vancouver Island, and author/humorist Stephen Leacock. Library and Archives Canada offers a site called AVITUS (*collectionscanada.ca/databases/avitus*), which allows users to search a collection of databases, catalogues, and websites for genealogical and historical information by keyword and subject. As well, Dr Susan Neylan, a history professor at Wilfrid Laurier University in Waterloo, Ontario, maintains a website (*canadianhistoryontheweb.ca*) with links to dozens of digitized Canadian history resources.

More and more archival items will be accessible online as material is digitized. The LAC has posted the complete diaries of former prime minister William Lyon Mackenzie King—50,000 pages of entries written between 1893 and 1950 that can be searched online (*www.collectionscanada.gc.ca/databases/king*). A search for the name *Winston Churchill* will turn up 107 references in entries written between 1904 and 1949. Library and Archives Canada also posts indexes of the diaries of soldiers who fought in the Boer War and the First World War; many have been scanned and can be viewed online. Scanned pages containing raw data collected for the national census of 1901 and the 1906 census of Alberta and Saskatchewan can be searched by city, town, or municipal unit. The 1871 census returns for Ontario have been converted into a database that can be searched by keyword, name, occupation, and ethnic origin. A complete list of LAC indexes and holdings accessible online is available through ArchiviaNet (*www.collectionscanada.ca/archivianet*). Provincial archives are also posting material online. The Archives of Ontario (*archives.gov.on.ca*) provides online access to exhibits that examine the War of 1812, what winter was like in early-twentieth-century Canada, and the exploits of renowned explorer and mapmaker David Thompson.

Visuals, film, and sound recordings

Archives preserve photographs, film clips, and audio recordings that can add texture and context to stories. The ArchiviaNet search engine mentioned above allows researchers to conduct online searches of 400,000 descriptions of photographs in LAC's photography collection. More than 10,000 of these images are accessible online and can be downloaded and used for free. LAC has created The Virtual Gramophone (*collectionscanada.gc.ca/gramophone/index-e.html*), a multimedia website containing audio files of recordings made during the early years of sound recording in Canada. The database includes images as well as biographies of musicians and information on the history of music and the recording industry in Canada. ArchiviaNet can be used to search a collection of 265,000 films, videos, and sound recordings. Descriptions of about 40,000 maps, plans, and charts in the archives can also be searched; approximately 4000 of these items have been scanned for free viewing and downloading. Most provincial archives offer online access to catalogues of the images and recordings in their collections as well as examples of their holdings.

Thousands of hours of the CBC's radio and television programming is accessible on the Internet in English (*archives.cbc.ca*) and in French (*archives.radio-canada.ca*). The archives contain more than 10,000 clips and new items are added weekly, with the oldest dating to the founding of radio in Canada in the 1920s and television in the early 1950s. The material is protected by copyright and intended for educational and other non-commercial use, but the CBC permits users to create links to their own websites and the clips posted—as well as those still tucked away in the broadcaster's vast archives—can be purchased for republication. The JournalismNet website (*journalismnet.com/video*) has links to other Canadian video archives.

Genealogical resources

Tracing people from the past relies on many of the resources journalists use to find people who are alive today, such as newspaper archives, city directories, court files, and property records. The passage of time means additional records considered confidential today may be available, including birth, marriage and death records, ships' passenger lists, and the census records of individual Canadians. Archives house much of this material to assist professional genealogists and people tracing their own family tree. Some material is available online for free, including early census returns, or, for a fee, through commercial sites such as Ancestry.ca. The website of Nova Scotia Archives and Records Management in Halifax (*www.gov.ns.ca/nsarm*), for instance, includes a searchable database containing close to a million records of births, marriages, and deaths in the province from 1763 to 1957. Resources such as these can be used to trace the family tree of a profile subject or for finding out more about those involved in historical events. For an overview of genealogical resources and how to use them, consult Angus Baxter's *In Search of Your Canadian Roots: Tracing Your Family Tree in Canada*.[11]

Suggestions for Further Reading

Hallowell, Gerald, ed. *The Oxford Companion to Canadian History*. Don Mills, ON: Oxford University Press, 2004.

Morton, Desmond. *A Short History of Canada*, 5th ed. Toronto: McClelland & Stewart, 2001.

Muise, D.A. *A Reader's Guide to Canadian History*, 2 vols. Toronto: University of Toronto Press, 1982.

CASE STUDY: Part II—Jim Bronskill

Q What was the name of your story/project?

A Putting Tasers to the Test.

Q Where was it published/broadcast?

A The CBC/Radio-Canada teamed up with the Canadian Press news agency to undertake an unprecedented multimedia analysis of the Taser and the RCMP's use of these stun guns.

The two news organizations, both with a long-standing interest in Tasers, collaborated on data analysis of RCMP stun-gun use, identification of vital trends, interviews and preparation of stories for newspapers, websites, radio and television—amplifying the impact of investigative journalism in the public interest.

At the same time, CBC/Radio-Canada commissioned the largest independent test of Tasers ever conducted. The scientific examination found that more than 10 per cent of units tested were either defective or behaving unexpectedly, with some discharging significantly more electrical current than the manufacturer's standard.

The Canadian Press–CBC/Radio-Canada investigation

- revealed the extent to which the RCMP was shielding details of Taser use, creating a public backlash that prompted the Mounties to disclose more information about stungun firings;
- showed how the RCMP was using the potent weapon contrary to internal policy; and
- raised serious questions about the safety of Taser guns through independent laboratory tests, leading the RCMP and several provinces to test Tasers for potentially dangerous flaws.

> Reporters: Sandra Bartlett, Frédéric Zalac, Jim Bronskill, Sue Bailey
> Producers: Susanne Reber, Alex Shprintsen, David McKie
> TV Camera: Georges Laszuk
> TV Editor: Kris Fleerackers
> Editorial Assistants: Kevin Wiltshire, Darlene Parsons
> Data analysis: Phil Harbord

Q   How did you get the idea for the story/project?

A   The Taser wasn't a big deal to most Canadians when both news organizations began exam-
    ining the way Canadian police officers in Canada use the weapon billed as a 'less-lethal'
    alternative to conventional firearms.

    The Canadian Press undertook one of the first in-depth examinations of Tasers with
    a 2004 series that raised questions about the adequacy of policy and training stan-
    dards. The investigation showed that RCMP officers must file a form each time a Taser is
    used, beginning a lengthy battle for records of stun-gun firings under the *Access to
    Information Act*.

    Radio-Canada began researching Tasers in 2005 and produced a TV documentary the
    following year on the success of its manufacturer, Taser International, in distributing the
    weapon first to hundreds, then thousands, of police forces without independent research
    on the device's safety. CBC/Radio-Canada broadcast a series that revealed, while most
    police services in Canada had intended the device to be used instead of the gun, it was in
    fact being fired more frequently in situations that were far less than critical or dangerous.

Q   What initial research did you do to confirm that the story was valid? What was your initial
    theory as to what the story would be?

A   The October 2007 death of Robert Dziekanski and the subsequent release of a shocking
    amateur videotape in which the Polish immigrant was hit by the stun gun with little warning
    raised an urgent question: Was this an isolated case, or was it typical of how the Mounties
    used their Tasers? The Canadian Press thought the use-of-force reporting data received so
    far, covering 2002 to 2005, might yield some answers.

    The primary finding was startling: analysis of 563 Taser firings indicated three-quarters
    of suspects were unarmed. The data also documented a host of related injuries—including
    head wounds, burns, and lacerations—linked to a weapon police have touted as less harm-
    ful than pepper spray or batons.

    The figures also revealed a disturbing tendency to painfully jolt suspects after only the
    most cursory interaction. Far from being a tool to defuse major conflicts that might other-
    wise have required lethal force, officers repeatedly used the Taser as a compliance tool.
    Numerous cases involved detainees—many of them Aboriginal—held in RCMP cells.

Q   Once you had confirmed that you had a story, how did you plan out your research?

A   Dziekanski's death persuaded CBC/Radio-Canada it was the right time to take a closer look
    at what kind of testing had been done by Canadian police authorities prior to adopting
    Tasers. It took access-to-information requests and six months of repeated calls to the
    RCMP to learn that little had been done to verify the electrical output of Tasers.

    Furthermore, in analyzing the research material the police force used in making deci-
    sions, we realized the RCMP had not only relied on some seriously flawed studies, but had
    accepted information from Taser International at face value. This was strong incentive for
    CBC/Radio-Canada to commission its own tests.

Q   What secondary source research was required? What primary sources did you use? How
    did they contribute to the story?

A   We found one of the many people who had been stunned with a Taser and featured in our pieces through discovery of his online comments in response to a CBC forum on stun guns. The files of the BC inquiry into Dziekanski's death were also helpful.

Q   What were the most important interviews for the story? Why?

A   The news organizations painted a fuller picture of Dziekanski's last hours through an extensive interview with his mother, Zofia Cisowski, and details from documents released by the Canada Border Services Agency under the *Access to Information Act*.

Interviews with RCMP Inspector Troy Lightfoot and Corporal Gregg Gillis, as well as RCMP complaints commission chair Paul Kennedy, were also key.

In the weeks after October 2007, editorial writers and citizens in Canada continued to speculate about whether the Taser killed Robert Dziekanski. There was no indication that the stun gun used on him was going to be tested.

Taser International maintained that its electric guns would effectively incapacitate suspects and still have a very high margin of safety. In 2006, the company proudly showed CBC/Radio-Canada every step of the assembly line at its plant in Scottsdale, Arizona. At that time, a Taser International executive told us that all Tasers are fired with exactly the same output, then none would perform outside the specified range. That assurance was repeated last spring, when the president of Taser International came to Vancouver to address the Braidwood Inquiry examining Dziekanski's death. He unequivocally stated that his device could not produce more power than the specifications because the weapon was already operating at 100 per cent. He was adamant that police forces need not test their Tasers.

CBC/Radio-Canada decided to undertake what became the largest independent testing of Tasers. Through sources and freedom-of-information laws, we obtained the studies and tests that Canadian authorities had relied on. Several experts analyzed the studies and concluded that they were either extremely limited or lacked scientific rigour. We also obtained a testing protocol drafted by Taser International, which was valuable in designing our tests.

We hired National Technical Services (*www.ntscorp.com*), an internationally accredited engineering and testing firm, to randomly test more than 40 units of the most popular model, the Taser X26. The guns, all used by US law-enforcement officers, came from several police departments. The results were troubling: more than 10 per cent of the guns were either defective or significantly off specifications—some of them putting out 50 per cent more electrical current than the manufacturer's standards, thus significantly reducing the safety margin. Also, low serial number units were much more likely to produce too much current.

Pierre Savard, a professor of biomedical engineering at Montreal's École Polytechnique, designed the technical procedure for our testing and analyzed the laboratory's results. He took part without payment because he felt there was a strong public interest in doing so. Other electrical engineers then reviewed his work.

Through freedom-of-information requests, we also discovered that police forces returned Tasers to the manufacturer at a rate of 15 to 30 per cent. This data confirmed some of the allegations from former employees who had testified in a shareholder lawsuit against the company. They had alleged that there was a very high percentage of defective units coming off of the assembly line and that there were a lot of returns to the company.

We tracked down some of those former employees and they told us that, at times, over 70 per cent of the units produced were defective, yet there was a lot of pressure, both from investors and police forces, to deliver them.

One very important part of the story was the analysis of our test results using an international electrical standard. The analysis conducted by Savard concluded that the risk of death could be very high in certain circumstances. We contacted some members of the international committee responsible for that standard to verify our findings. Immediately after the broadcast, we learned Taser was using a 20-year-old version of the international standard and was not aware of important changes included in the 2007 version.

In the course of our work, we contacted eight electrical engineers, and several medical doctors and researchers. We also talked to a dozen police officers, tracked down former Taser International employees and some of the company's distributors, and obtained an interview with the RCMP and the head of the Canadian Police Research Centre.

The morning after the Taser testing stories aired, the Quebec government announced all X26 Tasers used by the province's police forces would be pulled off the streets and tested. They also committed to randomly testing the more recent models. The RCMP followed with a similar announcement and within days, several provinces and major police forces across Canada said they would withdraw early Taser X26 models until they were properly tested. Some provinces, like British Columbia, announced they would begin regular testing of Tasers.

Taser International attacked the credibility and methodology of the study saying it was 'not relevant on a medical safety perspective.' Ironically, Taser International criticized part of the methodology from its own testing protocol. No correction or clarification was published or necessary. Experts who reviewed our test results confirmed the study was valid and significant.

Q   What methods did you use to organize your research or the material you found?

A   A variety of tools: old-fashioned file folders, a chronology created using Microsoft Excel® and Windows desktop folders.

Q   Did you use any computerized techniques to do or organize research? If so, what were these, and how did you use them.

A   We used Microsoft Access® to create a database of RCMP Taser reports and analyze them.

Q   Did you use any undercover reporting for the story? If so, what did you do?

A   No.

Q   Did you use freedom-of-information requests for the story? If so, what requests did you make, and how many?

A   After a wait of 15 months, the RCMP began releasing new data under the *Access to Information Act*. However, the Mounties stripped crucial information from the official report forms, including whether suspects were armed, the precise dates of firings and what police officers had done before resorting to the Taser. In fact, the force had excised some material from the 2002-to-2005 period that was previously released to the Canadian Press. In doing so, the RCMP had effectively reclassified information about Taser use.

Q How important were these requests for the story?

A The RCMP's refusal to be more forthcoming with the information it could locate formed the basis of the first story in the joint investigative series by the Canadian Press and CBC/Radio-Canada. Reaction was swift and widespread. A 26 March *Globe and Mail* editorial on the stripping of record details, 'Editing out the essence', castigated the national police force for its 'trust-us' mentality: 'It makes one wonder whether the new RCMP commissioner William Elliott, whose job was to change the national police force's insular culture, has not instead become captive to it. . . . The hiding of these details about Taser use is another reason for Public Safety Minister Stockwell Day to stop delaying and to reform the national police force.'

Elliott subsequently announced he had 'directed that a further review of the recently released material be conducted' to see if additional information could be disclosed.

A 31 March *Toronto Star* editorial, 'Transparency on Tasers', said,

One hopes this will prompt the RCMP to do the right thing and open up its records to more scrutiny. But it is disturbing that it took being publicly embarrassed for Elliott to act. . . . As police use of Tasers increases, and pressure builds to put them in the hands of more officers in Toronto and elsewhere, more, not less, transparency is in order.

An editorial cartoon in the same day's *Ottawa Citizen* was less subtle. It portrayed a reporter flat on his back, eyeglasses and papers askew, after being Tasered by a Mountie behind an 'RCMP Access to Information' service counter.

The review ordered by Elliott resulted in the RCMP releasing more data: We could now say whether people hit with the stun guns were armed, and whether they were drunk or high at the time. 'I believe we need to do a better job in assessing and factoring in the public interest,' Elliott would tell a gathering in April.

Despite these challenges, the investigative team spent weeks compiling the best picture possible of RCMP Taser use, painstakingly typing numerous incident details from thousands of individual forms into the computer database. This groundbreaking analysis, illustrated with vivid details of telling cases, revealed that RCMP use of the controversial stun guns had spiked to 1000 incidents annually from just 600 in 2005.

But there was more: Officers fired their Tasers more than once in almost half the confrontations. We found many people who had been Tasered three, four, five, or more times, and sometimes by more than one officer. RCMP policy in place since 2005 states that 'multiple deployment or continuous cycling of the CEW [conducted energy weapon] may be hazardous to a subject. Unless situational factors dictate otherwise, do not cycle the CEW repeatedly, for more than 15–20 seconds at a time against a subject.'

Despite those new rules, the percentage of Taser incidents in which the weapon was fired multiple times crept up to 45 per cent in 2007 from 42 per cent two years earlier.

We also discovered that nearly one-third of suspects jolted with stun guns later received medical treatment. Furthermore, cross-referencing with earlier data showed that some who required medical treatment did not get it. For example, in one incident report, a person shot with a Taser suffered 'burn marks' but was not examined at a medical facility. The actual number of people requiring medical attention may have been higher given the fact that many Taser reports had been filled out incorrectly.

New waves of indignation followed these revelations about how suspects were zapped repeatedly with a weapon that has not been independently proven as safe.

A 13 June editorial in the *National Post*, 'The shocks keep coming', said the Canadian Press–CBC investigation had introduced a 'distressing new data point' into the debate around Tasers.

> How can figures indicating an increasingly frequent use of a torturously painful push-button weapon be defended? Were criminals more violent in 2007 than they were in 2002? Did they gain height and weight? Did they become more intractable under arrest?
>
> Logic points toward the conclusion that has been supported mostly by anecdote until now: As time goes by, police forces equipped with the Taser become more casual toward its use, and less responsible, even when there are strong written guidelines supposedly in place.

The statistics and conclusions presented in the stories were not challenged. On the contrary, they were supported in the following months by two independent analyses.

The first report, prepared by the Commission for Public Complaints against the RCMP, confirmed our findings and, having access to uncensored data, underscored additional evidence that the weapon was often used inappropriately.

The second, written by a consultant hired by the RCMP, examined the force's decision to adopt the device and its subsequent use. It criticized the RCMP for relying too heavily on Taser International for research and scientific studies, sloppy use-of-force record keeping and failure to regularly test the weapons.

Q   Many projects have a turning point when it all seems to fall into place. Was there such a point for this project? If so, please describe in detail that turning point?

A   The RCMP released thousands of pages of Taser data the Thursday before Easter weekend. Out of fear of being scooped, we spent three days hand counting and broadly assessing the content disclosed. This led to our story on lack of disclosure about details of RCMP Taser use—a piece that also documented the significant rise in stun gun firings.

Q   Did your story change from your first theory? If so, how?

A   The goals of the two major threads of the investigation were clear from the outset: to document RCMP Taser use and to test the technical specifications of the devices. It was simply a question of the results—and, therefore, the stories—that would emerge.

Q   How many stories did you write?

A   Literally dozens of print, radio, television, and online pieces.

Q   What was the most challenging part about writing these stories?

A   The most challenging part was coordinating the deadline and stylistic demands of the various media formats across two large news organizations.

Q   Over how many days/broadcasts did the stories run?

A   Roughly 18.

Q   Did your story/project include Internet elements?

A   Yes.

Q   If so, what were these and how did they fit into the overall presentation?

A   The Canadian Press produced two Web videos and several graphics. The graphics accompanied written CBC.ca pieces that anchored the broadcaster's extensive online Taser coverage.

Q   On what dates did the stories run?

A   Principal stories were aired and published throughout 2008—beginning 30 and 31 January, then 24–30 March, 15 April, 11–12 and 17–18 June, and 4–6 and 11 December.

Q   What was the most difficult thing about doing this story/project? The most challenging?

A   Many RCMP Taser reports were poorly filled out. In fact, in tracing dates of some serious injuries and deaths reported in the media, we found no official reports of these Taser incidents at all. For several months, submitting the form to headquarters had been optional, meaning gaps in the record. In addition, there was considerable effort involved in finding an appropriate lab to do the Taser tests and ensure the integrity of the process.

Q   What was the most satisfying part of the project?

A   The most satisfying part of the project was bringing statistical and scientific rigour to a much-debated and highly polarized subject: the RCMP's use of Tasers.

Q   What other comments would you make about this project?

A   Revealing pieces prepared by colleagues across both news organizations augmented the core team's investigative work. Reporters from the agencies' Alberta bureaus collaborated on a story about Jason Doan, who died in Red Deer after being hit with a Taser. Reporters in Vancouver examined cases in which disabled people had been hit with stun guns; they also looked closely at the RCMP's cavalier emails to staff after Dziekanski's death.

Q   How long did the project take to research and write?

A   As you can now tell, the various strands of the project took more than a year to pull together. However, the work on building and analyzing the Taser data took about two and a half months.

Part III

Getting to the Heart of the Matter:
Special Investigations

Researching and Finding People

Recognize that the more organized and methodical you are in building your file of material, the more useful it will prove to be when you begin to write.

Introduction

When father-and-son entrepreneurs Michael and Mark Gobuty moved their federally funded garment factory from Manitoba to Florida in the early 1990s, CBC investigative journalists Cecil Rosner and Ross Rutherford smelled a story. Michael was a well-known entrepreneur in the city who had been an owner of the Winnipeg Jets NHL hockey club and of a local racetrack. He and son Mark started the garment factory after securing a loan from the federal Business Development Bank.[1]

'We discovered that the plant [Gobuty] had moved to Florida was bought with monies from a federal agency, monies that hadn't been repaid,' Rosner says. 'We set out to discover as much as we could about the Gobutys. In particular, we wanted to know all the details of the government support he had received while here.'

Those government-funding details, along with a wide array of other important details about the Gobutys' business practices, formed the basis of a probing investigative biography into the father and son. The approach Rosner and Rutherford used to research the Gobutys offers a case study in *backgrounding* individuals.

'In general, it's possible to build a road map of any person's life by thoroughly analyzing public records,' says Rosner. Using those records, they showed that the Gobutys reneged on a federal bank loan and misrepresented themselves to Florida officials, who provided them with a host of financial incentives to move south.[2]

Ever wonder how a journalist finds such detailed information on a subject of a profile or investigation? Or have you considered how private detectives track down people who would prefer not to be found? For the most part, these gumshoes rely on the records available to everyone. Online tools, phone directories, professional or trade records, court files, property filings, business registrations and other sources can be used to unearth addresses, phone numbers, and colleagues, and to build meticulous personal histories. In this chapter, we will outline the process of backgrounding people through public records. We'll also show how you can use the Internet, databases, and other resources to locate research subjects, sources, and experts relevant to your project.

As we live and breathe, we create an information trail. Everything from your personal loans to your driving record is on file somewhere. Most of that information is protected by privacy legislation. Such personally sensitive information such as your medical records and banking information, for example, are not a matter of public record. But an array of basic information about all of us—who we are, where we live, what we own, what we owe, how we make a living—is considered public in Canada and most other Western nations. And those records can be valuable tools in helping researchers pull together vital pieces of information about people involved in matters of public interest.

People, after all, are always at the centre of news. And that means journalists are frequently in the position of finding out all they can about the personalities that shape public issues. Whether it's a local politician, an alleged criminal, or a corporate chief executive officer, a range of public records and online tools exist that can help map the intersections where private lives meet the public interest.

In many ways this is a review chapter, pulling together the various resources and tools we've discussed so far with some special online tools for finding people. The purpose here is to get you thinking about backgrounding people in a strategic, exhaustive manner with a checklist of approaches to using the Internet and public records.

There are some basic questions to ask yourself before you begin the process of building a profile on an individual. What is their background? Have they been in the public spotlight? What has been written about them already? What is their relationship to others who might be relevant to the broader story you're researching? Where does this person fit in the larger context of the story? Who are the people around your subject who might be valuable sources of information? What does your subject do for a living? Is he or she a member of a regulated or licensed profession such an accountant, doctor, plumber, or exotic dancer? Have they had brushes with the law that would have produced court records? What has your subject written that might be publicly available? Putting together this sort of detailed character sketch is a good place to start. Human activities and relationships are often the starting point to figuring out what records might exist and where to look for them.

While our focus in this chapter is on public records and the Internet, it should be understood that interviews are often the most valuable resources for backgrounding individuals. Any detailed look into the characters at the centre of an important story should utilize good interviewing skills, as we discuss in the next chapter. The challenge is always in finding the people with the necessary perspectives who are willing to share them publicly. Finding these people will become part of the journey of your research. One piece of information will lead to the next until you build a web of connections. The kinds of public-record and Internet search techniques discussed here will help you find the names and contact information for people who can bring the factual information you find to life.

This is no small point. While an investigation must rely heavily on documentation and verifiable facts, it's not enough to stop there. It's the voices and insights from the sources you uncover in that research that will form the bulk of any good story you eventually craft.

One other bit of advice off the top: Get a file folder with lots of separate pockets, and label them. As you work through the various methods outlined here, you will gather records. It's essential that all the paper you gather be kept organized. If you're working on an in-depth project, you'll likely end up with stacks of pages of material that will become confusing. Even worse, essential things will get lost. When you come across a valuable website or online article, print it and also send it to an electronic folder in your computer. You'll want backups. And make plenty of written notes on your material to remind you later of what is important. It's also worth creating an electronic spreadsheet file in which you list all your phone calls, interviews, documents, and notes. Another useful file is a chronology of your subject's involvement in your story, allowing you to see the evolution of a story over time in a way that your brain simply won't be able to.

Organizational methods are personal; everyone has their own system. But recognize that the more organized and methodical you are in building your file of material, the more useful it will prove to be when you begin to write.

Online Backgrounding

Web searching

'The Internet doesn't make a stupid journalist smart, but it does make a smart journalist smarter,' says journalist Julian Sher. 'Most people just use it as a blind search engine and they don't even use it that well. But if you use it as a finely honed tool it can be very, very effective.'[3]

The first thing many journalists do when they need to find out about someone is to type the person's name into an Internet search engine. This is indeed a helpful 'first blush' approach, but it's hardly exhaustive. The information returned is usually voluminous, largely irrelevant, and even misleading. Imagine you are investigating a (fictional) Nova Scotian geneticist named David MacKinnon, for instance, who claims to have a cure for Alzheimer's disease. A search for 'David MacKinnon' will turn up thousands of documents that have nothing to do with this Dr MacKinnon. Of course, the more search terms you include, the better; typing 'David MacKinnon' alongside other search terms such as *researcher* or *geneticist* would help you narrow the search.

But experienced Web searchers will be more precise, using various *advanced search* options that filter out much of the irrelevant material. All of the major search engines provide instructions for navigating their particular advanced searches. It's worth learning the skills for several of them. No single search engine covers the whole Internet; most search only a small portion. The more engines you use, the broader your coverage.

Google obviously reigns as the most popular search tool on the Web. Skip the standard Google search bar entirely and go straight to the advanced search screen—it allows for far more control and precision in your search. We'll discuss below a number of search operators that allow you to filter out the sludge and pinpoint the material you really want.

And remember that while Google is great, you need to expand your search beyond a single source. Try plugging the same search terms into a range of reliable search engines and you'll likely see entirely new results and an ever widening scope of sources. Here's a sampling:

- Dogpile (*www.dogpile.com*)
- BlindSearch (*blindsearch.fejus.com*)
- Yahoo (*dir.yahoo.com*)
- Librarian's Internet Index (*lii.org*)
- Infomine (*infomine.ucr.edu*)
- Canadian Information by Subject (*www.collectionscanada.gc.ca/caninfo/ecaninfo.htm*)

While the specific instructions for conducting advanced searches differ from engine to engine, the general principles are largely consistent. Google, for example, offers many of these targeted searches on its Advanced Search page (find the link to the right of the main search bar in Google). With other search engines, you can type the operations into the main search fields once you understand the proper format. Check the help pages to find the particular operators each engine supports. The features essentially allow you to dig beyond simple keyword searches in an effort to isolate information.

The first step is to do some thinking about the question you're asking. Computers are literal. They have no ability to interpret a clumsy array of keywords into a meaningful query. Think about the connections between the individual names and the broader concepts you can add to the name to focus the search. In the case of our fictional David MacKinnon, you could try typing 'Alzheimer's' into the search field, but you should also consider words like 'heredity' and 'gene'.

It's useful to imagine the ideal document and the words it would contain. Remember that concepts can be expressed in a number of ways; your coming up with an exhaustive list of keywords will help you to unearth documents that might have never turned up in more superficial searches.

You can also eliminate unhelpful responses to your queries. If your search results are being muddied by hits about a person with the same name as your subject but who sells real estate in Calgary, for example, you can use the advanced search tools to eliminate all pages containing the words 'real estate'.

Some search engines let you do many complicated search techniques without having to type any special commands (called *operators*) into the search field. However, it is often quicker to learn the commands yourself than to navigate an engine's supposedly helpful interface.

Phrase searching

If you're looking for a term containing two or more words, most search engines won't be smart enough to understand that you want the whole phrase rather than isolated examples of each word. For example, a search tool told to find 'David MacKinnon' might suggest to you a document that mentions a David in the first paragraph, a MacKinnon in the 179th, and no David MacKinnons at all. To fix this, you need to surround the words with double quotation marks: "David MacKinnon".

Truncation

The so-called *wild card*, usually expressed as an asterisk, allows you to ask for the core of a word while ignoring variations in word endings. For example, if you're searching for information on that Alzheimer's researcher using keywords having to do with genetics, typing in 'genetic★' will give you documents containing the words 'genetic', 'geneticist', and 'genetics'. If you want to Canadianize search results, you can add 'canad★' to give you documents that include the words 'Canada', 'Canadian', and 'Canadians'.

Searching document titles

To find responses that are even more relevant to your search, try searching within the title of documents. Each search engine has its own way of doing this. For example, Google's advanced search offers a pull-down menu for specifying where you want to search for a term in a document. You can also use the operator 'intitle:' (for example, intitle:"david mackinnon"). In other search engines, the command may look something like the following (check the proper format for each engine):

title:"David MacKinnon"

In any case, this search will provide documents with 'David MacKinnon' in the title, a good indication that he is a central focus in the piece. You can go one better by combining this with the previous tips, adding other words to the search. If you use parentheses, you can separate off the other search terms so that the computer deals with them separately. The following example demonstrates this technique:

title:"David MacKinnon" AND (genetic* OR Alzheimer*)

That search would give you documents having David MacKinnon in the title, plus any of 'genetic', 'genetics', 'geneticist', 'Alzheimer', 'Alzheimer's', or 'Alzheimers' in the body of the document.

Domain and URL searches

Every website address ends with a top-level domain suffix such as *.ca* (common for Canadian sites) or *.uk* (for British ones). Many suffixes indicate the kind of organization that owns the site: *.com* is for companies and businesses, *.mil* for US military sites, *.edu* for US universities or colleges, and so on. Often, the correct operator to search for sites with a particular suffix is either 'site:' or 'domain:', as in the following:

    domain:edu AND "David MacKinnon" AND (Alzheimer* OR genetic*)

This would give you pages from US university sites that mention David MacKinnon and either a word beginning with 'Alzheimer' or a word beginning with 'genetic'.

Operators such as *site:* and *url:* search the Web addresses themselves, so you might be able to find a website maintained by David MacKinnon or documents and news stories about him by using the command

    url:"David MacKinnon"

In Google, the format is

    inurl:"David MacKinnon"

Host searches

These let you search large sites that do not have their own search functions. For example, if you're looking for references to David MacKinnon on the (fictional) site *www.canadianresearcher.ca*, you can type this:

    host:www.canadianresearcher.ca AND "David MacKinnon"

Google automates this process in the advanced search page by letting you simply type in a domain or site name.

Link search

When you hit the jackpot and find a site about the person or subject you are investigating, a link search can direct you to more valuable finds. If you've found a website at *www.DrDavidMacKinnon.org* that focuses entirely on the geneticist you're interested in, try the following:

    link:www.DrDavidMacKinnon.org

This should result in a list of sites that link to Dr David MacKinnon. These might be operated by friends, colleagues, professional connections, or even rivals.

Again, Google Advanced offers a link search at the bottom of its page, or, alternatively, you can use the *link:* operator.

Format Searches

Consider a document's format as a search option. Google Advanced, for example, lets you limit your search to PowerPoint presentations, Microsoft Excel spreadsheets, Adobe Acrobat files, and several others. There's potentially great value in finding, for example, a PowerPoint slide show on your subject posted online by an expert who used the presentation at a conference. Such presentations often contain the names of prominent people in the field, summaries of research or studies, contact information, statistical information, graphs, and point-form notes.

'It's a way to find someone really specific,' says Julian Sher. 'If you put *AIDS*, *orphans*, and *Africa* into a search engine, you'll get everybody. But if you ask for a slide show—who has bothered putting together a slide show and putting it up on a webpage? It's got to be an expert.'

In compiling data on your subject, a search for documents that bear the suffix *.xls* will filter out the flood of text-based records and focus solely on Microsoft Excel spreadsheets. And Adobe *.pdf* files can be useful for finding government documents (which are often created in this format), even if they're no longer posted on the government's website.

A final note on Web searches

Websites can prove a useful research tool for finding out about people, and not just because of the site's content. Tools exist to allow researchers to dig into information that isn't immediately apparent. At the site *www.allwhois.com*, for instance, an online directory lets you access information about the people behind any given website. Researchers can obtain information about the person or company name associated with a site, along with contact information; of course, sites are often registered in the names of technical contacts or agents rather than the individuals who actually run the organization posting the site, but this contact information may prove useful in certain circumstances nonetheless.

If the site you're looking for has disappeared, it may not be gone forever. An online archiving tool at *www.archive.org* can help you access websites that have been pulled down. By typing in the address, you'll get a list of dates on which the database archived the site. Click on a dated version of the site and it may well show up. It is, however, a hit-and-miss process.

Because it's easy to remove a website from the Internet instantly, it's always a good idea to save a copy of a site onto your hard drive if you know it's going to be important to your research. In some cases, people will pull their sites down once they get a sense that authorities or journalists are looking into their activities. If you haven't saved a copy, it may be difficult to prove what had been posted previously. The best method here is doing a *screen grab* of the site by saving an image of what is on screen to your hard drive.

News alerts

As we discussed earlier in this book, online news alerts are an increasingly useful tool for journalists, especially those who work on long-term projects and need to keep track of what's happening in their area of interest. Services such as Google Alerts (*www.google.com/alerts*) and Yahoo! Alerts (*beta.alerts.yahoo.com*) will serve up daily news headlines and stories based on your keywords.

Setting up Internet news alerts is one of the first things Julian Sher does when he begins an investigation. At any given time, he's got at least three or four alerts delivering stories to his email every day. 'If you're working on a long project, you want to be able to follow it as it evolves,' he says. 'It gives you leads you never would have thought of because names of people and experts come up.'

Expert directories

Finding experts was a lot more work before the Internet came along. Now, though, researchers and journalists have an amazing array of options for getting fast access to people with impressive expertise on virtually any subject, from the social impact of Madonna to the technicalities of bridge engineering.

Whatever you're researching, someone out there is spending a lot of time thinking, talking, and writing about it. The more obscure the topic, the more difficult it might be to find that perfect expert, but if the person works for a company, government, university, or college, chances are he or she can be found through an Internet-based expert-finding service. These are effectively online matchmaking services for journalists and experts, and they can extremely useful. Here is a sampling of some of the most useful expert database and search services online:

- ProfNet (*www.prnewswire.com*)—This is the pioneer expert-finding service with a long track record of getting journalists and experts on the phone together within hours. It works in two ways: you can either search a ProfNet database of expert profiles, or send a query for expert assistance which is then transmitted to thousands of news and information officers across North American institutions such as universities, governments, and non-profit agencies. You indicate what kind of institutions you would like the request to reach. Depending on the time of day, you could start getting responses within minutes by the phone or email contact information you include in your post. Because this is a largely US service, the vast majority of responses tend to come from sources in the States. You can, however, limit your request so that it reaches only Canadian sources.
- Sources (*www.sources.com*)—A regularly updated directory of Canadian experts with more than 5000 entries
- Experts.com (*www.experts.com*)—An international expert database
- ExpertPages.com (*www.expertpages.com*)—This is a resource most commonly used by lawyers looking for expert witnesses to testify in court proceedings; the service is obviously also useful for journalists.

Databases of authors are another potential source of expert comment. Those who have written books on your topic of research could become interview subjects. Some of the most extensive author directories are actually operated by online booksellers like *Amazon.ca*. The retail site can double as a research tool. The Chapters/Indigo website (*www.chapters.indigo.ca*) is another alternative.

There's another kind of 'expert' that journalists often fail to consider. Activists can be incredibly useful sources despite their obvious biases. Using the Internet to get their message out, they provide journalists with gushers of studies, documents, and networks of human sources that could otherwise take weeks to collect.

'I assume that on every story there are some people out there that are much more fanatical about the story and much more obsessed—one way or the other—than I am,' says Sher. 'For example, there are numerous biker sites where biker groupies and biker advocates catalogue every single blip, news [item], arrest, or event going on in the biker world. It's fabulous because these people live and breathe your topic.'

As long as you remain aware of an activist's partiality, the information can still prove useful. Many activists or advocacy groups also collect official records such as government studies and reports, along with newspaper clippings, that come from legitimate and credible sources. A tip: To improve your chances of finding activist websites, consider the kind of language that impassioned campaigners are likely to use. For instance, Sher suggests that, when researching bikers, you might plug into your search a phrase such as 'police intimidation'.

Newsgroups and mailing lists

Newsgroups and mailing lists can be useful research areas, although they can also be frustrating due to the widely varying quality of debate. But many experienced researchers have used these sources to find people worth interviewing.

Newsgroups
These online public forums—also known as *chat groups* or *Usenet*—are the Wild West of the Internet. There's a certain lawlessness in these public forums that often leads to loud, meandering, and sometimes profanity-filled debates that resemble schoolyard clashes. In other cases, the free-flowing nature of newsgroups leads to wonderfully open, candid debate. Anyone can drop in or leave at any time and there are few rules about what is said.

Newsgroups are quickly being superseded by newer forms of online chat technologies such as Web forums and social-networking sites. But they are still worth a look on specific issues where there could still be a core group of quality sources gathered.

One of the biggest challenges producers faced in making a CBC documentary on Steven Truscott's conviction for a murder committed more than 40 years earlier was finding people who were in the small Ontario town of Clinton at the time.

'They're now adults. They've moved from Clinton, the women had changed their names. It was an almost impossible task,' Julian Sher recalls. 'A lot of the kids had scattered to the wind.' A newsgroup called *can.military.brat* proved to be a vital tool for tracking them down. The chat group, devoted to discussion of children brought up in Canadian military families, seemed like a good place to look, considering Clinton's close proximity to a military base at the time. That intuition paid off.

'We struck gold. We could post messages there. We could find people. We got video from somebody's mother [that she] had taken in 1959. . . . Some of the messages would lead to webpages where we could find names of people we were looking for.'

There are a number of specialized search tools for finding newsgroups. But for now, we'll focus on Google. (Follow the 'Groups' link above the search bar in Google under 'more'—this tool searches newsgroup discussion lists rather than Web content.)

Type in a keyword such as *aids*. The results will be a long list of postings that include references to AIDS contained in discussion lists with names like *sci.med. aids* and *misc.health.aids*. The prefixes *sci* and *misc* refer to general categories. The *sci* newsgroups deal with applied science or social science issues. The following parts categorize in more detail. In this case, *med* refers to medical issues; *aids* specifies that the topic is AIDS. *Misc* is, unsurprisingly, a miscellaneous category. *Biz* groups deal with business topics. *Talk* groups cover current affairs. *Humanities* groups discuss fine art and literature topics.

Newsgroup communities are bound together by topic, not geography, so the participants and the content are overwhelmingly non-Canadian. Some newsgroup topics do depend on geography, however, and Canadian-based newsgroups exist to discuss issues from a Canadian perspective.

Before asking a newsgroup member for an interview, you might want to get a more complete sense of the person by looking at all of their public posts to newsgroups. You can do that in Google Groups by choosing the 'view profile' option next to the poster's name. For a deeper backgrounding, click on the 'more options' link next to the name, then select 'find messages by this author'.

'If somebody says, "I've got a great story about CIA malfeasance," I want to check to make sure they haven't actively participated in the alien abduction chat groups before I'm going to bother wasting my time with them,' says Sher.

It's always a good idea to familiarize yourself with a newsgroup or mailing list before you post a message there. Understand that when you send a message to a newsgroup, it is posted for everyone around the world to read. Be careful what you say—it's public and it lasts forever. Some journalists have ended up in hot water by saying too much online about a company or individual they were investigating. Don't say anything online that you wouldn't want to see quoted in the newspapers or cited in court. Be polite. Respond quickly to those who get in touch with you. And be generous. If someone helps you on a board, make sure you also offer your help whenever you can.

Mailing lists

Compared to newsgroups, mailing lists—many of which are hosted by universities— provide much greater odds of thoughtful debate. The limitation here is that many mailing lists have died off in recent years as newer forms of Internet communication have evolved. Still, if you can tap into a vibrant list on a subject you're researching in depth, there remain big advantages that will likely be overlooked by other journalists.

As with newsgroups, the first step is to find relevant mailing lists. Among the best search tools is Catalist (*www.lsoft.com/catalist.html*), which gives a general description of mailing lists, the email address for subscribing, and instructions on how to send the initial request to subscribe. Generally speaking, it means sending an email to the appropriate address with words like 'SUBSCRIBE HIVGROUP' in the body of the message.

Before subscribing, you may want to contact the mailing list's owner for some information on the list's focus, interests, and membership. If you are considering approaching subscribers to request interviews, ask the list owner or moderator whether this is welcome.

You may not be able to determine the quality of a list before subscribing, but the number of subscribers gives you a general indication of the traffic flow—a few dozen probably means you will get a handful of messages each month; a list with thousands of subscribers, on the other hand, will generate several messages a day.

Online telephone directories

Assuming you know the name of the person you're looking for, or where they work, you can search for them in online telephone directories. The snag is that not everyone is included in phone listings. If someone isn't in the regular phone book, then they likely won't be listed in an online directory either. But for locating anyone else, these resources provide you with a telephone number and address. The various online telephone listings services work in essentially the same way, but many catalogue information from different sources. If you're not successful at first, it is worth trying other databases.

Some of the tools below also provide reverse searching by address or phone number. This can be extremely useful. If you have an address or phone number and nothing else, running that information through a reverse search tool will provide the person's name, along with contact details.

A basic but useful reminder: many people list themselves in the phone book with only a first initial. If you enter 'David' as a first name and the person listed himself as 'D', or even used his spouse's first name, your search won't turn up the correct information.

Below, we look at some of the best Canadian telephone directories.

White and Yellow Pages
The following websites offer reverse searching, and provide numbers and addresses for residences and businesses:

- Canada 411 (*www.canada411.ca*)—this one also offers a keyword search for toll-free numbers
- SuperPages.ca (*www.superpages.ca*)
- Telus (*www.mytelus.com/phonebook*)

- White Pages (*www.whitepages.ca*)
- Canpages (*www.canpages.ca*)

Government employee telephone directories

If you're looking for civil servants in the federal or provincial governments, there are several online telephone databases that let you search by name. They are available at the following government sites:

- Federal government (*sage-geds.tpsgc-pwgsc.gc.ca*)
- Alberta (*alberta.ca/home/directory.cfm*)
- British Columbia (*www.dir.gov.bc.ca*)
- Manitoba (*web2.gov.mb.ca/contact/index.php*)
- New Brunswick (*www.gnb.ca*)
- Newfoundland and Labrador (*www.tw.gov.nl.ca/TelephoneDirectory/*)
- Northwest Territories (*www.gov.nt.ca*)
- Nova Scotia (*www.gov.ns.ca*)
- Nunavut (*www.gov.nu.ca*)
- Ontario (*www.infogo.gov.on.ca/infogo/mainPage.do*)
- Prince Edward Island (*www.gov.pe.ca/phone*)
- Quebec (*www.reptel.gouv.qc.ca/?lang=en*)
- Saskatchewan (*gtds.gov.sk.ca*)
- Yukon (*www.gov.yk.ca/phone*)

Social-networking sites

The social-networking phenomenon has largely attracted attention for reacquainting long-lost friends and family and serving as an online headquarters for modern socializing. But tools such as Facebook, LinkedIn, and Twitter have also been quickly adopted by journalists as a means of finding sources.

Think of these sites as massive databases of people. In some cases, it's possible to search them by name or interest. In other cases, a broadly published request for anyone suffering with a rare disease or engaged in a social struggle can ferret out hard-to-find human voices to illustrate an important story.

When a Sikorsky helicopter bound for the Grand Banks oil rigs off the coast of Newfoundland crashed into the Atlantic Ocean on 12 March 2009, Facebook was the first place *Toronto Star* reporter Robyn Doolittle turned.

Emergency crews pulled one survivor, Robert Decker, out of the water not long after impact. They also recovered a body. That meant 16 people, including the pilots, were still missing. Within hours, the *Star* was making arrangements to send a reporter to Newfoundland. Doolittle's job was to find addresses of the missing people's families by the time her colleague landed there.

Officials with the oil rigs were saying nothing. The Joint Rescue Coordination Centre was saying nothing. So where to start?

'For me, the answer is almost always Facebook,' says Doolittle.

As with many stories such as this, she began hours of searching the massive social-networking site (it has more than 175 million users) for clues about the identities of anyone on board the ill-fated helicopter.

Facebook's privacy settings mean getting at an individual's information isn't nearly as simple as typing names into the search field. Most profiles are closed off to anyone who isn't already on their list of 'friends'.

That meant Doolittle could see little more than tiny headshots. She couldn't get at any of the photos posted on people's profiles.

So she had to find a back door.

'Even if profiles are closed, normally you have access to the person's friend list—and really even a name is a great start,' she says. 'It's also a safe bet that when tragedy happens, people will turn to the Internet for support. So for the ill-fated Cougar helicopter flight, I launched a search for memorial sites.'

Her first step was to choose key words: 'helicopter', 'cougar', 'crash', '12 March', 'rest in peace'. This kind of needle-in-haystack detective work necessitates a lot of trial and error on the part of the journalist. When she found a relevant site, Doolittle checked the far right side for 'Related Groups' in an effort to follow the digital trail to other memorial sites.

'Almost immediately, I found three sites. Always go for the biggest first. Even after only a few hours, there were hundreds of wall postings on the group "Cougar Helicopter Crash, March 12th". If you have the time, read every one.'

Sure enough, buried in the voluminous postings, someone attached a link to a separate memorial page called 'In Loving Memory of Allison Maher'.

'Since it had only been a few hours since the crash, and none of the other bodies had been found, this was obviously the identity of the body rescue workers had recovered,' Doolittle says.

She joined the group, poured through photos, and recorded the name of family members who were 'tagged' in the pictures. Next, she turned to wall postings and discussion boards.

'Often, people will write something like "I'm so sorry, my cousin is missing,"' Doolittle says. 'Every time you come across these people, first see if their profiles are open.'

None were. But she clicked on their friend lists—which were open—and printed them out. Once Doolittle built a growing list of people, she started to see an overlapping pattern of friends.

'Someone will say, "My cousin is dead." Another will say, "I know who you're talking about, because they're my best friend." If you go through the friend lists of both of those people and find the overlap, you know you've likely found a missing person.'

Using that method of cross-referencing along with recurring first and last names and similar photos, Doolittle was able to identify five of the missing people by the time her *Star* colleague landed in Newfoundland.

Here are some other search tips:

- Consider the variations on a name when you do your searching (Rob, Robert, Bob, Robbie, Robb, Bobby).
- Study the posted details, such as a person's birthday, hometown, relationship status, and school, to make sure you've got the right person.
- Be sure to read the information feature on each profile for a list of likes and dislikes, and check contact info for details and potential colour.
- Once you find the person you're after, do a *screen grab* (on a PC, hit 'alt/print screen' at the same time, open the Paint program, hit ctrl/v at the same time, and save the file. On a Mac, hit command/shift/4). Facebook pages are sometimes pulled down in an instant when someone is suddenly in the news.
- If you can access the photos posted on a person's page, it's a good idea to save those to a file on your hard drive for future reference. They may come in very handy when it comes time to start contacting friends and family and helping identify people.
- Pay special attention to photos in which your subject is 'tagged' by someone else. It means the image was likely posted by a friend or family member who, in the body of the photograph, identifies your subject in a kind of caption. The tagger is someone who likely knows your subject well, spends time with the person, and is, therefore, likely to be a useful contact. Email the tagger.
- A person may have hundreds of friends listed on his or her profile, but chances are that many of those people are distant acquaintances. The trick is finding out who the real friends are. In some cases, people actually list their 'top friends', which makes things easy. If not, look for people who went to the same school, live in the same city, are about the same age or list similar interests.
- If there is a stabbing in a local school or a food-borne illness outbreak linked to a local processing plant, type the institution name into Facebook's search field. People often list where they work or go to school in their profiles. A search by institution name can turn up students, employees, friends, and colleagues.

Another social-networking site, Twitter, with its constant flow of 140-character mini-feeds (personal updates popularly known as *tweets*) posted by millions of subscribers around the world, is also a standard new-age journalistic tool. Twitter's application does lean more toward breaking-news stories, although there are also ways to use the site for more in-depth reporting.

With a Twitter account and a large network of 'followers', a journalist can build what amounts to a large body of potential sources with experiences, views, and contacts that cover a vast territory of issues. And they're all instantly reachable by posting a brief message. A message—or tweet—seeking parents caught off guard by a city daycare workers strike, for example, can generate dozens of tips in minutes—a task that often took hours in the pre-digital era. For specific individuals, use the 'find people' search tool.

Of most use for more issues-based reporting, however, is *search.twitter.com*, which allows you to search tweets by keyword. Type in 'listeria' and find a voluminous list of messages referencing everything from scientific papers to victims to the food-borne pathogen.

As with most search tools, use double quotation marks for phrase searching and a minus sign followed by unwanted words to filter out posts containing a word. For example: *"Tiger Woods"–golf* (italics used here for clarity) will give you tweets that mention Tiger Woods but not golf.

One search trick unique to Twitter is the use of the hash tag # to group messages around a specific topic. For example, type "#globalwarming" into the Twitter search field to cast a wide net for messages filed by posters under that general topic description. The results will be overwhelming. But a scan through the list will begin to reveal the names or organizations most engaged in the issue on Twitter and possibly provide some interesting leads from opinion leaders or insiders with a story to tell.

Once you've found those people, be sure to 'follow' them so you get their updates. And you can also search for messages they've posted. If, for example, you want to see all recent tweets by the Canadian Association of Journalists (CAJ), search "from:caj". If you want to further limit the search by keyword, try "from:caj sources".

To search all messages that make reference to an individual or organization, simply put a "@" sign before the user name in the search box: "@caj".

For all postings from a specific person or organizations type "from:" followed by their Twitter name. For all messages sent to them, type "to:" followed by their name.

Here are some other Twitter search tips:

- Location searches: If you want to find postings with the word 'reporter' sent by people around Halifax, type, "reporter near:Halifax".
- To limit results by date, add the phrase, "since:2009-01-01" or "until: 2009-01-01".
- Twitter Search also has an advanced search link that automates most of these techniques in a series of query boxes.
- Use "Happn.in" to search Twitter geographically by city or country. What you'll get here is a survey of postings from users in cities such as Toronto, Calgary, and Vancouver arranged into categories.

By following a quality group of Twitter posters, reporters are also able to learn about breaking stories from every corner of the planet as they're unfolding. Many stories hit Twitter lines before they ever reach the news wires. That's good, of course. And bad. The complete lack of verification should always be at the top of your mind when you're reading Twitter posts. Think of Twitter as an endless stream of unedited free-associative thoughts. It's instant and far-reaching. But it requires care.

Social-networking search tools

There are a growing number of search tools that catalogue blogs and social-networking sites. Google, for example, has a blog-specific search engine.

- Pipl (*www.pipl.com*) is a remarkable online backgrounding tool that pulls together a vast collection of electronic data on people by simply searching their names and locations. Search by name, email, username, or phone number. Blog posts and mailing-list posts dating back nearly two decades, news articles, website references, published documents, references on networking sites such as Flickr and Classmates.com, online photos, and professional designations all display themselves in seconds.
- Spokeo (*www.spokeo.com*) is a probing search tool and people finder that scans a wide range of social-networking sites for multimedia breadcrumbs such as photos, blog postings, and videos that can lead you to the individual you seek.
- SocialMention (*www.socialmention.com*): This is an alert service focusing on social-media sites. Create an alert based on the name of an individual or company and the site will deliver postings to your email address.
- WhosTalkin (*www.whostalkin.com*): With its lengthy list of online social-networking sources, this tool returns a rich array of material based on keyword or name searches.
- BlogDigger (*www.blogdigger.com*): BlogDigger is a helpful tool for finding bloggers who write about what you're researching.
- Technorati (*technorati.com*): This is a quality indexing tool for the blogosphere.
- Wink People Search (*wink.com*) is an effective social-network information finder if you have a name and a location.
- ZoomInfo (*www.zoominfo.com*): While ZoomInfo is geared to recruiters, it provides journalists with a wealth of information drawn from the Web on individuals.
- Address Book (*www.internetaddressbook.com*) offers a similar name search of networking sites including Facebook, MySpace, Friendster, LinkedIn, and Flickr.
- ConvoTrack (*convotrack.com*) digs into comments posted on social-network sites including Twitter, FriendFeed, Digg, Reddit and blogs.

The online classified giant Craigslist also has practical utility for journalists looking to find people talking about issues they're covering. The 'Rants and Raves' sections in each city are filled with opinions about hot topics along with plenty of ready-made story ideas that tap the public consciousness.

The Public-Records Checklist

In Chapter 4, we surveyed some basic personal records in the public domain. Let's now look at those records in action, and supplement the list with other less official, but still important, sources of accessible information. This list of examples could also act as a kind of checklist of items for when you are faced with the task of finding out background information about a person, or you're just looking for names of key people.

Media databases

Before writing a single word about anyone, you should know everything that's already been written. That means a thorough search of media databases and the Internet. Study previous stories carefully, make notes, and keep the material on hand as you work through your story. Look for the unanswered questions in those stories, issues that need to be followed, and names of sources who might be able to help you.

It's also important not to limit yourself too much in terms of the scope of your reading. In the process of producing a documentary and a book on the David Milgaard story in the early 1990s, Cecil Rosner read two years' worth of *Saskatoon StarPhoenix* newspapers prior to the Gail Miller murder.[4]

'This provided valuable context about the nature of the community, the attitudes to hippies and counter-culture which played a role in police activities, the nature of the police force itself, the attitudes of the police chief, etc. It gave me information I would have never thought to ask about.'

Searching media databases can be daunting. Putting a couple of keywords into a database can turn up thousands of hits. So you'll need to develop techniques for limiting such searches to find the major pieces you need to know. Consider limiting the results to stories that are 1000 words or over; this filter will remove small news stories and focus your search on more in-depth pieces.

Also, consider the less obvious information published in the media, such as obituaries. Julian Sher recalls the challenge of finding the family of a dead pilot from Halifax with a common surname.

'We did the standard directory searches in Halifax, then moved outward to Nova Scotia and then the Maritimes,' he recalls. 'My editor suggested quite wisely that we do a special search for the obit. Sure enough, in the obit, they mentioned all the next of kin and then we found the mother. And from the mother we were able to find the brother and we got a great interview.'

Be sure to save or copy important stories from media databases, as you will likely need to consult them later. Mark them up. Highlight key facts. Put question marks around issues you need to explore. Circle names of people you'll want to talk to. Spending a few hours—or days—just reading is likely the best way to get your brain thinking critically about how to proceed.

School records and former teachers

Say you discover what secondary school your subject was attending prior to his or her registration at the University of Toronto. Check the school yearbooks and alumni associations for information.

When *Toronto Star* reporters conducted in-depth research into the country's biggest kingpin in minor hockey—a man who had purchased an interest, or control, of an unprecedented collection of nearly one hundred youth hockey teams—they found his 1982 secondary school yearbook. This allowed them to begin one story as follows:

> A graduating student named Stuart Hyman summarized his aspirations this way: 'To be a dominant, powerful and persuasive public figure.' Twenty-two years later, he's making it happen.[5]

That detail gave a useful insight into the character at the centre of the story, which involved a controversy over rising fees and alleged profiteering in non-profit youth hockey.

Consider also school newspaper clippings, transcripts, and awards for achievement in academics, sports, or drama. Finding a veteran teacher or principal with a good memory can be the best way of tracking down school records for your subject, and building a character profile.

One more tip: we've already recommended getting hold of the person's thesis; don't forget to read the acknowledgments section of the work, as it might provide useful contacts.

Evidence related to lifestyle and hobbies

If your subject is an amateur pilot, that fact should lead you directly to Transport Canada for a public-records search (*www.tc.gc.ca/CivilAviation*). Or perhaps your subject is an avid boater with a weekend yacht; registration details are also logged by Transport Canada (*www.tc.gc.ca/marinesafety*), which lets you search by the name of the owner, the boat, and so on. If you are researching someone who dabbles in amateur radio, you would visit the Canadian Amateur Radio Callsign Database (*www.rac.ca/callbook*). If the person plays recreational hockey, his or her stats may appear on league websites, which could tell you whether you're dealing with a goon who is always in the penalty box, or a talent with team-leading goals or assists.

Biographical information

There's no shortage of material out there documenting the lives and accomplishments of notable Canadians. But be careful about the source of the information. In many cases, current 'biographical information' is actually written by the person in question, often without verification by the publisher. Even so, such miniature autobiographies can be interesting.

Toronto Star reporters Dale Brazao and Patricia Orwen turned to biographical resources in 2000 to help explain the story of Mark Suddick, one of Ontario's more prominent deadbeat dads. After eight years of ignoring a court order and repeated reminders to pay child support, Suddick owed more than $100,000 to his former wife, the newspaper reported. The province claimed it was unable to find Suddick, who was dividing his time between Ontario and Florida.

Facing three warrants for his arrest in the United States, Suddick left his posh Sarasota home and returned to Ontario in 2000, where the reporters found him living in an exclusive subdivision near Toronto. While Suddick earned only a modest living, the reporters found his high-end lifestyle came compliments of a successful father.

'Suddick's father Patrick is a retired Honeywell Canada executive whose lifetime accomplishments, including being a member of a Canadian delegation to the North Atlantic Treaty Organization (NATO), were listed in the 1988 edition of the *Canadian Who's Who*,' Brazao and Orwen reported. In an interview, the senior Suddick explained his support for his son this way: 'Unfortunately, Mark has got some problems. He is not completely capable of handling himself properly. . . . What would you have us do? Kick him out on the street?'[6]

Here are some of the most useful and authoritative Canadian biographical resources for researching people whose names are already in the public domain:

Canadian Who's Who
Perhaps the most consulted contemporary biographical resource with information on about 15,000 prominent Canadians. The 2010 edition is available in book form or CD-ROM at most public libraries.

The Canadian Encyclopedia
Available at *thecanadianencyclopedia.com*, this classic research tool of high-school students on tight deadlines can be a helpful quick glance for researchers looking for a primer on a high-profile Canadian from a more historical point of view.

Dictionary of Canadian Biography Online
At *www.biographi.ca*, this federal government database features biographical information about important people who died before 1930.

Resumés

Resumés are the calling cards of the working world. They also document how people choose to represent themselves to potential employers. One of the most valuable documents Rosner and Rutherford obtained in their investigation was Michael Gobuty's resumé.

'This is an undervalued resource,' says Rosner. 'It provides a road map to a person's life and career, and is invaluable in any investigation. It is often filed with public applications, and therefore is often publicly available.'[7]

Rosner and Rutherford got Michael Gobuty's resumé from a filing with a federal immigrant investor program. The document contained a number of valuable pieces of information that assisted the CBC investigation. For example, it included exact dates of his involvements with his various companies, which allowed reporters to chart a chronology of his career. It contained his personal references, including Manitoba premier Gary Filmon and ambassador Ken Taylor (then Canadian ambassador to the United States). A check with those people allowed the journalists to say in their story that Filmon had never given Gobuty permission to use his name.

'It also listed as a professional reference Iain Brown, president and CEO of First National Bank in the Turks and Caicos Islands, an interesting contact for Gobuty, who claimed around this same time to have annual income of less than $3000 per year,' says Rosner.

If your subject's resumé isn't available as part of a public document such as a funding application, you may have some digging to do. The simplest thing is to ask for it directly, of course. The odds of success with this approach will depend largely on the context of your research, and possibly your own tact. In some instances, you might find your subject's resumé posted on a personal website. In other cases, it might be available from sources such as the person's colleagues.

As with other documents, don't assume the information contained in a resumé is true. You should report only information you have verified. Resumés do open up research possibilities, however, and often mention references who can be added to your interview list.

Disciplinary records

In Chapter 4, we mentioned the many trades licensed by municipalities; the businesses—from restaurants to daycare facilities—that are routinely inspected by city inspectors; and the professionals, such as dentists and home builders, whom are subject to regulatory organizations. To exemplify how fruitful these records can be, we should consider the investigation into Dr Kenneth Bradley, which was conducted by *Toronto Star* journalists in 2001.

After building a database containing every disciplinary decision by the Ontario College of Physicians and Surgeons over a six-year period, the journalists noticed how Bradley's name was among a number of physicians with a troubled medical history in the province. This led them to uncover more details of Bradley's long trail of medical negligence. A remarkable story began to unfold in the records of medical regulatory bodies in three different jurisdictions.

In two disciplinary hearings in Ontario, Bradley was found to have committed serious errors in surgical judgment and to have failed to maintain standards of patient care—lapses that resulted in the deaths of two patients. In the written decisions, college officials called his surgical techniques 'indefensible' and 'the most serious of cases of failure to meet the standards of the profession.'[8]

Despite the serious breaches, the college did not revoke the doctor's licence, choosing instead to impose lighter penalties such as retraining, probation, and restrictions. This approach failed to protect the public. Even before the college issued a decision in Bradley's second disciplinary case, the surgeon was in the process of relocating to Virginia, where he obtained a licence to practise without disclosing his troubling professional record in Ontario.[9] College documents showed that Ontario officials had been well aware of Bradley's move to Virginia and had done nothing to inform Virginia officials of his troubling past.[10]

Using US physician registries and Internet searches, the reporters traced Bradley's path to Virginia and discovered a stunning documented history of medical misconduct that raised serious questions about how doctors were regulated. Virginia Board of Medicine records showed how, between 1994 and 1996, Bradley's actions resulted in the death of six people and the medical mistreatment of two others.[11] Among the deaths was that of a 71-year-old man on whom Bradley conducted a gallbladder operation. The records described how Bradley was 'unable to identify the gallbladder' during the operation. It wasn't there. The man's gallbladder had been removed 26 years earlier.[12]

While the Virginia Board of Medicine pondered what to do with Bradley, the doctor applied for a medical licence in Alaska. That state's request to see Bradley's record was found by reporters, who then obtained Bradley's application, complete with a photograph he had submitted—a photo that ran on the front page. Based on a tip from a reader, reporters then searched property records in Ontario's cottage country to find Bradley's summer home. He was there in May 2001, back from a Caribbean trip on his yacht.

'Kenneth Bradley has left the dead, injured, and maimed who suffered beneath his surgical knife far behind him,' the *Star* reported. 'Life is good these days for the former chief surgeon of the Milton District Hospital. Retired after a career marred by incidents of negligence that caused at least six deaths and numerous injuries, Bradley has retreated to secluded splendour in eastern Ontario cottage country.'[13]

Following the series of stories, the College of Physicians and Surgeons of Ontario posted disciplinary records for all Ontario doctors on its website—the first medical college in Canada to do so. In June 2002, two decades after becoming aware of problems with Kenneth Bradley, the college revoked his licence to practise medicine.

Police and court records

Returning to the Michael Gobuty story, we can see how important it is not to ignore the small-claims courts when investigating individuals. The information that emerges in the minor cases handled by these courts can be vital for researchers.

'[Small-claims courts] are often overlooked because they are so small,' says Cecil Rosner. 'Some of our most valuable information came from these, along with leads from lawyers and others who provided information. One example: We secured Michael Gobuty's income-tax information from such a filing. He argued that he could not pay a small debt, because he had insufficient income.' To support his claim, Gobuty had to submit his income details as evidence.

Rosner and Rutherford also turned to court searches in the United States for information they couldn't get in Canada: 'The [Federal Business Development Bank (FBDB)] refused comment. As a bank, they are also exempt from the *Access to Information Act*. But when they seek to recover monies, they have to file information in open court. We checked with the Florida county courts and found the FBDB filing a detailed application seeking to recover their loan.'

In Chapter 5, we mentioned the police records called *informations*, which provide the name of a person charged, the date charges were laid, and so on. In researching the David Milgaard story, Rosner used informations to get at some of the most vital material:

I think our most important contribution to the case came in discovering the pattern associated with Larry Fisher's other victims. I proceeded by getting the original informations from police records on all of Fisher's victims. This gave us their names and some addresses at the time. I took those to the Saskatoon Public Library and checked old city directories. From this, we created a map of where his victims lived, and where they were attacked. At least two of the victims lived in the same neighbourhood as Gail Miller, and it appeared they could well have taken the same bus route as Miller. This was key, as we discovered that his modus operandi involved following victims from bus stops. All of this was a revelation to Milgaard and his lawyers at the time, and it provided a turning point in the case.

Motor vehicle records

Most of us drive. And driving is among the many public activities that produces documentation. Our licences, vehicle ownerships, plate registrations, and driving records all generate information held by provincial motor vehicle departments. Driving-related charges are public records held by the appropriate courthouse. These may well be relevant to the subject you are researching.

The records played an important role in the *Toronto Star*'s investigation of deadbeat dad Mark Suddick. While the provincial government can revoke driver's licences belonging to those delinquent in child-support payments, it took no such action against one of the province's most notorious deadbeat dads, reported Brazao and Orwen.

'Ministry of Transportation records show Suddick's driver's licence was suspended on Sept. 22, 1999—but for non-payment of traffic fines, not child support. Suddick paid the fines and the suspension was lifted this week, after Suddick was asked by *Star* reporters how he could drive for a living with a suspended licence.' A ministry spokesperson 'wouldn't say why the government didn't suspend Suddick's licence over his child support debt,' the paper reported.[14]

In another investigation, then *Toronto Star* reporters John Duncanson and Phinjo Gombu relied on motor vehicle records to report that Michael Di Biase, former mayor of Vaughan, Ontario, had been charged with running three red lights in 15 months. There was an added hint of intrigue behind those tickets.

'Two of the tickets were withdrawn when officers didn't show up in court, records show. The third, laid after a December 2002 accident, simply disappeared,' the *Star* reported. 'Nowhere does the provincial offence act ticket issued to Di Biase on Dec. 12, 2002, show up in the Ministry of the Attorney-General's main computer tracking system, called ICON.' A ministry spokesperson responded simply, 'We can't find it [i.e., the ticket].'[15]

In 2006, *Star* reporters used motor vehicle records to prove driving instructors with numerous demerit points were allowed to keep teaching teenagers the rules of the road.[16] Among them was a Markham driving instructor with seven demerit points from five separate speeding convictions.

'In one case, a driving instructor was caught driving 99 km/h in a 50 km/h zone. Another was convicted for doing 141 km/h and 140 km/h in a 100 km/h area on two separate occasions. But none has hit the provincial limit of eight demerit points, a ceiling experts say is too high and risks public safety.'[17]

Following the story, the province dramatically tightened the rules governing driving instructors.

Reporters in Ontario routinely conduct motor vehicle searches using the province's so-called *Used Vehicle Information Package*, available in public kiosks, usually in shopping malls, across the province. With a licence plate or a vehicle information number, reporters access a history on the car, the current owner's name and city where they live. That makes it a useful tool for tracking down people.

For example, even when reporters are prevented from entering crime scenes, running licence plate numbers from cars parked near the home or building can provide leads about who may be a victim in a homicide or a person killed during a police chase.

Tribunal or licensing bodies

Licensed professionals must meet standards that, to varying degrees, are policed by officials. Within that system is a mechanism for handling those that fail to meet minimum professional standards.

Those bodies are always worth a thorough check. They generally hold hearings into allegations of wrongdoing. And most often the results of those hearing are public records.

In the driving instructor story, reporters uncovered City of Toronto licensing tribunal records that documented detailed complaints about companies and individuals who teach young people to drive.

'Muhammad Yousaf's students have accused the Scarborough driving instructor of swearing at them during lessons, uttering racial epithets and using an instruction vehicle without a passenger-side brake,' the *Star* reported from the documents that included the names of complainants and their detailed allegations.[18]

'One former student who filed a complaint with the city alleged that Yousaf "grabbed her purse, bruised her wrist and called her a 'bitch'"....Themesia Fernandes, one of the 19 complainants, says Yousaf dumped her at the side of the road in winter during her first lesson.'[19]

Lien searches

The supplementary information provided by lien records can be as useful as the main details of a person's loan. For instance, you might find a subject's date of birth, address, vehicle make and model, and vehicle identification number, allowing you to do a vehicle record search. Or, in the case of the Gobutys, you might find out all about their sewing machines.

'From this check, we discovered that the Gobutys had used, as security for their [FBDB] loan, all the sewing machines in their factory,' says Rosner. 'We also learned the loan had not yet been repaid. All of which made the relocation of this equipment to the US more interesting, especially since they were using the same machines as collateral for loans in Florida.'

Land-title and assessment searches

Julian Sher, in researching his 2003 book about the Hells Angels (*The Road to Hell: How the Biker Gangs are Conquering Canada*, co-authored by William Marsden), used land-title searches across the country in order to show the extent of wealth among individual gang members. 'To be able to say the president of the Vancouver chapter has a house worth over $500,000, [and] his number two had a house worth over $1 million, was one of the cases where it was important for background but actually became a very important part of the book,' says Sher. 'It caused a big stir when we were able to say, "Look this clothing store, this restaurant, this café is owned by a member of the Hells Angels."'

Bankruptcy

This is a standard backgrounding search for many investigative journalists digging into stories that focus on specific individuals. The information provides further insight into an individual's financial situation over time and can raise interesting questions about their business dealings. For example, a chronic history of bankruptcy filings will prompt questions that might lead a researcher to the individual's creditors. In some cases, the details of a single filing might raise interesting questions.

Take, for example, the case of John and Aldo Martino, who owned a chain of Hamilton-based nursing and retirement homes. They filed for personal bankruptcy in 2002, each claiming to have $10,000 in assets and each listing more than $180 million in liabilities, mostly related to their businesses.

Hamilton Spectator reporter Steve Buist found a trustee's report, however, which showed that they earned a combined $4 million over the previous six years. Buist described how they continued to live an 'extravagant and luxurious' lifestyle despite their bankruptcy. The filing raised questions about 'unexplained financial transactions, unusual business practices, extravagant spending and lack of disclosure by the Martinos both before and during their respective bankruptcies,' Buist reported.[20] The long series of stories in the *Spectator* catalogued how the brothers continued to live in homes each assessed at nearly $1 million, drive luxury cars, and own a large boat and expensive 'toys'. Royal Crest Lifecare, the nursing-home chain owned by the two brothers, declared bankruptcy in 2003, listing nearly $85 million in debts. When the chain collapsed, it owed more than $18 million to taxpayers. In February 2004, the Ontario Health Ministry launched an independent probe into the matter.

'The case of Royal Crest and the Martinos is an excellent example of how a bankruptcy filing can drag a large and interesting array of documents into the public record,' says Buist. 'More importantly, it's a perfect illustration of how sensitive documents that a bankrupt person never expected to be publicly available can be viewed openly by a journalist, thanks to a bankruptcy filing.'[21]

Building permits and zoning variances

These may not be terribly interesting. But you never know. They can, on occasion, provide an interesting bit of detail. In backgrounding the owner of several 'holistic' treatment centres in Toronto, *Toronto Star* reporters obtained a copy of a zoning variance application she had filed with the city. It showed the woman had applied for a variance in order to open a business 'offering services such as aromatherapy treatment as well as reiki, and therapeutic touch, along with other stress management services.'

In its written decision, the committee approved the application, noting that it was 'desirable for the appropriate development and use of the subject property and does maintain the general intent and purpose of the zoning code and the official plan.'

With variance approved, the woman received a city-issued holistic licence to operate. Shortly after, municipal inspectors conducted an undercover investigation and laid 37 charges related to offering sexual services to clients.[22]

Corporate records

These are dealt with elsewhere in this book; suffice to say that, while they primarily tell the stories of companies, they can also be extremely useful for research on individuals associated with companies. They tell us, for example, when executives of public companies buy or unload stock, or make moves within a corporation. By following the advice on investigating businesses (see Chapter 9), you might come across public comments that your subject has made regarding their professional endeavours. Corporate documents can clarify names of officers and directors, outline financial indebtedness, detail business successes and failures, and tell us about the fiscal fortunes of individuals. The websites and online groups that discuss corporations may offer more informal public perceptions about high-profile business people and how they conduct themselves.

Privacy Concerns and Dealing with Confidential Information

Invasion of privacy

The privacy rights of Canadians are not well established in law.[23] As we make clear in this chapter, personal information about individuals is accessible though an array of public records. Journalists, however, could face prosecution or a lawsuit if they use illegal or covert methods to collect information, harass the subjects of their investigations, or invade someone's personal privacy.[24] The courts are only beginning to define the scope of this form of civil action under Canadian law, and only a few cases deal directly with the newsgathering activities of journalists.

In Saskatchewan, Manitoba, British Columbia, and Newfoundland and Labrador, privacy legislation prohibits eavesdropping on private conversations, stalking or following someone, unauthorized use of diaries or other personal papers, and using a person's name or likeness to advertise products without consent.[25] These restrictions do not apply where there is a public interest in the information or the material is considered privileged under defamation law, which exempts most news coverage.[26]

Saskatchewan's law goes a step further and specifically exempts newsgathering by journalists.[27] The federal government introduced a law in 2000 that controls the use of personal information in the hands of private businesses but recognizes the media's right to gather news; the law does not apply to anyone who 'collects, uses or discloses' personal information for 'journalistic, artistic or literary purposes.'[28]

Several rulings have helped to define the scope of British Columbia's privacy law and suggest where other courts may draw the line. A television station, for instance, did not invade the privacy of a businessman by airing footage of his scuffle with a camera crew during a labour dispute. While the parking lot where the scuffle occurred was private property, a judge ruled anyone walking by could have witnessed it and the labour dispute was a matter of public interest.[29]

Another British Columbia man failed to prevent the broadcast of an interview in which he was asked about his conviction for a drug offence. The man's criminal record and the fact he had been pardoned were matters of public record, a judge ruled, and did not invade his privacy.[30] A television station was sued in 1996 for broadcasting video of a bald man undergoing a procedure to restore his hair. While the company that offered the service was found liable for invasion of privacy, a court dismissed a claim against the TV station because the company had assured it the footage could be used.[31]

Quebec's civil law provides a general right to sue for injuries, including harm caused by invasion of privacy.[32] In addition, the province's *Charter of Human Rights and Freedoms* protects privacy, confidential information and the 'dignity, honour and reputation' of Quebec residents.[33] A teacher won $37,500 in damages in 1991 after the *Montreal Gazette* identified him as having AIDS. The newspaper did not name the teacher, but a court ruled enough details were reported to identify him and his right to keep his illness and sexual orientation private had been violated.[34] Lawyers for Karla Homolka, who served 12 years in prison for manslaughter in the deaths of two teenaged girls, tried to prevent the media from reporting on her private life after her release from jail in July 2005. A Quebec judge rejected the request, ruling there was a public interest in Homolka's crimes and she could not escape media scrutiny after her release.[35]

The media's use of photos or video images of someone without his or her knowledge or permission also raises privacy concerns. Photographers and videographers usually seek a subject's consent before an image or clip is published or broadcast. This may not always be possible, especially if the target of an investigative article or a person accused of wrongdoing refuses to co-operate.

After reviewing a Quebec woman's complaint about the use of her photo to illustrate a news article, the Supreme Court of Canada ruled that images of public figures captured in a public place can be published or broadcast without consent. Politicians, professional athletes, artists, and others whose careers depend on publicity must expect some intrusion into their personal lives. The media are also free to capture and use images of anyone, regardless of the person's stature, who is caught up in a matter of public interest, such as a business-fraud trial or a political scandal.[36]

In provinces that do not have privacy legislation, lawsuits seeking damages for invasion of privacy have set some limits for reporting on private lives. A leading decision describes invasion of privacy as an emerging basis for a civil action, and one likely to succeed only when a claimant has been subjected to 'harassing behaviour or an intentional invasion of privacy.'[37] It appears, for example, that a journalist is entitled to remove someone's garbage from the curbside in search of information. The Supreme Court of Canada ruled in 2009 that it is not an invasion of privacy for police to collect and search the garbage of a suspect. Garbage put out for collection is accessible to anyone who passes by, the court ruled, and any privacy interest in the contents is lost.[38]

Two recent cases dealing with how journalists gather information are also instructive. In 2008, an Ontario judge allowed a lawsuit claiming invasion of privacy to proceed against *The Globe and Mail* and journalist Jan Wong, who worked as a maid to research a series exploring the world of Toronto's working poor. Wong used her real name to get a job with a cleaning service but her employer, co-workers, and the service's clients were not aware she was a journalist. A Toronto family sued, claiming damages for embarrassment, mental distress, and loss of dignity, based on 'deceit' and 'invasion of property', over an article in which Wong described ironing oversized clothing and cleaning a soiled bathroom in their 'monster home'. The homeowners were not named but their suburb was, and the lawsuit claimed acquaintances recognized the family based on Wong's description of their home and belongings.

A judge refused to dismiss the lawsuit before trial, saying a full hearing was needed to examine the competing interests involved: the right to privacy versus the guarantee of press freedom enshrined in the *Charter of Rights and Freedoms* and 'the ability of investigative journalists to play their role in a free and democratic society.'[39] The *Globe* issued an apology on 2 January 2010, saying it and Wong did not intend to identify the home's owners and expressing regret for any harm caused by the publication of Wong's stories. The case suggests journalists should explore other ways to tell a story before working undercover, tell as few lies as possible, and avoid detailed descriptions of people and places that are not central to the story.

In another case, a Nova Scotia judge refused in 2009 to prevent *The Halifax Chronicle Herald* from publishing a conversation between a federal minister and one of her aides. The aide inadvertently recorded more than five hours of candid comments about political issues and other federal MPs, then mislaid her recording device in a Parliament Hill washroom. The device was given to the *Herald's* Ottawa correspondent, who informed the aide and repeatedly asked her to drop by his office to retrieve it. She never did and five months later, after the same aide lost her job for leaving confidential briefing notes at a television station, the journalist listened to the recording device's contents and advised her that he would be using parts in an article. The deposed aide sought an injunction to block publication, claiming invasion of privacy and improper use of her personal property (the recording device and its contents). But the judge ruled the conversation was not private—it took place during a long drive and was overheard by a chauffeur—and the journalist's restraint showed no evidence of intentional invasion of privacy.

'It is wrong,' the judge concluded, 'to deprive the press, and the public it serves, of remarks made privately, but not confidentially in the sense of trade secrets or privileged communications, after those remarks became available because of poor record keeping or management.'[40] The ruling suggests courts will seriously consider the media's right to gather news when deciding whether privacy has been invaded.[41]

Confidential and stolen information

A journalist can be charged with theft of documents or with possessing documents that have been stolen by someone else.[42] As well, a journalist who encouraged a source to steal documents or other property could be prosecuted under criminal law as a party to the offence.[43] But when a television reporter was charged in 1989 with possession of stolen goods—a pamphlet on the yet-to-be-released federal budget—a judge ruled that information itself cannot be 'stolen' within the meaning of criminal law. The reporter could be prosecuted only for possessing the paper the information was written on, which had little if any value, prompting the judge to toss out the charge as politically motivated and an abuse of the court process.[44]

In another case, a judge ruled that a journalist who photocopied a stolen document was not in possession of stolen goods because information transferred to a copy is not stolen.[45] It is a criminal offence, however, to hack into a computer system to access data or programs. It is also an offence to use a password to hack into a computer system or to supply a password to another person to enable that person to break into a system.[46]

Courts may have the power to prevent the publication of confidential information and to order its return. The Canadian Press was barred from publishing stories based on a leaked draft of the Canadian Transportation Accident Investigation and Safety Board's investigation into a 1998 ferry accident, as these reports are considered confidential under federal law. The news service was also ordered to hand over the draft and any copies its journalists had made.[47]

In another case, the CBC was ordered not to broadcast the contents of documents about a controversial development project because the disclosure would violate solicitor–client confidentiality. The client had the legal right to force the media to keep the information confidential.[48] A journalist who misuses confidential information about individuals or companies risks being sued for any harm caused by the release of the information.[49]

Harassment and trespassing

While investigative journalists should be vigilant and thorough in their research, they do not have a right to hound people for information or comment. Reporters are expected to seek comment from the subjects of their stories, but their efforts must be reasonable and they cannot subject people to harassment.

Making repeated telephone calls intended 'to harass any person' is a criminal offence.[50] A few calls does not amount to harassment; dozens made in a short time period or after someone refuses to comment could cross the line. And journalists who put their subjects under surveillance at their home or business must avoid being mistaken for stalkers. The offence of stalking or criminal harassment is defined as 'repeatedly following or communicating with someone, or staking out or watching a person's home or workplace.' While there must be evidence that the person who was targeted feared for his or her safety, there is no exemption for newsgathering and journalists cannot be certain how their actions will be interpreted.[51]

Journalists must respect private property and newsgathering does not give them the right to trespass. They must respect fences and NO TRESPASSING signs and, if a property owner, employee, or security guard demands that they leave a property, they must do so. Trespassing is considered a minor offence but a journalist could be fined or jailed and could also be sued for damages. A private home and its outdoor property, including gardens, orchards, and farm fields under culti- vation, are considered off limits unless a person has permission to enter.[52] In Ontario, the restriction extends to a body of water on private property and to ships, vehicles, trains, and aircraft.[53] It is a criminal offence to trespass on the grounds of a private home at night.[54]

Journalists and camera operators can enter a property to knock on the front door of a home or to ring the doorbell. They are also entitled to enter stores, shopping centres, transportation terminals, and the reception areas of offices. But if someone who answers the door or is in control of the property orders them to leave, they must comply or they can be ejected by force and charged with trespassing.

Streets, sidewalks, and roads that do not cross private land are public places and journalists can use them as vantage points to observe or to capture images on adjoining private property.

Some stories may be of sufficient importance and public interest to be worth the risk of being prosecuted for trespassing. A Quebec television crew, for example, entered an unguarded hydro-electric dam and power plant in 2005 to expose lax security. No charges were laid and their reports forced Hydro-Québec to hire additional security guards and utilities in other provinces to review their security measures.[55]

Recording phone interviews and private conversations

Canadian law allows journalists to record interviews conducted over the tele- phone without the knowledge of the person on the other end of the line. One of the people taking part in the conversation must consent to the recording, and that person can be the journalist making the recording.[56]

It would be a criminal offence, however, to report the contents of a phone conversation another person taped without the consent of those taking part in the call.[57] While journalists can record their phone interviews, the recordings can be used only for note-taking; broadcasting a recorded telephone conversation with- out the consent of the person interviewed is a violation of CRTC regulations.[58]

It is a criminal offence to record a conversation between other people if it occurs in a private place or where those involved expect they will not be over- heard.[59] This does not prevent clandestine videotaping of people speaking if no sound is recorded.[60]

Wiretaps and cellular calls

It is a criminal offence to use or disclose information the police have collected through a wiretap, and the media are prohibited from disclosing that a wiretap or intercepted phone conversation exists. The existence of wiretaps and their con- tents, however, can be reported once the information is revealed in court during a criminal or civil case.[61] A British Columbia judge brought some flexibility to this restriction in a 1999 ruling permitting the media to disclose that police had used wiretap evidence to obtain a search warrant in a high-profile investigation.[62]

It is also a criminal offence to use or disclose the contents of cellular calls, which can be picked up over a radio scanner; it is even an offence to reveal that an intercepted cell phone conversation exists unless one of the people involved in the conversation agrees to the disclosure.[63]

It is also an offence under the *Radiocommunications Act* to divulge or use cellular calls, or information gathered from them, without permission.[64] As is the case with police wiretaps, journalists can report the contents of cellular calls if they are disclosed in court. The law does not apply to print reports of conversations overheard on a police scanner or a citizens-band radio, but broadcasting these conversations without permission is a violation of the *Radiocommunications Act*.[65]

Connecting the Dots

A thorough background research job attempts to trace the labyrinthine path of a person's life, following a document trail to find how various activities are recorded. No matter how structured and methodical your approach, your progress will be determined by the information you gather, the order in which it comes, and where it points. One piece of information inevitably leads to the next, and you will find that the lines blur at times between researching an individual and investigating a company. In trying to find out about a person or dig up names of new potential interviewees, therefore, your checklist of tasks and avenues of investigation will draw also from the other chapters in this book. Be open to new lines of inquiry, and each time you get a relevant document, consider not only what it tells you but also where it might lead you.

A name, for example, might prompt a lien search that reveals a home address and business address. A reverse search on the business address might provide the name of a company. The name of the company might prompt a corporate search that turns up other officers and directors who are business partners of the person you're researching. A lien search on the company might provide still more details such as the company's level of debt and list of creditors—more potential sources of information. It might also provide information on property or vehicles that can lead to other material from motor vehicle searches and land-title inquiries. A bankruptcy search can provide details such as a person's net worth at a point in time and whether your subject lives in the lap of luxury or on the edge of a financial cliff.

A basic Internet search might give you a personal website that describes how this character likes to skydive. That could direct you to newsgroups or online chat sites about skydiving (to which your subject might be a contributor), and perhaps the discovery of other people within that online community who know your subject well.

A deep Internet backgrounding task using the tools we describe above can produce a thick file of messages, news stories, postings, photographs, and documents about your subject dating back decades.

Whatever your searches turn up, it's important to go back and read documents again, days or weeks after you obtain them. Names, addresses, or company numbers that meant little to you when you first encountered them may suddenly ring bells when you examine them later with the benefit of further research.

There are as many possibilities for research into people as there are human activities. The most important thing is to develop a mindset that prompts you to consider all of the potential research possibilities, to find alternative ways of accessing information when roadblocks appear, and always to keep digging.

Getting People to Talk:
The Art of the Interview

The question list is the backbone of your interview. It forms the anticipated structure, and gives your interview strength so it can support whatever unexpected movements the discussion may make.

When *Vancouver Sun* reporter Lindsay Kines began investigating the unexplained disappearances of drug addicts and prostitutes from Canada's poorest neighbourhood—Vancouver's Downtown Eastside—he had to rely heavily on people to find the story. On this assignment, there wasn't an extensive repository of documentary information ready to be unearthed by an enterprising reporter. Instead, Kines had to build trust with subjects who were slow to trust outsiders: the people of Vancouver's skid row and the police. He ended up doing hundreds of interviews.

'I'd done a lot of stories on the Downtown Eastside even before going on the police beat, so I already had some sources there. But, really, there was no real secret to it—just spending time with people, listening to their stories, and quoting them accurately helped build trust.'[1] Kines would eventually help unearth the largest serial murder case in Canadian history.

No matter how good you get at digging through documents, trolling databases, and unearthing archival material, a thorough investigation must involve talking to people. You begin dealing with people from the very beginning of a project: experts, tipsters, government bureaucrats, clerks, secretaries, accident witnesses, and so on. In some cases, when not many documents are available, human sources may give you much of your story.

Investigative interviewing shares characteristics with that done by daily-reporting journalists, but investigators are more likely to face special situations such as interviews with reluctant or hostile subjects. Investigative reporters usually do many more interviews for one story, with each interview providing a few patches of information that will be assembled into the complete quilt, so to speak. In the following sections, we'll break down the process.

The Basic Interview

You have no doubt heard that an interview is just a conversation, and the more like casual conversation it is, the more the subject will reveal. We'd like to advance the proposition that an interview isn't much like ordinary conversation at all. Certainly, you want the tone to be similar, you may even want the person being interviewed to believe it is a conversation, but an interview is actually a unique verbal form. Mastering the process takes hard work, a dose of psychology, and a willingness to learn from your mistakes.

Ordinary conversation darts from one topic to another, following paths that have little to do with what was being talked about just moments before. The participants are often likely to avoid a subject that creates discomfort. A good interview, by contrast, is structured and deliberate. Its purpose is to facilitate a largely one-way transfer of information from source to interviewer. Difficult topics are often the whole point of the exercise.

An interview is characterized by a delicate balance of power. The interviewer largely controls the topics; the interviewee controls the information. Conducting an interview effectively is a kind of verbal seduction. Both parties may enjoy the experience, but at least one may be initially reluctant to engage. A big part of your job is to increase the comfort level of your subject so he or she will want to talk.

A number of factors are necessary for a successful interview. You must do sufficient research to prepare. Questions must be based on that research, and organized so the interview has a logical flow. Finally, the interviewer's approach must provoke answers that are useful for broadcast or publication. It's a tall order, and only a distant relative of the casual conversation. It's hardly a surprise that interviewing is often the task that most confounds young and experienced journalists alike.

The Successful Investigative Interview

What to prepare

You need to understand your topic, the role your interviewee plays, and as much as you can about the interviewee personally. Stewart Harral wrote about this latter requirement as far back as 1954: 'If time permits, use all available sources to secure information about the person with whom you are going to talk. Read the clip files in the office, talk with the man's acquaintances, look up his connections, check biographical reference books, talk with other staff members—use all possible sources.'[2] Such work saves you from having to ask basic questions during the interview.

Pulitzer Prize–winning investigative journalist Eric Nalder argues you should prepare thoroughly even when facing a tough deadline. 'It's empowerment,' he says. 'When you know something about someone . . . you are going to exude a confidence that you did not have when you called them out of the blue.'[3]

What to ask

The actual content of your questions is, of course, determined by what you need to find out, but some basic principles can help you deliver the goods. For the purposes of this discussion, we are grouping questions into three broad categories.

The names of these categories are quite arbitrary. The point is that you can divide questions up according to the degree of emotional content. In the first edition of this book, we adopted the terms *personal, impersonal*, and *abstract* questions. We are adopting different wording this time, although with the same intent. We are now calling them *hot, neutral*, and *cool* questions, according to the degree of emotional involvement.

Hot questions probe into personal experience—that is, the individual's details, role, and direct observations. *Neutral* questions tap people's knowledge of matters in which they are not involved so directly (e.g., a public-relations officer's description of company operations as opposed to the daily grind of being a public relations officer). *Cool* questions deal with concepts, such as the law or a scientific principle; these primarily engage the intellect.

Hot questions engage an interviewee more emotionally, helping you harvest rich anecdotes. It is easy to understand the difference in response to the hot question, 'What were you thinking about as you stepped up to the altar?' compared to the cool question, 'What do you think about the institution of marriage?' Some people are uncomfortable answering hot questions, while others prefer this territory. As we will see, moving from the intensely personal toward a cooler inquiry can act as a pressure-relief valve in an interview. Conversely, starting with cooler questions before warming things up can help some subjects open up in an interview.

Obviously, the mix of question types will hinge somewhat on who you are interviewing and why. An interview with a person who suffered radiation poisoning after a childhood spent playing on a nuclear waste dump, for instance, may be driven primarily by hot questions. On the other hand, an interview with a political figure about a new policy to crack down on irresponsible nuclear-waste handlers may be driven primarily by the neutral sort. Finally, an interview with a university professor on the long-term effects of radiation exposure may be dominated by cool questions.

The form of the question is just as important. The overriding message here must be that old saw, 'Keep it simple, stupid.' Writer Sally Adams put it particularly well: 'Since the first interview requirement is to communicate, common sense dictates that short questions are better than long ones, simple questions better than convoluted ones, clear questions better than abstruse ones.'[4]

We must also pay homage to the groundbreaking work of investigative writer John Sawatsky. The author of two best-sellers on Canada's spy establishment, and an unauthorized biography of former prime minister Brian Mulroney, Sawatsky is one of the few people who has actually studied thousands of interviews to assess what kinds of questions work most of the time, and which ones fail. His basic message is that interviewers should stay in what he calls 'input' mode, asking simple, evocative, open-ended questions that encourage interview subjects to describe and explain, instead of asking aggressive, closed-ended questions that require only that the subject confirm or deny.

Sawatsky argues that closed questions such as 'Were you surprised?' or 'Are you a racist?', while sometimes sounding informed and tough, allow interviewees to answer simply yes or no, then stitch on whatever information they choose. 'Socially, people are taught to add a postscript to a confirmation or a denial,' says Sawatsky. 'As journalists, we hope the "p.s." will describe or explain the issue we've raised. That's interviewing by accident. If you get somebody who doesn't want to play, you're in trouble.'[5]

He also counsels against

- long-winded questions weighed down by unnecessary or leading statements— 'How should people react to that? I've heard many people are angry.';
- questions that betray the opinion of the interviewer—'Isn't it true that your company has poisoned thousands of children?';
- multiple questions that allow an interviewee to choose one or the other to answer—'Why did you do that? Didn't you consider the consequences?'; and
- questions that include what Sawatsky calls 'trigger words', which prompt the respondent to address the word rather than the query—'Why did you do such a reprehensible thing?' (Likely answer: 'We are not reprehensible at all. In fact, our nuclear by-products management program is second to none.')[6]

Of course, closed-ended questions can help you to confirm basic facts (e.g., 'Did you attend the meeting?' or 'You were born in Vancouver, correct?').

Open-ended questions on the other hand, force people to think. 'Genuinely tough questions compel people to go further than they otherwise would,' Sawatsky says.[7] Examples are 'Why did you do that?', 'How did that happen?', 'What did you see?', or 'What went through your mind?' While sounding easier, these actually make it much more difficult for an experienced subject who has taken media training to hijack your question to deliver a pre-planned message track, fully loaded with talking points.

Once more, and at the risk of being repetitive: A thought-out list of questions is imperative so that you make the most of your interview time and don't leave out anything crucial. The question list is the backbone of your interview. It forms the anticipated structure, and gives your interview strength so it can support whatever unexpected movements the discussion may make.

Where to do it

For the most part, this is usually a choice between using a telephone and meeting the person face to face.

In your investigative work, telephone interviews will play an important role, especially for the many foundational interviews that develop your knowledge of a subject. Generally speaking, interviews that seek to gather facts and context are more easily done by telephone, or via an Internet video-conferencing service such as Skype or Google Chat, than those that seek personal details or insights. This is because it is difficult to develop a personal rapport using voice/video contact alone. Also, confrontational interviews, which often necessitate some hot questions, are usually more challenging to do with a voice or video feed—more on these later.

The most important interviews should be done in person. You can make eye contact and read body language; it is a more human relationship. The best location may be in the person's natural environment, such as an office or home, which may offer evidence of personal or professional interests in the form of mementos, certificates, family pictures, and so on. Often, discussing such objects can provide the perfect icebreaker. For example, if you have no choice but to speak on the telephone, you can ask the subject to describe the room he or she is in.[8]

A variant of the in-person interview is one done at the 'scene of the crime'. If your investigation involves an incident with a specific locale, or if there is a regular spot where the person you are interviewing was involved in the story—an example might be a busker on a particular street corner—by all means arrange to do the interview there. Being at a location can provide you with scenes to describe, and prompt useful questions, as well as help the interviewee to remember experiences more acutely. Steve Buttry, director of tailored programs at the American Press Institute, suggests trying a 'moving' interview: 'Start out in the workplace, go out to eat, ride home in the character's vehicle, ask her to show you the house and the yard.'[9]

If you are approaching people in public places—as Kines did when working on the story of Vancouver's missing women—you should probably approach without a notebook or recording device, and begin with casual conversation before moving into interview mode. You should still identify yourself quickly (unless you're working undercover, of course), but you may decide not to take notes. Instead, you can jot down your recollections of the conversation shortly after it occurs, much as police officers do after assessing incidents. You will need to judge when enough trust has developed to introduce more formal interview activities such as note-taking; you might talk to an interviewee a number of times before that level of trust develops.

How to act

It sounds obvious to say that a good interviewer needs to listen well, but you would be surprised how often interviewers don't. A great many things can distract us: hearing the hubbub in a newsroom, taking excessive notes, thinking about the next question, looking at other things in the room, worrying about a sick child, wondering what to cook for dinner tonight, or contemplating the attractive man or woman who just walked past the window.

Listening well has two advantages: First, you will, obviously, absorb what the other person is saying and remain alert to the progress of the interview. Second, your subject will notice if you are listening or, more to the point, if you are not.

'To be a good listener means more than just asking questions,' counsels expert John Brady. 'It means being attentive, leaning forward, nodding, and making sounds or gestures of approval. A good listener is active, not passive.'[10] If you bury yourself in notes, fidget, look out the window, yawn, slouch, or fail to make eye contact, the subject's ego gets insulted and you may soon face monosyllabic answers.

How to strategize

A good interview is like a story, with a beginning, a middle, and an end, with some high points and other junctures where it is just cruising along. But unlike a story, over which the writer has control, an interview unfolds on the fly. In fact, the interviewer is a bit like an air-traffic controller contending with aircraft that may not understand or follow directions—and that may suddenly take off when they are supposed to be landing. An interviewer needs a plan.

Most interviewees will naturally be wary. The fact that you are an investigative reporter and have identified yourself as such will only contribute to that. Your strategy probably begins, therefore, with some sort of icebreaker. This might be something unrelated to the interview or simply a piece of flattery—for example, if you have chosen to speak to someone because they are the undoubted expert in a given field, then say so. Perhaps you will ask how the person learned so much. It doesn't matter if you know the answer; the purpose is psychological, to ease the person into the interview, to get him talking on comfortable ground, so that he can warm up to you. Generally, the more personal the interview topic, the more personal the icebreaker. More impersonal topics might require an icebreaker that is simply a straightforward opening question. If you have only 15 minutes with the deputy minister on the phone, of course, you might want to skip the icebreaker altogether and get to the point. For more intense interviews, for example with victims, you may need a significant icebreaking period before you can slide gently into the actual interview.

Next, you would usually move to factual questions, which will help establish points of agreement with your interviewee. To take up the hypothetical nuclear waste story mentioned earlier, you might have to interview the CEO of the waste company; let's call it Wasteglow. You would develop a factual consensus on the manner in which waste is stored, transported, and handled, and the measures the company has in place to ensure this is done safely.

This done, it is time to hike together into more difficult terrain, and tackle contentious or personal questions. It is a lot easier for both parties to do this once they are acquainted, and are comfortable with the basic geography. Make sure, though, that you save a couple of easier, non-essential questions to give yourselves a rest in a tough situation. You can always ask those questions at the end if you don't need them earlier.

At this point in your interview with the nuclear waste company executive, you might present some of the known criticisms of the nuclear-waste-disposal industry, and some of the concerns of the radiation victim. You may also move into more personal (hot) territory, if that suits the needs of your story.

Next, you aim for the peak, presenting your own findings that Wasteglow deliberately buried dangerous nuclear waste in the landfill without obtaining the proper regulatory approvals. You will move into this phase earlier or later in the interview, depending on the amount of such material you must cover. The key is to get the housekeeping and moderately contentious material out of the way first, in case bringing up an explosive topic prompts your interviewee to suddenly have a pressing appointment. You want the answers to most of your questions safely tucked into your notebook before such a calamity happens. (If the entire purpose of the interview is to discuss your findings, and this is understood in advance, you will likely introduce the material sooner.)

You can also reduce the chance of prematurely derailing your interview by keeping your questions non-judgmental. Rather than accusing the Wasteglow CEO of illegally burying waste, you should ask incremental, factual questions that get to the point of the illegality without being accusatory. A good beginning might be, 'We have found *Document X*, which says that Wasteglow buried nuclear waste in the landfill between 2001 and 2005. What do you have to say about this document?' You could then ask what the rules are for burial, then how the waste was buried, whether this followed the rules, why the company proceeded even though the regulations prohibited it. This approach has a greater chance of eliciting an admission than a blunt question such as, 'We know you buried nuclear waste in that dump. Why did you do that?'

Once you have dealt with the toughest questions, you will be near the end of your interview. A good technique is to signal that you are finished with this stage of the interview, using a quick comment—'Good that we dealt with that'—before proceeding to wrap up the conversation. Because people tend to remember best what happened most recently, and because you may wish to talk to this person again, it is important to reach comfort level again in the interview's denouement. Often, you have leeway here to ask a more personal (hotter) question, one that will put the subject back on comfortable ground. For example, you might ask the CEO what it's like to constantly fend off these accusations, or why the nuclear waste industry is always under attack. The very fact that you have signalled reduced tension can sometimes prompt the interviewee to open up more on such questions. If you already have interviewing experience, you know that some of the best material emerges at the end.

As you conclude, it is standard practice to ask if the subject would like to address anything that you may not have covered. This is polite because it ensures the person has the opportunity to say everything she had planned to say. Some trained interviewees will use this opportunity to retread a planned message track, but if so, you have lost nothing. It is also important to ask about who else you should talk to, and why. The person may well suggest someone you have never heard of, or have overlooked.

Lastly, as in any interview, check the spelling of your subject's name, and if you are in broadcasting, its proper pronunciation.

Other useful tips

Use the brake

You are cruising along in your interview, and your question plan is unfolding as you thought it would, when you notice that your subject has become increasingly uncomfortable with your line of questions. The answers are becoming curt, the interviewee is disengaging, you can see your conversation heading for a 12-car pileup. The moment has come to apply the brakes. Of course, an interviewer doesn't have a set of brake pedals ready for a little squeeze from the right foot. What you do have are the easier, more neutral, questions you saved up earlier. This is where you can use such a question to divert the interviewee onto more comfortable ground. Having done so, you can then gradually work your way back to the sensitive territory from a slightly different direction.

The key thing to remember is that an interviewer is not just a relentless information gatherer. This is, after all, still a social undertaking. Consider the impact your questions are having.

Use silence

Novice interviewers often make the mistake of jumping right in with another question just as soon as the subject has finished speaking. Resist this impulse. Especially when you have asked a difficult question, and the interviewee has uttered the words she may have planned to say in this circumstance, wait a few seconds. Silence in an interview is like a vacuum; it's in people's nature to abhor it. The person may fill that awkward silence, and go beyond what they originally intended to say, and even be more honest about it.

'The pause may draw out the answer your question didn't,' Steve Buttry says. 'You want thoughtful answers, so give the character time to think. This is not a stubborn staredown. You casually take a few moments to catch up on your notes, to take a few notes about the setting, or your subject's appearance and mannerisms. Just shut up and listen.'[11]

Sally Adams suggests waiting four seconds, adding, 'If you need extra persuasion to keep silent, bear in mind that the more you interrupt, the less you listen and the less they will talk.'[12]

Stay calm

If your subject becomes angry or rude, don't reply in kind. In a social sense, the person then owes you one. To make up for their boorishness, they are liable to be more gracious later. You can use this to your advantage.[13]

Be on time

This one goes without saying, but in our busy lives it is easy to forget social niceties such as punctuality. Getting to your interview a little early not only indicates that you take your subject's time seriously, but you might even get a cup of coffee.

Stop them when you don't understand

Brady counsels journalists not to pretend they are experts. 'Stop your subject when he gives you some complex information. "Let me make sure I understand what you are saying," you can say. Then summarize what he has said and repeat it. This will clear up any misunderstandings that can occur when an interviewer just goes with the flow of a tech-talking source.'[14]

As well, whenever an interview subject leaves something partially unexplained, or the logic doesn't make sense to you, keep asking probing questions, such as, 'Why did you do that?' or 'How did that work?' to get the explanations you need. You won't always have the opportunity to go back to the source later for elaboration.

Offer encouragement

Keep the person talking with affirming questions such as, 'What happened next?' and 'What did you think of that?' When someone makes a statement of fact, ask 'How do you know that?'

Interviewing experts suggest developing a list of standard questions you can use to keep a conversation going.[15] Leading someone through a chronology is a particularly useful tool. Nalder recommends using a chronology as a way to get somebody to open up. 'There's a logic the person needs to fill in—as though they were filling in a form—in that chronology,' he has said. 'The chronology also takes you to the place at which they're doing the things that are interesting to you.'

Be flexible

When the source surprises you with an unexpected direction, try to accommodate the shift—you may discover completely unexpected information. Because you have a plan, you know where you need to return once you have finished exploring. Joan Walters, who often uses investigative techniques in her work at *The Hamilton Spectator*, had one such experience in the early 1980s:

> I was at Queen's Park for the Canadian Press and had been trolling annual reports of each of the ministries for potential stories. . . . An entry for the purchase of three obviously luxury cars caught my eye and I set up an interview to talk with a senior civil servant. . . . The civil servant was agitated and hostile, offended that I would question expenditures on cars when 'so much else' wrong was going on in other ministries. I probed. . . . In the end, I managed to conclude that he was referring to something that involved Gordon Walker, who was then a minister in the Bill Davis cabinet and a rogue candidate for the PC Ontario leadership in the expectation that Davis would eventually be stepping down. . . . What I eventually discovered was that Gordon Walker had given untendered contracts using money from three ministries he headed to a political adviser who was working on his behind-the-scenes leadership campaign, including

self-publication of an autobiography-style book by Walker on the politics of the right. It was a stunning story, which effectively precluded Walker from leadership candidacy when Davis finally did retire in 1985. It took me weeks of working sources, quietly pursuing possibilities, before the story finally slapped me in the face and I was able to write it. Had it not been for that civil servant trying to divert me from a story harmful to his own ministry, I never would have tripped on the Walker story.[16]

Keep a low profile

Doing your interviews in the correct sequence is just as important as organizing the flow within each interview. In our hypothetical example of Wasteglow's nuclear-waste dumping, you wouldn't approach Wasteglow first. Likely, you'd wait until most of your other interviews were completed. Generally, investigators work from the outside in, advancing through a series of concentric rings until they reach the target of the investigation, at the very centre.

The outside ring might consist of complainants, such as the radiation victim. From there, you might go to generic expert sources: people who are familiar with the problem at a high level, but who are not involved with the specifics. You might proceed to people closer to the responsibility, such as the public officials in charge of overseeing nuclear-waste disposal. Finally, you would reach the target. You should limit, as much as possible, the chance that word of your activities will reach the centre while you work through the outer rings. The more warning the target has, the easier it is to develop a public-relations strategy to counter your research, or to try to squelch contacts who might speak to you.

By starting with people who are antagonistic to the target, moving through people who are essentially neutral, and on to people who may be closer to the target, you improve your chances of working undetected for the longest period of time.

Some might feel uncomfortable about this technique, that it is something akin to an ambush. Really, though, it is simply a matter of keeping your investigation confidential in order to avoid contaminating the story by influencing it yourself, much as a scientist avoids having an effect on an experiment aimed at testing a hypothesis.

Keep your eyes open

You are doing more than asking questions and listening to responses. Your eyes are just as important as your ears. What does your subject do while speaking to you? Does the CEO lean forward, engaged in the discussion, or lean back, apparently bored? Does the person assume a position of power behind a desk, or invite you to sit casually on a couch? What's in the room? Is there a shelf full of books? If so, what books?

Such observations provoke additional questions and provide you with the detail to help a story come alive.

Recording the Answers

In an investigative context, you must record a person's answers in detail. You're not just looking for a few good quotations. You want the context in which your subject says things, the order, the emotional tone of voice, and—often as important as what is said—what is not said. Did the person avoid some of your questions?

To capture an interview in such detail, you either need an electronic recording device or some form of shorthand or speedwriting. Longhand notes are fine as a way of capturing the highlights of an interview you are also recording, but few people can write longhand fast enough to keep up with the average speaker, who talks at about 120 words per minute. Also, you don't want to spend all of your time during an interview taking notes, because this destroys the human contact between you and your source.

Recording electronically is always the preferred method in any kind of controversial investigation, since it allows you to prove what someone said. It is important to work out with your editor the custodial arrangements for any recordings in instances where a libel suit is possible. If you possess the material, a court could order you to hand it over. Some reporters have, therefore, been known to hand over notes or tapes to a third party, who then places them in an unknown location. However, these matters must be discussed with your supervisors and/or legal counsel *before* they become an issue.

Electronic recording devices in use today are of three basic types: those that use regular or mini-cassette tapes, purpose-built digital recorders, and hand-held devices such as Apple's iPod Touch, or even your cell phone, that can be adapted to record audio. Other digital formats, such as those using removable discs or digital audio tapes, are nearing obsolescence.

Analogue tape devices are fairly reliable so long as you don't buy the cheapest model. The recording medium is cheap to use. The devices are compact, with removable tape cassettes that are easily stored. All you need are a small sticky label and a pen, along with a shoebox, and your storage system is ready to go. As of 2010, audio cassettes are still widely available, but it may become more difficult over time to obtain the tapes, much as it has become more difficult to buy photographic film.

Tape has disadvantages. To find a particular spot on the tape, you need to wind forward or backward, referring to your notes and the tape counter; this can be annoying and time-consuming. Cassette recorders—other than professional-quality units designed for broadcasting—also deliver lower sound quality.

Digital recorders store your interviews on either an internal memory chip, or a removable memory card. Some provide several hours of recording time. Their biggest advantage is speedy access to any point in the recording. Some suffer from poor sound quality, however, and limited recording time, so watch out for these problems if you are buying one. You may wish to seek out a unit designed for professional use if audio quality is a significant concern. The Zoom units produced by Samson have a built-in microphone and produce acceptable sound quality for broadcast or online news use. Make sure you buy yourself enough memory to do the job—you don't want to run out of space in the middle of a crucial interview.

It is also possible to use devices such as the iPod Touch or iPhone to record audio. The Canadian firm Vericorder markets software and a companion microphone to turn either device into a portable audio recorder and digital editing studio. An obvious advantage is that one device can serve many purposes, and with the built-in wireless or wireless connectivity, the devices can be used to send your recorded audio to a remote location for broadcast or posting.

If sound quality is important, you should consider buying an external microphone to go with any device you use. Even a relatively inexpensive microphone will usually increase the distance at which the recorder will pick up sounds, and improve the ability to pick out a voice from a noisy environment. More expensive microphones, paired with a high-quality recorder, can deliver broadcast-quality sound.

Whatever type of equipment you are using, you will want to consider transcribing at least your most important interviews. Transcription alerts you to subtleties that get missed when taking notes. For legally sensitive material, such as when you make allegations about an identified person or corporation, transcription of major interviews is almost mandatory to ensure you have got all the points right and are not overlooking something.

Whatever you do in this regard, it is crucial to review each interview after completing it to see how the person's answers have helped supply necessary information and to determine what new questions have been raised. Lastly, remember that all recording devices can fail. You should ensure the recorder is working at the beginning of the interview, and if you can, glance at it occasionally to ensure it is still running.

How to Get People to Talk to You

Not every interviewee has the same desire to share information. The head of a public-interest group decrying nuclear-waste pollution may be delighted to speak about such a controversial topic, but the head of Wasteglow will likely be reluctant. People's willingness depends, unsurprisingly, on whether they expect your story to have a positive or negative impact for them. Still, if your investigation is to be successful, you need to get reluctant sources to talk.

As we have said regarding other aspects of the investigator's craft, the most important thing here is preparation. The Wasteglow chief is more likely to speak to you if you already have the guts of the story. It won't be possible for the company to halt your investigation merely by not speaking with you. In fact, you can advance the legitimate argument that it will be in the subject's interest to speak to you to ensure that the firm's point of view is heard. You also will have the compelling argument that by speaking to you, Wasteglow will ensure the accuracy of your story.

People like to feel important and you can use this to your advantage. If someone is reluctant to speak to you, emphasize the significance of their role in whatever issue you are investigating. One approach might be, 'It's important that we hear from you because you probably know more about this than anyone.' Take advantage of the research you did on the person before you called to talk.

People also like to be helpful, and journalists often need help. 'I'd like your help to understand this better' is one, less confrontational, way to approach someone.

If you are having particular difficulty reaching someone, or the person is repeatedly putting you off, you may need to resort to stronger tactics. You could make it clear to your prospective interviewee that the consequence of not speaking is to be left out of the mix and to miss the opportunity to respond to the story's findings, or to comments from others. This sentiment can be expressed in a positive way, by telling the source you value having his or her point of view in the story.

Especially when a story contains findings that will cast an organization or person(s) in a poor light, it is important that you make every effort to obtain an interview or statement. If you get nowhere with telephone calls, and emails and BlackBerry messages are ignored, you may need to send a letter—best by registered mail—repeating the request for the interview and outlining the areas you wish to cover in the interview, as well as key allegations or facts to which you are seeking a response. While this will not shield you from possible defamation action later—the best way to do that is to get the facts right, but we deal with defamation in Chapter 12—it will help establish that you made every possible effort to give the person or organization a say.

But above all, be courteous. No matter how wretched an activity is under discussion, being accusatory will not take you far. Remember that your goal is to get the information. You are not on show. Be fair in all interviews and discussions, right from the beginning. Don't take sides, even if your story will have a distinct point of view. Don't badmouth subjects you may talk to later. (Better still, don't badmouth anyone.) Word of your activities will spread, and you don't want to reinforce the subject's suspicions about investigative reporters. Ken Metzler put it well in *Creative Interviewing: The Writer's Guide to Gathering Information by Asking Questions*: 'In communities where people know each other, your presence as a journalist gives them something to talk about. After the first interview, your reputation will precede you. That will make subsequent interviews easier or harder depending on the perception of the first . . . bad vibes travel on express lanes.'[17]

Ultimately, the more you know, and the more accurately you know it, the more likely reluctant interviewees will be to speak to you—if only to ensure that their own point of view is put on the record. Your career reputation is also important in this regard. If you can, point to other work you have done to demonstrate that you are a fair and reasonable reporter. If people understand that you do substantial, serious work, they may be more likely to speak to you.

The Dilemma of 'Off the Record'

Determining what your subject means and wants

Sooner or later, you will hear an interviewee say the following: 'This is off the record.' It is one of the most overused and misunderstood phrases in journalism.

Traditionally, 'off the record' meant you could not use the information at all, except as a starting point to develop questions aimed at extracting the same information from others who spoke 'on the record'. In our experience, most people really mean, 'Don't use my name.' This is more properly called 'not for attribution' or 'going on background'. If someone asks for their comments to be off the record, politely inquire what they mean.

You commonly see unnamed sources used in political stories, but less often in investigative work. Unquoted sources may well be used in investigations to provide hints, leads, and advice, but they don't appear in print that frequently. This is because an investigative story needs to rely on what is established and, therefore, on the record. This said, it is extremely important to understand the different types of attribution, what they mean, and the implications they carry both for reporters and sources.

On the record
If your contact is on the record, then you can quote the source by name and use the information provided without restriction. This is where you want to be all the time if possible. The audience knows who is speaking, and the speaker takes responsibility for his or her words.

Not for attribution
This means you cannot quote the source by name, but you can fully use the information and in most cases describe the person generally, using a euphemism like 'a government insider'. Depending on your understanding with the source, you may be able to run direct quotations. A promise of confidentiality is implied, although this should be negotiated at the time of the interview. As we note below, however, be extremely careful about undertaking such agreements.

On background
The information may be used, but is generally not to be attributed to anyone, nor quoted directly. A promise of confidentiality is implied. This is a stance commonly assumed by government sources.

On deep background
This typically means the information may not be used—and certainly not quoted directly—in a story. It can, however, be used to corroborate other information, and can be the basis for questions put to others who may be able to provide the same information on the record. A promise of confidentiality is presumed.

Off the record

As mentioned, this theoretically means the same as 'on deep background'; in practice, however, it can mean almost anything, so you need to clarify it with the person.

Confidentiality

If you do promise confidentiality, journalistic ethics bind you not to reveal the name of the source, ever, or until such time as the source releases you from the agreement. Such promises should be made with caution and only in exceptional circumstances, because Canadian law does not give journalists an absolute right to shield their sources. The shield laws that protect journalists' sources in many American states[18] do not exist in Canada, and a federal private-members' bill introduced in 2007 to create one in criminal cases did not become law.[19] Courts have the power to demand the name of a source regardless of a promise of confidentiality, if the source's identity is required to investigate wrongdoing or to ensure justice is done. A refusal to comply can be punished with a fine or imprisonment. While few Canadian journalists have been jailed for protecting a source,[20] judges decide on a case-by-case basis whether a source is worthy of protection.

As investigative reporters have become more aggressive in their pursuit of stories, the courts have come under increasing pressure to expose confidential sources. Since 2001, three major legal battles have helped to clarify when a court may be willing to allow a journalist to protect a source. Andrew McIntosh became the target of a police investigation after a bank document was leaked to him during his National Post investigation of federal aid to businesses in then prime minister Jean Chrétien's Shawinigan riding. The document, which was allegedly forged, suggested Chrétien stood to benefit personally from a loan to Shawinigan's Grand-Mère Inn, a hotel he once owned. Officers with the RCMP obtained a search warrant to seize the document and the envelope used to mail it, and to analyze both items for fingerprints or traces of DNA that could identify the leaker. Since the document came from a source McIntosh had promised to protect, the *National Post* challenged the warrant in court and won at the trial level.[21] Justice Mary Lou Benotto of the Ontario Superior Court ruled in 2004 that journalists have the right to protect sources when reporting on matters of intense public interest, such as the conduct of a key elected official.

The Ontario Court of Appeal reversed Benotto's ruling in 2008, however, and ordered McIntosh and the *Post* to hand over the document and envelope.[22] While Justice Benotto felt it was more important to protect McIntosh's source than to allow the police investigation to proceed, the appeal court felt this deprived the RCMP of evidence of what could be 'an especially grave and heinous crime'—a criminal conspiracy designed to create controversy and possibly drive a prime minister from office. The right to protect a source, the court ruled, 'loses much of its force' when used 'to protect the identity of a potential criminal or to conceal possible evidence of a crime'. The *Post* appealed, but in a May 2010 ruling, which applies across the country, the Supreme Court of Canada refused to give journalists a blanket right to protect sources.[23] The constitutional protection of press freedom puts the media in a 'special position', the court said, and judges should strive to 'protect the media's secret sources where such protection is in the public interest'. Attempts to shield sources, however, will be considered on a case-by-case basis, and journalists must demonstrate that protecting a source is more important than uncovering information vital to a police investigation or the outcome of a legal dispute. When the claim is tied to a source accused of a crime or with information that could help solve a crime, it will be harder—but not impossible—to shield the source. 'The bottom line', Justice Ian Binnie noted in the court's majority ruling, 'is that no journalist can give a source a total assurance of confidentiality. All such arrangements necessarily carry an element of risk that the source's identity will eventually be revealed.'[24]

The high court heard another source-protection case in the fall of 2009, and a ruling was still pending at the time of writing. A Quebec court ruled that *Globe and Mail* reporter Daniel Leblanc could be questioned about a key source he had used to investigate the notorious federal sponsorship program, a.k.a. AdScam. A judicial inquiry credited Leblanc's diligent reporting for exposing some of the worst abuses of the program, which saw tens of millions of dollars directed to politically connected Quebec advertising firms, in some cases based on inflated invoices or for work not completed. The federal government is suing one of these companies to recover $35 million, and lawyers defending the company want to identify the journalist's source. A Quebec judge has allowed the firm's lawyer to ask 22 federal employees if they passed information to Leblanc, and to question the reporter as well, depending on the outcome at the Supreme Court. Since Leblanc's source is not being sought as part of a police investigation and is not suspected of wrongdoing, the *National Post* ruling suggests the court may be more willing to respect his promise of confidentiality.

In the third case, an Ontario judge found *Hamilton Spectator* reporter Ken Peters in contempt in 2004 for refusing to identify a source. Peters was a key witness in a lawsuit: a nursing home claimed it was defamed by the City of Hamilton when someone leaked documents to Peters alleging mistreatment of the home's residents and staff. Justice David Crane of the Ontario Superior Court ruled that Peters's refusal to reveal his sources threatened to deprive the plaintiff of crucial evidence and ordered the *Spectator* to pay $31,600 in costs.[25] The newspaper appealed, and the Ontario Court of Appeal overturned the finding of contempt as well as the fine.[26] The ruling faulted Justice Crane for moving too swiftly and imposing an 'excessive' penalty, and warned other judges that citing a journalist for contempt should be a last resort. Peters's source came forward on his own, the court noted, and journalists trying to protect a source should be treated with respect, not as if their goal is to defy the court or subvert justice. That ruling was not appealed.

In light of these rulings, here are some suggestions for dealing with a source's request to remain confidential:

- Avoid using unnamed sources. The public has a right to know who's behind the information and allegations that the media disseminate; this makes sources accountable and lends credibility to what is reported. Many news organizations require an editor or producer to approve the use of unnamed sources and may require at least one other source to verify the information. The Canadian Association of Journalists' *Statement of Principles for Investigative Journalism* declares that journalists should promise confidentiality only when a source's co-operation 'puts them at risk of harm or personal hardship (i.e., a whistle-blower who might lose his/her job, or a mole within organized crime).'[27]
- Clarify what the source is seeking. Is it a matter of attributing quotes and information to an unnamed source? Does the source expect his or her identity will never be revealed? Or something in between?
- Never promise complete anonymity. Journalists are obliged, under defamation laws, to disclose a source's identity an editor or producer, who has a duty to verify the information a reporter gathers before it is published or broadcast.[28]
- Level with the source and negotiate an exit strategy. Journalists should warn sources that it is impossible, under Canadian law, to offer an ironclad promise of confidentiality. A journalist can promise, for instance, not to reveal the source's identity (other than to a direct supervisor) unless ordered to do so by a court. Or the source may agree that, if the journalist ever faces a fine or jail time for refusing to testify, he or she will come forward at that point.
- Insist on the fine print. 'If you are willing to go to jail to protect a source, say so,' the CAJ advises in its *Statement of Principles*. 'Otherwise, spell out the conditions.' Whatever promise is made, journalists must ensure that they can follow through and that their employer is willing, if necessary, to absorb the legal costs of defending a promise of confidentiality. Journalists also should heed the lessons of the Maher Arar case, where unnamed government sources used the media to smear Arar, a Canadian detained and tortured in Syria, as a terrorist.[29] The CAJ believes sources should be on notice that, if they lie or knowingly provide false information, all deals are off, and the journalist is free to expose them.

Sometimes, sources will tell you that they don't want their name used *after* they have provided you with some information, or at the end of an interview. The classic stance, in this instance, is that a source cannot withdraw his or her name after speaking the words. The request must come first. As with any rule, this one has nuances in its application. Certainly, any official source—a police officer, politician, senior bureaucrat, and so on—ought to know the rules of the game, and so should not be given leeway. But what about an ordinary citizen you have contacted out of the blue in the midst of your investigation, one who tells you the whole story, then thinks better of it? In such a situation, there cannot be an expectation that the person knows the rules. Depending on the context, you may choose to be merciful. However, if the person's information is vital to the story—if he or she is providing important corroborating information, for example—you may have no choice but to use the person's name. It is difficult, but a journalist's first obligation is to the audience. Ideally, you will find another source who can provide the same information, and then you can sidestep using the first source, but this will not be possible sometimes. Every situation must be weighed on its own merits. If you are unsure of what to do, consult a senior editor or producer.

Some reporters refuse to allow anyone to speak anonymously. There are valid arguments for this, perhaps the most compelling being that people who don't attach their name to their words don't have to be accountable for them. It is far easier to float half-truths or attack somebody's reputation from a position of anonymity. If someone absolutely insists on speaking anonymously but you need them on the record, Eric Nalder recommends going back over not-for-attribution portions of an interview, at the time of the interview or later, to see if the subject can be coaxed into letting certain sections be attributed. Once the person has agreed to a few things, you coax more out of them, in a process that Nalder calls 'ratcheting': 'Sometimes they'll say, "Okay, I could say that," or sometimes they'll say, "Well, I couldn't really say it that way, but I could say *this*," and they'll start telling me what I could say.'[30]

John Brady offers several tips on the use of unnamed sources. He suggests reporters and sources agree on what 'off the record' will mean from the beginning of the interview, to 'make it clear that the subject is the one who needs to take action to put information off the record,' and to 'verify all off-the-record information before using it in your story.'[31]

He adds, 'If the off-the-record information cannot be confirmed, remember the old newsroom axiom: Sometimes it's better to kill a story than to be killed by a story.'[32]

Interviewing Online

Email

Our first piece of advice would be to avoid email, whenever possible, at least for substantive interviews. While it may seem convenient, an emailed Q&A is far too open to manipulation, to prepackaged statements, and to media-relations spinning. You cannot see or hear the interviewee. Spontaneity is non-existent, and follow-up questions require another email exchange, allowing a chance for the person to simply end the discussion.

That said, there can be circumstances when email is an acceptable means to get quotations for a story. One of these is if the person cannot be reached any other way. A scientist at the South Pole may be impossible to reach on the telephone, but be accessible via email. Similarly, a corporate CEO who doesn't have time to speak to you in person might answer a few quick questions on a BlackBerry.

Sometimes, you may have little choice. Journalists covering federal politics, for example, report that media-relations officials are increasingly insisting that reporters provide emailed questions in advance so that the governing party can keep tight control of the daily 'script' on Parliament Hill. It is best to push hard for an in-person interview, but the media-relations gatekeepers may hold most or all of the cards, thus forcing you to go along in order to get *something* for your story.

Email is better than no interview at all

You might also use email to get quick additional comments from somebody you have already interviewed, close to your deadline. If all you are doing is quickly clarifying a point, or seeking additional details, this may be just the ticket.

As we mentioned, media-relations officials in government, who work the front lines in answering politically explosive questions from the press, will often insist that you pose your questions in an email ahead of time. It is up to you and your editors to decide whether to do this. Officials want to labour over possible answers for hours, or days, and finally dish up the carefully phrased and weighed responses in an email. This prospect is not appetizing for journalists.

Every investigative reporter who has been doing the work for a long time will have had the experience of having the same canned answers recited over and over, no matter what the question. In those cases, at least the emailed answer is easier to cut and paste into the story. The real work in such instances is often to read between the lines, even between the words, to try to decipher some meaning from the released statements.

Email may also be a viable alternative for students or reporters with small-market media, as they likely have difficulty getting responses from government or business officials who fancy themselves too busy to spare time for the small fry.

Instant messaging and BlackBerrys instead of email

Instant messaging or cell phone 'texting' are probably not the best tools for important investigative interviews, because either party can break off the 'conversation' instantly (and with less drama than slamming down the telephone). But one advantage is that these methods can sometimes allow you to get past filters such as receptionists. Many executives and bureaucrats have assistants who receive their emails for them, but this may not be practical for instant messaging or text messages because the filtering person ruins the immediacy in an email environment. The lack of a filter makes the ubiquitous BlackBerry an attractive option. Many journalists have discovered the usefulness of these devices in allowing them to communicate privately with one another—and BlackBerrys offer a great way to make connections with sources. You could get access to a high-powered executive who would otherwise be difficult to reach any other way.

Working with Media-Relations People

There was a time when journalists could reach most sources directly, or through a personal secretary or receptionist. However, an enormous media-relations industry has sprung up and grown dramatically in Canada over the past several decades. Its machinery is increasingly sophisticated and intrusive. Media-relations officers are very likely to be involved when you call any sizable private company or public institution. Their primary job is often to ensure that nothing is said that doesn't fit a preordained organization line. Even if you get to talk to the people in charge, or to mid-level functionaries, the media-relations officers will be involved in arranging the interview, and may insist on sitting in on your discussion.

Of course, journalists will always develop and nurture sources within organizations, but when it comes to official public contact, the media-relations office will usually intervene. Many employees of private companies and public bodies are under strict orders to refer any media calls to the press office, sometimes on pain of dismissal.

You might as well develop the best relationship you can with these people. Many are former journalists who have discovered better pay and working conditions in public relations. Preparation is, as ever, the best tactic. Try to know as much as you can going in, with hopes of recognizing subterfuge and misinformation when you see it. Treat media-relations staff with the same respect and courtesy you would anyone else, but be insistent on having your questions answered; make it clear that if a source refuses to answer questions, your story will say so.

A valuable reason for staying on good terms with media-relations officers is that they are often the gatekeepers who control access to the people with whom you really need to speak. With courtesy and honest disclosure of your subject matter, you can turn many press officers into allies. At the very least, you can avoid being placed on their mental blacklist of rude reporters.

When it comes to the key accountability interviews, you must speak to the people who are truly accountable. Media officers will try to insist on answering your questions themselves. Make no mistake; this is a power struggle. The media person wants to keep the accountable person out of the spotlight, away from the heat, so to speak. You need the accountable official because readers, viewers, and listeners aren't stupid. They know the difference in heft between the public-relations officer and the head honcho.

In this scenario, you start softly and shift toward a harder position until you land the interview.

You can begin by politely explaining that you need to put your questions to the person in charge in order that the company or public body's position carries the most weight with the audience. If that doesn't do the job, be more insistent. In many cases, the media-relations person will be bluffing, in the hope you accept him or her as the source. That, after all, is what this person is paid to do. You may need to tell the media person categorically that only an interview with the responsible official will be acceptable and that you will make it clear in the story that the truly accountable person refused to speak if that is the case. Often, the realization that you are willing to play hardball will turn the tide.

You shouldn't accept an accountability interview with a media-relations person without putting up a vigorous fight.

A Final Note on Media Training

In Chapter 1 we mentioned media trainer George Merlis, who counsels his clients to develop *intentional message statements* (ISMs) that they can drop into interviews to ensure the company line is delivered and to pay 'factual lip service' to questions before 'bridging' to one of the message tracks. We also discussed the McLoughlin Wedge®, a method to introduce pre-planned content throughout an interview.

Merlis and Barry McLoughlin are among a growing army of consultants, many of them former reporters, who train senior politicians, bureaucrats, and company officials to deftly handle interviews. They put clients through simulated interviews and teach them how to take control by watching for the 'exit ramps' that will allow them to move to their canned messages. Make no mistake, when you face one of these trained people, you are dealing with a real adversary, and one who has been trained to think of you in exactly those terms. Among the favourite tricks of trained interviewees are

- Ignoring the question and simply saying whatever they want to.
- Refusing to answer on the basis of 'privacy, security, or budget secrecy.'
- Having the final word by recapping the canned message at the end of the interview.[33]

Because Canada is a free country, we can't stop interview subjects from learning and practising these methods. But there are simple things you can do to counter their wall of training. The most basic is to be persistent—if a source doesn't answer a question, or 'bridges' to other territory, politely bridge back and ask your question again. Ultimately, the person isn't obliged to answer it, but you want to have that refusal to answer on the record. Investigative reporters need to be alert and aware of these stonewalling techniques so as not to cede control of the interview to the subject. For this, of course, you need to listen closely and focus on the information you need, so that you know if your question was answered satisfactorily in the first place.

Use silences. Remember John Sawatsky's advice on open-ended questions. Finally, just as the media trainers have studied the media, we should study the media trainers. Borrow Merlis's book from the library and buy a copy of McLoughlin's media strategies guide.

Interviewing step by step

- Identify the appropriate source.
- Be prepared. Do your research.
- Prepare questions based on your research.
- Decide on a location—in person is best.
- Have a strategy for the interview.
- If possible, keep all interviews on the record.
- Record the interview if possible.
- Transcribe the results for important interviews.

Suggestions for Further Reading

McLaughlin, Paul. *Asking Questions: The Art of the Media Interview*, self-published (available from author, www.paulmclaughlin.ca).

McLoughlin Media. *Encountering the Media Strategies and Techniques Pocket Tips*. Ottawa: McLoughlin Multimedia Publishing Ltd, 2005.

9 Following the Money: Seeing the Business Angle in Any Story

Only by developing a good understanding of the numbers can you find the compelling story. Numbers do lie. So it's important to ask questions, and, when possible, do the math yourself.

Introduction

Our goal in this chapter is not to turn you into a business reporter; it is to provide you with tools and strategies for conducting research on non-profit entities, institutions, and businesses involved in your investigation. Beyond this, we want to emphasize the importance of the financial angle in all sorts of stories. Whether you're focusing on a local sports team, an arts group, a government department, a nursing-home chain, a small company promising lots of jobs, or a political scandal, you will always find it useful to 'follow the money'. This means asking simple questions: Who is making money? Who is losing it? Where does it come from? Why has some of it gone missing. The answers help you determine why something is happening.

A journalist must be comfortable with basic mathematics and financial statements, and should be able to research beyond a company's products or services to discover things like its level of debt, the jobs of key executives, lawsuits that may be eroding its bottom line, and accounting irregularities. Only by developing a good understanding of the numbers can you find the compelling story. Numbers do lie. So it's important to ask questions, and, when possible, do the math yourself.

As former business reporter David Stewart-Patterson once told a conference of journalists,

What's the number that really matters? Why does that number matter? What does it say about real people in their real lives? You're trying to get away from the charts. You're trying to get away from the numbers as fast as possible and as far as possible. Because what all business and what all economics boils down to is real people making real choices about their lives.[1]

Stewart-Patterson is right, but his advice conceals a paradox: in order to get away from the numbers, you first need to get close to them.

Case Study: Nursing-Home-Chain Disaster

Recognizing that many of the best stories are about money and how it's made, spent, and wasted leads you to ask out-of-the-ordinary questions. It helps you to get past the spin and to uncover truths that should be public. Such was the case with a collapse of a nursing-home chain that, when the dust finally settled, would become the largest such failure in Canadian history, leaving creditors, taxpayers, nursing-home workers, and residents on the hook for millions of dollars.

'Any time I see someone go bankrupt, the first thing I am is skeptical,' says Steve Buist, an investigations editor at *The Hamilton Spectator*, who began covering the nursing-home story in 2003. 'Every time someone comes back to me and says I just got these bankruptcy documents, what do you think? My first thought is, I'm going to look at this with a very critical eye. Do the numbers add up? Does the explanation for why they went bankrupt make sense? Where was the money going? Are there any connections that seem questionable? Who is owed money and who is handing out the money?'[2]

These were all key questions Buist attempted to answer in the 45 stories he wrote between January 2003 and February 2008 about John and Aldo Martino, two brothers who ran the Royal Crest Lifecare Group Inc., a company that owned 17 nursing and retirement homes in southern Ontario, and similar homes in the United States. 'The one theme was that there was this huge, staggering amount of money that didn't seem to be easily accounted for. And the second major theme was that a lot of taxpayer dollars were at stake here.'[3]

Buist's entry into the story began when he returned from Christmas holidays in January 2003. He had just completed a number of features and was fishing for some new ideas. So Buist did what all good journalists should do: He contacted a source and asked if there were any issues worth pursuing. After a long pause, his police contact said, 'Yes, there is.' He asked Buist if he knew anything about the Martinos. At the time, there had been a number of stories about the company seeking protection from creditors while it presumably figured out ways to pay its bills. The *Spectator* had done a number of stories about what would happen to the homes if the company declared bankruptcy.

'He said, "Something's going on." I said, "What,"' recalls Buist. 'And he just repeated, "Something's going on. That's all I can tell you." And I said, "Okay." And that was all I needed. The next day, they declared bankruptcy. And a whole bunch of dominoes began to fall. And there was the possibility of some sort of police, or criminal, investigation into the business.'[4]

Like most reporters working a general beat, Buist knew little about bankruptcy law and where to look for information about a company—in this case, one that had major creditors such as the Bank of Nova Scotia and National Trust pulling the plug on Royal Crest's operations for failure to collect their money.[5] Fortunately, he was able to use the services of the regional office of the Office of the Superintendent of Bankruptcy Canada (OSB), the federal agency that oversees bankruptcies.[6] The OSB publishes monthly, quarterly, and annual statistics on the number of insolvencies—that is, bankruptcies and proposals—filed by consumers and businesses in Canada.[7] We will talk more about the OSB later in this chapter.

However, apart from filing statistics that can be turned into general stories, the OSB can become a one-stop shop—or at the very least, a starting point for your investigation. For Steve Buist, this meant 'hundreds and hundreds of pages of material which was being added to on a regular basis.'[8]

One of the first documents was filed by Ernst and Young, the trustee. In *The First Report of the Trustee*, the firm outlined the case history of Royal Crest's problems, complete with names of creditors and dates.[9] As a starting point, such a document is invaluable to journalists following a company that is seeking protection from creditors.

There was so much material, that Buist and his editors decided to tell the unfolding narrative in bite-sized chunks, rather than overwhelm readers with dense stories with too much detail. 'Then, every so often, I'd pull back and present a longer piece tying together a number of themes or issues.'[10]

Essentially, the documents revealed that while the company was not paying its bills, the Martino brothers were still paying themselves, and handsomely at that. In the words of one bankruptcy judge, '. . . the failure of the two Bankrupts to reduce their draws to ease the company's cash shortages, while failing to remit the funds withheld from employees, is morally inexcusable even if not actually dishonest.'[11]

'Basically, the allegation is that money came in the front door through (Ontario) government funding. And they (the Martino brothers) said, "Thank you very much," and they went out the back door with their dividends and payments to . . . suppliers or family suppliers,' said David Debenham, an Ottawa-based forensic accountant who reviewed a government-commissioned audit[12] that concluded 'based on the patterns seen, there is a strong possibility of criminal conduct, including conspiracy to defraud, conversion of property, bankruptcy fraud and tax evasion.'[13] The Ontario Provincial Police did investigate, but its health squad investigations unit couldn't find enough evidence to press charges.[14] Still, there are many unanswered questions about where the millions of dollars went, the role of the Ontario government's auditors, and how such failures can be prevented from happening again.

For Steve Buist, who is now responsible for mentoring young investigative journalists at his newspaper, it's important to question the numbers, dig deeper when they don't add up, and look for answers in a range of sources, including secondary documents, land-registry records, and court documents, which we learned about in Chapters 2, 4, and 5, respectively.[15]

Though Royal Crest was a private company, its file became an open book because it was thrust into bankruptcy, which, as we'll learn later in this chapter, is a public process. Both brothers also filed for personal bankruptcy. One of the brothers, John Martino, has since died. Aldo still owes $300,000. And the Ministry of Health is still trying to collect $4.1 million.[16] So the story continues.

Getting the Numbers

The closer we get to the numbers, the better stories we are able to find. Sadly, though, many journalists are unaware of what information to ask for and where to get it. Many actually take pride in the fact that they got into journalism to avoid working with numbers!

'Reporters often joke that they get into journalism to avoid math,' writes Conrad C. Fink in *Bottom Line Writing: Reporting the Sense of Dollars*. 'Many reporters will do anything to avoid dealing with numbers in earnings reports or even government and school board budgets. But reporters who take the time to learn about finance and accounting have a great advantage over their colleagues that will add perspective and depth. . . . Follow the numbers and you'll be surprised where that takes you.'[17]

The easiest financial numbers to get are those of public companies, which is why they tend to dominate the business coverage. Firms such as Nortel are required to open their books regularly, providing updates on how much money they're making or losing, whether they have any liabilities, if they're getting sued, if they've recently taken over another company, and so on. Failure to provide that information on time can itself become a story.

Private businesses present a greater challenge, unless, of course, they're forced into bankruptcy, as was the case with Royal Crest. Private businesses are more secretive about their financial performance because, under normal circumstances, they are not obliged to disclose information to the public. What makes this troubling is that most businesses or business-minded entities in the communities journalists cover are, indeed, private. People can't buy shares in them on the Toronto Stock Exchange (TSX) or New York Stock Exchange (NYSE). Private companies usually do not publish financial statements, or if they do, the documents are usually watered-down versions. The closest glimpse you may get of a private company's inner workings is in whatever documentation it chooses to publicize or information an inside source chooses to provide. The key is finding documents— in addition to insolvency records filed with the OSB, the courts, and bankruptcy trustees and receivers—that they don't want you to see. When it comes to non-profit entities, the rules on disclosure vary. As mentioned in Chapter 4, a registered charity must submit financial information to the federal government, and some of these records are available online. Smaller organizations, however, may be just as secretive as small private businesses.

We'll address each category in turn here—public, private, and not-for-profit—and discuss what information may lurk within the organizations, and how to get at it.

Public companies

Public companies are required to file a wealth of material. And because many of the big companies in Canada are multinationals or indigenous companies that trade on US stock exchanges, they must file financial information in the United States. The deadlines for these filings often arrive before the ones in Canada, but such companies usually file simultaneously in both jurisdictions. If the company trades stock only in the United States, then it is legally obliged to file financial information just in that country, meaning that you can only obtain key details for your investigation from stateside sources such as the website of the US Securities and Exchange Commission (SEC). Though there are many types of corporate filings, we'll focus here on the ones that can produce the best stories.

Form 8-K, which in Canada is called *Publication of Material Change*, contains juicy information that may not be in the company's news release. These forms must be filed with the regulator after a 'materially important event occurs.' The SEC now requires companies to file these documents within two days after the event occurs. In Canada, the requirement is 10 days. Journalist Leah Beth Ward clarifies the point well: 'Legally, something is materially important if its disclosure would affect the shareholders' decision to buy or sell the security.'[18] These newsworthy events include a decision to file for bankruptcy, or a company's decision to name a new CEO. While these may be announced in a news release, the details that the company does not want the general public to know are contained in the 8-K forms or *Publication of Material Change*. These might include the intricacies of the pay-and-bonus package for the new CEO at a time when the company's share prices are plummeting.

In the *Form 10-K*, which in Canada is broken up into three separate documents called *Financial Statements*, *MD&A*, and the *Annual Information Form*, the company must report how much money it's really making, or losing, bad loans it may have been forced to assume, and lawsuits it is facing. If the company has changed its outside auditor, then it must give reasons in its *10-K*. The form is filed annually, 75 days after the end of the company's fiscal year, which means that the reports should become available in March. In Canada, the deadline for filing is 90 days after the end of the fiscal year. In addition, the *10-Ks* provide a detailed history of the company, the number of employees on the payroll, and the property the company owns. For journalists looking to write a profile of the company, in addition to digging up newsworthy nuggets, the *10-K* is invaluable.

Form 10-Q (or *Interim Financial Statement* in Canada) differs from *10-K* in that it is filed quarterly (hence, the letter *Q*) and it is unaudited, meaning that the numbers haven't been verified by an outside auditor. You can use the information in a *10-Q* to compare the quarter with the previous one, or the equivalent quarter of a previous year. The *10-Q* is due 45 days after each quarter ends. (This applies only to the first three fiscal quarters since the fourth *10-Q* is actually the *10-K*.) The *10-Qs* also contain information about lawsuits or market risks that the company learned of during that quarter. It's important to emphasize that, though newsworthy, the *10-Q* is but a snapshot of how the company has performed during a particular three-month period.

The *Annual Information Form*, or annual report, gives the company a chance to show off its stuff. These documents are usually replete with beautiful pictures and optimistic language about the company's future. The annual report is the company's way of communicating with shareholders (and indirectly with members of the public; all the reports are also available on the company's website under a category usually called 'investor relations', or alternatively on the website of the securities regulator). The report contains a lot of non-financial details including marketing plans. The best information can be found in the *Management Discussion and Analysis (MD&A)*, which is tailored to answer the question that many shareholders have in mind: 'How's business?'[19] Stories may be contained in certain line items. For instance, it is interesting to examine how much the company is spending on marketing as opposed to research and development (R&D). This is an especially important piece of information if the company has been saying publicly that it needs tax breaks so it can spend more money on R&D. A good story might be one that points out how more money is being spent to promote the old product than to make a better one.

The *MD&A* is the portion of the annual report required by regulators. It is usually found near the back. It summarizes the company's financial results and provides richer and more frank detail about the financial performance. In the rest of the annual report, however, companies are free to pick and choose what they tell shareholders. So obviously, it's important to read the *MD&A* for context and story ideas.

Proxy statements can be viewed at the same time as annual reports. They notify shareholders when and where their annual meeting will be held. These statements provide background information regarding changes which require shareholder approval, such as the election of board members, the selection of outside auditors, and even the approval of a stock option plan.[20] The statements contain story ideas because, at the meeting, any shareholder can place items for discussion on the ballot; it's worth paying attention to the topics that might be controversial. Social or environmental activists, for instance, may want to dissuade the company from making decisions that could lead to instability in a particular community or harm the environment. As is the case with *8-Ks*, proxies also contain information on salaries, bonuses, and stock options for the highest-paid employees. It's always interesting to find out how much money executives are really making, especially when those executives may be telling their rank-and-file employees to make do with less because the company is enduring hard times.

So financial statements can be seen as tip sheets to be mined for story ideas or questions that few people thought to ask.[21]

How to read a public company's financial statement

We will look here at a financial statement filed by Nortel, which was once one of those companies that could do no wrong. It made lots of money, had good products, and was the darling of the investment community. When it failed to file its quarterly statements in 2004, people in the business community wondered what the problem was. The delay turned out to be caused by a disastrous case of fiddling the accounts. The company was in the middle of revisiting its numbers from the previous four years, during which time it had been misrepresenting the figures to cover up major problems. When Nortel finally came clean on this issue in its 2004 *10-K*, the real numbers made sobering reading for its investors.

The accompanying table is part of Nortel's financial statement in the *10-K* it filed with the Security and Exchange Commission (SEC) and the Ontario Securities Commission (OSC). It covers the years from 2000 to 2004. Because it was trading on the stock exchanges in Canada and the United States, the company filed its financial statement simultaneously with both securities regulators.

The table in the *10-K* is called the *results of operation*, which is like an income statement, according to Bill Lawson, a retired finance professor at Carleton University's Sprott School of Business. The results of operation provides a partial window into the company's financial health. The first line item on the left-hand side is *revenues* or sales, which we can see have diminished. This might not be surprising, given the general hard times that hit many high-tech firms. Lawson says reporters should provide context for those revenue figures by comparing them to similar figures for other competing companies. Be sure to compare similar-sized companies that operate in the same marketplace. A good analyst who studies the sector can be a handy source for a reporter looking to achieve such context.

Research and development (R&D) has also diminished. This could be a troubling figure for a company that needs to be innovative in order to stay ahead of its competitors and make money. Lawson points out that this declining figure is not necessarily bad; it could indicate that the company is streamlining its R&D to specific products. Instead of leaping to conclusions, you ought to look for an explanation of this in the management's discussion of the financial statement or the notes.

The *special charges* category is divided in two. The first, *goodwill impairment*, refers to investments that the company has made in the past. The term *goodwill* covers the amount of money Nortel paid to acquire a company over and above the book value of its assets. Let's say that a company's assets were valued at $500 million, but Nortel decided to make the purchase for $600 million. That extra $100 million is considered to be goodwill. In other words, it's the extra money you're giving the company as goodwill because it has a good reputation and a good name. If the company's value diminishes, so does the amount of the goodwill—hence the term 'goodwill impairment'. If the company's value diminishes from $600 million to $550 million, then the goodwill impairment would be $50 million. The amount can be written off as a loss.

The second category is called *other special charges*. The word 'other' can be an important red flag for reporters. It means that something is unusual—perhaps it happens only once and has nothing to do with making a product. Lawson says that, in this instance, we could be talking about the costs such as severance pay to laid-off employees.

The next line down is *operating earnings*, also known as operating income. This is the money that the company makes from its telecommunications products. When the figure appears in brackets, it means that Nortel is losing money.

Table of Contents

(millions of US dollars except per share amounts)	2004	2003	2002	2001	
Results of Operations					
Revenues	$ 9,828	$ 10,193	$ 11,008	$ 18,900	
Research and development expense	1,959	1,960	2,083	3,116	
Special charges					
Goodwill impairment	——	——	595	11,426	
Other special charges	180	284	1,500	3,390	
Operating earnings (loss)	(111)	45	(3,072)	(25,020)	
Other income (expense) – net	231	445	(5)	(506)	
Income tax benefit (expense)	29	80	468	2,751	
Net earnings (loss) from continuing operations	(100)	262	(2,893)	(23,270)	
Net earnings (loss) from discontinued operations – net of tax	49	184	(101)	(2,467)	
Cumulative effect of accounting changes – net of tax	——	(12)	——	15	
Net earnings (loss)	(51)	434	(2,994)	(25,722)	
Basic earnings (loss) per common share					
— from continuing operations	(0.02)	0.06	(0.75)	(7.30)	
— from discontinued operations	0.01	0.04	(0.03)	(0.78)	
Basic earnings (loss) per common share	(0.01)	0.10	(0.78)	(8.08)	
Diluted earnings (loss) per common share					
— from continuing operations	(0.02)	0.06	(0.75)	(7.30)	
— from discontinued operations	0.01	0.04	(0.03)	(0.78)	
Diluted earnings (loss) per common share	(0.01)	0.10	(0.78)	(8.08)	
Dividends declared per common share	——	——	——	0.0375	

(millions of US dollars)	2004	2003	2002	2001	2000
Financial Position as of December 31					
Total assets	$ 16,984	$ 16,591	$ 16,961	$ 21,971	$ 44,337
Total debt (a)	3,902	4,027	4,233	5,212	2,454
Minority interests in subsidiary companies	630	617	631	654	758
Total shareholders' equity	3,987	3,945	3,053	4,808	27,862

(a) Total debt includes long-term debt, long-term debt due within one year and notes payable.

In *other income*, we see the word 'other' once more; this is income derived from unusual or one-time events, which could include selling off businesses. Unlike revenue from its normal business, Nortel can't benefit from this other source of income year after year, but at least it has been able to use the income to help stabilize its finances.

Next is *income tax benefit*. The reason it's called a 'benefit' is that Nortel is able to recover some of the early taxes it paid when the company was earning more money.

In short, Nortel gets money back (unless the figure appears in brackets, in which case it refers to an expense).

Now we're getting into the *net* category; that is, closer to Nortel's bottom line. In general, 'net' is money available after taxes are paid. We see that Nortel's net earnings from continuing operations (the word 'continuing' refers to its normal line of business) has diminished. It has been able to generate some income from its discontinued operations, which means money from products it no longer sells.

The following line items, which mention *earnings per share*, do not add much new information for us, since they are calculations based on the 'net' numbers just provided. The figures do not actually tell us about the trading prices for Nortel shares. But they do indicate that investors were not happy with Nortel.

Finally, we see the *total assets* and *total debt*. An asset is cash, inventory (a product that's sitting in the store waiting to be sold), or property that can be can be sold or converted into cash. To relate this to personal finances, if you own a bicycle, it would be considered an asset. So would a car, although the value of an automobile does not remain the same as when you bought it—it is a quickly diminishing asset over time.

'Total debt' includes the money Nortel owes to the banks and other creditors (i.e., the companies from which it buys its supplies). If the 'total assets', or available cash, is more than the total debts, then the company should live to fight another day. If the debts are larger than the total assets, the company is in trouble. Because Nortel has gained much of its income from selling businesses, it has been able to generate enough cash to offset its declining sales.

The table excerpting Nortel's financial statement can provide many story ideas. What new products will Nortel develop to allow it to compete? What businesses did it sell, and could they have made more money for Nortel had it kept them and sold something else? How much longer can it tolerate a decline in sales? If the explanations in the management's discussion contained in the *10-K* are unsatisfactory, or if there are numbers that still don't seem to make sense, you would have an issue to pursue with the company and outside experts.

If reporters had access to these figures during the company's heyday, the stories about Nortel would have been harder-hitting and more reflective of the company's actual performance; shareholders would not have been misled into thinking the company was doing well, and the impact on people's investments would not have been so devastating and abrupt.

Of course, Nortel has now entered a new phase in its history, which could spell the end of the company. Many of the details of the company's financial woes are not only included in financial forms, but also in court documents that are now part of the company's bankruptcy proceedings.

Seeking protection from creditors

When companies, such as Royal Crest and Nortel, or individuals can't pay their bills, a process often unfolds that can end with the ultimate form of insolvency: bankruptcy. The Office of the Superintendent of Bankruptcy (OSB) supervises the administration of the *Bankruptcy and Insolvency Act* (BIA), which includes maintaining 'a publicly accessible record of bankruptcy and insolvency proceedings.'[22]

There are many records filed during the insolvency process. The basic records that deal with the nuts and bolts of the insolvency by a consumer or business are filed with the OSB, and as such can be excellent tip sheets. In addition, there are provincial court records in some files of consumers (with contested matters or large bankruptcies and proposals) and in all bankruptcies and proposals filed by corporations. The court records contain the documents that can be found at the OSB but also in many cases, the court records may contain additional, detailed information.[23]

For instance, if a company is attempting to avoid bankruptcy, it can file a document with the OSB called a *Notice of Intention to File a Proposal*, a legal document stating that the individual or company intends to file a proposal to repay its debts. 'Notice of intention is just saying we intend to cut a deal with our creditors,' explains David Debenham, an Ottawa-based lawyer and forensic accountant.[24]

The notice, which journalists can obtain from the regional OSB office, includes the name of the licensed trustee, the creditors owed more than $250 and the amounts of their claims and the court file number. You can also find the name of the court, a detail which the trustee filing the notice may choose to include or leave out.[25] This document becomes an excellent road map for journalists. Other documents filed with the OSB include the proposal itself, the report from the trustee on the proposal and the minutes of the creditors' meeting, held to decide whether to accept or refuse the proposal. These documents are then filed in court. The court records may, as mentioned before, also contain additional information that could result in stories. You can also contact the trustee, whose office will have many—if not all—of the documents related to the case.

The *Notice of Intention* is the beginning of a process that could unfold with all the drama that is usually contained in many instances where companies face the prospect of going out of business. Journalists wanting to get the real story must follow the paper trail, which can begin with the OSB, then wind its way to a court file containing more material related to the case, and eventually to interviews with the major players in the drama—be they creditors demanding their money; company executives fighting for their corporate lives; or employees battling to hold on to their pensions, severance packages, or jobs.[26]

Entegrity Wind Systems Inc. provides a useful example. In the spring of 2009, the Prince Edward Island–based company was the subject of favourable headlines. On 30 March, *The Guardian* carried a story entitled, 'A sign of wind energy times: Prince Edward Island's Entegrity Wind Systems Inc. expands into new sales territory in the United States and Canada'.[27] The headline seemed to say it all. Entegrity was an expanding company, full of promise for its product: 50-kilowatt wind turbine generators designed to supplement electric power for clients such as large buildings, farms, and schools.

And yet some three-and-a-half months later, another headline placed more prominently in *The Guardian* told a bleaker story: 'Wind turbine maker going into receivership: Province plans financial help for Entegrity Wind Systems'.[28] It turns out that the company's 50 workers hadn't been paid since mid-May, not long after the initial story boasted about expansion plans.

'They closed their doors and their employees didn't get paid for the last month,' *Guardian* political reporter Teresa Wright recalls after going to press with her story about Entegrity's troubles and promises on the part of the province to help keep the jobs on the island. 'The employees were trying to figure out what was going on. And then we found out that the business sought protection from its creditors.'

While reporters can discover the names of the creditors in Entegrity's *Notice of Intention*, they'll have to consult the material in the court file to obtain more details. 'There's all sorts of business strategy involved in [insolvency] that you can only get a look at when it all goes to court,' says Debenham, who believes that journalists covering these cases frequently miss the real story because they don't take the time to read the court documents and understand the contents. 'Ninety-nine percent of business is done behind closed doors. This is your one chance to pull back the veil and see what's going on.'

Because Entegrity is a private company, it's impossible to wait for a quarterly or annual statement to examine items such as income statements, balance sheets, and cash-flow statements, as is the case with public companies such as Nortel. Instead, Entegrity's story will unfold. Justice Wayne Cheverie, of the Prince Edward Island Court of Appeal, denied the company's request for more time to sort out its finances, forcing it to declare bankruptcy.[29]

There's another avenue companies pursue when they can't pay their bills. Firms with debts more than $5 million dollars can file for protection from their creditors under a different act called the *Companies' Creditors Arrangement Act* (CCAA). Firms such as Air Canada have used this route to restructure their affairs while staying in business. During the process, one that can end in bankruptcy, the company and other interested parties (e.g., creditors) file documents such as affidavits, which contain lots of detail about why the company is in trouble. Company executives may also file for personal bankruptcy, as was the case with John and Aldo Martino.[30] These documents also become part of the court file.

Journalists seeking information about these large companies can find them in court, and, depending on where you reside in Canada, some of the documents can be located using online databases such as CanLII, which allows users to search for documents in cases that have had rulings.[31] As with OSB files, CanLII can be used as a tip sheet because, among other things, the documents contain the court file number. You can find out what a judge ruled, but you won't have access to the documents upon which he or she depended to make that ruling. If the decision is a newsworthy one, then it's worth the effort to consult the court file for the rest of the material.

With CanLII, you see the sausage after it's been made. But some of the interesting stuff is the evidence being made in the sausage. The documents found on CanLII are basically saying, at the end of the day, this is what the judge decided. 'Well, that's interesting, but what evidence was he looking at?' asks Debenham.[32]

Private companies

Privately owned companies don't always receive the critical attention they deserve, unless, of course, they declare some sort of insolvency, as was the case with Royal Crest or Entegrity. The problem is that by the time the company hits the skids, it may be too late to inform people such as nursing-home residents, employees, customers, suppliers, or creditors that something is wrong.

For the most part, stories about small businesses run the risk of being too complimentary, particularly when a new firm is moving into a community such as Charlottetown, Prince Edward Island, and creating badly needed jobs, or if an entrepreneur is offering a unique service, as we saw in the case of Entegrity. This is not necessarily because journalists are failing to be watchdogs. Instead, it can happen because private companies are obliged to tell you only what they want. And in most cases, the news that sees the light of day is positive, even though the real story may be something entirely different.

Because they're private, these companies are not legally obliged to file the same kind of information that is required of public companies like Nortel, meaning that under normal circumstances, there's no surefire way to know how much money they're making or losing. But you needn't give up just yet. There are ways to poke around for controversial information that the company would rather keep secret. It's all in the way you approach your investigation.

As we have seen in Chapter 5, court documents are a rich source of data. The CEO or president of a private company may not want to divulge the degree to which her company is enriching a bank account (legally or illegally), but may have no choice in a bankruptcy, divorce hearing, or lawsuit. In court, people often have to disclose details about their worth and how they make their money. If the information is damaging, a person may apply to have the information sealed.

Key financial information, or even allegations of embezzlement, can also be obtained from former employees who may have left the company after trying to blow the whistle but failing to make any headway. In the case of Entegrity's former employees, there might be people willing to talk about some of the real reasons the company's initial financial projections turned out to be overly optimistic.

A company's competitor may also have good stories to tell. The same thing goes for creditors with whom the company under investigation does business. If creditors are constantly owed money, or if payments are continually behind schedule, then that would tell you about the company's ability to make ends meet. And this is why it's helpful to have lists of creditors, such as the Entegrity Wind System's *Notice of Intention* described earlier in this chapter. Perhaps trouble with creditors is a signal that the firm is short of cash, just as with an individual who is constantly late paying bills. It is important to recognize all the potential players and institutions involved in the unfolding drama that involves the private firm you're investigating.

As we saw in Chapter 4, government departments and agencies that regulate business can also be wonderful sources of information. You won't necessarily find out how much money the company is making or losing, but you will discover a thing or two about its products and track record as a corporate citizen. This is information that the company often isn't eager to make public.

In addition to determining whether or not a company is private or public, it's important for you to find out how a particular business is regulated. If the private company makes prescription drugs, for instance, then its activities are monitored by Health Canada and the US Food and Drug Administration (FDA), which will take action if one of the company's drugs turns out to be harmful. These regulatory bodies work with companies to issue what are called 'Dear Health Care Professional' letters or public alerts, spelling out any new dangers. So, if a company is praising one of its products such as a new flu vaccine, conduct a search on Health Canada's website to determine the drug's safety record.

Businesses are also regulated by labour ministries to ensure that they are providing a safe workplace environment for their employees. There's hardly a week that goes by when we don't hear about a worker seriously injured or killed on the job. How many workers have died from similar accidents at a particular company? How has the provincial or federal ministry of labour ordered the employer to improve its safety record? Is the company flouting employment standard rules by forcing employees to work unpaid overtime? Answers to some of these questions can be found on provincial Ministry of Labour websites, which track investigations, naming the company and the reason it got into trouble. For Ontario, consult the Enforcement Activities: Prosecution and Conviction Statistics, a yearly tally of companies that have run afoul of the *Employments Standards Act*.[33] If the online information doesn't go back very far, call the ministry and ask if you can obtain data from an earlier time period.

Although you may be unable to determine if a company is making or losing money, these other approaches can take you beyond the company's news releases or the rosy information on its website.

Non-profits

There are many entities that operate like businesses, but with one difference—they do not have the goal of making a profit to be shared by the owners. These non-profit entities include charities, foundations, Crown corporations, and agencies.

Charities

One of the less-obvious lessons from the fallout of the 11 September 2001 terrorist attacks in the United States was that journalists need to ask more probing questions about charities. Some groups took advantage of the disaster by pretending to collect money to help the victims. In the worst cases, that money was used to support criminal or illegal activities; in other cases, the groups were simply sloppy operators.

During periodic drives to support charities, or during times of the year such as Christmas when the emphasis is on giving, journalists should take a harder look at certain charities to determine how they're spending the money they collect. For instance, as part of its ongoing investigation into charities, the *Toronto Star* was able to demonstrate that the group Mothers Against Driving Drunk (MADD) spent an inordinate amount of the money it collected from donors on paid fundraisers. 'A little bit of analysis, and we found that 81 cents of every dollar raised went to pay fundraisers and administrators. The charity had to make some big changes after that story,' writes Kevin Donovan, the paper's editor of investigations.[34]

We have already mentioned that registered charities file basic information with the Canada Revenue Agency.[35] You can download the most up-to-date list of registered charities on the CRA website, and view the information in a database manager such as Access® or a spreadsheet such as the 2007 version of Excel®. You can also find out which charities have been added to the database and which ones have had their charitable status revoked. There may be a perfectly innocuous reason behind a revocation, but then again, maybe there isn't. If the charity you're investigating has had its status revoked, find out why.

Following the trail of the charity with the revoked status could lead somewhere. For instance, it helps to know the names of the individual directors, since you can use these to perform the kind of background searches that we described in Chapter 7. Have they ever been sued? Do they have a dubious business background? This is why it's also helpful to request a CD—free of charge—from the Revenue Agency that contains all the financial information on each charity that goes beyond what's available on the agency's website.

Foundations and airport authorities

Increasingly, governments are depending on arms-length agencies to deliver services. The federal government under the Chrétien–Martin Liberal regime created Millennium Scholarships to dole out money that benefits post-secondary students, even though the responsibility for education resides with the provinces.

The feds have created other foundations to deliver a range of services, including health research and projects to promote sustainable development. Foundations such as Millennium Scholarships have websites where you'll find information such as annual reports.[36] When investigating a foundation, it's important to read audits and annual reports, then find out how it is organized. Ask the same questions as when investigating charities: Who sits on the board of directors? What kinds of histories do these individuals have? Did they ever make political donations or accept any money from the government through consulting firms? We can also go further by demanding what reports the foundation is obliged to file to the minister in charge. Is it only an annual report? Or is it something else? Ask when the foundation was last audited and the reason for the audit. Airport authorities also exist at an arm's length from the federal government. They were created just after the federal Liberals swept back to power in October 1993, on the heels of two terms of majority Tory rule. It was good politics to talk about smaller government. The Liberal transport minister at the time, Doug Young, initiated the partial dismantlement of his ministry by getting it out of the business of running major airports such as the ones in Vancouver, Toronto, Ottawa, Montreal, Halifax, and St John's. That task was handed over to non-profit airport authorities. Such outfits were also created for medium-sized airports, including those in Kingston (Ontario) and Cranbrook (British Columbia). These new entities stressed that they could run the airports more efficiently, raising money not through tax increases that would hit everyone, but through measures such as fees charged to passengers and air carriers. The heads of these authorities are frequently quoted in newspapers, on television, and on the radio, usually complaining about the leasing agreements they have with the federal government or defending themselves against complaints about user fees, which always seem to be increasing. For journalists, these authorities should be covered with the same diligence as any business that is offering a vital service. For instance, airport authorities are obliged to file reports about steps they're taking to secure a safe environment for planes to take off and land. Finding out when these reports are filed, and obtaining them—usually through an access-to-information request—can reveal details about problems the authority may have with problems such as keeping birds away from its airspace.[37]

As entities that operate like businesses, airport authorities are allowed to borrow money, which means that they are rated, just like any other corporation, according to their ability to pay debts on time. An airport authority that has a dubious track record in this regard may have trouble raising the necessary cash for that needed expansion, which might increase the pressure for more user fees.

Crown corporations
Crown corporations are extensions of the federal and provincial governments, but some operate at a greater arm's length than others. Like foundations, they have a separate board of directors that makes decisions independently of government. A cabinet minister usually appoints people to sit on the board, and the directors must file reports and financial statements to a cabinet minister. These reports should be available for the asking, either informally or through access to information.

Crown corporations—including operations such as the CBC and Canada Post, which are considered to be 'commercial' Crown corporations—are now covered by the *Access to Information Act*. To be sure, they publish annual reports and other information on their websites but it may not be the kind of juicy material that embroiled Canada Post in the Chrétien–Martin sponsorship scandal (AdScam), when it was involved in dubious advertising schemes. During the time of AdScam in the early 2000s, the Canada Post website never divulged the details that led to the resignation of Canada Post's CEO, former Liberal cabinet minister André Ouelette, after questions were raised about his spending habits. Some of that information is contained in detailed audits, which, as we saw during the Gomery Inquiry that investigated the scandal, aren't always made available. In other instances, reporters can use access to information to demand the expense accounts of the executives running these corporations. If the expenses are exorbitant at a time when the corporation is experiencing financial problems, then you have a good story that leads to more questions.

Some audits may appear to be available on the corporation websites but these are often mere summaries that leave out details about spending habits. During the Gomery Inquiry, journalists learned just how misleading these abridged versions of audits can be. As a reporter, you must never be satisfied with the summarized versions. The details are the key to your story, so always ask for as many as possible.

Agencies

Agencies are also separate from the government, and are supposed to be run more efficiently because they have more flexibility to hire and fire staff as they see fit—just as a private business would do. They include the Canadian Food Inspection Agency (CFIA), which was at the heart of the listeriosis crisis that erupted in the summer of 2008 when 22 Canadians died after eating tainted meat from a Maple Leaf Foods meat-processing plant in Toronto. Stories, including those produced by a joint CBC-*Toronto Star* investigation, raised serious questions about the agency's ability to ensure food safety at a time when food companies are assuming more responsibility for policing themselves.[38] Fortunately, agencies such as the CFIA are covered by access-to-information legislation, which means journalists can obtain records that the agencies may not want to share. This was the case when the CBC and the *Toronto Star* used the *Access to Information Act* to obtain inspection records from the CFIA that shed light on the level at which the Maple Leaf plant was being monitored months leading up to what would become the largest food recall in Canadian history.[39]

Getting Information from Outside the Company

Consumer complaints

Consumers must have access to venues designed to handle their complaints, be it with the level of service or the quality of a product. Larger companies usually have their own in-house complaints procedures. Companies that are regulated may be answerable to a quasi-judicial body. Still, for small companies in your community, places such as the Better Business Bureau (*www.bbb.org/canada*) and the Consumers' Association of Canada (*www.consumer.ca*) should be kept in mind when looking for stories.

Quasi-judicial bodies

Quasi-judicial bodies are established by governments to adjudicate on matters from the adequacy of airline services to electricity rates to the abuse of human rights on the job.

For instance, people dissatisfied with carriers such as Air Canada or WestJet can complain to the air travel complaints commissioner, whose semi-annual reports are made public on the website of the Canadian Transportation Agency (*www.cta-otc.gc.ca*).

These bodies, which can also be government departments such as Health Canada, establish rules of conduct for many industries responsible for the food we eat, the drugs we consume, and the pollutants in the air we breathe. When companies break those rules, they are punished, usually through fines. Therefore, when you're on Health Canada's or the FDA's website, you should be looking for documents such as warning letters and enforcement actions.[40] The agencies also pass judgment on the quality of the products they regulate.

One case in point involves Relenza, a drug designed to combat influenza. Glaxo Wellcome Inc, known at the time (1999) as GlaxoSmithKline, hailed this product as a wonder drug. The headlines in the Canadian print and broadcast media reflected that optimistic assessment. The problem was that Relenza was no miracle; in fact, if the reporters had bothered to do a quick check on the FDA's website by plugging in the drug's name into the search engine, they would have seen that the agency's assessment was more lukewarm, concluding that the drug was of only 'modest benefit'.[41]

It's also important to know which legislative committees, be they at the federal or provincial level, are responsible for monitoring certain sectors of the economy. It becomes useful to examine the pieces of legislation that committees review, the witnesses they call before them, and so on. And, because many of the businesses we cover tend to operate in the United States—drug companies and car makers being among them—it's useful to peruse the legislative committees in that country. For instance, Democratic congressman Bart Stupak had his staff pull together information about the drug Accutane after his teenage son committed suicide while on the drug.[42] Research like this may be available to you on US congressional websites. You should also search *Hansard* in Canada for committee minutes.

Analysts

If you're researching a public company, and you've located an analyst who may be a good contact, then you'll want to find out what that analyst and others have written about the industry. As with any source, it's important to determine the analyst's potential bias. If the analyst in question has only positive things to say about a company, make sure that the person doesn't have a financial stake in how well the company performs. Any conflict of interest should be stated up front. This aside, the analyst and the journalist share much in common.

'In a way, both the reporter and the analyst are in the same job,' writes Chris Roush in his book, *Show Me the Money*. 'They both inform people about companies, and they both go about their jobs by asking questions and examining a company's operations. The only difference is that a reporter does his or her job to better inform readers, whereas the analyst does his or her job to better inform investors.' Roush goes on to recommend that reporters find analysts who have shown themselves willing to be critical of companies.[43]

Journalists can also find experts at universities and colleges that have schools of business. The same credibility checks should be performed to determine possible conflicts of interest, but business professors are often more independent than professional analysts. Their expertise may be gained by studying the company for the purposes of teaching courses such as business ethics.

Unions

The power of trade unions isn't what it used to be. Only a fraction of the workforce in Canada and the United States is unionized. Still, many employees for large employers such as automakers and federal government agencies such as the Canadian Food Inspection Agency belong to unions that study the industry very carefully.[44] Because the unions negotiate contract provisions, such as wages and working conditions, they can provide insight into the company as an employer. As well, they may be in touch with whistle-blowers seeking job protection over internal complaints about unethical, or even illegal, practices. These days, some unions use access-to-information and freedom-of information laws to extract even more data. The union might be concerned about the company's increasing tendency to cut corners and save money by flouting certain safety regulations. To get documented proof of such activities, the union might have pursued inspection reports or correspondence within Transport Canada, the CFIA, or the provincial agriculture ministry.

A union may not be interested in painting its employer in too positive a light, especially during contract negotiations, so use its information with that in mind. Nevertheless, unions should not be overlooked. It's worth establishing good relations with people in the union, everyone from the executives in the head office to the shop stewards who tend to be in closer contact with the workers and so are most likely to know which workers have complained about profligate spending or unsafe working conditions.

Finding former employees

Former employees may or may not be able to talk. You may be able to locate them with the help of a union, but if the workplace is non-unionized or the person was an executive, then you have to depend on your own legwork. In many instances, former employees are forced to sign confidentiality agreements, under which they receive 'hush money' in exchange for promising to keep quiet. In other instances, the employee may not want to talk, preferring instead to leave the past behind and move on, especially if the person still works in the same industry. However, there are times when former employees want to come forward, either because it's a matter of extreme public interest, or simply because they've never been approached by reporters and they like the attention. The possibility that someone may talk means journalists should always be on the hunt for ex-employees. Perhaps they've been quoted in newspaper articles. Perhaps they have their own website, blog, or account on a social-networking site such as Facebook or Twitter. Or perhaps they've been referred to in a discussion group or listserv. They may even have already complained to a regulatory body.

Julie Ireton, a business reporter for the CBC, tracked down a former Nortel employee in Texas who had complained about the company to the Securities and Exchange Commission back in the late 1990s. Nothing ever came of the complaint, and the man moved on to become a university professor. Unconcerned about the confidentiality agreement he had signed with Nortel, the former employee agreed to talk and, even more importantly, appear on camera, helping Ireton's story on Nortel lead CBC's *The National* two nights in a row.[45]

Conclusion

The ability to follow the money on any beat separates the great journalist from the mediocre one and helps tell stories that matter most to your readers, listeners, and viewers. The way people and institutions spend money can tell us more about their character than just about any of their other actions or what they say about themselves in public. The money angle also helps us avoid the spin.

In the case of Royal Crest Lifecare Group Inc., Steve Buist of *The Hamilton Spectator* used court documents in a bankruptcy case to peel back the veil of a private corporation that ran nursing and retirement homes in a dubious fashion to the dismay of creditors, government officials, nursing-home workers, and residents. Enhanced scrutiny is important at a time when an increasing number of for-profit companies are operating public facilities such as nursing homes and daycare centres in communities across the country.

Larger publicly traded companies are always in the news, and, as such, we may feel intimidated about finding new and damaging information on them. But, as we saw in the case of Nortel, it is important to persist and read the fine print of large companies' financial statements.

We also saw, for smaller companies, the benefits of mining public documents in insolvency cases such as the one for Entegrity Wind Systems.

Companies, whether they are public or private, have a sphere of influence that goes well behind the enterprise itself, which means it is essential for journalists to hold them to account, either as corporate citizens, employers, or producers of certain products.

You need to look for documents, people, websites . . . anything that sheds light on areas that businesses would rather keep hidden from public scrutiny. You need to identify where to look and what questions to ask. Keep track of the dates when public companies must file their reports with the securities regulators. As soon as the reports are filed, scour them for news such as lawsuits, lost earnings or surprising numbers you won't find in news releases. Develop a good rapport with an expert who can help you compare the information contained in the numbers to what the company is saying publicly. The larger the disconnect, the better the story. Keep track of insolvency cases to find out if employers in your area are at risk of going under.

Above all, do not take companies at their word. Be skeptical—but not cynical. Get your own information from the regulators, consumers, courts, competitors, and creditors, particularly from people who are angry with the company and, therefore, won't mind sharing their information, which still needs to be verified.

Be relentless. Follow the money.

Suggestions for Further Reading

Fink, Conrad C. *Bottom Line Writing: Reporting the Sense of Dollars*. Ames, IA: Iowa State University Press, 2000, Chapters 6–8.

Roush, Chris. *Show Me the Money: Writing Business and Economics Stories for Mass Communications*. New York: Lawrence Erlbaum Associates, 2004, Chapters 1–4.

Taparia, Jay. *Understanding Financial Statements: A Journalist's Guide*. Portland, OR: Marion Street Press, 2004, Chapters 1–5.

Exercises

1. Use the bankruptcy statistics from the Office of the Superintendent of Bankruptcy Canada (*www.ic.gc.ca/eic/site/bsf-osb.nsf/eng/h_br01011.html*) to monitor business and consumer insolvencies, as Teresa Wright from *The Guardian* did with her story entitled, 'Number of Islanders filing for bankruptcy takes dramatic rise: Numbers up by almost 37 per cent in a year'.[46]

2. Find a company in your area that is facing insolvency. Follow the developments and read the documents for stories that other people aren't telling or that the company is avoiding.

3. Choose a publicly traded company that is also a major employer in your market and use proxy statements to track what their executives have been making during a three-to-five-year period. You'll have to dump the numbers into a spreadsheet and do the math yourself. Once you've completed the calculations, contrast the executives' wage hikes with the salary increases of

the company's front-line workers. If there's a large disparity that has gone unnoticed, then you have a good story. Increasingly, this is what newspapers such as *The New York Times* are doing.[47]

4. Perform the same task, this time with executives who work for the public sector in your province or territory. In jurisdictions such as Ontario, governments post salaries of bureaucrats who make more than $100,000 a year.[48] Included in these databases are large salaries of CEOs of hospitals and Crown corporations, who may have trouble balancing budgets and giving their employees decent raises but are receiving handsome salaries and yearly wage increases nonetheless.

5. Use some basic ratios—profit margin, operating margin, return on equity, return on assets, price-to-earnings ratio—to analyze a publicly traded companies for a three-to-five-year period.[49] For definitions of these ratios, please see Appendix C of this book on page 317. In his book *Understanding Financial Statements*, Jay Taparia writes, 'Entering the figures into a spreadsheet will help you learn the numbers. Not only will you start to understand the business, you will also start to see trends (and maybe even some parts of the story).'[50]

10

Getting Behind Closed Doors:
Using the Information Laws

Some of the most important knowledge we have about how we are governed has come from disclosures under access-to-information and freedom-of-information laws.

Introduction

Hidden somewhere in a thick pile of federal sponsorship funding documents, Daniel Leblanc and Campbell Clark uncovered what would lead to their light-bulb moment. It came in an inconspicuous reference to an advertising firm report commissioned by the federal government to provide the Liberal Party of Canada with advice on increasing their public visibility. The *Globe and Mail* reporters filed an access-to-information request for the document. It never came. But the report's absence, rather than its contents, became the real story that launched a political scandal. Two years later, bureaucrats finally admitted there was no such report.

The story Leblanc had been casually pursuing on federal government spon-sorships of community events across the country suddenly took on a dramatic new dimension, he recalls. '[The story] was suddenly about a probable fraud case instead of just wacky spending,' Leblanc says.

In March 2002, Leblanc and Clark reported in the *Globe* that the Jean Chrétien government paid $550,000 for a report by the Liberal-friendly Group-action Marketing 'of which no trace can be found.'[1]

'Documents also show, in a separate $575,000 contract signed with the gov-ernment, Groupaction agreed to undertake two specific tasks, but the company only delivered on one. Groupaction said it did a partial job after reaching an agreement with the bureaucrat in charge of the program,' the story reported. 'It will now prove difficult for the government to defend the $1.1 million in contracts to a generous Liberal donor, with little to show for its payment but 122 pages for the second report.'[2]

The story was among the first in a Pandora's box of revelations about the waste of millions of taxpayer dollars, soon generating headlines and dominating news broadcasts across the country. The stories would trigger deep public outrage, a high-profile inquiry and prompt criminal charges against a federal bureaucrat and the heads of three advertising firms. Federal access-to-information (ATI) and provincial freedom-of-information (FOI) legislation is our most forceful legal expression of the public's right to know. These laws give citizens the legal right to request records held by governments at all levels. They offer journalists, researchers, and any Canadian citizen the ability to look beyond the public record to learn more about hidden government actions, policies, and decisions.

'The overarching purpose of access to information legislation is to facilitate democracy,' according to a 1997 judgment by former Supreme Court of Canada justice Gerard La Forest. 'It does so in two related ways. It helps to ensure first, that citizens have the information required to participate meaningfully in the democratic process, and secondly, that politicians and bureaucrats remain accountable to the citizenry.'[3]

Access-to-information and freedom-of-information laws have long been used by journalists, politicians, citizens, community groups, researchers, and companies to obtain numerous public records, including data, correspondence, briefing notes, and memos. For the investigative journalist, access requests are a basic research tool. The legislation opens the door for in-depth research into the machinations of government, the reasons why decisions are made, and their impact on the public. If used strategically, information laws can help us discover how taxpayer dollars are spent, warn us of public health risks, uncover corruption, and hold elected officials to account.

Some of the most important knowledge we have about how we are governed has come from disclosures under access-to-information and freedom-of-information laws. These disclosures have helped inform us about the troubling conduct of Canadian soldiers in Somalia and police officers in Toronto. They have detailed the misspending of public money, including cost overruns at the firearms registry and the so-called 'billion-dollar boondoggle' at Human Resources Development Canada in the 1990s. They have allowed us to know about the neglect of elderly people in nursing homes and the abuse of children in daycares. And they have brought to our attention health threats like food-borne illnesses, safety inspection oversights, and potentially fatal adverse drug reactions.

Ideally, there would be no need for legislation dictating formal procedures for requesting and accessing public records. Governments would release information of this nature upon request as a matter of routine in the service of the public interest. But human and political instincts dictate otherwise. And information laws, while valuable, are by no means an assurance that important information will be made public. Any routine user of information laws knows that it can be extremely difficult to obtain public records if governments don't wish to release them.

There are growing concerns about the accessibility of public information in Canada, especially among journalists. Canadians do not read, see, or hear nearly as many access-to-information stories as fill US newspapers and news reports, largely because Canadian journalists cannot access records that are routinely available in the States. Many fear the regulatory regime is getting increasingly restrictive.

Countless volumes of public information in Canada are locked in government filing cabinets, tightly guarded by eagle-eyed bureaucrats. Often, it takes months, even years, to access information that should be provided within days. Often, high fees for the records put them beyond the reach of many requesters. And even when records are released, the contents can be 'severed'—or blacked out—thus rendering documents meaningless.

A philosophical bent toward self-protection and secrecy dominates many government offices across Canada. And while freedom-of-information laws act as a counter to those human tendencies, their efficacy is highly limited and remains subject to the whims of bureaucrats. It is the product of what former federal information commissioner John Reid calls a 'culture of secrecy' within government.

'The greatest shortcomings in the right of access are not shortcomings in the words of the [*Access to Information*] *Act* but in the deeds of those who administer the Act,' Reid wrote in his 2000/01 annual report. 'The Act is administered all too often as a secrecy statute. All too often the test used by officials is: "If in doubt, keep it secret"—a test which has been specifically rejected by the Federal Court.'[4] Bureaucratic rejection of fundamental rules of public access is an expression of resistance against the surrender of control to legislation that would make powerful, potentially damaging, information part of the public record, he wrote.

'The access law—with a positive right of access by anyone present in Canada to most records held by government, coupled with a deadline for response—constitutes a frontal attack on both of these perceived virtues of secrecy. Consequently, there is every incentive for officials to resist, if not impede, the operation of the law.'[5]

When they do, there's little in the way of consequences.

In 2009, then-information commissioner Robert Marleau lamented the lack of enforcement mechanisms in the legislation when bureaucrats undermine the spirit of the act. 'There are few incentives to comply with the Act's requirements, and even fewer consequences for not doing so,' he wrote in his 2008/09 annual report. 'Much more is needed to bring about a true culture of openness and transparency, and allow Canada to regain its status as a leader in the area of access to information.'[6]

While criticism of government secrecy from within the government is rare (except from information commissioners, charged with the duty of monitoring the issue), other high-ranking officials have occasionally expressed concern. In his final report to the House of Commons in 2001, titled *Reflections on a Decade of Serving Parliament*, former auditor general Denis Desautels made candid observations about government secrecy:

There is a reluctance to let Parliament and the public know how government programs are working, because if things are going badly you may be giving your opponents the stick to beat you with. And even when a minister is not personally concerned about this, senior public servants assume this fear on the minister's behalf. The people who write government performance reports seem to try to say as little as possible that would expose their department to criticism.[7]

Desautels added that government aversion to openness has much to do with the outdated concept of 'ministerial accountability' in the Canadian political system:

> In every Westminster-style government, ministers are responsible to Parliament for the state of their departments. Unlike other countries, however, Canada has never modernized its doctrine to distinguish between the minister's area of public responsibility and that of his senior public servants. To me, there is a certain lack of realism in holding ministers ultimately accountable for everything. Overall, our system makes it difficult to be candid and therefore Parliament has a hard time in discussing certain issues with officials.'[8]

As it stands, the prevailing bureaucratic mindset encourages public servants to protect their political bosses by withholding potentially damaging information from public release, regardless of the information laws. One of the most troublesome expressions of those internal efforts to undermine public access to records is the practice of failing to keep records in the first place. Records that don't exist can't be released to the public, goes the logic.

That unspoken technique was exposed most notoriously in the wake of AdScam, the federal sponsorship scandal of the early 2000s. Charles Guité, the former bureaucrat at the centre of the controversial program, testified under oath before the Public Accounts Committee that sponsorship records were not kept in order to evade the *Access to Information Act*.[9]

In the aftermath of a public inquiry into AdScam, the presiding Justice—John Gomery—said the public's ability to access information about its government has fallen into crisis. 'In Canada, official secrecy continues to operate as the governing culture,' he said in 2009. 'Canada compares very poorly to almost every other democracy in the world.'[10]

What all of this means—the culture of secrecy along with outdated and restrictive legislation—is that requests for what is often clearly public information can be routinely denied or delayed far beyond reason. It means Canadians know far less than they should about government actions and their implications.

Despite those challenges, there are ways to access important public records, to learn the system, and to challenge unreasonable delays and denials from overly secretive bureaucrats. In this chapter, we explain those ways.

The Laws

One might assume that legislation designed to provide access to public records would be heavily used by journalists. But a relatively small percentage of reporters actually file requests as a matter of routine—evidence of how cumbersome and slow the process can be.

Usually, ATI and FOI requests are not useful for reporters working on tight deadlines. It's not generally a tool for breaking news stories. It is a method of pursuing issues that are likely to be as important in a month or two as they are now, stories that go beyond the press release or official comment of the day. And it's a way of pursuing issues that aren't part of the public debate at all, but should be.

Because this is a practical research guide, we will not dwell too long on legal details of the various information laws across the country. It is important, however, to understand the basic legal foundations upon which citizens file requests for information to governments. The general principles underlying provincial and federal information laws are the same: to establish a right to access government-held documents, to detail the limits or 'exemptions' to that right, and to establish an appeal procedure if access is denied. The laws express the democratic belief that governments must be open and accountable.

In Canada, we have a federal *Access to Information Act* as well as separate provincial and territorial freedom-of-information laws. The fundamental utility of these is similar. They generally impose a 30-day deadline for government departments to respond to written requests for information; the departments can, however, request extensions. The laws outline fees for access, including fees for receiving filed requests, compiling the records, and providing copies of documents. They list the agencies covered by the legislation and the specific records that are exempt.

The various laws differ in their specific exemptions to access, the relative effectiveness of the appeals processes, and the fees imposed. Delays in accessing records can also vary widely among government departments across the country.

Exemptions

Legislated exemptions to access often present the most serious challenge to obtaining government records. All information laws in Canada detail specific records that cannot be released. These might include internal government deliberations, business secrets, documents that could breach solicitor–client privilege, records containing personal information, cabinet confidences, law-enforcement and national-security records, and documents covering federal–provincial relations. Some of those exemptions are considered 'discretionary' and are therefore open to interpretation. As such, they can be challenged by requesters.

It's not uncommon to receive hundreds of pages of records from an ATI request only to find the vast majority of words blacked out in response to specific legislated exemptions. Variation also exists in how wide a net the different laws cast over the institutions they cover. For example, some provincial freedom-of-information laws apply to universities and professional self-regulatory bodies, but in much of the country, those institutions—which carry out vital public interest work—are beyond the reach of legislated public scrutiny.

Institutions or specific documents excluded by the information laws are, by definition, outside the scope of public access. Requesters have virtually no recourse in these circumstances. Although they can appeal a request denial, the chances of success are extremely low. Any piece of legislation is open to interpretation, however, and when it comes to information laws, those interpretations can play a vital role in determining whether a record should be made public. Many ATI and FOI researchers say governments frequently interpret exemptions and limitations to the widest possible extent in order to argue against release of records. Rather than presuming a right of access, experienced researchers in Canada often brace for the bureaucratic default position of 'No' when filing sensitive information requests.

'When you're asking for information, you're going against the natural bureaucratic tendency to be cautious,' says Alasdair Roberts, a leading Canadian scholar on information laws.[11]

Clear restrictions in the legislation need to be fairly and judiciously observed, but many requesters and experts argue that exemptions are applied in ways that block the release of information that should be public. Government departments 'often don't bother with reasons to support secrecy, unless and until there is a complaint,' John Reid wrote in his 2003/04 annual report. 'Too often, departments have been content to address only the question: "May the requested records be kept secret?"'[12]

Fees

Fees for accessing government records in Canada vary from province to province. The three main fees are an initial application fee, the cost of retrieving the records, and the cost of appealing information-request decisions.

The initial fee to file a request is $5 at the federal level and in some provinces. Other provinces do not charge for this. The highest fee is in Alberta, where requesters are charged $25 up front.

By far the most onerous fees associated with information requests are those charged for researching, retrieving, and vetting the records. Once a government department researches your request and locates the records, it will estimate the cost of researching and preparing them. It may assign no fee if the request was precise and specific to a single record or two. Large requests, asking for hundreds of pages of documents or requiring computer work to prepare a government database for release, can cause fee estimates to balloon to thousands of dollars.

Federally, your $5 request buys you a few hours of research time before the extra fees apply. So dividing large requests into several smaller requests helps maximize the bonus search time you receive. At the provincial level, the initial fee for filing a request generally includes no search time, so the costs start to add up the moment civil servants begin the work of locating the records. That means fee estimates at the provincial and municipal levels are often higher.

Requesters generally have the right to request fee waivers for retrieval and photocopying based on either an inability to pay for the records or because releasing the information would serve the public interest. This requires a written appeal outlining the reasons. While journalistic requests are clearly made in the public interest—as opposed to personal or business requests that serve private interests—government officials rarely award the fee waivers without additional compelling arguments.

The third major fee, related to appeal submissions, also varies. Some provinces let you file appeals free of charge, but most don't. In Ontario, for example, an appeal to the provincial information and privacy commissioner must be accompanied by a cheque for $25. The varying menu of fees in different jurisdictions can produce very different financial burdens for requesters. High fees represent a significant impediment to access because, while major media outlets may be able to afford hundreds or thousands of dollars for records of vital importance, smaller outlets or individuals may not. For the public, those financial restrictions can spell the difference between learning about matters of importance and remaining in the dark.

Some government officials argue that administering information laws is expensive, requiring rising fees in order to ensure 'cost recovery'. It's a position quickly challenged by access advocates who call access to public information a right as fundamental as voting.

Delays

The legislation may impose a 20- or 30-day deadline by which government records are to be provided to requesters, but that deadline frequently comes and goes without disclosure. Requesters have waited many months, even years, for records to be released.

While straightforward requests for simple reports or studies are often fulfilled within the statutory time limit, more complex requests dealing with large numbers of records or politically sensitive documents generally take much longer. Many journalists tell stories of information requests that dragged on well beyond reasonable time frames, sometimes reaching into years.

A sweeping 2008 study of global information laws by Canadian journalist Stanley Tromp found Canada's federal law fails to meet international standards on 12 key points set out by a London-based human-rights organization and endorsed by the United Nations Special Rapporteur on Freedom of Opinion and Expression.

'Some departments are so backlogged that they automatically add extensions of more than 100 days to most, if not all, requests,' writes Tromp. 'Other agencies grant themselves a 240-day extension—three times the previous average.'[13]

There is a strongly held belief in journalistic circles that bureaucratic delay is an intentional—and often effective—technique for undermining the public's right to know. In many journalistic cases, information delayed is information denied. Time-sensitive records can lose all value if their release is significantly delayed. Consider, for example, a government decision on whether to protect a particular green space or deport someone to his or her native country. Records explaining the context and details surrounding those decisions could have a vital impact on the public debate, but only if they are made public in a timely way. If release is withheld until after the person is deported or the green space has given way to a tower block, that information is clearly not much use any more, and citizens have been robbed of their ability to engage fully in public debate.

In 2004, *Edmonton Journal* reporters Karen Kleiss and Charles Rusnell filed a request for 'all records related to the flight logs for all government aircraft' for a 17-month period. It would take a six-month battle and $900 in fees before the records were finally released—two days after the 2004 provincial election. What the records showed—and what Albertans weren't allowed to know when they cast their ballots—was that then-premier Ralph Klein's government had a fleet of four aircraft that cost taxpayers more than $3.5 million a year to operate, the *Journal* reported. 'Planes flew empty 235 times, travelling enough kilometres to circle the Earth more than 1½ times, at a cost of at least $250,000,' wrote Kleiss and Rusnell. 'There is virtually no oversight to ensure the fleet is not being used for personal or political reasons.'[14]

Alberta's privacy commissioner later ruled in 2007 that the Klein government 'deliberately and for political purposes withheld information about the government's use of aircraft until after the 2004 provincial election.'[15]

'When one places the timeline of events regarding the processing of the request up against the timelines of the provincial election, it is very difficult to come to a different conclusion,' the commissioner stated. 'The public body would have me believe that two sets of events are purely coincidental and that it was impossible to make the records available any sooner. The evidence does not support such a finding.'[16]

Government departments negotiate delays by requesting extensions to their 30-day deadlines. While requesters can appeal those extensions, it is often more productive to allow the first of these because an appeal will stop the entire process while the issue is resolved. Time extensions of 30 or even 60 days may, in some cases, be justified by the volume of records that need to be collected and reviewed. Challenging necessary delays may serve only to incite an adversarial relationship with government officials that could lead to even more procrastination.

When delays become unreasonable, with one extension turning into two or three, and when it becomes clear that a department or agency is dragging its feet, it may be time to file a formal appeal. We'll deal with this process in detail later.

Here are links to the various information laws and appeal bodies across the country:

Federal
- *Access to Information Act*: http://laws.justice.gc.ca/en/A-1
- Office of the Information Commissioner: *www.infocom.gc.ca*
- Office of the Privacy Commissioner: *www.privcom.gc.ca*

Alberta
- *Alberta Freedom of Information and Protection of Privacy Act*: http://foip.alberta.ca
- Office of the Information and Privacy Commissioner of Alberta: *www.oipc.ab.ca*

British Columbia
- *BC Freedom of Information and Protection of Privacy Act*: *www.oipcbc.org/legislation.htm*
- BC Information and Privacy Commissioner: *www.oipcbc.org*

Manitoba
* *Freedom of Information and Protection of Privacy Act*: *www.gov.mb.ca/chc/fippa/*
* Office of the Manitoba Ombudsman: *www.ombudsman.mb.ca*

New Brunswick
* *Right to Information and Protection of Privacy Act*: *www.gnb.ca/0062/acts/acts/ r-10-6.htm*
* Office of the Ombudsman: *www.gnb.ca/0073/index-e.asp*

Northwest Territories
* *Access to Information and Protection of Privacy Act*: *www.justice.gov.nt.ca/PDF/ ACTS/Access_to_Information.pdf*
* Information and Privacy Commissioner: *www.justice.gov.nt.ca/ATIPP/index. shtml*

Nova Scotia
* *Freedom of Information and Protection of Privacy Act*: *www.gov.ns.ca/legislature/legc/ statutes/freedom.htm*
* Freedom of Information and Protection of Privacy Review Office: *www. foipop.ns.ca*

Nunavut
* *Access to Information and Protection of Privacy Act*: *www.info-privacy.nu.ca/en/ legislation*
* Information and Privacy Commissioner: *www.info-privacy.nu.ca*

Ontario
* *Access to Information and Protection of Privacy Act*: *www.e-laws.gov.on.ca/html/statutes/ english/elaws_statutes_90f31_e.htm*
* *Municipal Freedom of Information and Protection of Privacy Act*: *www.e-laws.gov. on.ca/html/statutes/english/elaws_statutes_90m56_e.htm*
* Information and Privacy Commissioner: *www.ipc.on.ca*

Prince Edward Island
* *Freedom of Information and Protection of Privacy Act*: *www.gov.pe.ca/attorneygeneral*
* Office of the Information and Privacy Commissioner: *www.assembly.pe.ca/ foipp/index.php*

Quebec
* *An Act Respecting Access to Documents Held By Public Bodies and the Protection of Personal Information*: *www2.publicationsduquebec.gouv.qc.ca/dynamicSearch/ telecharge.php?type=2&file=/A_2_1/A2_1_A.html*
* Commission d'accès à l'information du Québec: *www.cai.gouv.qc.ca/index-en. html*

Saskatchewan

- *Freedom of Information and Protection of Privacy Act*: *www.justice.gov.sk.ca/ Freedom-of-Information-and-Protection-of-Privacy-Act*
- Freedom of Information and Privacy Commissioner: *www.justice.gov.sk.ca/ AP-IPC*

Yukon

- *Access to Information and Protection of Privacy Act*: *www.atipp.gov.yk.ca*
- Yukon Ombudsman and Information & Privacy Commissioner: *www. ombudsman.yk.ca*

How to Make Your Request

Researching

The first step in obtaining government records is not filing an information request. In fact, filing a formal written request should only happen after exhausting all informal methods of obtaining the records. Simply asking for them is the best initial approach. It may be that you need to ask the question in different ways or tailor the request to respond to any concerns from government officials. But if you're able to get what you need informally, you will almost certainly be far ahead in terms of time and effort. It's always worth pointing out to government officials that information laws in Canada were not designed to replace routine disclosure of information.

In many cases, however, formal information requests are unavoidable. As a matter of course, many public servants refer all requests for information, regardless of how simple or straightforward, to ATI and FOI offices. Getting past that reflex response can be difficult, but there are basic public records that fall under what should be 'routine disclosure' by governments. If the documents you seek clearly fall within that category, it's important to make a strong case for routine disclosure. Citing the appropriate law and what it says about routine disclosure might help you avoid having to go the formal route.

If you're seeking records that contain personal information, potentially sensitive material, or that deal with companies or government conduct, a written request will almost certainly be required. You still need to do research before filing a request, however. The more informed and detailed your question, the more complete and precise the response will have to be. Filing a well-crafted information request can take a lot of work. You may need details of a government department's record-keeping and managerial processes, or a company's subsidiaries and regulatory background. The more you know about the question, the better your chances of plucking out the most relevant and important records from government files.

There are effectively two kinds of ATI requests:

The fishing expedition

These requests are broader in scope and use open-ended language. Fishing expeditions tend to be requests for records about a particular subject using phrases such as: 'including, but not limited to, memos, reports, studies and briefing notes regarding . . .'

Requesters who use this approach deliberately employ all-encompassing language as a means of capturing records which they may not know exist. You can't always find out the names of specific records you want before you file a request. Information requests of this kind are often used as a method of determining what records exist on a particular matter and what they contain. The danger with open-ended requests of this nature is the volume of material they can cover. While you want to know as much as you can about the records you're seeking, such a broad approach can land you a vast pile of documents, containing little of interest and slowing down your work. And a voluminous stash of records generally entails fee estimates ranging into the hundreds or thousands of dollars.

You may need to streamline a broad request in order to reduce fees. When surrendering some records in order to reduce volume, many researchers attempt to get a catalogue of the potentially relevant records so they're aware of both what they're getting and what they're not. The fishing expedition can result in an inventory of government records including document titles and basic details about them. That information, while not the records themselves, can be extremely valuable. Once you understand what records exist, what they're called, and how they're maintained, subsequent requests can be far more specific and precise.

The surgical approach

Your best footing for an information request comes when you know the specific question you want answered, or, even better, the specific documents or records that contain those answers. The more specific the question, the more specific the response must be. A request for a government study of illegal immigration, named by title and date, will trigger a much faster and positive response than a request for all records related to illegal immigration over the past 10 years. Likewise, a request asking for a particular inspection database, detailing the individual fields of interest and the time frame you wish to cover, will generate a more helpful reply than if you ask for all data from a large number of inspections, some of which may contain personal information and other exempted material. The goal is to compile a well-researched, unambiguous question. Vague, indecipherable requests are doomed to languish in fees and delays.

Whether you're filing a broader request or a surgical one, you'd be well advised to do as much research up front as possible so that your wording is as clear and defined as possible. That means doing a good deal of reconnaissance work before filing requests, to get a good understanding of how a government department maintains its records, what the records contain, and what they're called internally.

One of the best ways to do this is to speak to insiders at the particular government department who are willing to help you understand the issues that are going to raise alarm bells, and who can give you advice on how to address these. Such people are a great resource for helping to craft a specific request; their knowledge of a department's paper trail can be immensely valuable.

In cases of government tender requests, unsuccessful bidders can be helpful in providing background on the players and procedures behind the scenes.

When requesting databases, you should attempt to find out as much as possible about the data, how it's stored, and what fields it contains. Ask the department's officials for a one-page printout of a sample of the data, listing its fields. From there, you can determine which fields are likely to be protected by privacy legislation and which should be public. That lets you craft a far more specific request, which is likely to succeed. Doing such work up front saves time later.

Public directories are good sources if they outline the sorts of records that governmental departments maintain, what these records are called, and what they contain. A number of resources provide such information, although it can often be selective or unclear. In Chapter 4, we describe some of these. One to emphasize at the federal level is Info Source (*www.infosource.gc.ca*), an immensely useful directory of government records subject to access-to-information requests, listed by department and agency. Choose 'Sources of Federal Government Information', then choose 'List of Institutions' in the left-hand column. Then, select the ministry or department of interest from the list; next, click on 'Institution-Specific Classes of Records' on the left.

The online catalogue at Info Source provides a complete list of records by name with content descriptions and program record numbers which the departments use to identify the materials. If you're researching refugee issues, for example, you might be interested in a catalogue of records held by the federal Immigration and Refugee Board. Info Source tells you about such records as the Immigration Appeal Division Case Files (program record number: IRB OPS 005), which detail individual appeals including '[i]nformation, evidence, exhibits, arguments and submissions upon which the Board makes its decisions.'

The Transportation Safety Board, which investigates transportation accidents or concerns, lists among its records all marine, air, rail, and pipeline investigation reports, including 'safety deficiencies, safety recommendations, and advisories.'

It's also helpful to review the 'Standard Classes of Records' listed in the left-hand column for a more general listing of federal records.

Filing the request

The federal government and many provincial/territorial governments provide standard forms for access-to-information requests. In some cases, those forms may be mandatory but usually a simple letter is sufficient. Always use clear language and consider any imprecision in your wording that could trigger confusion and delays.

It's also helpful to predict any potential problems and address them in advance. For example, if the records you are requesting are likely to contain personal information that would be covered by privacy exemptions, then you should specify that you are waiving any demand for that material.

Address your request to the appropriate information coordinator or municipal officials in the department or office responsible for the information, and include any required payment for filing the request in the form of a cheque attached to your request. Officials will probably not begin processing your request until they have received payment.

The initial response

In most cases, government departments should respond, within a week or so, with a standard form letter indicating that your request has been received and that the department has begun researching the records. You might also receive a phone call from a government official asking for clarification. If your request is overly broad, you may receive an early warning about the potential cost or delays. This is an early opportunity to refine your request to speed up the process without sacrificing essential material.

Time and space are two common parameters for limiting requests. If you've asked for 10 years' worth of records, for example, cutting that time frame in half should quickly reduce response time and cost. Likewise, rather than asking for records for the entire province or region, limiting the request to a particular city or rural area should reduce the number of offices involved in collecting the records and, therefore, cut research time and cost.

It's a good idea to get a sense whether the ATI or FOI department plans to meet the legislated deadline for responding to your request. The earlier in the process you get a sense of the department's planned time frame, the better equipped you'll be either to edit your request or begin planning whether you want to appeal any extensions the department claims it needs.

Governments are obliged to respond in some way by the initial deadline. If that response is a denial or a partial disclosure of the records, the department must explain its decision by citing the specific exemptions that apply.

The next step

Journalists facing denials, long delays, or substantial fees for access to important public records have several options. These include abandoning the request altogether, requesting a detailed accounting of the costs, amending the request to reduce fees or, when all else fails, appealing the government department's decision. It's an important strategic decision in the investigative process.

Abandonment

Assuming you have a reasonable and important question, for which the answer remains hidden, walking away from a request should not be your instinctive response to a high fee estimate. It may be exactly what government bureaucrats are hoping for though. There is almost always another step in the negotiating process that can turn a closed door into one that is slightly ajar. You should be satisfied with abandoning the request only when you are certain that the questions or curiosity that launched your request are false or no longer valid. Even if you or your media outlet can't afford the fee levied by officials, there are strategies worth attempting before you give up.

Accounting

Exorbitant fees for FOI requests are a common complaint. Those fees may well be justifiable based on the staff time that would be required to compile the records. Government departments estimate fees based upon formulas regarding the cost of compiling, severing, and photocopying records. Those calculations should be made available to you, either in the response from the department or upon demand. Study the math carefully. It's up to you to understand and determine whether the rates are being fairly calculated.

Your being able to do that relies partly on understanding how the records are kept. For example, if you're asking for records that you know are already compiled in a database or single government file, you know that the work of producing them is fairly straightforward. If the records are spread out among various government offices across the province or the country, however, the compiling process will clearly take more time and effort, justifying greater fees.

If you feel the strain on staff time is being unfairly assessed, you can certainly request a detailed explanation of how the figure was calculated and argue for a reduced fee based on a more reasonable assessment.

Amendment

The most common method of addressing high fee estimates is amending your request. As we suggested earlier, you could reduce the number of records you want to request, or the geographical area to which they apply. If you asked for all records related to a massive subject area, get more surgical with your request.

It's a good idea to work through such amendments in consultation with the department's information coordinator. Talking through possible changes with a person familiar with the scope of your request and the rationale behind the fees should help you devise a new plan that will bring the costs down significantly and still provide enough material to make the records meaningful.

Be careful when you compromise on aspects of the request. If you're looking at how a particular government program has served the public, cutting down your request to six months' worth of records instead of a year's worth might render your resulting analysis vulnerable to criticism for failing to account for unique circumstances in that limited period of time. In the same way, a request that filters out important research can give rise to charges of unfair reporting. If you obtain reports critical of a particular foreign policy option without seeing contradictory material presented to officials, the resulting story could be dangerously one-sided.

When you begin shrinking your window of research, therefore, make sure the results reflect reality and allow you to report accurately. Ask officials what you would not be getting once you limit a request, and make sure you understand the limitations you will face when you begin writing.

It may be that such limitations are unavoidable because of cost and timing issues. If so, your responsibility is to be open and clear with your audience about what you do not know. Don't represent your research material as exhaustive when it is not. The records may still form the basis of an important story, but you should acknowledge any shortcomings in your evidence. You might also use the opportunity to question publicly why the public records are so difficult to access.

Appeals

There are a number of situations in which you should consider appealing a government department's decision not to let you have information. They include

- when governments have made an unreasonable use of exemptions to deny information;
- when fees imposed for access to the records are unreasonable; and
- when delays for accessing the records are unreasonable.

Appeals are directed to one of two offices depending on the level of government you're dealing with. For federal requests, you approach the federal information commission; provincial/territorial or municipal appeals are handled by access and privacy officials in each province and territory. Most Canadian jurisdictions have an appeals process in which ombudsmen or adjudicators consider submissions from both sides before issuing a decision based on the legislation. A mediator may first be assigned to attempt an informal resolution to the dispute.

In some cases, appeal rulings are binding. Ontario's information and privacy commissioner, for example, has the power to compel the release of records deemed to be public. The federal information commissioner and some provincial appeal bodies, however, don't have this power. Even if they rule in favour of the requester, the final decision regarding release of the records remains with government officials. Generally speaking, the moral suasion of an appeal decision is sufficient. If not, the appeal body may sometimes take the cases to court on behalf of the requester. Likewise, requesters who are unsatisfied with the findings of an appeal body can take their cases to court on their own.

Remember our earlier caution: appealing at the fee-estimate stage comes with a major pitfall, in that the access process stops the moment an appeal is filed. It does not resume until the conclusion of the appeal, which could take months.

Appealing is a more complex process than filing a request but it is entirely possible to conduct an appeal yourself without the assistance of a lawyer. That said, a good media lawyer will likely make the process easier. Journalists arguing for access to denied records most often make a case that release is in the public interest considering the media's ability to use such information to shed light on important issues, engage citizens in needed debate, and uncover matters worthy of public attention. A typical journalistic appeal argues that publishing the information benefits the public so much that the exemptions should be overridden. An interest is generally considered compelling if it triggers strong public attention, fosters accountability, or helps ensure the public's right to know matters of vital importance. That argument is, of course, subject to careful consideration by adjudicators and commissioners. Its merits are measured according to the nature of the specific information and the potential public-interest benefits. But appeals bodies across the country have accepted this argument and released exempted information in cases where the records fostered public scrutiny of government actions.[17]

In one example, the *Toronto Star* appealed a decision by Ontario's Ministry of Public Safety and Security to deny full access to a 21-page fire marshal's report into a pipeline explosion that destroyed a house near Hamilton in 2000. The ministry cited personal privacy exemption to deny access to the information. The *Star* argued that the public needed to know about the explosion and how such incidents were investigated. 'In the circumstances of this appeal, this public interest clearly overrides the purpose of the [personal privacy] exemption,' the newspaper argued in its submission.

The adjudicator found that the records did contain personal information subject to exemption, but he also found that the disclosure of the records

> is desirable for the purpose of subjecting the activities of the Government of Ontario and its agencies to public scrutiny.... Although the factors weighing against disclosure are not insignificant, I find that the factors weighing in favour of disclosure carry sufficient weight to override the nondisclosure factors. As a result, I find that the information may be disclosed because disclosure would not constitute an unjustified invasion of the privacy of the witnesses.[18]

Even if you win the appeal, and the fees are reduced or removed altogether, you will have been stuck in a process that likely took months in order to access the records. That's a long time in journalism, especially when you're after time-sensitive data. If you are simply appealing the fees, therefore, it's generally best to avoid an appeal at this stage of the process. The alternative approach that some media outlets have chosen is to pay the exorbitant charges, publish the information, then appeal the fees after the fact. This allows important stories to be told with credible, complete records in a timely way, while still addressing the cost issue. It means taking a big risk, though, because if the appeal fails, you and your media outlet will not be reimbursed.

That said, there have been some favourable judgments for journalists appealing high access fees after the fact. A year after the *Toronto Star*'s series in 2003 on the dramatic problems inside nursing homes, an adjudicator in Ontario's Office of the Information and Privacy Commissioner ruled in favour of the newspaper's appeal of a $5000 fee it paid to access nursing-home inspection records.[19] The appeal body ordered the provincial health ministry to refund the money because the newspaper's stories 'benefited the health and safety of the public in Ontario.'[20] Incidentally, the *Star* obtained the records in 2003 after a nine-month process during which it narrowed its FOI requests several times to bring the fee down from $13,835 to $5000.[21]

The Challenges

Despite holding a legally protected right to access public records, many information requesters in Canada find the process slow and intimidating. Requesters need to pose their questions properly, pursue the progress of requests with officials, and be vigorous about appealing decisions that fall short of statutory requirements. Records containing potentially sensitive or embarrassing information are likely to raise alarms within government bureaucracies and lead to problems with access.

'Government departments are increasingly sophisticated in identifying politically sensitive requests, and most major departments will have procedures for dealing with communications implications of sensitive requests,' says Alasdair Roberts. 'If you're making a politically sensitive request, your request will be delayed. You should also assume that communications advisors in government are looking at your request and developing "communications products" to help the department deal with the fallout from your request.'

'Communications products' is a bureaucratic phrase that refers to advice for ministers and spokespeople on how to respond to public questions raised as a result of an information request once the information is published. Government department staffers also routinely prepare notes for ministers on how to address questions in the legislature. Keep in mind that those records are also subject to information legislation, meaning that individuals who wish to know how their request was handled behind the scenes can file separate requests for the material. The records should show when the request was received, the office that held the records, whether there were consultations with communications staff and ministerial advisors, and the back-and-forth communications between officials on the process of handling the request.

A request for a database of Ontario career college complaints and inspection results by Robert Cribb of the *Toronto Star* in 2006 triggered a two-year battle with the Ministry of Training, Colleges and Universities, including an appeal for denied portions of the data that were ordered released by the provincial information and privacy commissioner.

A follow-up FOI request in 2009 for all the records related to that battle provided a blow-by-blow account of the ministry's handling of the protracted request. The internal records document, for example, how officials categorized the request as 'contentious' and identified the requester as 'a member of the media' in internal correspondence. One document, titled 'FOI Sign-Off Sheet', indicates such sensitive records are sent to the assistant deputy minister for review. The original request for the data also prompted ministry staff to write messaging materials for spokespeople. One such record, called an 'FOI Contentions Issues Briefing Note', sets out the department's response to potential questions about delays in release:

> The ministry takes its obligations under the *Freedom of Information and Protection of Privacy Act* very seriously. . . . The ministry will make the responsive record, or portions thereof, available to the requester in accordance with the provisions of the Act.

A more detailed communications–issues plan lays out the ministry's tactics for addressing negative press about the state of inspection and enforcement of career colleges that breach provincial regulations: 'Circulate . . . story to key ethnic media —include quote from third party spokesperson(s),' it reads. 'Take advantage of good news events or milestones to issue news release.'

The records also help outline the key concerns that officials have about their own programs.

A document titled 'Issues Management' cites a list of perceived vulnerabilities in the ministry's oversight of career colleges including 'colleges still not registered or colleges out of compliance,' 'lack of enforcement on behalf of the government, i.e., too few inspectors to ensure all schools are in compliance,' 'accusations about flight schools being a hotbed for terrorists,' and 'exaggerated promises in a college's marketing materials.'

All of this provides a rich and detailed foundation upon which to make further inquiries, ask questions, and request other records.

Amber lighting

In some government departments, the process of flagging politically sensitive requests is known as *amber lighting*. And while that process may go by different names in different governments, formal research and the experience of journalists have shown it's not uncommon for lower-level bureaucrats to treat sensitive requests with special care. The result is careful vetting by senior officials and ministers, long delays in the processing of requests, and carefully stage-managed responses from governments.

In 2008, the federal information commissioner published the findings of its investigation into a complaint from the Canadian Newspaper Association alleging federal officials applied 'secret rules' to media requests that resulted in 'systematic discrimination and unjustifiable delays in the processing of media requests.'[22]

While the commissioner was unable to conclude secret rules were in place, the investigation did find that labelling access requests with words or phrases such as 'sensitive' or 'amber light' do result in delays 'for unacceptably long periods.'[23]

Alasdair Roberts has traced the handling of sensitive requests from journalists at the federal level. 'In a major federal department,' he says, 'when a request comes in from a journalist, the access officer will note in the log that it's a media request.

Usually, every week, a list of media requests is compiled and reviewed by individuals from the communications office, the minister's office, and the access office. At that meeting, a decision is made about the requests thought to be most sensitive.' When the records are ready for release, they go to the minister's office for review along with the aforementioned communication products that relate to the request. Only then are the records given to the journalist.

That same level of scrutiny is not applied to access-to-information requests from other members of the public, Roberts says. Amber lighting can prove highly problematic to journalists for a couple of reasons: 'Firstly, there's clear evidence at the federal level that these practices delay response times,' he says. 'And [secondly,] in the process of handling politically sensitive requests, the personal information of the requesters could be shared, which is a violation of privacy rights and it might influence disclosure decisions as to how much information is released.'

Public–private partnerships

Modern Canadian governments have become ubiquitous brides, anxious to marry into partnerships with private industry for the purposes of delivering public services. It's a trend that has swept both federal and provincial/territorial governments looking to do more—or as much—with less. Private industry has answered the call, forging alliances with governments in the form of new agencies or public service bodies that do everything from inspect elevators to manage air space.

The arrangements are generally billed as good news for taxpayers since partnerships reduce the cost of operating a program, provide private-sector jobs, and maintain vital services. But these partnerships have also created an expanding black hole of public information. That's because the internal financial and organizational details of private companies are not subject to information laws. And they generally want to keep it that way for competitive reasons.

As the number of private–public agencies grows, more and more public business takes place outside the scope of information laws. This effectively means that public works, paid for with public money, are falling outside the reach of public scrutiny.

'The federal government has tried to undercut the [ATI] law by creating new organizations to provide public service but failing to include those new organizations under the law,' says Roberts.

There are many examples of essential public interest work being done by some public–private partnerships that now fall outside the law. Among them are Canadian Blood Services (which manages the safety of Canada's blood supply); the (Nuclear) Waste Management Organization (which oversees the management of nuclear waste); Nav Canada (which plays a key role in aviation safety in managing air traffic); the Greater Toronto Airport Authority and other major airport authorities across the country; the Canadian Institute for Health Information; Canada Health Infoway Inc.; and the Canada Pension Plan Investment Board. In all, more than 100 public institutions sit beyond the reach of public access.

A researcher looking to access expense records for Ontario judges, for example, might expect such records to be available through the provincial attorney general. But while judges fall under the department's jurisdiction, expense records are kept by the Office of the Chief Justice. That body is not subject to provincial FOI legislation. So, expense records of those public officials, funded by public money, are not accessible.

What You Can Get

This brings us to a brief survey of the types of records commonly sought (and successfully accessed) under ATI and FOI laws. It cannot be an exhaustive listing but, as with other similar sections in this book, this survey should serve as a jumping-off point, getting you to think about the sorts of items to which you might want access.

Expense records

Among the most high-profile documents obtained through information requests are expense records submitted by public officials. These form the basis for one of the classic watchdog roles of the press: keeping an eye on how public money is spent. This material can contain startling revelations about how taxpayers finance meals, travel, and other expenses for officials operating without proper account- ability. Such cases have been documented at all levels of government across the country.

As we discussed earlier, federal disclosure rules now make it mandatory for ministries to post travel and hospitality spending on their websites. But other expense records remain within the domain of formal information requests. And routine disclosure of travel and hospitality expenses is not always customary at other levels of government.

A 2009 *Ottawa Citizen* story reported then-natural resources minister Lisa Raitt spent nearly $80,000 on travel and hospitality during her last two years as head of the Toronto Port Authority before running federally for election. The records, obtained through a formal information request, documented $28,000 in hospitality charges from 2007 through to the fall of 2008, the newspaper reported.[24]

The same year, *Calgary Herald* reporters used provincial freedom-of-informa- tion legislation to access expense records showing the city's mayor spent $28,076 in taxpayer dollars on a one-day speaker's event for top city bureaucrats. Included in the expenses were '$1863 for a general manager's office chair, $390 for maga- zines in one department, and thousands of dollars for managers' meals and hotel stays,' the *Herald* reported.[25]

The Vancouver Sun's Chad Skelton used British Columbia's freedom-of-infor- mation law in 2004 to report on how provincial BC Hydro executives 'routinely eat at some of the most expensive restaurants in the city and end up paying exorbitant prices for airfare[s] by booking at the last minute in business class—even when travelling to conferences whose dates are set months in advance.'

Police, justice, and security records

Documents related to law enforcement are among the most difficult for researchers and the public to access. Many records are protected by exemptions, and police departments tend to be especially conservative in their approach to releasing information to the public.

The most high-profile journalistic investigation into police conduct in recent times was the *Toronto Star*'s Race and Crime series in 2002, which we discussed briefly earlier in the book. The comprehensive series of stories relied on Toronto police data, obtained through a freedom-of-information request, to report that a black person arrested for simple drug possession was twice as likely as a white person to be held for a bail hearing.[26]

The analysis was based on six years of police arrest records contained in a database that had never before been released to the public. The stories triggered a fierce debate about police actions in Toronto and across the country, and led to a $2.7 billion class-action libel suit by the police against the *Star*, alleging the series portrayed all Toronto police officers as racist. (Three courts ruled successively that the suit could not proceed because the series could not be 'reasonably understood' to imply that every officer was racist.)[27] Federal justice records have been the source of some high-profile public-interest stories. Ottawa journalist Jim Bronskill routinely pursues federal justice and security records through access-to-information requests. Many of the documents he has obtained through hundreds of formal requests have contained information never before revealed to the public. For example, he used ATI-obtained documents in 2000 to report on the startling extent to which witnesses, judges, and prosecutors involved in the country's justice system face intimidation and threats.[28]

The briefs, written by justice officials from across the country, cited 'instances of bulletproof vests being issued to Toronto prosecutors, witnesses in Nova Scotia who refused to testify, and members of the Edmonton Police Service who were outfitted with home alarms and panic-button systems because of threats to them and their families,' Bronskill reported.

In 2004, Bronskill obtained an RCMP report through access to information that revealed 'at least 600 foreign women and girls are coerced into joining the Canadian sex trade each year by human traffickers. Case figures indicate 1500 to 2200 people are trafficked from Canada into the United States annually, though the RCMP stresses the numbers may be only a fraction of the actual total.'[29] Requests like this, which bring important public-interest issues to light, represent the power of public-access information laws. But even for experienced requesters like Bronskill, not every question produces interesting answers.

'In baseball terms, if you get a hit in one out of every three at-bats, you're doing well. The same goes for access. One request might yield a story, another some interesting background material and the third could be a strikeout,' says Bronskill. 'I think the best request ideas flow from intuition. They could come from reading a news item, noting something said by a cabinet minister or following up on a hunch.'

One such hunch came to Bronskill in a March 2004 report from the federal auditor general, Sheila Fraser. The report found that Canadian watch lists used to screen visa applicants, refugee claimants, and travellers were filled with inaccuracies.

'I was curious to see what the government was doing to follow up on her recommendations,' Bronskill recalls. 'This is a valuable technique because while the media generally make a one-day wonder out of auditor's reports, [the reports] often trigger a flurry of ongoing work behind government scenes.'

He submitted various requests to a number of federal departments: Canada Border Services Agency, Citizenship and Immigration, Foreign Affairs, the Privy Council Office, Public Safety and Emergency Preparedness, and Transport Canada. A request filed to several of the agencies asked for 'Reports, studies, memos, and briefing notes produced by or for the department in 2004 concerning efforts to improve the quality and reliability of security watch lists.'

Records released by Public Safety and Emergency Preparedness included memos and a draft report on the challenge of consolidating watch lists. This resulted in a Bronskill story that reported, 'Efforts to keep terrorists from obtaining travel documents or boarding airplanes will falter as long as federal agencies rely on an incoherent array of watch lists, an internal government report warns.'[30]

Memos, briefing notes, reports, and studies

Journalists are frequently interested in documenting the hidden influences behind important government actions. That often requires accessing records that reveal the deliberations, decisions, and conduct of public servants regarding public-policy issues.

Government memos, briefing notes, and studies are all common records sought by researchers through access-to-information requests. They can show the inner workings of government decision-making, how those decisions are defended, and their impact on the public. As well, memos and briefing notes are among the easiest records to obtain.

Many difficult stories have unfolded on the public record thanks to such internal records. They have provided insights into everything from public spending to emergency response, to the management of public institutions and decisions on policy issues such as same-sex marriage and missile defence.[31] Among the stories that entered the public consciousness as a result of such records is the case of the controversial shooting death of a First Nations man by Ontario Provincial Police during a 1995 standoff at Ipperwash Provincial Park.

Natives were protesting against the province's failure to protect their ancestral burial grounds in the park. In the explosive situation that followed, police shot and killed an unarmed protestor named Dudley George. Immediate questions arose about how this occurred, and about the role of the new provincial Tory government. But the answers were slow to come. Tight-lipped politicians and public servants offered little in the way of explanation.

In 1996, then-Ontario attorney-general Charles Harnick said the government had no knowledge of a sacred burial ground on the site. Some *Globe and Mail* journalists used FOI legislation to obtain Harnick's briefing notes from the time of the crisis. These suggested a different story, and allowed reporter Martin Mittelstaedt to quote the notes prepared for Harnick in 1995, which specified that '[the] occupiers allege that the park lands are theirs [without explaining how] and that there is a burial site in the park.'[32]

Reports and studies form the theoretical basis for government deliberations on matters of public interest. Their findings are cited by politicians, but for in-depth research, it's important to see the documents in their entirety and not rely on such selective interpretation. The research material that politicians rely on to make their case can be more textured or even contradictory than they might portray in front of the media.

In 1998, then-Ontario Minister of Natural Resources John Snobelen pointed to a 1972 provincial government report to support his case that there was no evidence of a Native burial ground at Ipperwash. '[We] have an archaeological survey of Ipperwash Provincial Park in 1972,' Snobelen told the legislature at the time. 'That report indicated that there were no finds made and recommended that no further archaeological work of any kind be carried out there.'[33]

Toronto Star reporters Peter Edwards and Harold Levy obtained documents through a freedom-of-information request in 2000 that added important subtext to Snobelen's claim: there was a warning attached to the 1972 report from a Ministry of Natural Resources officer who questioned the reliability of the information. 'The methodology used at the time [1972] does not agree with current archaeological survey standards,' read the memo cited by the *Star*. 'This report cannot be used to say, with authority, there are no burial sites within Ipperwash Provincial Park. The methodology as described in the report would not likely uncover possible sites.'[34]

Edwards and Levy's long series of investigative reports into the Ipperwash affair involved long battles with government officials over freedom-of-information requests.

'The government was extremely unwilling to grant requests,' recalls Edwards. 'I think we had roughly 100 [FOI requests] in total and I can't recall anything coming back in less than a year, unless it was a rejection. We fought for a year for one batch of information that in the end included some of our own articles.'

In 2003, reporter Ann Rees investigated the mysterious lack of public information related to the Ipperwash case and the lengthy delays in processing information requests on the subject. She found an internal briefing memo from the Ministry of Natural Resources stating it used exemptions that '[were] "weak at best" to block freedom of information (FOI) requests for records that said then-premier Mike Harris wanted the protesters out of the park "and nothing else".' Rees concluded that the Ontario government 'knew it was using questionable tactics to delay and obstruct the release of freedom-of-information records' around the Dudley George shooting.[35]

There are a range of reports and studies generated by bureaucracies. Asking questions about how each identifies their reports can form the basis of quality information requests. Many government departments, for example, create 'situation' or 'incident' reports that document important public-interest issues.

Citing 34 'Quality Care Situation Reports' obtained through provincial freedom-of-information laws in 2009, the Canadian Press reported nurses in Halifax-area hospitals complained of 'unsafe' conditions for patients as a result of staffing shortages. 'There were 17 instances when nurses with the Capital District Health Authority were assigned between 10 to 12 patients,' the story reads. 'Managers say the normal ratio is four or five patients per nurse on the units involved.'[36]

Contract information

Documenting public spending is one of the foremost preoccupations of journalists and public-interest researchers. The reasons are obvious. Canadians hand over billions of dollars in earnings to governments every year. Government officials, in turn, routinely vow to safeguard that public money. Information laws are among the most important tools researchers use to scrutinize government spending. And among the most common records they seek out with regard to public finances are contracts with private industry. The documents or data outline the names of private companies hired by governments to do work for public money, the amounts awarded, and details of the agreements.

Most often, those contract arrangements with private firms are carried out responsibly. Government issues a request for bids, reviews the responses, and chooses a winner. The results are documented and publicly available. Sometimes, those records reveal waste and mismanagement.

A series of freedom-of-information disclosures into an Ontario electronic health agency in 2009 triggered visceral public anger, firings and resignations of top executives, and a political scandal.

Records obtained by the provincial opposition Tories and media outlets contained an eye-widening array of revelations about eHealth Ontario, a provincial agency charged with establishing an electronic record-keeping system to reduce health-care costs and medical errors.

Reports based on FOI documents revealed that there were $5 million in eHealth contracts doled out without the mandatory open-bidding procedure.[37] They also provided details on $2700-a-day bills charged by consultants working for eHealth, right down to $3.99 for Choco Bites, $5.69 for Tetley tea bags, and $1.39 for a muffin.[38] As well, the agency's CEO collected a $114,000 bonus after only five months' work at eHealth, newspapers reported.[39]

Correspondence

Researchers generally seek correspondence records as a way of digging into the background behind specific policy decisions or relationships between governments and private organizations or companies. Letters and emails often contain personal information, however, which complicates their release under access legislation. Some information may need to be extracted from the records before they are made public, but the overall records are covered and subject to release.

CanWest journalist Sarah Schmidt used freedom-of-information laws to obtain correspondence between University of British Columbia officials that documented 'an eight-month effort to limit enrolment in courses for the purpose of improving UBC's fifth-place finish' in the influential *Maclean's* magazine university rankings.[40]

'Before I filed a formal access request, I called around different department heads, asking about capping class sizes with an eye to do better on *Maclean's*. I didn't get anywhere, so I decided to file a formal access request,' says Schmidt. 'The only reason I was able to land this story is because BC includes universities under its FOI legislation.'[41]

Schmidt filed her FOI request with university officials on 22 August 2003, asking for 'any and all documents and correspondence in the President's Office and all dean's offices, including electronic correspondence, related to: UBC's ranking in the "*Maclean's* Special 2002 Edition: Exclusive Rankings" (published 18 November 2002) and the upcoming *Maclean's* ranking for 2003, to be published in November 2003.'

The records that eventually arrived as a result of that request allowed Schmidt to report that university administrators 'pressured faculty members to manipulate course enrolments and in some cases capped class sizes' to improve its fortunes in the annual rankings. Among the letters and memos Schmidt quotes is correspondence from a university administrator to a faculty department head saying, 'I realize that you have mapped course capacity to room capacity, but now we are being asked to respect *Maclean's* breakpoints in term one, rather than fill classrooms to capacity. I realize by capping these courses, we are, in effect, controlling the number of majors in linguistics, which may not be a good thing.'[42] While universities are subject to FOI requests in BC, Quebec, Ontario, Nova Scotia, Alberta, and Newfoundland and Labrador, they are among the conspicuous black holes in other provincial freedom-of-information laws. Even in British Columbia, accessing the records wasn't easy, Schmidt found. She filed a complaint to British Columbia's information and privacy commissioner after the university refused to meet deadlines for responding to her request. The records arrived shortly after she filed her complaint.

'The wait was worth it,' she says. She received over 500 pages of correspondence, much of it printouts of emails between senior administrators and department chairs. But there were many blanked out sections in the correspondence she received—a common problem with correspondence records obtained through ATI and FOI requests. So, after filing her original story, Schmidt decided to appeal the university's decision to blank out this material. Following a mediation process, the university released further information to Schmidt that included previously severed comments. That material served as the basis for a second story citing a memo in which a university official called the university's campaign for higher rankings in *Maclean's* a 'sham'.[43]

Meeting minutes

As we explained in Chapter 4, meeting minutes can provide important background about how a particular agency or government department is handling important issues, where the various decision-makers sit on the relevant issues, and how the debate is unfolding. They can reveal the champions behind specific decisions, those pushing against a particular policy direction, or details of a decision made in secret.

For example, *Vancouver Sun* reporters used freedom of information in 2009 to obtain city council minutes from an in-camera meeting that showed a former city manager's severance agreement cost the city $571,788.[44]

Accessing meeting minutes first requires some knowledge of the public institution or department you're researching. If it's a government committee, for example, begin by finding out about its mandate and a schedule of meetings and how and where minutes are kept.

Audit and financial details

While audits are generally public documents, they often make reference to questionable payments that aren't detailed. Learning more about the recipients of government largesse and the financial details of the arrangements usually requires filing a request.

In 2004, *Calgary Herald* reporter Suzanne Wilton was curious about a botched land deal that cost taxpayers millions of dollars. While the deal had been the subject of a city audit, important details, such as how things went wrong and who was responsible, were not made public.

There was much at stake. 'It cost the city $3 million to get out of the deal; the money was paid to private developers,' Wilton reported. 'Another $1.5 million was spent to redo planning for the area. It will cost yet another $25 million for the necessary infrastructure upgrades to set the stage for redevelopment.'[45]

Wilton filed several information requests to get at the details behind the failed downtown redevelopment project.

'Although senior managers and executives were fired for mishandling the deal, no one ever outright assigned blame,' Wilton says. 'I wanted the uncensored version of the audit to see if there were details that were withheld from the public.'[46] She eventually obtained documents that showed how four senior city staff were paid more than $1 million in severance in the aftermath of the botched redevelopment project. One of those city officials received more than $97,000 plus indemnity from 'any claim which may be taken against me personally based upon actions which occurred within the scope of my employment,' according to the story. Another official received $135,000 along with a vacation bonus.

Such vital public-spending information can go unreported without some digging into the numbers using information requests.

Polls

Public-opinion polls are published and broadcast in the news every week. Polling firms, media outlets, research institutes, and other organizations commission polls measuring public sentiments on a range of social and economic issues. But there is another realm of public-opinion polling intended entirely for the internal use of governments trying to gauge public attitudes and priorities. Many political parties hire internal pollsters or outside agencies to tell them how Canadians are feeling about the party leaders, the economy, and issues like same-sex marriage. The results of these internal polls can provide insights into the issues capturing the attention of governments—and the public—at any given moment, and they can prove valuable in measuring how a government's public-policy steps mesh with public opinion.

In 2003, *The Globe and Mail* was able to report that the federal government's own internal polling found the vast majority of Canadians surveyed said the country's health-care system had 'stayed the same or worsened in the past two years' despite a $23.4 billion federal investment.[47] The pollster concluded that 'splashy government announcements are not enough to convince people that the $100-billion-a-year health-care system—which they believe is fraught with waste and inefficiency—is being fixed.' The Finance Department, which commissioned the poll, unsurprisingly chose not to publicize this.

The Globe and Mail revealed in 2007 the firing of the BC Lottery Corporation's CEO and president came one day after an internal poll showed public trust in the corporation had 'plummeted' following warnings of fraud by some retailers.

The polling results, obtained through a freedom-of-information request, also showed the move didn't work. Another poll taken a month later showed the firing of the LotteryCorp's CEO and president 'had done little to restore public confidence, and public estimates of ongoing retailer theft had barely changed.'[48]

Inspections and audits

The front page of *The Vancouver Sun* on 14 December 2004 blared out an attention-grabbing headline: 'Secret tests reveal cattle feed contaminated by animal parts'. The story, written by Chad Skelton, was based on federal government inspection records that found 'more than half the feed tested contained animal parts not listed in the ingredients.' The findings raised serious questions about the safety of the country's feed system.[49] 'What surprised me ... was that such a high percentage of the feed tested contained animal protein,' Skelton recalls.[50]

Among the most important responsibilities of governments is the maintenance of public safety and security. Governments at all levels monitor industries and public services through regular vigilance of inspections. Inspection records are among the most compelling public records available to researchers interested in how a particular government system operates—and how well it protects the public interest. They generally provide the insights of government inspectors who monitor everything from water quality to pipelines to food safety. Generally, inspectors make such visits on a regular schedule. The results of those inspections tend to exist both on paper and in government databases. Working with inspection records often requires a three-step process.

Understand how the inspection system works

Consider the kinds of questions that might help you understand how things work in the field you're researching and what documents or data might exist to help you. If it's an area of government regulation, how do officials exercise their regulatory authority? What's the process by which public officials document their actions? Perhaps the most basic question for any public official responsible for protecting the public interest is simply this: 'When something goes wrong, where do you write it down?' Answers to that question will often provide a starting point that will help you understand where to go next.

Inspection records are one of the places where problems are written down. The authors of those reports are government officials who are presumably unbiased, informed, and acting in the public interest. But it's important to understand how a particular inspection system works. For example, how often do officials conduct their inspections? Are there mandatory time frames? Do they call the company ahead of time or make surprise visits? What exactly do they look for? Where do they record what they see? What are the names of those records? What kind of information is in them? When inspectors get back to the office after one of these inspections, what do they do with their findings? Do they squirrel them away in an office filing cabinet? Are the results input into a database? If so, what's the database called? Is it public? Just as important, what's missing? How reliable are the records? Do the inspection results trigger specific designations? Can they trigger charges? Under which piece of legislation?

All of those questions will help you build a clear picture of how governments tackle specific areas of public concern, and will help you gradually understand how well they might be accomplishing that goal.

When a listeria outbreak linked to cold cuts claimed 22 lives in 2008, journalists at the *Toronto Star* and the CBC joined together to file a series of access-to-information requests, including records on inspection oversight at the Maple Leaf Foods plant at the centre of the tragedy.

The daily inspection sheets covering the 19 months leading up to the outbreak revealed the level of inspection at the Toronto-area plant. After inputting the number of minutes inspectors were on site at the plant each day into a spreadsheet and analyzing the results, the *Star* and the CBC reported federal inspectors spent less than two hours a day at the facility—often dropping in for as little as 15 minutes. 'As much as two-thirds of the time each week was devoted to administration and recordkeeping rather than inspection,' the *Star* reported.[51]

Remember also that, in some cases, the inspection-record paper trail shouldn't be limited to Canada. Since we import many products from elsewhere, it might be revealing to obtain inspection records on equipment, food, or other products that come here from other countries.

For a series on medical devices in 2002, CBC Radio reporters obtained inspection reports from Mentor, a major US firm that has captured half of the breast-implant market on both sides of the border. The inspection records, obtained through US freedom of information legislation, showed the company had been slapped with safety violations after numerous inspections. That information had deep relevance for many Canadian women with Mentor implants that were deflating or deteriorating too quickly.

Request the records

Now that you know how inspection records are created and maintained, the next step is to access them. Because they might contain private information, one idea is to ask for a blank copy of the inspection form or the fields contained in any resulting database.

Reasonable government officials should be helpful with such an innocuous request. If not, working your way up the bureaucratic level might help. The blank forms will let you see how the department or ministry catalogues its inspection information.

There may be some portions of the database that will obviously contain personal information. Putting those aside, you can ask specifically for inspection records that don't include any of that personal information. This will likely amount to cumulative data—records that show the findings of numerous inspections or tests without identifying the individual companies or persons involved. For example, Chad Skelton's revealing research, based on records he obtained from the Canadian Food Inspection Agency, reported that, of the 70 feed samples labelled as vegetable-only tested by the agency between January and March of 2004, '41 (59 per cent) were found to contain "undeclared animal materials".'

Digging deeper

Cumulative data might prompt further questions. If you access data that shows problems in several water-testing plants, it would be in the public interest to identify which ones in particular. For this level of detail, where you'll likely be seeking information about private companies or individuals, you'll almost certainly have to file formal information requests.

Nursing-home inspection records opened the doors on the appalling conditions faced by many elderly residents in a 2003 *Toronto Star* series by Moira Welsh and Kevin Donovan. The series documented the disturbing treatment of many seniors in Ontario nursing homes including a 72-year-old diabetic man who was 'so neglected that an infected toe rotted and his foot had to be amputated. . . . Seniors in homes in Toronto and across the province were found to be malnourished, dehydrated and living in desperate conditions.'[52] Again, the series of stories, based on freedom-of-information requests for nursing-home inspection records, named the individual homes where the most serious problems were discovered.

'When I started looking at the issue of nursing homes in Ontario, I heard many anecdotal stories of terrible care, rotting bedsores, malnutrition, and neglect,' Welsh recalls. 'I needed to find a way to get as much data as I could so the story became an actual study of nursing home care.'[53]

Obtaining the records was only the first step. Analyzing them and ensuring accuracy turned out to be a painstaking process as well, Welsh says. 'You can never accept at face value the accuracy of the government's information. For example, after speaking with families, I found that the ministry had in some cases never contacted them regarding their concerns, and concluded that the complaint was "not verified" based only on a phone call to the nursing home.'

An important element in analyzing inspection records is understanding how the system works—and doesn't work, Welsh says. '[Inspection] reports showed numerous problems within the homes. I was surprised to learn, however, that the results were skewed in favour of the homes because the ministry gave administrators of each home several weeks notice of their annual inspection.'

In the end, 20,000 records gathered into three different databases produced results that Welsh says were startling: 'Seniors in as many as four out of five Ontario nursing homes were living in neglect.'

Cabinet documents

The deliberations that take place behind federal cabinet doors represent one of the controversial black holes of Canada's access-to-information laws. The law places a 20-year moratorium on cabinet records.

Nevertheless, journalists routinely seek access to cabinet records after the 20-year period has passed. Those records have provided unique historical insights into the workings of government at the time, how top officials handled high-profile issues from the FLQ crisis to defining public-policy issues.

For example, Dean Beeby of the Canadian Press obtained cabinet records in 2002 that showed Jean Chrétien 'helped launch a move to radically reform marijuana laws when he was justice minister in 1981.'[54]

As part of his involvement in the marijuana debate at the time, Chrétien (who was prime minister when the story was published in 2002) 'pressed cabinet to lower fines, reduce jail sentences and eliminate the criminal records of Canadians convicted of possessing small amounts of marijuana,' Beeby reported. 'Chrétien also tabled a discussion paper at cabinet that, among other things, raised the possibility of legalizing marijuana.'

These records document history rather than current events, but historical events can often still be relevant after 20 years. In many cases, they say interesting things about people or institutions that continue to matter in public life.

Conclusion

The deck often seems stacked against those seeking public information. While the public ultimately owns the information, governments are the custodians. And they can be exceedingly careful in what they choose to reveal. For more than two decades, federal information commissioners have lamented the state of public access to information in their annual reports, recommending legislative changes that would meet the expectations Parliament had intended when it passed the *Access to Information Act* in 1983. Those recommendations have generally fallen on the deaf ears of successive governments. In his 2003/04 report, Information Commissioner John Reid wrote, 'For twenty years, Canadians seeking information—especially about any subject the government considered "sensitive"—have been met by a wall of obstruction, obfuscation and delay.'[55]

All of this has triggered growing calls for government reforms that would create a culture of respect for the public's right to know. In 2004, Ontario's information and privacy commissioner, Ann Cavoukian, made a rare open call for greater government transparency in a 'blueprint for action' that called for 'direct personal action by the premier to help create a government culture of openness.'[56]

One expression of the frustration many journalists and researchers feel about the state of government openness in Canada is the Code of Silence Award, an ironic tribute awarded each year by the Canadian Association of Journalists (CAJ) to what it considers 'the most secretive government department or agency in Canada.'[57] The actual award is a plaque featuring a padlock hanging from chains.

Nominees have included the RCMP and police forces across Canada for refusing to release information about Taser use, Transport Canada for 'doggedly fighting for four years to keep basic aviation safety data out of the hands of journalists and the public,' Charlottetown's city council for refusing to open committee meetings to the public, and the Ontario Ministry of the Environment for 'withholding information about the Walkerton water tragedy that claimed six lives and sickened hundreds more.'

In 2008, the CFIA was 'honoured' for its efforts 'to prevent the public from learning details about fatal failures in food safety,' including lengthy delays in releasing records related to the listeria outbreak.

Perhaps the most conspicuous government department to appear on the annual list of Code of Silence Award nominees is Health Canada. The federal health department has been nominated three times. In 2004, it was distinguished with the award for denying 'access to a database of prescription drugs that could harm or even kill Canadians,' the CAJ stated.[58]

Access advocates have proposed a wide array of legislative changes to make Canadian laws more responsive to the public's right to know, including making all records created for the purposes of administering a publicly funded program subject to access laws, making all exemptions discretionary and limited, and imposing penalties against departments that withhold records illegally or release records only after chronic delays. But those proposed solutions have had little impact within the halls of governments. While they've earned the occasional receptive ear from opposition politicians, that receptivity frequently disappears when those same opposition pols wind up in government.

'There's no evidence that these laws create a culture of openness,' says Alasdair Roberts. 'They provide tools for individuals who want to access information, but you're always fighting against the governmental tendency to want to withhold information.'

11

Computer-Assisted Reporting

CAR stories do not write themselves. Journalists need to be creative when trying to translate the numbers into a narrative.

Introduction

The reporter's ability to obtain, analyze, and publish electronic data with the aid of database software and spreadsheets creates new possibilities for storytelling. Some journalists have an aversion to statistics and math, and find the concept of computer-assisted reporting (CAR) intimidating. In this chapter, we will show why you do not need to be afraid of CAR, why it is simply a matter of using the best tools for the investigative job at hand.

The umbrella term CAR can describe many activities: surfing the Internet for information or conducting searches using commercial online services such as LexisNexis; using spreadsheet programs to do repetitive mathematical calculations and to sort data; obtaining databases from government and other public institutions and then analyzing them with database software; building databases within the news organization itself; using mapping software to plot data on maps; manipulating sophisticated statistical and social-networking software to do in-depth analysis of communities and human relationships; and using Web frameworks to produce websites that visualize data for the audience.

Some of these activities are esoteric, but the use of database and spreadsheet programs has become an indispensable part of investigative reporting, and underpins the bulk of our discussion here.

The Development of CAR

The techniques that eventually became computer-assisted reporting were first practised in the United States and advanced rapidly with the arrival of desktop computing in the 1980s. Today, CAR is used in hundreds of newsrooms throughout the United States and is supported by online mailing lists, websites, university journalism programs, and a unique organization called the National Institute for Computer-Assisted Reporting, part of the Missouri-based group, Investigative Reporters and Editors. The institute runs training camps, gathers and sells data to news organizations at cost, and organizes an annual conference that brings together CAR practitioners from around the world.

The Canadian evolution of these techniques began in the mid-1990s, when a handful of curious journalists began to tap into the growing expertise south of the border. They did stories of remarkable sophistication almost from the start but few outside of these media outlets and their readers and listeners were aware of the efforts. That started to change when the Canadian Association of Journalists (CAJ), which for years had awarded prizes for the best investigative journalism in Canada, added a new category for the best story using computer-assisted reporting. The first winner of that prize (for work published in 1998) was Peter Cheney, then of the *Toronto Star*, for his Taxi series, about which we will have more to say later.

In more recent years, publicity created by the new award, as well as notable successes, such as the *Star's* Race and Crime series on the Toronto police, have further raised awareness of CAR. The technique is used in more and more print and broadcast newsrooms, and also by freelancers. While CAR is still not used in many smaller Canadian newsrooms, one need only read newspapers, surf the Web, and tune in to broadcasters such as the CBC to discover how data analysis using computers is now driving many important stories—ones that are forcing real and profound change.[1]

As well, more and more training is being offered. The Canadian Association of Journalists offers basic CAR training at its annual conferences, various journalism schools in universities and community colleges have added at least some CAR-related instruction to their curricula, and the University of King's College in Halifax has offered annual week-long CAR training sessions in the summer since 2008.

More and more often, data is moving online. A commercial service called Caspio is used by many newspapers, the CBC, and others to make simple database searches available to the public.

The leading edge of CAR, as has always been so, is in the United States, where a new kind of journalist has evolved: a hybrid reporter–computer programmer. These innovative journalists are using tools such as the Django Web framework (*www.djangoproject.com*) to make data available to the audience in graphic, searchable form. Rather than data simply being used as a research tool for reporters, it is becoming part of the end product. One journalism site, *PolitiFact.com*, won a Pulitzer Prize in 2009.

CAR Tools

We deal with online resources thoroughly in other parts of this book, so we'll skip that aspect of CAR for this chapter. Here, we focus instead on the basic use of spreadsheet and database programs to assist with investigative reporting. The higher-end tools, and advanced use of spreadsheets and databases require a more detailed how-to guide than we can offer here. Those interested in a complete guide should read Fred Vallance-Jones and David McKie's *Computer-Assisted Reporting: A Comprehensive Primer*, a companion volume to this book.

Spreadsheets

Spreadsheets are like calculators on steroids. They allow hundreds or thousands of calculations to be done simultaneously and make working out percentages and percentage changes a breeze. Spreadsheets can also perform basic data manipulation. Examples include Microsoft Excel®, Corel Quattro Pro®, iWork® (for Macs), and the free programs OpenOffice® (downloadable at *www.openoffice.org*) and NeoOffice (downloadable at *www.neoffice.org*).

Google also offers a spreadsheet through its online Google Docs service. Unlike other programs, the data doesn't reside on your computer. Instead, it sits on Google's server and you access the spreadsheet through your Web browser. The free service was quite primitive when it began, but as features are added, it is becoming a legitimate alternative to traditional spreadsheet programs for basic number crunching, especially when smaller amounts of data are involved. It has a huge advantage in that users in different locations can access the sheet, making it an excellent collaborative tool. Microsoft is introducing an online version of its Office suite as part of the Office 2010 release.

Whatever their type, spreadsheets are all based on the same concept. They are a bit like the kids' game *Battleship*™. They see the world as a grid, with rows numbered along the left side of the computer screen, and columns labelled with letters, across the top. The intersections of the rows and columns are called *cells*, named according to the row and column to which they belong. For example, the first cell on the sheet, at the top-left corner, is called *A1* because it is located at the intersection of Column A and Row 1. Mathematical formulas are entered using the cell references instead of the numbers in the cells. The formula *A1+B1*, for example, tells the computer to add whatever numbers are in *A1* and *B1*.

Conventional spreadsheet software can do math of just about any kind, but most of the time journalists will stick to sums, percentages, and means.

Spreadsheets are also good at sorting and filtering information. A sheet can be reordered, or sorted, based on the contents of one or more columns. So, for example, a spreadsheet of city hall expenditures could be sorted from largest to smallest expenditure. The filtering functions of most spreadsheets allow a user to see only entries that meet certain criteria. For more detailed information on how to actually use a spreadsheet, see Appendix A on page 280.

Database managers

If spreadsheets are king with numbers, database managers come into their own for the 'heavy lifting' of data. Spreadsheets can do simple sorting and filtering, but most can deal with only about 65,000 rows of information on any given sheet (the newest versions of Excel can handle up to a million rows). As soon as you get into extensive data crunching, you need to move to a database manager.

Databases have been at the heart of many of the big CAR stories done in Canada. In addition to the *Star*'s Race and Crime series, several other prominent examples featured in this book have relied on CAR, including the joint CBC–Canadian Press investigation of Taser use by the RCMP, and *The Hamilton Spectator*'s Smokescreen series on the fraud and ineffectiveness in Drive Clean, Ontario's mandatory emissions-testing program.

Database programs fall into two groups: desktop programs such as Microsoft Access®, able to handle small- to medium-sized databases; and server programs such as Microsoft SQL Server and the open-source applications MySQL and PostgreSQL, both of which handle databases of nearly limitless size. The latter two programs run on Macs as well as PCs.

Like spreadsheets, databases organize the world into rows (called *records*) and columns (called *fields*), although how the two types of programs work for the user are completely different. Depending on the program, a database can hold hundreds of thousands or millions of data records, and information is extracted by running *queries*.

The data may be divided into several different tables that refer to each other. This means that a single piece of data such as a person's name or address can be kept in one table and combined with other data when needed. You can even get the computer to grab data from several different tables and produce a list combining them. By doing this, the software can, for example, tell you which political donors (listed in one database) are getting big government contracts (listed in another).

Database programs are harder to learn to use than spreadsheets, but are much more powerful. Server databases can slice through millions of data records, producing summary results in seconds or minutes. Even Microsoft Access® can handle hundreds or thousands of records with no trouble, and server programs can crunch though millions or tens of millions (Appendix B on page 303 explains more about databases).

How the Tools Are Used

Searching

This is probably the simplest application of CAR, and differs little from what many already do with word-processor documents, PDFs, and websites. Both databases and spreadsheets can be used to find information such as a person's address from a set of driver's-licence records. Database managers are more powerful, however, in that a user is able to isolate information with a query, then save that query so it can be run again at any time.

Searching is one of the simplest ways to spot something newsworthy. In the 1990s, Rob Washburn, then of the *Cobourg Star*, broke a story about the municipality spending $80,000 per year to maintain an abandoned dump. He came across the story only after having entered the budget figures into a spreadsheet, then searching through them.

Counting

It can be useful to count the number of times that something happens or the number of times an entry is found in a database. This technique of analyzing data can produce newsworthy information that may contradict conventional wisdom.

Adrian Humphreys, now a reporter with the *National Post*, shared some of his CAR tips in a *Media Magazine* column. For instance, when faced with a story put out by police about a reduction in the number of drunk-driving incidents, Humphreys decided to use a spreadsheet to crunch the numbers himself. He phoned half a dozen police forces in major cities across the country to obtain raw spot-check data; he asked for the number of vehicles stopped and the number of impaired-driving charges laid for each year over the previous five years.[2]

Humphreys then entered the data into a spreadsheet, and compared the rate of impaired charges with the number of cars stopped by the police. He noticed that the number of checks had dropped significantly—in Toronto, this number had fallen by 66 per cent in five years—and that this decline had not been mentioned by officials who bragged about how the government's policies had stopped people from drinking and driving. Not surprisingly, the number of charges had dropped dramatically along with the reduced police surveillance; by running the data through his spreadsheet, Humphreys was able to see how that dubious statistic had been conjured up by police and government—then he reported on it.

Sorting

This is a method of ranking facts or numbers in order from largest to smallest or vice versa. When a US newspaper reporter learned from a source that police officers were making a lot of money working overtime, the paper bought a computer tape that contained the city's payroll records. From this, the reporter calculated the total paid to every city worker during the course of one year. Next, these totals were sorted from largest to smallest. The result? From the complicated mess of data emerged a strikingly clear picture: patrol officers who worked double shifts for several months earned more than the governor did for that year.[3]

Comparing

Comparing entails looking for matches in the information contained in two or more databases or spreadsheets. In 2002, *The Hamilton Spectator* used this technique to match the names of donors to Ontario political parties with those of participants in the new, free-market electricity sector created by the Progressive Conservative government. The story revealed that dozens of firms that benefited from the creation of the open market were generous supporters of the PCs.

Calculating

Whether using databases or spreadsheets, journalists often use software to do repetitive or complex mathematical calculations. Perhaps the most common involve percentages, or percentage changes, extracted from tall columns of numbers, something spreadsheets are particularly adept at doing. Spreadsheets are also used to find averages and medians, as well as to do more sophisticated statistical calculations such as finding the standard deviation from the mean in a range of values. To cite the Drive Clean example again, *The Hamilton Spectator* used a database to calculate the time elapsed between tests for hundreds of thousands of vehicles that had failed their initial tests. The results showed that cars had passed new tests within minutes of failing, suggesting fraud, which the newspaper then confirmed through traditional reporting and freedom-of-information requests.

Visualizing

Computer programs can be used in a number of ways to help you 'see' data. For example, a spreadsheet can produce a graph to show a trend, such as an increase in the number of accidents at a particular intersection over the years. Such graphs, especially when a great number of entries are involved, make trends easier to perceive than the plain digits on a computer screen can do.

Incidentally, *mapping programs*—which we cannot address in much detail here—are all about seeing. Also called *geographic information systems*, they take a list of coordinates and plot them on a map. This would be useful if you had a set of data on the location of, say, toxic-waste dumps, and wanted to see the information represented visually. If you then wanted to see the proximity of these dumps to people's homes, and you have a street base map, you can get the computer to layer the two sets of data, thus allowing you to compare them.

As with spreadsheet graphs, maps produced this way can help a journalist better understand data. The maps can also be published, used in a TV production, or posted on the Internet, allowing the reader, viewer, or listener to also 'see' the results of the reporter's work.

Some mapping functions no longer require expensive mapping applications. Most readers will be familiar with Google Maps and its ability to create custom maps. The service becomes more sophisticated by the year, and now has the ability to *geocode* addresses (i.e., place them on a map). Other online geocoding and mapping services such as batchgeo.com and geocommons.com can also help you create impressive Web-based maps at little or no cost. For an example of the latter application, see the maps at http://gambling.kingsjournalism.com.

CAR in Action: A Detailed Case Study

Let's look at a Canadian story that would have been impossible to tell without CAR: the award-winning series by Peter Cheney on the taxi industry in Toronto.

The idea for the Taxi series emerged when Cheney, a self-described car afi-cionado (as in 'motor car'), began wondering why so many of Toronto's cabs were in such horrible condition.

> I remember one car where the shift lever had been splinted with a piece of wood and some duct tape, and another where the driver had to get out and open the door for me because the inside latch didn't work. . . . Many of the drivers told me about Toronto's system of taxi-licensing, and how it had helped create the horrors I was seeing.[4]

Cheney was told that the licence plate needed to operate the taxi was worth $90,000, and the waiting list to get one from the city was 15 years. In the mean-time, drivers had to rent the plates from people who had them; the fees often amounted to about half their earnings, which made it impossible to get better cars. Many cabbies used dilapidated ex–police cruisers rented from garages, and drove the vehicles into the ground in order to make as much money as possible.

He discovered that there were 3477 cab licences in Toronto. A source helped him get access to the confidential list of licence owners, after the reporter's access-to-information requests had failed. Cheney scanned the paper list into his com-puter using optical character-recognition software, then spent three weeks fixing all the typographical errors that this introduced. Once that task was completed, he discovered that more than half the plates were held by corporations that con-cealed the identity of the people behind them. 'To get the names of the people behind the names, I did more than a thousand corporate searches, then punched in the names, addresses and telephone numbers that came up,' Cheney explains.[5]

He also noticed that many were held by the estates of deceased people. 'How was it, I wondered, that a licence to operate a taxi was held by a dead person when so many live drivers couldn't get one?'[6]

While he was building his database, Cheney continued to try the access-to-information route to get names of corporate plate holders. He finally managed to obtain a list from the municipal government, but it didn't match some of the information he had obtained earlier from his anonymous source. This was a major worry. Databases are only useful if they are precise; apart from the inherent prob-lem of unreliable information, many errors can also ruin the ability to search, count, sort, compare, or do calculations. He spent the next two weeks correcting inconsistencies in the data. The problem was that over the years, corporations had bartered and sold plates, which made it difficult to get an accurate snapshot of who owned what at any given time. The task was made easier when Cheney real-ized that the meetings of the Metro Licensing Commission were public. He obtained 15 years' worth of transcribed minutes on disk, then pasted them into a large word-processing document that ran more than 5000 pages. He used the search function to look for plate numbers and names. These searches allowed him to determine who had bought and sold plates over the years, and who had been suspended, thus resolving some of the conflicts in his data.

Once Cheney completed the spreadsheet, he began to notice patterns, such as the fact that more than 75 per cent of the plates were in the hands of people who didn't drive a taxi.

'I began hunting down the names,' he wrote in one account of the investigation. 'Among the plate-holders were dentists, airline pilots, Bay Street tycoons, and people who had won their plates in a card game. Many of the plate-holders didn't even live in Canada—many lived overseas, and collected income off their plates by renting them to out-of-work drivers.'[7]

Cheney also discovered that many owners held dozens of plates, with the biggest owner possessing more than 152. Since drivers couldn't operate without them, the licence plates were hot commodities. 'Once I [built] the database, I saw who owned the plates. I saw there was also this person called an *agent*, who handled the plates for people who didn't want to have anything to do with them day to day. You wouldn't see any of that without CAR.'[8]

The cabbies would pay $1000 per month to rent the plates through the agents, who also forced the drivers to purchase vehicles at exorbitant prices. Cheney profiled a man who was charged an interest rate of 28 per cent. These stories about the cab industry had never been told before and his work exposed major corruption in the taxi business.

CAR as a Tool

Those new to computer-assisted reporting, reporters and managers alike, make a number of common mistakes. Most of these are rooted in misconceptions about the nature of CAR and unreasonable expectations about what it can achieve. Just because a particular CAR story prompted government to change a policy, or forced a business to clean up its act, that doesn't mean the application of CAR techniques will automatically lead to such results every time. People sometimes confuse the results with the technique.

This can have a couple of unfortunate consequences. First, the reporter may be set up to fail, because the expectations for success are so high as to be unachievable. Second, editors may lose faith in CAR after the stories don't measure up to what they expected.

This is unfortunate, because we don't create similar expectations for other tools; nobody expects the telephone to produce groundbreaking stories by its mere use, for instance. Neither do we expect the use of a word processor to instantly result in Michener Award–winning copy. Computer-assisted reporting is simply a tool that, in the hands of talented and creative journalists, can help produce great stories. The techniques themselves help a reporter analyze and understand impressive volumes of digital information; it is the *reporting*, however, that can bring home the awards.

If overestimating CAR is one of the most common mistakes journalists make, underestimating it is another. Journalism, like any craft or profession, has its baggage, its own set of assumptions, principles, and prejudices. One of the deepest-set beliefs is that 'real journalism is about developing sources. Anything you need, you can find out or get if you cultivate the right relationships.'

As we've explored elsewhere in this book, developing relationships is absolutely crucial, as is doing effective interviews, but relying on sources alone is like farming without fertilizer. The crops will grow, just not as vigorously.

Getting past the fear of numbers

More than a few journalists have been heard to comment that they chose reporting as a career because they flunked math and wanted to avoid it at all costs. This fear often extends to things that are particularly technical. Hence, as soon as many journalists hear the term *computer-assisted reporting*, they want to run as fast as they can in the other direction. They fall back on the old notions of what journalism is really about, and dismiss CAR because they are afraid of it. That said, much of this is changing as CAR gradually merges with advanced online journalism to create a new hybrid, *programmer-reporter*, what some are calling 'computational journalism.'

There is no question that CAR often involves a bit of number crunching, sometimes a lot. But the good news is that the math doesn't get much more complicated than it did in grade 5 or 6. The main tasks are adding, dividing, multiplication, and subtraction. No complex algebra, calculus, or trigonometry is required. With a few moments taken to refresh basic elementary-school concepts such as working out a percentage or an average, you are on your way. The nice thing with CAR is that you don't even have to do these things yourself—the computer will take care of the work for you.

What makes a good data investigation?

The answer to this is much the same as the answer to what makes any good investigation, but there are some special cautions to be exercised when working with data. Generally speaking, the more that a database records something that directly affects people, as with Peter Cheney's Taxi series, the more likely it is to be the basis for a compelling investigation.

Effects on people can be measured in many ways. For example, a database of adverse drug reactions provides information of acute importance to people: dangerous side effects from drugs. Similarly, a database of police arrests applies to intensely personal experiences. Reporters have also used CAR to investigate meat-packing plants, doctor discipline, vehicular arsons, political patronage, pollution, slum landlords, and faulty medical devices. The closer the data gets to people's lives, the more impact your stories are likely to have.

Don't make the mistake of believing that just because something is recorded in a database you can miraculously make a story appear from it. Analyzing boring data will produce a boring story.

Steps in the development of a database investigation

Database investigations generally begin in much the same way as more conventional probes. A tip comes in, an editor, producer, or reporter sees something in the community, a neighbour mentions a problem, and so on. This leads to the same kind of preliminary legwork that we discussed in Chapter 2.

Where a database investigation starts to differ is in the process of obtaining or building the data that will help drive the story. Once a story subject has been identified, the reporter explores as to whether there is a public database that might shine light on the problem. The need for data may not present itself immediately, of course. In some cases, the existence of a database or the likely utility of database analysis does not become apparent until later.

If the matter under investigation is one that falls under some form of government regulation, there may well be a database. Almost any time a government agency administers, tracks, or inspects something, the results will be collected in such a system. Think of the number of times you have been to a government office and have filled out a form. The information from those forms almost certainly ends up in a database somewhere. It is faster and far more efficient than using paper storage. Data from the past can be looked up with ease. Every time you call a government service number and they look up your file, that search is being done on a database.

As we've discussed several times in this text, federal, provincial, and municipal officials inspect or test myriad things. The results of this activity, usually going back many years, are typically recorded in databases. Governments also track and record incidents and events, including fires, earthquakes, workplace, railway and traffic accidents, environmental mishaps, arrests, parking and traffic violations, and more. Records of complaints and other correspondence from the public are also kept in databases, as are requests made under the federal and provincial access and freedom-of-information statutes. Governments keep thousands of databases, big and small, and much, if not most, of this information can be obtained by enterprising journalists.

If you have obtained the database from a government agency or other outside source, you will have to take some time to come to understand the data. We'll discuss some of the technical details of Microsoft Access® in Appendix B on page 303, but in general, the first thing you need to do is come to understand what's in the database. This means opening the tables, seeing what fields are present, and what kind of data each field holds (plain text, numbers, dates, etc). You also need to figure out what any codes in the database mean, and see if any 'dirty data' is present. Dirty data includes misspellings of names, fields that are empty when they should be filled, and mistakes. Details on advanced skills such as data cleaning can be found in Vallance-Jones and McKie's *Computer-Assisted Reporting: A Comprehensive Primer.*

You probably have a basic idea of what you want to find out from the data, so the next step is to make a list of queries you would like to run. From there, you create and save your queries, keeping track of what each one is for, and start developing a list of questions, based on the data, that you will take to human sources. Interviews, further paper-based research, and rigorous accuracy checks on your results will follow. As well, you will need to look for examples on the ground to illustrate trends that have appeared in your data. If you can't find your great story in the real world, you should question whether the story is real at all.

Once the data work is done, the investigation differs little from the conventional pattern, except that you hope your database analysis will have given you a solid foundation that will infuse your story with the significance and impact it would have otherwise lacked.

Obtaining data

Getting data from government agencies can be as simple as making a call to an official who then sends you an email with the data attached. Or it can be as difficult as fighting an access-to-information battle that drags on for months or years. Although this is changing, for many government officials in Canada, a request for information in electronic form is still a novelty. Public servants tend to be creatures of procedure, and many will be reluctant to do things that aren't covered by existing rules. Officials may not have analyzed the data themselves, leaving them unsure what you will do with it. Therefore, you may face resistance. The approach you take from the very beginning can be the difference between getting a data file in a few hours or years later.

The first thing you need to do is find out as much as you can about the data, and the real-world situation that is being tracked. Look up secondary sources. Talk with people who are familiar with the issue or the information. Obtain any public annual reports or summaries produced from the data. These may give you a good sense as to what would be stored in a database. Most of the annual summaries will have been generated from the data, and will contain narrative sections that may help. Don't forget to look in the official access guides, such as Info Source, the federal directory of records published by the Treasury Board—these sources often contain detailed descriptions of the databases. And if you can, get a copy of the form that is used to gather data. The questions may resemble the fields under which information is stored.

Armed with this knowledge, contact the people who manage the information and ask how they store it. Particularly, find out if the system they use runs an up-to-date program such as Access® or Oracle®, or is some kind of old mainframe system (the latter problem has largely disappeared but you will still encounter it from time to time). You want to know how large the database file is, and whether they can make you a copy. Get a copy of the record layout now, if you can. A *record layout* (sometimes called a *field list*) will contain the name of each field, its data type (see Appendix B for a brief discussion of data types), and the length of the field in bytes.

You may also want to cultivate a source in the information technology or data systems branch of the agency. These people know the data far better than their superiors do, and usually know far more than the media-relations people.

Ask for the database on CD, DVD, or some other easily transportable medium. Often, just asking will get it for you. If necessary, talk or meet with the bureaucrats in charge to calm their fears. Carry a USB drive with you when you visit government departments. Getting the data could be as easy as having a friendly official copy it for you, right onto your thumb drive.

Using freedom-of-information requests to obtain data

If you have been unable to obtain the data set through informal negotiations, you may have no choice but to file a formal request under the appropriate provincial or territorial freedom-of-information statute, or the federal *Access to Information Act*, as we explained in the previous chapter. It's worth supplementing that discussion here with some special considerations that apply to data requests.

The request: A checklist
- Describe the database as specifically as possible, using the information you gathered beforehand.
- Ask that it be provided in Microsoft Access®, Excel®, delimited ASCII, or some other electronic format you can work with. Try to avoid having data provided in PDF format, as this makes it difficult to extract the data for analysis. (If the PDF file has been password-protected by the creators, it could be nearly impossible to do anything more than look at it on the computer screen.)
- If you don't have them already, ask for full details on the record layout, all codes used in the database, and the file format.

The reply
If you are lucky, the agency will send you a data disk. Just as likely, they'll say one of the following things:

- 'It doesn't exist in electronic form.'
- 'We can't provide it in electronic form, but would you like paper?'
- 'Technically, we could do it, but we don't have to.'
- 'We can provide it in electronic form, but it will cost you $7800 for programming.'
- 'We use a Complicator III computer system, and it's just too difficult to produce what you want.'

What do you do? The key is to be armed with knowledge. It is very unlikely that any modern government agency will use anything but computers to track things such as grant programs, inspections, permits, safety violations, and the like.

If you have done your homework, you probably know the electronic format exists. Even if they claim it doesn't, there may be dead giveaways, such as paper records that are obviously computer printouts, or detailed tabulations of program performance in annual reports, which were undoubtedly created by a computer. If the agency can generate a printout it should be able to provide an electronic version just as easily.

If an agency sends you a large cost estimate, ask the official to explain what it is for. If they mention the hours of programming time that will be required to generate the information, ask them why this is so. Get them to give you a detailed breakdown of the charges. Compare them with what is allowed in the applicable FOI fee regulations. Ask them what would happen if a top bureaucrat requested the same information. Would it take three days then? Suggest that you will do a story about how long it takes to extract such basic information from the agency's database.

The bottom line here is that database systems are designed to make data extraction easy. Programming should almost never be required, and if it is, it shouldn't have to be extensive or expensive. Occasionally, you will run into so-called 'legacy' systems, computer systems designed long ago that really do pose problems for people trying to extract data. Luckily, you will run into this less and less often; many of the legacy systems were weeded out when agencies upgraded to overcome Y2K (year 2000) issues. Even if an agency is using one of these legacy systems, reporters shouldn't be made to pay for antiquated data storage.

If a agency people say their system is too complicated to allow them to provide the information you want, ask them to explain *why* it is so complicated. Get them to give you details on the system, the vendor, etc. Don't be afraid to ask for a face-to-face meeting with the bureaucrat in charge of the database. Run their explanation by other CAR people by posting a question on NICAR-L (*www.ire.org/ membership/subscribe/nicar-l.html*) or another online mailing list. If necessary, you can phone the vendor of the computer system to ask how to extract the information you want. Most technical 'impossibilities' are just like huge cost estimates— ploys to make you go away. You should always persist, and eventually the agency may have to give in to you.

Often, agencies simply don't want to hand over electronic information because they know what you could do with it. They want to control the data. Or they're just nervous because no one ever asked before.

Sometimes, agencies will say a portion of the information in the database you want can be withheld under legal exemptions. Knowing what you need is the key here. If you don't need names, for example, tell the agency to strip them off. If you don't need street addresses, do the same. Think about what you really need to do your story. If the information is critical, consider their argument and appeal if necessary.

If you persevere long enough, you can get the data. But if all goes well, you will get it long before you even whisper the words 'freedom of information'.

Building your own database

Even if there is no existing database, or data that exists can't be obtained, journalists can employ the power of database software by building their own data sets, using documents, direct observation, or other source materials.

A favourite subject for database building has been murder. In 1997, *Hamilton Spectator* reporter Adrian Humphreys built a database of more than 100 murders, and then wrote one of Canada's earliest major CAR projects. In 2008, the CBC and the Canadian Press teamed up to build a database of RCMP Taser use, using paper use-of-force reports obtained under the *Access to Information Act* as their source. The story won a Michener Award, considered the highest honour in Canadian journalism.

One advantage of custom building a database is that the journalist will have an intimate understanding of the data by the time the work is completed.

Caution

One of the dangers of computer-assisted reporting is that wrong results look as good as the right ones. The old expression 'garbage in, garbage out' is especially applicable to CAR. This means that you have to pay careful attention to detail. Sort data in individual fields to look for unusually large or unusually small entries, called *outliers*. These may be mistakes that could add up to bigger mistakes for you. Verify these outliers using external sources such as printed reports, or people familiar with the data.

Look for fields with no data in them. If data has been collected inconsistently, any summary results will be questionable, and you shouldn't publish, broadcast, or post anything based on the results until you are certain the omissions won't render your conclusions invalid.

Go back and check your original data, as well as your queries and spreadsheet formulas, to make you sure you haven't made mistakes. Maybe ask a colleague or someone in the accounting or finance department double-check your numbers.

Be especially careful if a pattern you found in the data cannot be verified in the real world. If you don't see real examples of what you think you have found, you have to go back and question your results. You might also want to run your results by experts in statistics or data analysis to ensure that your methodology and conclusions are sound.

Finally, don't hesitate to present your main results to the authorities who control the data. You will want to do this in any case, in order to get their comments on the record. If officials protest that your results are wrong, take heed and be wary. Find out why they are saying this before you proceed to base your reputation on the work you have done.

Databases as reference sources and tip sheets

Sometimes it's not the big picture that counts, but the fine details.

While large CAR investigations often involve extensive data analysis, just scanning through a data set can give you story ideas. Databases kept on your hard drive (and updated from time to time) can provide you with quick reference material for day-to-day stories.

Let's say you analyzed a database of traffic accidents in your community in order to find the most dangerous intersections in town. If you keep the data on hand, you can later check how many accidents have occurred at a particular location whenever there is a big accident there. With all the time and effort that can go into obtaining a data set, squeezing more value out of it in this way just makes sense. Over time, it pays to maintain and update your databases.

Combining CAR with traditional reporting

As we said earlier in this chapter, computer-assisted reporting is an extremely powerful tool, but no amount of data analysis will produce a story on its own. To get the story, you need to combine CAR with traditional techniques.

Sometimes, computer analysis will provide rock-solid, irrefutable facts that can themselves be highlighted in a story. This was the case with *The Hamilton Spectator*'s series about emissions tests on cars in Ontario. Just as often, analysis will provide you with good questions to ask. If you determine an intersection has more accidents than any other, you still have work to do to find out why. What are the traffic volumes along that section of roadway, and what effect do they have on accidents? What physical features might obstruct views and lead to accidents? Is there a problem with the traffic signals?

To answer such questions, you may need to interview traffic officials, accident victims, pedestrians, and local residents, as well as find documents such as detailed accident reports, and so on. The data can point you to the story, but only reporting will land it. This is why it is called computer-assisted reporting, and not reporter-assisted computing.

Getting help

There are specialized online resources to help you with your CAR work.

* *http://goingdeeper.kingsjournalism.com* is a website devoted to investigative reporting including CAR.
* NICAR maintains a website at *data.nicar.org*.

Conclusion

The stories we've referred to in this chapter benefited from reporters who used CAR to bring attention to structural problems in public institutions by uncovering information that would have remained hidden from public view. As with any form of journalism, however, CAR must overcome obstacles. We want to draw attention to four of these.

First, the availability of Canadian data. The Canadian Newspaper Association's 2008 freedom-of-information audits have shown that requests for electronic data under the various access regimes across Canada are more likely to be subject to fee estimates, to have information removed, and to take longer to process. A number of federal departments refused to release records in database format, preferring the static PDF format instead. As well, some provincial access laws were still putting restrictions on access.

Second, there must be a change in mentality when it comes to the use of statistics. Working journalists will frequently make light of their aversion to statistics and math. Despite the fact that journalism schools in the United States and Canada are introducing statistics into their curricula, Philip Meyer still argues there is resistance. 'That's what drive me nuts,' he says, 'because the journalism schools actually market themselves as the place to go to school if you want to lead a math-free life. And that's a lie. You can't get away with that in journalism anymore.'[9]

Third, more managers need to realize that CAR is as useful a skill as the ability to develop good sources, track down elusive people, interview subjects, and write sparkling prose. Such a realization would make it easier for journalists to argue for the time and money it takes to negotiate for and build databases.

The fourth challenge is a more direct one for the journalist: turning CAR stories into compelling narratives that will capture the imagination or indignation of readers, listeners, or viewers. Journalists must understand that just because they have uncovered an important piece of information in a database, people will not automatically be impressed by all the hard work and ingenuity it took to get it. CAR stories do not write themselves. Journalists need to be creative when trying to translate the numbers into a narrative.

Suggestions for Further Reading

Cohen, Sarah. *Numbers in the Newsroom: Using Math and Statistics in News.* Columbia, MO: Investigative Reporters and Editors, 2001.

Paul, Nora, and Kathleen A. Hansen. *Computer-Assisted Research: Information Strategies and Tools for Journalists.* Columbia, MO: Investigative Reporters and Editors, 2007.

Vallance-Jones, Fred, and David McKie. *Computer-Assisted Reporting: A Comprehensive Primer.* Don Mills, ON: Oxford University Press, 2008.

CASE STUDY: Part III—Steve Buist

Q   What was the name of your story/project?

A   Royal Crest and the Martinos.

Q   About Steve Buist

A   He's been at *The Hamilton Spectator* for 23 years. Buist started out as a sports reporter, but now is the investigations editor who is responsible for the large projects, bringing along younger reporters, and teaching them about investigative techniques.

   At the outset of his *Spectator* tenure, Buist was doing mostly features and science writing. His degree is in human biology, and he was filing a lot of medical and health-issue stories.

   'And then this one [the Royal Crest–Martinos story] just kind of came out of the blue.'

   'I had just come back from Christmas vacation, and I had finished some stuff at the end of 2002 related to environment and landfill issues. I completed all that stuff before Christmas and had a clean slate. I was looking for something to do and called up a police contact and said, "Give me a scoop," jokingly. He paused, and asked, "What do you know about the Martinos?" At the time, they had been in the news because the nursing homes had gone into CCAA [*Companies' Creditors Arrangement Act*] protection. There had been a flurry of stories about what was going to happen to the homes.

   'He said, "Something's going on." I said, "What." And he said, "Something's going on. That's all I can tell you." And I said, "Okay." And that was all I needed. The next day, they [the nursing homes] declared bankruptcy. And a whole bunch of dominoes began to fall. And there was the possibility of some sort of police, or criminal, investigation into the business.'

   They [the police] had been perusing the stories from the consumer side of things, rather than the business. And there were none of the documents suggesting tens of millions of dollars of fraud.

   'There were a couple of feet-thick files of documents in the bankruptcy office here in Hamilton. Going through them took hours and hours and it became clear that there were things that just didn't add up.'

Q   What events occurred at this point?

A   There were bankruptcy filings, which led to the creditors meetings . . . that Buist attended. 'I didn't identify who I was. I just sat there like anyone else.' He developed a good relationship with the trustee handling the case.

   As for the Martino brothers, a lot of liabilities listed on their personal bankruptcies were business-related bankruptcies. He can't remember the number of documents, but there were 'hundreds and hundreds of pages of material which was being added to on a regular basis.'

Q   What was the narrative that started to emerge?

A   'Two major themes emerged: There seemed to be huge amounts of money that weren't easily accounted for. And there were a lot of interconnections between numbered companies and third parties that had relationships with the principals of Royal Crest. They set things up in what you could call suspicious ways. For instance, they would buy all of their supplies from a third party company that acted as a broker. And then it turns out there was a connection between that third-party company and the Martinos. So they had found interesting ways to double and triple dip.

'One theme involved this huge, staggering amount of money that didn't seem to be easily accounted for. And the second major theme was that a lot of taxpayer dollars were at stake here. There didn't seem to be any interest in any of the public institutions to get this money back. In large part, the money that was at stake was in the form of security or mortgages held on the properties themselves and were insured by CMHC or something. Or the banks, which were owed the lion's share of the money, had that in some form of mortgage security that was insured. So at the end of the day, the smallest creditors, the people who worked in the nursing homes, the residents—their dollar amounts (owed) seemed puny compared to the large dollar amounts owed to the larger creditors.'

Ernst and Young's job was to find buyers. A couple of the small homes were sold, with ministry approval, to Joe Melo, who was a contractor for the Martinos. He used to do maintenance and construction work in their nursing homes and was frequently seen at their head office at King Street East. 'Because there was nothing preventing it, he bought these homes.'

Buist did a story about this. The ministry attempted to do a forensic audit, hiring a low-profile audit.

Q   Why not hire Ernst and Young, which had control of all Royal Crest documents?

A   Buist thinks the ministry did it on the cheap and didn't get anything for their audit.

'There were so many threads to pick at with this story that it wasn't difficult to keep it alive. I would hope they were interesting for people to read. The judge's decision in the personal bankruptcy case had reinforced what people had been reading in the Spectator. We weren't crazy, and the judge saw it the same way. That's what good investigative journalism does: shine a light.'

The decision came down in March 2004, when Justice Lane announced that he wouldn't let them off the hook until they paid the $300,000 that they owed. Buist learned about corporate and bankruptcy law, how to ask the right questions, and 'just dealt with lawyers through email, never spoke to John or Aldo Martino.' All through producing 30, full-page articles, Buist saw the Martinos in court, but never spoke to them.

'I tried to be a very organized person, maybe because I came through the science stream when I was younger. Science is all about order and method and walking through your results.'

'It's really important for a story of this complexity, that you be organized in how you collect your information, where you put it, and how you name your folders and documents. Because, four and five months down the road, you're not going to remember what you did.

So you need to be organized in your thinking and approach to collecting information. You need to be able to figure out how to track down one little fact. That's where the Internet was invaluable, especially on the US side of the story. Just because you hit a roadblock, doesn't mean that the information isn't there somewhere else and you didn't have a way of finding it. I had to do this on my own, so it was trial and error for me in terms of learning bankruptcy law and corporate law and doing property searches.'

Q Land-title offices

A 'Don't just look at who owns the piece of property. Go look at the mortgage document because it may lead you to a numbered company that's listed as a guarantor. And then that numbered company may lead you to three more numbered companies. There were probably two dozen or more numbered companies. In some cases, they would set it up where one numbered company would own the retirement home and the other would own the land. Keeping track of those connections was complex.'

Q Documents

A 'There were trustee reports from early on, where the trustee had to resume the situation. They gave good information about the amount of money going into the business.'

The mortgage and property-search documents hinted at some of the unknown connections. For the personal bankruptcy report, the Office of the Superintendent of Bankruptcy (OSB) interviewed the Martino brothers. 'These are recorded and transcribed.'

Q Potential assets of the Martinos

A 'They had a Port Dover vacation property, a $500,000 waterfront property in Port Dover that was registered to a trust—it was the initials of all the kids, plus the husband and wife put together. How could a 14-year-old kid be a trustee?

'I don't think they realized that you create quite a paper trail in your life, especially the way the Martinos conducted their business. There came a point where I think they realized that they wanted to go off the grid, and that's when their business went into bankruptcy protection. I think it came as a complete surprise to them that they had created this huge paper trail along the way and you can't put the genie back in the bottle after it has happened. There were probably times they sat there and said, "When is this going to end? How does he keep finding all this stuff?" And they didn't realize that once it's created, it's there.

'We even tried to do some creative things to see if we could get a hold of more documents. If you're a creditor, then you have a few more rights than if you're just a person off the street. And then I discovered you can take the place of a creditor, almost like buying someone's debt. I found a creditor who was owed a small amount of money. And she agreed to do a transaction with me. We even went as far as to draft a document (a proxy, in which she indicates that you are now the creditor), and then we discovered that because she was party only to the corporate bankruptcy, it wasn't going to help us. The personal bankruptcies were of more interest to us. And, again, that was another thing that I learned. I even went to our business department to see if they owed us any money for advertising, but discovered that we caught on to them years ago and forced them to pay cash—because we got stuck with some bills in the past.

'It was useful to do little things like attending the creditors' meeting and seeing who shows up. Everyone who goes has to sign in. The meetings have to be publicly noted.'

Q   Some general advice to reporters

A   'When covering these kinds of in-depth cases, keep in mind that most bankruptcies happen for unfortunate but legitimate reasons. But any time I see someone go bankrupt, the first thing I am is skeptical. Every time a colleague comes back to me and says, "I just got these bankruptcy documents, what do you think?" my first thought is, "I'm going to look at this with a very critical eye." Always look to see if it makes sense. Do the numbers add up? Does the explanation for why the person(s) went bankrupt make sense? Where was the money going? Are there any connections that seem questionable? Who is owed money and who is handing out the money?'

Part IV

Putting It All to Work

12 Organizing, Writing, and Libel-Proofing the Investigative Story

Narrative journalism—using storytelling techniques to engage, explain, and illuminate—brings together the immediacy of journalism and the allure of other narrative writing to produce extraordinary stories.

A stack of documents has been amassed. Interviews with the key figures are complete and transcribed. The research phase of the investigative story is complete. It is time to start writing. But where should the story begin? What has the investigation uncovered? Will the story make damaging allegations that could attract a libel suit? How should the information be structured, and what is the best way to tell the story? 'The successful investigative story packs a double appeal to readers; it engages their curiosity and surprises them with the results,' says Pulitzer Prize–winning investigative reporter and author James B. Stewart.[1] The writer's task is to convey the information gleaned from countless sources in a coherent fashion, while at the same time catching and holding the attention of the reader, viewer, or listener. In short, the writer must tell the story truthfully and effectively.

Preparing to Write, Right From the Start

In the first chapter, we talked about organization as one the 12 keys to a successful investigation. There is no question that being organized will save you countless hours and a great deal of stress. When you get to the writing stage, you want to be able to access information quickly and avoid being distracted as you search for the bits and pieces you need to tell the story. You must be in control of your material—it must not control you. This means getting organized early and staying organized. If you have followed the advice earlier in the book, you should, at the moment of writing, have the following prepared:

- **Well-managed research**
  (i) *List of documents and interviews*
    Whether kept electronically or on paper, this should detail the author of each document, where and how it was created, the essential points it contains, and why you found the document useful. A similar approach works in organizing interview transcripts. The records may be numbered for easy reference.
  (ii) *List of online resources*
    This may take the form of a website that you have created with links to the relevant sites.

- **Key points**
Important facts or questions that came to mind while reading documents or interviewing sources should be noted and ideally grouped into themes or patterns, perhaps filed on index cards or kept in a spreadsheet file.

- **Chronology**
This keeps track of every date that came up in your investigation, including those dates mentioned by sources during interviews, the dates of meetings, the dates on the documents you have obtained, and when important scholarly papers were published. The sequence of events exposes inconsistencies in explanations and contradictions between what people say they knew and what they must have known. It also serves as a roadmap for your story and can be reworked into a sidebar.

- **Transcribed notes and interviews**
Having typed out your notes after completing interviews, or having transcribed audio recordings, you may have written preliminary paragraphs to capture the essence while it is fresh in your mind. You may have kept a 'good quote' file of comments to use in the finished piece, saving time and ensuring you do not overlook important voices. If some audio recordings are not transcribed, you have at least noted the time when important quotes were uttered so you can find these easily. Your notes also include descriptions of things you saw during each interview—the subject's mannerisms, appearance, personal objects in the room, and so on. These paragraphs may not make it into your story exactly as written, but they will now prove invaluable as you sit down to write.

- **Facts checked**
All journalists aim to be accurate, but tight deadlines and the pressure to get the news out while it is still news means errors sometimes slip through. Investigative journalists, however, have no excuse for being sloppy. The credibility of their work hinges on getting the facts right. Usually, they also have more time to check and double-check the facts. This process continues throughout the writing and the editing stage.

Writing the Investigative Story

Prepare an outline

When you are confident of what you are saying, that you have assembled the evidence to prove it, and all necessary points of view have been canvassed, you are ready to start outlining your story. Review the main points you want to make in the story and the material that will support these points. This may include quotations from interviews, passages in documents, or material drawn from online sources. No doubt you have had a good idea for some time as to what the story will focus on. Now is the opportunity to put that in writing.

The first step is to organize the main points into a logical order. Who are the most important sources? Who are the key players? What are the strongest statements that you can make based on your research? What are the subsidiary points that support those statements? What background material and statistics will you need? In some cases, the logical order of the story may be chronological. In others, the story may have a logic of its own. Whatever order you choose, your list of points will become the outline for your story.

Once you have a good sense of the order in which you plan to present your material, you will need to mark up your summaries and any highlighted portions of interviews and research materials, indicating what goes where in keeping with your outline. Some journalists like to do elaborate outlines, defining blocks of material and then methodically writing each block. Others feel this can lead to a story that sounds choppy, and prefer to let the writing flow from one point to the next, from beginning to end.

Once you feel you are ready to begin to write, tell a colleague or friend in a few sentences what the story is about. Reducing the story to a short statement forces you to organize the major facts and important points in a logical manner. Complex events and technical jargon must be put into everyday language. Explaining things aloud forces you to get to the heart of the story and why it is important.

The better prepared you are, the more fluid the writing process will be. It takes some work up front to get organized, but it's always worth it. Reviewing your material, organizing interviews and documents into categories, creating a chronology, and reminding yourself of important scenes or sources will help you formulate an approach.

Focus on the central idea

Boiling down a stack of information and weeks or months of research is no easy task. It requires a good deal of thought. But a strong, clearly declared focus at the start of the story is essential if you are to carry the tale—and the reader—through the thousands of words that follow. Investigative stories flow out of these central themes. By whittling down the information to a single core idea, you are charting the path of your story.

Based on your outline and conversations with colleagues or friends, you should be able now to reduce your research to that one- or two-sentence revelation or argument. This can be turned into a paragraph ready to sit near the top of your story; this is known as the *nut graf* in print and as the *focus statement* in broadcasting.

In doing so, make sure you emphasize the information that is of the most relevance to your audience, not the information that was hardest to obtain. The public interest, and not behind-the-scenes journalistic challenges, should always be the defining consideration in choosing where to focus an investigative story. A newspaper reader will have little interest in battles to pry information out of reluctant bureaucrats or how difficult it was to track down a source. Some of the toughest battles for information ultimately produce documents of little relevance that never make it into a story. What matters is what you have discovered and what it means for your audience. If behind-the-scenes battles will help your audience understand the story, the details can be reported as a sidebar or as a brief explanatory item.

Think about the thrust of the story. What information means the most to your audience and reveals something new? Your conversations with others regarding this story should not just be an opportunity for you to articulate your views; pay attention also to which elements they find most interesting. Their views may differ from your own assumptions, as it is easy to lose perspective when you live with a story for a long time. Finding the central public-interest issue often requires stepping back to rediscover what most intrigues, fascinates, or concerns your audience.

The central story idea will drive the writing. It will help you decide how to begin your piece, how to structure it, and which facts are the most essential. When you find yourself lost in a mountain of unfocused material, your central story idea provides a constant reminder about what you are trying to say. Every paragraph in the piece should function to support that fundamental premise. Make sure you have it right before launching into a first draft.

Once you have nailed down the central idea, consider how to bring it home to your audience. How does this central idea play out in the real world? What are the anecdotes, events, and conflicts that best illustrate its impact? Make sure your examples are relevant. If you do not have strong illustrations of your main point, it's likely time to rethink it. The information you collect through documents and data should hold true in the real world. If it does not, is it because the data is incomplete or improperly gathered? Could you have collected records that prove one side of an issue and missed documents that reveal contrary evidence? You must test your conclusions and carefully consider any discrepancies between what you have researched and what you see and hear. If research and real-life reporting do not match up, find out why before spending time writing a story with a potentially flawed central focus. Go back and consider whether you are on the right track or the real story lies somewhere else in your research. Forget the documents and data for a moment and think about what you are seeing and hearing. Then go back and consider why those issues might not be showing up in your paper and data research. Re-interview your data. Go back to officials who provided you with documents and ask if they can direct you to other relevant information. Get to the bottom of it.

It is pointless to begin writing until you are locked and loaded on your main theme and where you are going to take it. Trying to write a complex story without a strong command of your material, ideas, and approach is a frustrating and futile exercise. So be willing to recognize fundamental flaws that present themselves at this stage. It is better to return to the research now than to forge ahead regardless.

Humanize

Now is also the time to think harder about the characters who will be featured in the story. The best journalism is always about people. A story based on solid data and documents will read like an academic study if it doesn't have people to provide impact and context. If your research has been thorough, you will have spoken to far more people than you could ever include in the story. Choose the ones who best represent the various elements and can bring facts and numbers to life. They are the main characters of your piece. Facts and figures should play the role of a supporting cast.

Manage the data

When you select these facts and figures, be ruthlesss. You may have done an exhaustive analysis of a database the public has never before seen, but falling in love with your data can be dangerous. Think of the facts and figures you have collected as the journey rather than the destination. A database may tell you where to look. It may take you to the particular city, school, person, business, or accident site. It may tell you how that specific incident relates to all other similar incidents. But it does not tell a story. You must take the extra step of going to that city, school, person, business, or accident site to find the scenes, voices, and real-life texture that will make the numbers come to life.

A number tossed into a story without context has virtually no value. Is a 7 per cent increase in pollution emissions significant or not? Is the environment being damaged, or does the apparent increase stem from a change in the way the figures are calculated? It is not enough to tell your audience that city hall spends $2 million a year defending lawsuits against police officers; you need to explain how this compares to the amount spent by comparable cities in Canada and, perhaps, the United States. Take the extra step of adding other kinds of context, too. For example, the figure $2 million has more meaning if you note how many daycare spaces or other services this amount of money would fund.

Get 'narragative'

Stories have a beginning, a middle, and an end. They have characters, structure, and pacing. And at their best, they utilize narrative techniques that are as old as storytelling itself. There's no single approach to writing an investigative feature; there are as many approaches as there are investigations. The writing choices you make when turning your facts into a story will determine whether the story hits home and is understood. Because investigative work is so firmly rooted in complex, in-depth research, the process of presenting that research can sometimes become an afterthought. But confusing or uninspired writing can blunt the impact of the important facts presented in the story.

Some stories demand a declarative, factual lead paragraph that states simply and clearly the fundamental finding of your research. Other stories beg for softer openings that create a sense of time and place and gradually unveil the elements that need to be understood in the complex tale ahead. We cannot offer hard-and-fast rules or a formula except to say that the right narrative techniques can bring an investigative project alive.

Narrative journalism—using storytelling techniques to engage, explain, and illuminate—brings together the immediacy of journalism and the allure of other narrative writing to produce extraordinary stories. Presenting facts within the context of compelling writing only reinforces their power and impact. While narrative techniques have generally been focused on feature writing, investigative reporting is an area of journalism where this approach often works well.

We refer to this approach as *narragative writing*—a technique that combines the investigative reporter's unwavering commitment to fact with narrative techniques such as setting, conflict, scenes, suspense, motive, dialogue, and character development. While this can be a challenge, if you can find a balance you will make a thicket of information and numbers far more readable and understandable. Human activity is the engine of a narragative story, so consider the action that relates to your central theme. Start by thinking about the most important images, incidents, and scenes that will put flesh on the bones of your research. Where are the points of conflict in the story and how can you present them in a human way? Can you recreate an incident that will let your audience in on a crucial moment in your story? These are the nuggets that will fill the mind of your reader with visual images that bring the information home. Spread them throughout the story and avoid jamming them all at the top. Readers, viewers, and listeners will stick with a story if they sense they are in the hands of a storyteller who is taking them on a journey that offers interesting elements along the way.

'Show, don't tell' is an often-repeated rule of narrative writing—and for good reason. It is not enough to say that child poverty is endemic and growing worse, according to statistics and public records. Such factual and statistical information must be in the story, as a function of your role as a researcher; as a storyteller, your job is to appeal to the heart. You need to combine the simple, declarative statements with strong, visual examples. Do this enough times in the course of your story and you will earn the trust of your audience. Strong narrative writing reinforced by reputable evidence builds a gradual sense that the story is comprehensive and authoritative.

The information has to feel authentic. Too often, journalists lose the faith of their audience by being too simplistic. Black-and-white truths are rare; most important human endeavours are rendered in shades of grey. Stories that reduce complicated issues to good-versus-evil scenarios risk losing their sense of authenticity. Always present the grey areas in your story with the knowledge that these complexities only enrich the authenticity of what you write. A person, company, or government department portrayed as a one-dimensional villain is far less interesting than a fully realized, complex subject.

Roy Peter Clark, a celebrated writing coach and senior scholar with the Florida-based Poynter Institute, has done a great deal of analysis of tools for journalistic narrative writing and recommends a number of well-tested, basic writing techniques for bringing sleepy prose to life. Among them,

- Use verbs in the strongest form, the simple present or past. Strong verbs create action, save words, and reveal the players.
- Dig for the concrete and specific: the name of the dog and the brand of the beer. Seek details that appeal to the senses.
- Prefer the simple over the technical: shorter words, sentences, and paragraphs at the points of greatest complexity.
- Control the pace of the story by varying sentence and paragraph length.

Clark also points to a number of narrative techniques that can apply to investigative writing. For example, one of his tools urges writers to 'use internal cliff-hangers to move readers to turn the page.'[2] Consider the stunning opening paragraphs to a series of news stories written by US journalist Anne Hull, entitled Metal to Bone:

> It was just the two of them, father and son, living in a tiny apartment where the only luster was a gold picture frame that held the boy's school photo.
> Their neighborhood stole the young. The father clutched his son fiercely.
> 'I don't want you making the same mistakes I did,' he said, the voice of a thousand fathers.
> On July 4, 1992, at exactly six minutes before midnight, the son stepped from his father's shadow. 'I just wanted to be known,' he would later say.
> For his coldblooded debut, he picked a police officer whose back was turned.
> The sound she heard from the gun would reverberate for months.
> Click.
> It was the same sound the key in the lock makes as the father comes home now to the empty apartment, greeted by the boy in the golden frame.
> A file at the Hillsborough County Courthouse Annex contains all the information pertinent to the case, but no hint of all the things that were lost on Independence Day.[3]

So begins a narrative series that takes thousands of words over several days to reveal the details of what happened that night between the young man and the police officer. But throughout, there are intriguingly crafted sections like this, which draw readers along.

Clark draws a distinction between writing a report and writing a story. 'Story elements, call them anecdotes, appear in many news reports. But few pieces in a newspaper earn the title of "story". Most items we call stories are actually reports.' Turning reports into stories, he writes, means rethinking the traditional five Ws (*who, what, when, where,* and *why,* as well as *how*). 'Who becomes Character. What becomes Action (what happened). Where becomes Setting. When becomes Chronology. Why becomes Motivation or Causality. How becomes Process (how it happened).'[4]

Structure the story

Most daily journalism utilizes the traditional inverted pyramid form, with the most important facts at the top and the remainder of the information arranged in decreasing importance as the story progresses to its ending. That is not the best approach for investigative writing. A series of paragraphs at the top of your story listing all of your findings without context or explanation, followed by hundreds or thousands of words that merely repeat and elucidate those points, is hardly an example of compelling craftsmanship. Chances are that most of your readers, faced with such a daunting structure, will simply give up after the first two dozen paragraphs.

Narrative techniques offer a number of alternatives to the inverted pyramid. The ancient storytelling structure of beginning, middle, and end is a possibility for some investigative stories suitable for being told around specific events or incidents that follow a clear chronology. Another option is the cinematic structure, introducing conflict between characters or, perhaps, policy directions, leading to a climax and resolution. Other writers have approached investigative stories as a series of scenes involving several characters; the writers insert occasional passages to give background, present data or documents, and anchor the story in a public-interest context. Regardless of the technique used, it is vital to include a nut graf or focus statement high in the story—you need to explain the story's implications and why it is important and newsworthy.

If it is going to be a long and involved series—as we saw in Chapter 9 with *The Hamilton Spectator*'s treatment of the bankrupt nursing-home chain, Royal Crest—it may be necessary to serialize the material. Break it up in chunks, as Steve Buist did by telling bits of the story at a time and then once in a while stepping back for a broader look at some of the underlying issues and the people affected by Royal Crest.

Rewrite

The suggestions put forward so far are enough to guide you into writing a first draft. That is not the end of the battle, however. Rewriting is the most important part of writing, especially on a major investigative story filled with potentially controversial information. Go through your story with a red pen, sentence by sentence. It's time to be a tough self-editor. Pare down wordy passages and long sections that regurgitate needless statistics from your database or other research. Simplify your language. Consider whether your overall structure is working from a storytelling point of view. Think about word choice and whether other words would provide greater clarity. Cut redundancies. Most writers incorporate too much of their notebook into their story. Never use four examples when one or two will make the point. One succinct, memorable quote from the right source is more effective than four meaningless quotes from others. 'Just as brilliant quotes bring a story to life, quotes used poorly or in heaping quantities can smother it,' warns writing coach Don Gibb, a retired professor who taught reporting for 20 years at Ryerson University's School of Journalism. 'Quotes that do nothing more than introduce factual, routine information—easily paraphrased—drag down a story.'[5]

Make sure every anecdote illustrates a different point. Read each example with an eye to whether it is contributing to the primary focus you articulated in the nut graf. Have you wandered off course somewhere? If so, readers will be confused and annoyed. The moment they get that aimless feeling, chances are they will move on. Finally, make sure narrative techniques have not compromised the facts. In journalism, unlike the writing of fiction, fact is the highest master.

Writing for Broadcast

Telling complicated investigative stories on radio or television is a challenge. Broadcast journalists need to take a minimalist approach. Their stories cannot be cluttered with details and numbers, and there is little time to explain methodology and complicated details, though, these days, a lot of those details can be put on a website that accompanies the story or series. And while it is true that a great narrative works in any medium, there are differences between print and broadcast that must be highlighted. North Americans get most of their information from television. If broadcasters do not find ways to tell better investigative stories, many Canadians will be deprived of information about important issues.

On television or radio, the audience gets only one crack at the information before it disappears into the ether. While broadcasters increase the shelf life of their stories by posting them online, it is still important to realize that viewers or listeners won't necessarily stick around just because the item is only a mouse click away. The story is still king, which is why broadcasters emphasize techniques such as simple writing, scene setting, and using memorable characters who 'project' well—by analogy to the way actors project their voices in a large theatre. All of this helps to lift information off the television screen, or out of the radio speaker, and convey it into the consciousness and memory of the audience.

Simple writing

Keep sentences short, declarative, and full of movement. Instead of using an adjective to describe something, use a verb. Why describe someone as a happy person? Why not explain that the person smiles a lot and even laughs at corny jokes? The verbs *smile* and *laughs* convey far more information than the adjective *happy*.

Simplicity also applies to the use of numbers, which should be kept to a minimum on television and radio. Too many numbers can be deadly. Broadcasters would do well to heed the advice offered by David Stewart-Patterson when he was CTV's business specialist:

> What you're trying to do, I think, especially in broadcast, is to give people an understanding of the forces at work. In a broad sense, things are getting better, or things are getting worse. But the underlying goal is giving people a better understanding of . . . what forces are affecting their lives.'[6]

Use numbers sparingly—just enough to get your point across. Viewers and listeners who want more information can be directed to additional information posted on the broadcaster's website.

Scene-setting

One of the aspects of storytelling that some journalists forget is place. Where did an event occur? What was the weather like when the murder took place? These are elements that contribute to setting the scene. When putting together a long investigative report for broadcast, journalists often break down the narrative in terms of scenes in which people are doing things. For the scenes to work, there must be memorable signposts that give the audience a sense of place. In Overdosed: The Drugging of Canadian Seniors, CBC Radio documentarist Bob Carty began his story this way:

> Bev McKay and her husband live in a large, beautiful cabin in the wilderness about 50 kilometres outside of Calgary. It is a peaceful, almost idyllic setting.
> But in her small home office, Bev McKay has pictures on display that tell tragic stories of pain, abuse, and death that are anything but serene.[7]

Note how, in the opening line, Carty takes his audience to a place in the wilderness, then contrasts that scene with Bev McKay's small office, lined with pictures. Such scenes, however brief they may be, take people to places and help move the narrative along.

Memorable characters

Later in the same documentary, Carty introduces us to another person, Stephanie Baziuk. She sent John Lisoway, her 76-year-old father, to a nursing home; he was suffering from dementia and was no longer able to take care of himself. Her father was given anti-psychotic medication to keep him calm but, while on the pills, he acted strangely. He would shuffle, avoid eye contact, and make strange piercing noises. The behaviour was so bizarre that Baziuk captured it on videotape. As the video's audio track plays in the radio documentary, Carty tells his audience, 'You see him in his bedroom, pacing the floor, his arms flailing. With every in-breath there is a piercing groan . . . the sound of agony . . . and in his eyes, a look of pure fear.'[8]

The haunting sound of John Lisoway pacing and groaning turned him into a memorable character in Carty's documentary. Even though Stephanie's father did not speak a word in the documentary—he passed away a few years after the video was shot—he was an unforgettable character, and his cameo appearance was a powerful one. Memorable characters may stick in a listener's mind because of the sound of their voices or the way they use words. A person may be memorable on television because of a disfigurement that makes it painful to talk or move. The point is, what makes someone memorable in broadcast can be different from what makes them stand out in a print story. A newspaper story can use selective quotes, great photographs, and snappy writing to bring a person to life. In broadcast, sources must do much of this 'heavy lifting' themselves. This is why it's important to find people who can express themselves well, or whose appearance helps amplify the story.

Don Gibb stresses the need to make these people integral parts of the story. They cannot be introduced at the beginning, then forgotten and tacked on at the end. He offers the advice to print reporters, but it works equally well for broadcasters, underscoring the point that memorable characters are important in any medium:

> When you do have someone to illustrate your story, be sure not to give the person short shrift. The person should be an integral part of telling your story. . . .
> - Make sure your person is a perfect fit for the story theme. The person has to know what she is talking about beyond clichés and generalizations.
> - Don't allow someone into your story simply because you talked to him. Or worse, because you have no one else. A person who has nothing to say to advance your story should be omitted.
> - Ask yourself these questions: Does the person add to my story? Does the person help readers see and feel the story? Does the person answer questions you would expect readers to ask? Do I need this person?
> - Try to avoid the standard open-with-the-person, end-with-the-person [approach]. It's a nice technique, but it's better to bring the person in throughout your story. Why? Stories often bog down in the middle with too many statistics and too many talking head experts.[9]

These techniques fit into a mindset used by many of the best investigators and storytellers who write for broadcast. They tend to think of their stories as real-life drama. The script is the screenplay. The interviewees are the actors, who in a sense are auditioned. For every three people interviewed for a long-form documentary, perhaps one will make it into the 'final cut' because he or she is a good speaker or has more of a presence. The others fail the audition and never make it into the broadcast. While such discrimination may seem heartless, Gibb points out that this is the nature of the legwork that goes into airing good stories. And for all the numbers a producer may have, if there is no person, no character to illustrate the dilemma, chances are the story will not get told.

The same is true for print, but for broadcast, it's a golden rule that is seldom broken. Memorable people make great radio and television.

Libel-Proofing the Story

The investigative story can be hard-hitting. It may accuse a politician of conflict of interest or a company of cheating customers or polluting the environment. It may allege a crime or other wrongdoing has been committed and it may name the names of those alleged to be responsible. Most investigative stories published or broadcast on issues of public interest uncover information that may make someone, somewhere look bad. For these reasons, investigative reporting carries a greater risk than daily journalism that a person or company whose reputation has been challenged could sue for defamation—or libel, as it is more commonly known.[10]

Investigative reporters must ensure the information they report is accurate and complete. Allegations must be based on verifiable facts and come from sources that are reliable and credible. Their stories must be fair and strike a balance between differing points of view. And they must make every effort to offer those accused of wrongdoing a chance to refute the allegations against them.

Journalists should view the law of defamation not as a barrier to reporting, but as a guarantee of quality journalism. If reporters were free to report whatever they liked about whoever they liked, any notion of media credibility would vanish. Rumours, hearsay, the conclusions of a reporter's cursory investigation, the ravings of every conspiracy theorist who walks through the newsroom door—all would be fair game. 'If no one had any redress for libel,' British columnist Paul Foot once noted, 'no one would ever believe a word we wrote.'[11] While libel law imposes limits on free speech to protect the reputations of individuals, it also helps to ensure that the information reaching the public is reliable, fair, and fact-based. It fosters and protects good journalism. If journalists conduct themselves professionally and responsibly, the chances of facing a defamation action—let alone losing one—become remote. And, as the development of the new libel defence of *responsible communication* on matters of public interest shows, the courts increasingly expect the conduct of journalists and media organizations to be consistent with the ethical standards of the profession.

This section offers an overview of the law of defamation and the steps investigative reporters can take to ensure their stories will withstand legal scrutiny. If the story is controversial or puts someone's reputation into question, the media organization's lawyers undoubtedly will be called in to vet the piece and offer advice on how to handle passages that may be vulnerable to a lawsuit. But the task of libel-proofing a story should not be left to editors and lawyers. Journalists should be able to spot potential problems in their stories at the reporting and writing stage, and they should know what needs to be done to minimize the legal risk of running the story.

Understanding defamation

Any statement that is published or broadcast and capable of damaging the reputation of a specific person could be considered defamatory. The classic definition of a libel is any statement that tends to discredit or lower an individual 'in the estimation of right-thinking members of society generally.' The same goes for a statement that may cause others to shun or avoid a person, or tends to expose the person to 'hatred, ridicule, or contempt'. Put another way, a false statement about someone, made to that person's discredit, would be defamatory.[12] Law professor Robert Martin has suggested a more down-to-earth definition of the kinds of statements that should be a warning flag for journalists: 'A libel,' he says, 'is simply something you would not like to see said in public about yourself.'[13]

Who can sue for libel?

The law of defamation is concerned with protecting the reputations of identifiable individuals. For a claim to succeed, the person suing—known as a plaintiff—must establish that he or she is the person portrayed in a bad light in a media report.[14] Corporations are considered 'persons' under Canadian law, and have the right to sue to protect their reputations. Courts have ruled that incorporated entities such as unions and non-profit groups can sue for libel. While the right to sue does not extend to a body without legal status, such as an ad-hoc citizen's committee, individuals belonging to this sort of group could bring an action if they could show that a statement related to their personal conduct. In the case of a company, the allegation must relate to the way it conducts its affairs (e.g., by defrauding customers).[15] A corporation cannot sue over allegations arising from the actions of individual officials or employees, but such persons would be free to launch their own libel suits. Governments cannot sue for libel: an Ontario judge ruled in 2006 that citizens must be able to question and criticize government actions and policies without fear of being sued. But individual politicians and civil servants still have the right to sue to protect their own reputations.[16] The person defamed must be alive; relatives and descendants cannot pursue a libel action on behalf of the person's estate.

In most cases, a group of people cannot sue for libel. An assertion that police officers take bribes, while obviously false, would be immune to a libel action because individual police officers could not show that the allegation refers specifically to them. In 2003, an Ontario court refused to allow Toronto's police union to sue the *Toronto Star* over stories alleging that officers engaged in racial profiling, ruling that the stories did not defame specific officers.[17] But journalists must be conscious of the size and nature of the group involved. The smaller the group and the more specific the reference, the greater the risk someone will be able to establish defamation. If a newspaper reports that police are targeting motorcycle gangs with connections to organized crime, for instance, and name a small-town club with only a few members, the members may be able to sue. The Alberta courts allowed 25 correctional officers to sue over a story describing guards at a particular jail as 'goons' and 'not having the brains to be Nazis', even though none of the guards was named, because the generalizations tainted the facility's entire staff.[18] In another case, a television report quoted a prostitute who claimed members of a narcotics squad who were 'high up—right up on top—take payoffs.' Nine members of the squad sued but the courts disallowed all actions except those of the squad's two senior officers, who had a strong case for claiming the report referred to them.[19]

Because of US law, it is difficult for politicians and others deemed to be public figures to sue for libel—and even erroneous news reports are protected from legal action as long as the journalist has not acted with malice.[20] In Canada, however, politicians have the same right to sue for defamation as any other citizen. The Supreme Court of Canada rejected an attempt to import the US practice into Canada in a 1995 ruling. In the court's opinion, 'it is not requiring too much of individuals that they ascertain the truth of the allegations they publish.'[21]

What can be considered libel?

Statements once considered libellous may now be as likely to make someone's reputation as to destroy it. 'What used to be called shame and humiliation is now called publicity,' satirist P.J. O'Rourke has joked. 'If you say a modern celebrity is an adulterer, a pervert and a drug addict, all it means is that you've read his autobiography.'[22] Publicity seekers aside, most people would never wish to be described publicly in such terms. The courts ultimately decide whether the words published or broadcast are defamatory. What the writer *intended* the words to mean is irrelevant, but neither is there a guarantee that the plaintiff's interpretation of a statement will be accepted. Judges examine the plain meaning of the words in dispute and strive, as one ruling put it, to 'construe the words according to the meaning they would be given by reasonable persons of ordinary intelligence.'[23] If words or terms carry a number of possible meanings, judges hit the books, consulting dictionaries and even collections of slang terms for guidance. A British Columbia judge, for instance, has ruled it is not libellous to call someone a 'son of a bitch.' Adding the adjective 'sick' to the term, however, changes the meaning and the phrase 'sick son of a bitch' is defamatory.[24] Judges also look at the context of the words. A reference to a Soviet defector as a 'traitor' was found not to be defamatory because the description was accurate when considered within the context of the entire news story.[25] The bottom line for journalists: choose your words carefully and be wary of using loaded terms that strike at the heart of someone's honesty or morality. Is the police officer who shot the fleeing suspect a 'racist', as critics claim? Was the politician 'lying' when she denied knowing about the controversy, or was she misinformed by her staff? If someone is accused of breaking the law, corruption, or other form of wrongdoing, the courts will demand proof to support the allegation.

Innuendo—the message that can be read between the lines of a news report—may also be defamatory. Suppose a journalist reports that a politician has an expensive lifestyle, makes only a modest salary, and supports proposals put forward by a businessperson who is also a long-time friend. Each one of these facts, in isolation, may be true. But when tied together, they convey the defamatory impression that the politician is taking bribes or kickbacks, even though those words appear nowhere in the report. The politician could sue for libel and the journalist might have to prove that bribery or kickbacks occurred. Robert Martin warns journalists not to 'waste their time beating around the bush or coyly suggesting conclusions.' Reporters should not try to make up for the gaps in a story 'by hinting at things.'[26]

Finally, journalists cannot duck a libel action by claiming they have only repeated what someone else has said. While a source makes a defamatory statement to a single person— the journalist—it is the news organization that disseminates it to a wide audience, inflicting the real damage to reputation.

Defences against claims of defamation

A person suing for libel does not have to prove that what was written or broadcast is false. Plaintiffs need only establish the media report is about them and the words used are capable of ruining their reputation. It is then up to the media outlet to show that the allegations are true or fall within the bounds of one of the other defences to libel.

Truth or justification

The best protection against a libel action is to get the facts right. No matter how extreme the statement, no matter how damaging the allegation, if the information can be proven to be true it cannot be defamatory. The law only protects reputations against attacks based on information that is false or inaccurate. One media law text notes the facts and any innuendo they create must be true for this defence to succeed, but defendants do not have to prove the truth of every word used; the 'gist of the statement' must be true.[27]

Proving that a statement is true is not as straightforward as it may seem. What a journalist suspects or believes to be true is irrelevant. Witnesses must be produced to verify information and to prove that documents are genuine. Journalists cannot rely on anonymous informants or sources who are unwilling to appear in court. Witnesses must be believable; a judge or jury may not believe that someone who has a criminal record is telling the truth, so other witnesses or evidence may be required to bolster that person's credibility. As well, the information must be admissible in court. For instance, what a witness says someone else uttered or saw is hearsay and, in most instances, this cannot be used as evidence.

Journalists must ask themselves tough questions as they write their stories. Can information and allegations be verified, either through witnesses, documents, or recordings? Are there independent sources to back up the story and, if so, how many? Does the information come from a participant or someone who is merely repeating what they heard from others? Is the source believable? Would the person be willing to testify if a libel suit were launched? The investigative reporter builds a story in the same way that a prosecutor or defence lawyer builds a case in court: piece by piece, laying a solid foundation of fact that will support the story's findings and assertions.

Responsible communication on matters of public interest

The Supreme Court of Canada created the *responsible communication defence* in a pair of 2009 rulings that overturned large damage awards against the *Toronto Star* and the *Ottawa Citizen*.[28] In essence, this defence gives the media the right to be wrong. It prevents libel claims from succeeding against news stories on important public issues, even if they include errors or statements that damage someone's reputation, as long as journalists made reasonable efforts to confirm the facts and dealt fairly and professionally with the subjects of the story. The Supreme Court decision shifts the focus from *what* was published or broadcast to *how* the story was reported. A judge or jury will assess whether journalists acted responsibly and, despite their best efforts, some facts or allegations turned out to be wrong or false. This reflects the legal test applied to doctors, lawyers, and other professionals facing allegations of negligence. Journalists are expected to be skilled and competent but not perfect. Patients die on the operating table, but not every death is the result of malpractice. The issue is how the operation was conducted and whether the surgeon's actions were reasonable in the circumstances. 'Productive debate is dependent on the free flow of information,' the Supreme Court noted in explaining the rationale behind the defence, and demanding perfection leads to an 'inevitable silencing of critical comment.'[29]

The defence is based on the 'responsible journalism' defence developed in the British courts.[30] The Ontario courts implemented it in 2007 and 2008[31] and the Supreme Court's final rulings have added refinements that now apply across the country. The Court has taken many of the elements of professional, ethical reporting—being fair, using solid sources, chasing important stories—and recognized them in law.

Here's how the defence works: First, a media report containing a potential libel must address an issue of public interest. This 'is not synonymous with what interests the public,' the Supreme Court cautioned, and would not include 'mere curiosity or prurient interest' in the private lives of public figures or celebrities. Second, the issue need not be of national importance or of interest to a wide audience. A battle over development in a rural area may be of local interest, for instance, but involves wider issues of land use and environmental policy. In the Court's words, 'it is enough that some segment of the community would have a genuine interest in receiving information on the subject.' Third, stories can be about government, politics, or subjects 'ranging from science and the arts to the environment, religion, and morality.' The media reports that led to the creation of the defence offer good examples. One was an *Ottawa Citizen* story that alleged an

Ontario police officer had hampered rescue efforts at Ground Zero after the 11 September 2001 terrorist attacks. In the other, the *Toronto Star* reported allegations that an Ontario businessman's political connections helped win approval for a controversial golf-course expansion.

If the story meets the public interest test—and any serious piece of investigative reporting should qualify—a court will decide whether reasonable steps were taken to verify the story. The Supreme Court formulated a list of factors (based on the British responsible journalism defence) to consider:

- *The seriousness of the allegation:* The more serious and damaging the allegation, the more diligent the journalist must be in researching and verifying the story.
- *The public importance of the matter:* Not all subjects of public interest have the same weight or importance. Stories exploring 'grave matters of national security,' the Court said, will require more diligence to investigate than those on 'the prosaic business of everyday politics.'
- *The urgency of the matter:* The courts will defer to the need to file timely reports on important allegations and events, but mistakes made in the rush to score a scoop might not be forgiven if a reasonable delay would have prevented publication of the error.
- *The status and reliability of the source:* If sources are untrustworthy or have an ax to grind, a reporter will be expected to show extra diligence in verifying what the source says. Confidential and unnamed sources can be used, but the test will be whether it was reasonable to do so.
- *Whether the plaintiff's side of the story was sought and accurately reported:* It's not always necessary or possible to contact the target of a defamatory comment, but the reporter must show that efforts were made to be fair and to get all sides of the story.
- *Whether the inclusion of the defamatory statement was justifiable:* The defamatory statement must be relevant to the story, but the court acknowledged that 'generous scope' should be given to editorial choices made in the newsroom.
- *Whether the defamatory statement's public interest lay in the fact that it was made rather than its truth:* The court termed this the 'reportage' defence, and it may be the most significant facet of the ruling. It recognizes that the public may have an interest in the allegations and countercharges made in debates over important issues, regardless of whether these allegations are true. While the law punishes those who repeat a libel, in this context, the messenger would have a defence if
    - (a) the statement is attributed, 'preferably' to a named source;
    - (b) the news report indicates the statement has not been verified;
    - (c) both sides of the dispute are reported fairly; and
    - (d) the report sets out the context in which the statement was made.

How this defence will be interpreted remains to be seen, but it may be a boon to reporters covering heated exchanges between politicians or when it is difficult to determine who's telling the truth.

- *Any other relevant circumstances:* A catch-all provision for other aspects of the story, including the tone of the article. Sensationalism or a critical tone may be appropriate, the Court noted, and writers should not be held to 'a standard of stylistic blandness. . . . The best investigative reporting often takes a trenchant or adversarial position on pressing issues of the day.'

This defence does not give journalists a licence to destroy reputations. As this list makes clear, the courts will demand high standards of conduct and the defence will be of little or no use to reporters who are sloppy or fail to keep an open mind as they do their stories. The journalist's actions and methods and the news organization's code of conduct will be put under the microscope and measured against the accepted ethical standards of journalism. But the defence encourages investigative journalism. It lessens libel chill and modernizes laws that, for too long, have put reputations ahead of society's need for hard-hitting journalism on important public issues.

One other important point: The Supreme Court deliberately named this the defence of 'responsible communication' because the definition of the term *journalist* is expanding in our multimedia age. Anyone 'publishing material of public interest in any medium'—bloggers and non-journalists included—is covered. Established journalistic practices will be used to assess the conduct of 'journalists and non-journalists alike,' the Court said, and standards will evolve 'to keep pace with the norms of new communications media.' Defamation law and its defences already apply to publication on the Internet, but this is a significant development. The ruling may encourage more high-quality, public-interest reporting by bloggers and citizen journalists.

Here's an example of how the defence might work: A journalist investigates an accusation that a restaurant inspector has taken bribes in return for ignoring food-safety violations. Police confirm they are looking into the allegation but refuse to identify the inspector. Two city hall sources confirm his name and say he has been suspended. The mayor calls a news conference to assure citizens that the allegation is being taken seriously, suspicious restaurant inspections will be reviewed, and steps will be taken to ensure diners are not served tainted food. The reporter calls the inspector's office and home five times seeking comment, to no avail. The story, naming the inspector, runs on the front page under the headline, 'Bribe probe prompts health fears'.

The allegation turns out to be false. No charges are laid, the inspector is reinstated, and public safety was never at risk. The inspector's reputation clearly has been damaged, but would the responsible communication defence defeat a libel action? The story would meet the following criteria:

- The bribery allegation is clearly a matter of public interest.
- The sources were solid.
- The reporter made reasonable efforts to verify the information.
- The bribery allegation had some substance and was under police investigation.

- There was urgency in publishing—people's health might be at risk.
- Efforts were made to interview the inspector.
- The story was not sensationalized and allegations were not reported as fact.

The story came up short on two fronts. First, it did not reflect the imperilled inspector's view of events and, second, the seriousness of the false allegation compounded the damage to the inspector's reputation. But the story was of intense public importance and the reporting was solid. The newspaper should be able to claim the defence of responsible communication.

Qualified privilege

As we noted in Chapter 5, freedom of expression and the public's right to know sometimes demand that defamatory statements can be reported in the media without fear of attracting a libel action. 'There are occasions when plain speaking is a public service, if not a moral duty,' a British libel lawyer has noted.[32] Media reports of official proceedings and documents are protected by qualified privilege, which means that journalists cannot be sued for publishing the statements or allegations made within them. Public sessions of Parliament and provincial/territorial legislatures, city council and school board meetings, and hearings of other public bodies are covered by this privilege. The courts have said there must be some form of public control over the proceedings—press conferences, church sermons, lectures, and political rallies are not protected by privilege.[33] But official documents are protected if they have been issued by a public body or are on file at a registry or government office and open to public scrutiny. Qualified privilege applies to the rulings of courts, tribunals, and public inquiries and all documents produced as evidence at their proceedings. This privilege also attaches to information in public documents, which the courts have defined as information that government agencies are required, by law, to make part of the public record.[34] At least one court has said qualified privilege applies to documents obtained from government agencies through a freedom-of-information request.[35]

If someone is accused of theft or fraud in a court document, the person has no right to sue the journalist who reports the allegations, even if the accusations turn out to be untrue. But, as mentioned in our discussion of court records, this right to publish damning information is a 'qualified' privilege and certain criteria must be met. The news report must be a 'fair and accurate' representation of what happened; it should stress that allegations have not been proven in court; and journalists must give the target of the allegations a chance to respond. There must be no suggestion of malice (i.e., that the journalist published the information out of spite or for some other improper motive).

When writing a story, look for documents and other sources of information that are covered by privilege. Was the allegation made in the transcript of a session of Parliament? Is the sequence of events set out in an affidavit or other court filing? Was the information made public by a government agency or released to the journalist through a request filed under access legislation? Were the questionable links between the businessperson and the politician revealed in documents tabled at a public inquiry? Privileged information is the cornerstone of solid investigative journalism, helping to shield the writer and the news organization from a libel action.

Privilege can also protect someone who has a duty to report information to the police. It also protects any official agency that has a duty to receive such information. Teachers, for instance, have a legal duty to report suspected child abuse and cannot be sued for defamation if their suspicions prove to be unfounded. The courts have been hesitant to apply this defence to media reports, since it is difficult to show a story is so urgent and so important that the media have a duty to make it public and citizens, in turn, have an interest in receiving the information.[36] The responsible-communication defence that we outlined in the previous section incorporates this defence and tailors it to media reports.[37]

Fair comment

Journalists may argue that a defamatory statement is 'fair comment'—an opinion based on the facts. In 1981, a CBC Radio reporter investigated a Winnipeg slum landlord and ended the report by describing the landlord as a person with 'no morals, principles, or conscience.' The landlord sued over this attack on his character, not over the revelations of the poor conditions in his buildings. While the courts acknowledged these were 'strong words', the well-researched report left no doubt tenants were living in filthy, substandard properties. The statement was found to be fair comment and the lawsuit was dismissed.[38]

The Supreme Court of Canada revised and updated the law of fair comment in 2008, acknowledging the need for greater tolerance of comments on matters of public interest—even extreme opinions intended to shock rather than enlighten. 'We live in a free country where people have as much right to express outrageous and ridiculous opinions as moderate ones,' the court ruled in dismissing a libel claim against controversial Vancouver radio talk-show host Rafe Mair. 'An individual's reputation is not to be treated as regrettable but unavoidable road kill on the highway of public controversy, but nor should an overly solicitous regard for personal reputation be permitted to "chill" freewheeling debate on matters of public interest.'[39] Mair's observation was pointed: a prominent anti-gay activist's address to a public meeting, he told listeners, reminded him of former Alabama governor George Wallace 'standing on the steps of a schoolhouse shouting to the crowds that no negroes would get into Alabama schools.'

While this defence is designed to protect the expression of opinion, it is often used to defend investigative stories. Under the criteria set out by the Supreme Court in the Mair ruling, a defendant relying on the defence of fair comment must establish that the comment deals with a matter of public interest. The public interest 'is a broad concept,' the court stated, making this 'relatively easy to establish.' The opinions published or broadcast must be based on fact, and these facts must be proven. Not all of the supporting evidence has to be included in the article or broadcast, though. The facts can be 'indicated' and may be 'so notorious as to be already understood by the audience.'[40] As well, the comments must be an honest expression of the person's belief—in the words of the court, 'an opinion that could honestly have been expressed on the proved facts by a person prejudiced, exaggerated or obstinate in his views.' If the journalist does not believe what has been said and written, it follows that the comment cannot be considered fair.[41] Finally, the statement must not be malicious; the information must not be reported in a deliberate attempt to harm someone or ruin the person's reputation.

Consent

As strange as it sounds, a person can agree to be defamed. While the defence of consent rarely applies, it can be used if the subject of a story makes damning admissions, then tries to retract them after they are reported in the media. A Nova Scotia newspaper could have advanced this defence after a musician phoned one of its reporters to announce that he had filed for bankruptcy. Court offices were closed and the reporter was unable to reach the musician's lawyer or agent for confirmation before the story was published. The musician later admitted the story was a hoax designed to embarrass the paper.[42] His reputation was damaged as he faced a backlash from nervous creditors, but he could not sue for defamation because he had instigated the story and, in effect, consented to its publication.

Malicious reporting

Journalists must act professionally, investigate thoroughly, double-check facts, and strive to produce a story that is accurate, balanced, and fair. As noted, the defences of fair comment, qualified privilege, and responsible journalism will fail if a story was published or broadcast maliciously—if it is clear the journalist or media outlet was motivated by spite, acted in bad faith, or was out to 'get' someone. While motivation is difficult to prove, the courts have said that evidence of malice can include a sensational treatment of the news, exaggerating or distorting facts, or using words that are unnecessarily harsh. Journalists have been judged to have acted with malice for failing to contact the target of the story, not bothering to check whether information is accurate, leaving out key facts, taking statements out of context, or publishing information known to be false.[43] Evidence of malice may come directly from those who produced the story. In one libel case, where a serious allegation of political corruption turned out to be a fabrication, an editor had referred to the plaintiff as a 'sleaze' and the reporter had boasted of catching the plaintiff red-handed.[44]

Libel chill

Journalists sometimes complain that the threat of a libel suit means some important stories go unreported. But if sources turn out to be unreliable or journalists cannot confirm that information is true, the story should be spiked. The public interest is not served, however, if editors and large media companies discourage investigative reporting or suppress stories—regardless of the strength of the evidence uncovered—rather than risk paying legal fees to defend a lawsuit and even more money in damages if the plaintiff wins. Six-figure damage awards for libel have become common, particularly when the person defamed is a doctor, lawyer, engineer, or other professional whose livelihood hinges on his or her reputation. In another disturbing trend, higher damages have been awarded if the news organization responsible for the libel is considered authoritative or reaches a large audience. In awarding $950,000 to a doctor defamed by a report on CBC Television's *the fifth estate* about the use of a heart drug, the judge cited the program's 'remarkable potential and capacity to cause damage.' *The fifth estate's* reputation and national audience of more than a million viewers made it 'far more likely to cause damage than other less respected publications or broadcasts,' the judge noted, creating 'a greater responsibility upon those who produce such programs to ensure that the content is factually correct.'[45]

The risk of being sued for libel should be put into perspective. While virtually any allegation or harsh criticism is 'capable of defamation', relatively few libel actions are threatened, let alone filed. Most people who feel an inaccurate report has damaged their reputation only want to see a correction or clarification. Serious allegations that are unfounded may bring the threat of a lawsuit, but these complaints are often settled when the media outlet agrees to make a public apology or retracts the original story. Few people have the financial resources or the stamina to pursue a legal action that could take years to reach trial.

Good journalism: The best defence

Good journalism—reporting done professionally, accurately, and fairly—is the best defence against the threat of a libel suit. Here are some tips on how to avoid being sued.

Verify

Double-check facts against previous news stories, official reports, and any other document that may back up a controversial statement or assertion. Seek out at least one independent source to back up what the main source of the story says happened. Look for documents covered by qualified privilege—such as court records and transcripts of debates—that support the allegations or a source's version of events. Journalists scrambling to make deadline or to avoid being scooped may feel pressured into rushing stories into print or onto the air before they have been fully researched and verified. Many costly defamation cases could have been avoided if reporters and editors had taken more time to get the story right.

The courts have imposed a clear division of responsibility within the newsroom—reporters gather the facts, editors and producers have a duty to confirm those facts before publication or broadcast. 'It is the editor's responsibility,' one judge has noted, 'to know in detail before publication, the documentation to support the story and the reliability of the sources and so ensure its accuracy.'[46] Another judge chastised the executive producer of a broadcast-news program who failed to check a major investigative piece before it aired.[47]

Question

Many news stories develop from a tip or suspicion that proves, on closer examination, to be overblown or unfounded. If the story seems too good to be true, it probably is. To avoid tunnel vision in their investigations, journalists must constantly question their preconceived notions and assumptions. Analyze and question the information you have gathered: Is each source credible? Does a key piece of information come from a participant, or is it hearsay? Sources often have their own agendas to promote or axes to grind. Find out why a source has decided to come forward with information or allegations. Ask tough questions, and be wary of any source who objects to being challenged or second-guessed. As well, bear in mind that documents can be easily doctored or faked. Check with the author of a leaked report or memo to ensure the document is genuine.

Act professionally

During an investigation, avoid asking questions during an interview or in an email that could trigger a libel action on their own. If a journalist attacks a person's character when interviewing someone else, the comments have been *published* (in the legal sense of the term) and the journalist could be sued for libel. Never directly accuse someone of lying or stealing; ask the person to explain what happened and whether what was done was proper. Obtain a copy of every important document, keep good notes, and electronically record key interviews. Retain all research materials for at least six months, in case a libel action is threatened.

If someone sues, all information the journalist has gathered must be disclosed to the plaintiff and could become evidence in court. Avoid making statements that denigrate the subject of a story and never write derogatory comments in the margins of documents or notebooks. Even the filename or slug used to identify a story could suggest malice. Using the word *pervert* to designate your subject in a story about allegations of sexual harassment, for instance, could be seen as evidence of the writer's mindset or prejudice. Make it a practice to avoid saying or writing anything that you do not want to see made public.

Strive for balance

Be fair to all sides of an issue or controversy. Seek out information and opinions that do not fit the official line or an opponent's criticism. It is easy to portray an issue as black and white or as the good guys versus the bad, but the truth usually lies between such extremes. Make a genuine effort to contact anyone who is being criticized in a story, even if the result is a simple 'no comment'. If an explanation is offered, fairness demands that it be given prominence in the story even if it appears to be dubious or self-serving.

Show restraint

Present the facts without speculating on motives, unless there is evidence to back up an assertion that the businessperson lied or the government official personally benefited from a decision. Avoid sensationalism and do not use language that is unduly harsh or more judgmental than the facts will bear. Let the facts speak for themselves; viewers and readers will be able to draw their own conclusions.

Suggestions for Further Reading

Brown, Raymond E. *Defamation Law: A Primer.* Toronto: Carswell, 2003.

Canadian Journalism Project (J-Source). 'Journalists and the Law: Libel' and 'Internet Media Law', law section, *www.j-source.ca.*

Jobb, Dean. *Media Law for Canadian Journalists*, 2nd ed. Toronto: Emond Montgomery Publications, 2010, Chapters 4 and 12.

———. 'Journalists Win One in Court: The defense of "responsible journalism" can be used to head off libel suits', *Media Magazine*, vol. 14, no. 3 (Winter 2010), 18. Available at *www.caj.ca/mediamag/Media_Winter2010.pdf.*

Martin, Robert. *Media Law.* Toronto: Irwin Law, 2003, Chapter 4.

CASE STUDY: Part IV—Jeffrey Simpson

Jeffrey Simpson, a reporter with *The Halifax Chronicle Herald*, put Nova Scotia's motor vehicle inspection safety system to the test in 2007. He took an older car to five garages—receiving repair estimates ranging from $30 to almost $1000—then used government data and interviews with mechanics and consumers to expose a flawed regulatory regime. His stories forced the provincial government to revamp its inspection process, curbed abuses by unscrupulous mechanics and garage owners, and saved drivers money. Simpson, a 2004 winner of the Atlantic Journalism Award, has been reporting for the *Chronicle Herald* since 1996.

Q   What was the name of your story/project?

A   'It's the MVI lottery' was the headline on the original article that kicked off the project.

Q   How did you get the idea for the project?

A   The provincial government introduced an expanded system of motor vehicle inspections in 2007, upping both the list of things mechanics needed to check and the cost to car and truck owners. The government claimed this was necessary to improve public safety and cut down on deficient or fraudulent checks, but many measures seemingly had little to do with such concerns. The government didn't face much in the way of public scrutiny over the changes (or the original inspection system, because it had been in place for so long). Our paper gave it a bullseye in its weekly 'hits and misses' feature. But there had long been grumbling from mechanics and car owners about the system, so I decided to check it out. I thought about different ways to test the system, including going along with somebody taking their car to various mechanics. But I thought this might be a bit complicated to set up and could even result in mechanics carrying out the inspections differently than normal if a customer was accompanied by someone. So I decided to just take a car around myself—and not mention that I was a reporter until after the inspection was completed.

Q   What initial research did you do to confirm the story was valid?

A   I checked how motor vehicle inspections had changed and I also attempted to obtain some explanation about why this was done. I looked into how widely used such inspections systems are in Canada. Then it was a matter of taking the car for multiple inspections to see what happened.

Q   What was your initial theory as to what the story would be?

A   I worked at a service station when I was teenager, so I was well aware of the potential such places had for housing unscrupulous managers and mechanics preying upon unsuspecting customers. People have also long complained about the annual inspections, claiming some garages were tougher than others. So, while I expected to see discrepancies in the results, I really had no idea what would happen. It was a bit of an experiment and I went into it with an open mind. I didn't want to draw any premature conclusions or affect the results.

Q   Once you confirmed that you had a story, how did you plan out your research?

A   The big thing was figuring out how to proceed with the inspections. I wasn't going to identify myself as a journalist; obviously, the mechanics would be suspicious and either refuse the inspection or conduct it differently. But I had other concerns. I didn't want to misrepresent myself, I definitely didn't want to lie, and I didn't want the investigation to seem too contrived, like I was predetermining the outcome. My biggest concern was that there'd be no story and I'd have to come back to my boss and explain how I'd wasted a lot of work hours and money for nothing. The car could have been failed and deemed unfit for the road right off the bat, meaning that I wouldn't have been able to drive it away. A station could have refused to inspect it or asked some uncomfortable questions after seeing it had just been inspected the same week. It could have passed all five times or mechanics might have pointed out the same problems, making for a boring story.

Q   What secondary-source research was required?

A   I accessed each province's website for information on its motor vehicle regulations and through some of them learned about studies that had been done and, in some cases, influenced their decisions to scrap such inspections years earlier.

Q   What were the most important interviews for the story?

A   Service Nova Scotia Minister Jamie Muir, who was responsible for the inspection system, was important because he acknowledged from the beginning that the system was far from perfect yet he was seemingly in no hurry to make improvements.

Another important interview was with Patrick O'Malley, the province's inspection coordinator. He was in charge of inspections but unable to justify or explain why changes were made to the system. He also told me about punitive measures he could take against service stations, but wouldn't divulge any details. This gave me the subject of a freedom-of-information request and resulted in more follow-up stories.

And, of course, the interviews I conducted with service-station managers after their mechanics had checked the car I'd brought in. I phoned, told them who I was and what I did and gave them a chance to explain. Every mechanic I interviewed—at the time and subsequently—told me they know people in their industry are ripping off customers. It was an accepted fact. But they weren't happy about the stories. One asked me to bring the car back to have it checked again, but, as I have written about since, they wouldn't always provide a customer with that luxury—especially if the customer didn't pay for another inspection. I had all the written reports they'd provided me with, and I knew the car hadn't been touched between inspections.

Q   What methods did you use to organize your research?

A   I kept the written records of the safety inspections at hand and kept track of who I interviewed—and transcripts of my conversations with them—on my computer. Later, when I dug into the story again, I received the results of freedom-of-information requests.

Q   Did you use any computerized techniques to do or organize research?

A   I used an Excel® spreadsheet to examine the government's records of service stations that were investigated.

Q   Did you use any undercover reporting for the story?

A   I didn't want to misrepresent myself or lie, but I also didn't want the investigation to seem too contrived or predetermined. I took a colleague's 1997 Plymouth Breeze to five different garages. I wanted a sampling of different types of service stations, so I chose a Chrysler dealership, a Canadian Tire, a Petro-Canada service station, a Speedy, and a small independent garage with no sign, where the owner worked his way through a parking lot of customers' cars.

I first went to a Petro-Canada Certigard station, where mechanics failed it and found $738.72 worth of repairs. Not only that, they also recommended over $1000 of additional repairs (front sway bar link kit, horn not working, rear tires too worn, left rear wheel cylinder seized, and right rear brake drum scored). I went down the street to Canadian Tire and they passed it, charging $30.21. Then I went to Speedy. They failed it for the brake drum and two rear tires; the estimate was $319.41. Steele Chrysler failed it for the rear tires and brake tubing, which is expensive to replace due to labour costs. Their cost: $973.32. Ochterloney Service Station singled out the scored brake drum, rear tires, and the light bulb over the licence plate, totalling $289.27.

Q   Can you elaborate a bit on the freedom-of-information requests for the story?

A   When I interviewed the guy in charge of the inspections for the province, I couldn't get clear answers on why they changed the system or if it worked—it was carefully stage managed by the department's communications people. So I submitted freedom-of-information requests. One was to determine how many mechanics and service stations were penalized for conducting shoddy inspections. Another was to see what kind of records they had on my investigation, because the man in charge of inspections told me he'd investigated it.

Q   How important were these requests for the story?

A   Getting the records of shoddy inspections was helpful in advancing the story and putting more pressure on the Nova Scotia government to revamp the system.

Q   Many projects have a turning point when it all seems to fall into place. Was there such a point for this one?

A   The turning point for this story was after I took the car in for its second inspection. Because it differed so drastically from the first, I knew I had the makings of a story.

Q   How many stories did you write?

A   In an initial instalment of stories for the project, I wrote about people who faced similar problems and the pressure they felt to have the work done where they'd taken the car for an inspection, even if they were suspicious. One man was charged by police for driving his car home when it wasn't safety inspected. I later followed the case of a man who questioned a safety inspection, then wanted to lodge a complaint. The ensuing story illustrated a system that was arbitrary and too cumbersome to address driver complaints and ensure the public wasn't being taken for a ride.

Q   How long did the project take to research and write?

A   Taking the car to the different mechanics and then conducting the interviews and writing the stories for the initial three-part instalment took more than two weeks. For some service stations, I had to make appointments several days in advance. I later returned to the story, using the situation of a local man as a further example of how the system didn't work. And I also spent time filing freedom-of-information requests as I followed up.

Q   What was the most challenging part about writing these stories?

A   Probably explaining in simple language the discrepancies in inspections without getting bogged down in technical jargon. I also wanted to be fair to the businesses, so I in detailed their findings and explanations. It was a trickier story to write than it appears because there was always a lot of information but not unlimited space in the paper.

Q   Over how many days did the stories run?

A   Initially, over a three-day period. Then I dug back into it a year later, writing stories over several months as I documented the changes.

Q   Did your project include online elements?

A   We scanned the inspection reports and posted them on our website.

Q   On what dates did the stories run?

A   The first instalment came, 3–5 July 2007. The follow-ups were 12 December 2008; 2, 4, and 11 February 2009; and 1 April 2009.

Q   What was the most satisfying part of the project?

A   The most satisfying thing was that it performed a public service, helping to correct a government policy that was unfair. My work exposed a system that was arbitrary—mechanics and their customers agreed on this—and too cumbersome to address public complaints to ensure people weren't being exploited. Several hundred readers phoned and emailed me to share their frustrations with the system and to express their thanks. It was obvious from the minister's comments and inaction that the government wasn't going to fix the inspection system on its own.

   Thanks to public pressure resulting from my stories, the minister's hand was forced and he eventually announced that his department would be reviewing the inspection system. The day these stories were published, the provincial government announced it would be reviewing the motor vehicle inspection system. The department later made several changes, scaling down the inspection criteria and decreasing the frequency with which they must be performed.

Q   What other comments would you make about this project?

A   This goes a bit beyond a consumer story in my mind, because it's a mandatory government system from which the province and mechanics can make money. Meanwhile, there was little in the way of public protection. The Registry of Motor Vehicles was unable to adequately justify this public policy; it could neither explain why the most recent changes were warranted nor prove that the inspections were accomplishing their goal of keeping the streets safer. The province still hasn't explained or demonstrated why inspections are necessary in Nova Scotia and not in other jurisdictions.

Appendix A

Quick Guide to Spreadsheets

As we discussed in Chapter 11, the spreadsheet is probably the simplest of the CAR tools, and the one most adept at working with numbers. The purpose of this appendix is to demystify the topic of spreadsheets for anyone who finds them intimidating, to alert you to the useful things a spreadsheet can do, and to give a quick summary of how to use the basic features. We begin with some definitions:

Definitions

A **spreadsheet** is a computer program that allows you to do simple or complex calculations on a series of numbers at the same time. Whenever values in the spreadsheet change, any calculations dependent on those values will be redone automatically (unless you set them to be done manually).

Microsoft Excel® is a brand of spreadsheet. If you have another brand, you will find that most of the information in this section also applies to your program, albeit with slight tweaks.

A **worksheet** is a page with a grid, made up of rows, columns, and cells. It is similar to a city map, with letters running across the top and numbers down the left side. Just as the letters and numbers on maps allow you to find specific streets, the ones on a worksheet allow you to find locations on the worksheet called cells. Depending on the version you are using, an Excel® sheet can have between 256 and 16,384 columns and between 65,536 and 1,048,576 rows. The lower limits apply to Excel® versions up to 2003. For those who like really big numbers, that works out to between 16,777,216 and 17,179,869,184 cells per worksheet. You can open multiple worksheets and each one has the same number of cells.

The **cell pointer** is moved around the screen by the mouse. When you click on a cell, its border is highlighted to indicate it is the active cell, meaning the one in which you can add or change information. When you type information into a cell, anything that was in it before is erased. If you merely want to edit an entry, double-click on the cell, or edit it in the formula bar.

The **formula bar** is a horizontal bar across the top of the spreadsheet screen that shows the contents of the active cell, whether a formula, value, or label.

Toolbars are those bars across the top of the screen that contain little icons. The toolbars allow you to do many things quickly without having to open up menus or use keyboard commands (there are keyboard shortcuts for many Excel® features). Commonly used toolbar buttons include the *autosum* button, the *currency format* button, the *percentage format* button, and buttons that add or remove decimal places. Excel® has different toolbars for different purposes that can be added and removed. Right-clicking on the active toolbar will bring up a box with a list of toolbars that can be added and removed by checking and unchecking them.

A **column** runs down from the top of the worksheet page and is made up of individual cells. Each column is labelled with a letter, starting at *A* and running through to *Z*, and on through *AA*, *AB*, and ultimately to *IV* for column 256. **Rows** run across from the left. A row is also made up of individual cells.

A **cell** is a rectangular area in which text (labels), numbers (values), and formulas can be typed. Cells are known by their coordinates; e.g., cell *A1* is at the intersection of column *A* and row *1*.

Labels are any characters typed into a cell that aren't purely numeric. Excel® normally orients labels to the left of the cell. Labels are usually located along the far left, and across the top of the worksheet, to identify what all those numbers are. A spreadsheet without labels is mostly useless.

Values are numbers you type into cells. You can do calculations using values. Values are usually oriented to the right side of the cell. If you ever see a number oriented to the left, it means that somehow the spreadsheet is seeing it as a label or as text, and you won't be able to use it for calculations. This can happen sometimes when a database file is imported into Excel®. It also happens if an apostrophe is entered before a number in a cell. The apostrophe won't be visible, but it tells the program to treat the number as text.

Formulas are used to do calculations on one cell or a series of cells. For instance, the code *=A1+B1+C1* is a simple spreadsheet formula. The equal sign before the cell references tells the program that you are now entering a formula. As you enter this text, it will appear in the formula bar at the top of the screen. You can alter it there later by putting the cell pointer into the cell where you typed the formula. The results of formulas are automatically updated as soon as you change any of the values on which the formula is based, unless you have set up the program for manual recalculation. You would do this only on an extremely large worksheet where recalculation of thousands of values would slow the computer down.

Functions are used to make it easier to write formulas. Examples include *AVERAGE, MEDIAN*, and *SUM* (these are explained in the following section).

What a Spreadsheet Looks Like

The accompanying illustration shows an Excel® worksheet containing information on the population of census metropolitan areas in Canada in 2006 and 2008, in thousands. The data comes from Statistics Canada. Annotations on the illustration point out some of the main features of the worksheet. Note that the examples are illustrated using the traditional Excel® user interface—not only because it is still in wide use, but also because it is similar to the version of Excel® available for Apple Macintosh computers, and to other spreadsheet programs such as OpenOffice.org. For a comprehensive guide to the features of the newer versions of Excel® (2007 and 2010), as well as to more advanced spreadsheet features, you should obtain a copy of Fred Vallance-Jones and David McKie's *Computer-Assisted Reporting: A Comprehensive Primer*, available from Oxford University Press.

Using the Statistics Canada data, we are going to walk through the Excel® functions most often used by journalists. If you would like to follow along in your own copy of Excel®, you can copy the data directly from Statistics Canada's website (*www.statcan.ca*; look in the 'Summary Tables' section). If you are working with Microsoft Internet Explorer on a PC or Safari on a Mac, you simply have to select the table on the webpage by highlighting it, then copy and paste it into Excel®.

Annotations:
- Row 3
- Autosum button
- Sort in ascending or descending order
- Column E
- Add or remove decimal places
- Cell E3
- Display as currency

	A	B	C
1	CMA	2006	2008
2	Abbotsford-Mission, B.C.	164.3	170.7
3	Barrie, Ont.	183.9	188.2
4	Brantford, Ont.	135.4	136.6
5	Calgary, Alta.	1,123.90	1,182.40
6	Edmonton, Alta.	1,073.80	1,124.20
7	Greater Sudbury, Ont.	164.2	164.8
8	Guelph, Ont.	132.2	134.1
9	Halifax, N.S.	384.8	394.6
10	Hamilton, Ont.	719.9	731.5
11	Kelowna, B.C.	167.1	180.1
12	Kingston, Ont.	158	158.8
13	Kitchener, Ont.	470.7	482
14	London, Ont.	477.6	485.2
15	Moncton, N.B.	129.5	132.2
16	Montréal, Que.	3,685.00	3,750.50
17	Oshawa, Ont.	344.2	356.6
18	Ottawa-Gatineau, Ont.-Que.	1,169.00	1,198.70
19	Peterborough, Ont.	120.5	120.8
20	Québec, Que.	724.3	738.9
21	Regina, Sask.	200.1	206.7
22	Saguenay, Que.	152.5	153.3
23	Saint John, N.B.	125	125.8
24	Saskatoon, Sask.	240.5	250.4
25	Sherbrooke, Que.	188.7	191.4
26	St. Catharines-Niagara, Ont.	404.1	403.7
27	St. John's, N.L.	183.4	185.7
28	Thunder Bay, Ont.	127.1	124.6
29	Toronto, Ont.	5,336.10	5,531.30
30	Trois-Rivières, Que.	142.5	144.6
31	Vancouver, B.C.	2,190.10	2,271.20
32	Victoria, B.C.	339.8	348.2
33	Windsor, Ont.	336.1	333.6
34	Winnipeg, Man.	716.4	732.6

Basic math

Addition

Addition, or summing, is probably the most common thing you will do in a spreadsheet, whether with a few numbers at a time, as here, or with thousands, or tens of thousands. So the first thing we will do is add up the total population of the census's metropolitan areas.

To add a range of cells, we use this formula.

=SUM(CELL1:CELL3)

The colon between the cell references tells the program that we are dealing with a continuous range of cells, starting with the first one and running through to the last. If the cells aren't in a continuous range, separate them with commas:

=SUM(CELL1, CELL3)

You can also combine this to have several continuous ranges, separated by commas, as in =SUM(B3:B5,B8:B11).You type the formula where you want the answer to appear, as in this illustration:

	A	B	C	D	E
1	CMA	2006	2008		
2	Abbotsford-Mission, B.C.	164.3	170.7		
3	Barrie, Ont.	183.9	188.2		
4	Brantford, Ont.	135.4	136.6		
5	Calgary, Alta.	1,123.90	1,182.40		
6	Edmonton, Alta.	1,073.80	1,124.20		
7	Greater Sudbury, Ont.	164.2	164.8		
8	Guelph, Ont.	132.2	134.1		
9	Halifax, N.S.	384.8	394.6		
10	Hamilton, Ont.	719.9	731.5		
11	Kelowna, B.C.	167.1	180.1		
12	Kingston, Ont.	158	158.8		
13	Kitchener, Ont.	470.7	482		
14	London, Ont.	477.6	485.2		
15	Moncton, N.B.	129.5	132.2		
16	Montréal, Que.	3,685.00	3,750.50		
17	Oshawa, Ont.	344.2	356.6		
18	Ottawa-Gatineau, Ont.-Que.	1,169.00	1,198.70		
19	Peterborough, Ont.	120.5	120.8		
20	Québec, Que.	724.3	738.9		
21	Regina, Sask.	200.1	206.7		
22	Saguenay, Que.	152.5	153.3		
23	Saint John, N.B.	125	125.8		
24	Saskatoon, Sask.	240.5	250.4		
25	Sherbrooke, Que.	188.7	191.4		
26	St. Catharines-Niagara, Ont.	404.1	403.7		
27	St. John's, N.L.	183.4	185.7		
28	Thunder Bay, Ont.	127.1	124.6		
29	Toronto, Ont.	5,336.70	5,531.30		
30	Trois-Rivières, Que.	142.5	144.6		
31	Vancouver, B.C.	2,190.10	2,271.20		
32	Victoria, B.C.	339.8	348.2		
33	Windsor, Ont.	336.1	333.6		
34	Winnipeg, Man.	716.4	732.6		
35					
36		=SUM(B2:B34)			
37		SUM(number1, [number2], ...)			
38					

Microsoft Excel - DD2_ApAimg2.xls
MEDIAN   =SUM(B2:B34)
Sheet1 / Sheet2 / Sheet3

Notice that the formula also appears in the formula bar across the top of the screen. When you press *<Enter>*, the result appears in the cell.

The autosum button

There is a useful shortcut called the *autosum* button. By highlighting a cell underneath or to the left of the row or column of figures to be added, and then clicking on the symbol that looks like a letter *E* (it is actually the Greek letter sigma) on the toolbar, you can quickly add up the range of cells.

Copying a formula

From here, we could type the equivalent formula into the next cell to the right, to work out the total population for 2007. Instead, though, we will simply copy the formula by selecting the cell where we wrote it, then move the mouse pointer to the lower-right corner of the cell until a little '+' symbol appears. We will then hold onto the left mouse button and drag the '+' across to the right to copy the formula. When we let go of the mouse button, the formula will be automatically copied, as in the next illustration:

	A	B	C	D	E
1	CMA	2006	2008		
2	Abbotsford-Mission, B.C.	164.3	170.7		
3	Barrie, Ont.	183.9	188.2		
4	Brantford, Ont.	135.4	136.6		
5	Calgary, Alta.	1,123.90	1,182.40		
6	Edmonton, Alta.	1,073.80	1,124.20		
7	Greater Sudbury, Ont.	164.2	164.8		
8	Guelph, Ont.	132.2	134.1		
9	Halifax, N.S.	384.8	394.6		
10	Hamilton, Ont.	719.9	731.5		
11	Kelowna, B.C.	167.1	180.1		
12	Kingston, Ont.	158	158.8		
13	Kitchener, Ont.	470.7	482		
14	London, Ont.	477.6	485.2		
15	Moncton, N.B.	129.5	132.2		
16	Montréal, Que.	3,685.00	3,750.50		
17	Oshawa, Ont.	344.2	356.6		
18	Ottawa-Gatineau, Ont.-Que.	1,169.00	1,198.70		
19	Peterborough, Ont.	120.5	120.8		
20	Québec, Que.	724.3	738.9		
21	Regina, Sask.	200.1	206.7		
22	Saguenay, Que.	152.5	153.3		
23	Saint John, N.B.	125	125.8		
24	Saskatoon, Sask.	240.5	250.4		
25	Sherbrooke, Que.	188.7	191.4		
26	St. Catharines-Niagara, Ont.	404.1	403.7		
27	St. John's, N.L.	183.4	185.7		
28	Thunder Bay, Ont.	127.1	124.6		
29	Toronto, Ont.	5,336.70	5,531.30		
30	Trois-Rivières, Que.	142.5	144.6		
31	Vancouver, B.C.	2,190.10	2,271.20		
32	Victoria, B.C.	339.8	348.2		
33	Windsor, Ont.	336.1	333.6		
34	Winnipeg, Man.	716.4	732.6		
35					
36		22211.3	22834		

B36 ▼ ƒ= =SUM(B2:B34)

Microsoft Excel - DD2_ApAimg4.xls

Sum=45045.3

Other functions

There are many more spreadsheet functions in addition to summing. For example, 'AVERAGE' will calculate the average among a range of values (e.g., AVERAGE(A2:A26) will calculate the average value in the range of cells from A2 through A26). 'MEDIAN' will calculate the median. There are dozens more, including some mighty impressive statistical calculations.

Calculating percentages

After adding, the next most likely thing you will do with a spreadsheet is calculate percentages. Journalists love percentages because they are familiar and readers understand them.

It is easy to calculate a percentage in a spreadsheet as long as you remember this basic rule: you will probably have a smaller number that you want to see as a percentage of a bigger number. If so, remember this rule: take the smaller number and divide it by the bigger one. So, if you want to find out what 50 is as a percentage of 100, you divide 50 by 100. (Don't worry about multiplying by 100. The spreadsheet takes care of that for you, as you will see.)

To begin, we will insert a column after the existing column for 2006. To do this, we click at the top of an existing column to highlight it, as in this illustration:

	A	B	C	D	E
	CMA	2006	2008		
1					
2	Abbotsford-Mission, B.C.	164.3	170.7		
3	Barrie, Ont.	183.9	188.2		
4	Brantford, Ont.	135.4	136.6		
5	Calgary, Alta.	1,123.90	1,182.40		
6	Edmonton, Alta.	1,073.80	1,124.20		
7	Greater Sudbury, Ont.	164.2	164.8		
8	Guelph, Ont.	132.2	134.1		
9	Halifax, N.S.	384.8	394.6		
10	Hamilton, Ont.	719.9	731.5		
11	Kelowna, B.C.	167.1	180.1		
12	Kingston, Ont.	158	158.8		
13	Kitchener, Ont.	470.7	482		
14	London, Ont.	477.6	485.2		
15	Moncton, N.B.	129.5	132.2		
16	Montréal, Que.	3,685.00	3,750.50		
17	Oshawa, Ont.	344.2	356.6		
18	Ottawa-Gatineau, Ont.-Que.	1,169.00	1,198.70		
19	Peterborough, Ont.	120.5	120.8		
20	Québec, Que.	724.3	738.9		
21	Regina, Sask.	200.1	206.7		
22	Saguenay, Que.	152.5	153.3		
23	Saint John, N.B.	125	125.8		
24	Saskatoon, Sask.	240.5	250.4		
25	Sherbrooke, Que.	188.7	191.4		
26	St. Catharines-Niagara, Ont.	404.1	403.7		
27	St. John's, N.L.	183.4	185.7		
28	Thunder Bay, Ont.	127.1	124.6		
29	Toronto, Ont.	5,336.70	5,531.30		
30	Trois-Rivières, Que.	142.5	144.6		
31	Vancouver, B.C.	2,190.10	2,271.20		
32	Victoria, B.C.	339.8	348.2		
33	Windsor, Ont.	336.1	333.6		
34	Winnipeg, Man.	716.4	732.6		
35					
36		22211.3	22834		

Sheet1 / Sheet2 / Sheet3

Ready   Sum=47676

We then go to the Insert menu at the top of the screen and choose 'columns', as in this illustration:

	A			C	D	E
1	CM		2008			
2	Abbotsford-Miss		.3	170.7		
3	Barrie, Ont.		.9	188.2		
4	Brantford, Ont.		.4	136.6		
5	Calgary, Alta.		00	1,182.40		
6	Edmonton, Alta.		30	1,124.20		
7	Greater Sudbury		.2	164.8		
8	Guelph, Ont.		.2	134.1		
9	Halifax, N.S.		.8	394.6		
10	Hamilton, Ont.		.9	731.5		
11	Kelowna, B.C.		.1	180.1		
12	Kingston, Ont.		58	158.8		
13	Kitchener, Ont.		470.7	482		
14	London, Ont.		477.6	485.2		
15	Moncton, N.B.		129.5	132.2		
16	Montréal, Que.		3,685.00	3,750.50		
17	Oshawa, Ont.		344.2	356.6		
18	Ottawa-Gatineau, Ont.-Que.		1,169.00	1,198.70		
19	Peterborough, Ont.		120.5	120.8		
20	Québec, Que.		724.3	738.9		
21	Regina, Sask.		200.1	206.7		
22	Saguenay, Que.		152.5	153.3		
23	Saint John, N.B.		125	125.8		
24	Saskatoon, Sask.		240.5	250.4		
25	Sherbrooke, Que.		188.7	191.4		
26	St. Catharines-Niagara, Ont.		404.1	403.7		
27	St. John's, N.L.		183.4	185.7		
28	Thunder Bay, Ont.		127.1	124.6		
29	Toronto, Ont.		5,336.70	5,531.30		
30	Trois-Rivières, Que.		142.5	144.6		
31	Vancouver, B.C.		2,190.10	2,271.20		
32	Victoria, B.C.		339.8	348.2		
33	Windsor, Ont.		336.1	333.6		
34	Winnipeg, Man.		716.4	732.6		
35						
36			22211.3	22834		
37						

Sheet1 / Sheet2 / Sheet3 /

Ready   Sum=47676

As soon as we let go of the left mouse button, the new column will appear:

Microsoft Excel - DD2_ApAimg7.xls

File   Edit   View   Insert   Format   Tools   Data   Window   Help

Arial   9.5   B   U

C1

	A	B	C	D	E
1	CMA	2006		2008	
2	Abbotsford-Mission, B.C.	164.3		170.7	
3	Barrie, Ont.	183.9		188.2	
4	Brantford, Ont.	135.4		136.6	
5	Calgary, Alta.	1,123.90		1,182.40	
6	Edmonton, Alta.	1,073.80		1,124.20	
7	Greater Sudbury, Ont.	164.2		164.8	
8	Guelph, Ont.	132.2		134.1	
9	Halifax, N.S.	384.8		394.6	
10	Hamilton, Ont.	719.9		731.5	
11	Kelowna, B.C.	167.1		180.1	
12	Kingston, Ont.	158		158.8	
13	Kitchener, Ont.	470.7		482	
14	London, Ont.	477.6		485.2	
15	Moncton, N.B.	129.5		132.2	
16	Montréal, Que.	3,685.00		3,750.50	
17	Oshawa, Ont.	344.2		356.6	
18	Ottawa-Gatineau, Ont.-Que.	1,169.00		1,198.70	
19	Peterborough, Ont.	120.5		120.8	
20	Québec, Que.	724.3		738.9	
21	Regina, Sask.	200.1		206.7	
22	Saguenay, Que.	152.5		153.3	
23	Saint John, N.B.	125		125.8	
24	Saskatoon, Sask.	240.5		250.4	
25	Sherbrooke, Que.	188.7		191.4	
26	St. Catharines-Niagara, Ont.	404.1		403.7	
27	St. John's, N.L.	183.4		185.7	
28	Thunder Bay, Ont.	127.1		124.6	
29	Toronto, Ont.	5,336.70		5,531.30	
30	Trois-Rivières, Que.	142.5		144.6	
31	Vancouver, B.C.	2,190.10		2,271.20	
32	Victoria, B.C.	339.8		348.2	
33	Windsor, Ont.	336.1		333.6	
34	Winnipeg, Man.	716.4		732.6	
35					
36		22211.3		22834	

Sheet1 / Sheet2 / Sheet3 /

Ready

To actually do a percentage calculation, we select the cell where we want the answer to appear, then enter the formula for calculating a simple percentage. In this case, we might type *=B2/36.*

B2 contains the 2006 population of Abbotsford-Mission, British Columbia, and *B36* the total population of census metropolitan areas in 2006. (We are actually going to add a '$' character to this formula, typing *=B2/B$36.* The '$' is an instruction to Excel® to 'lock' that part of the calculation in place, regardless of what else moves around on the worksheet. We explain this technique more fully later on.)

	A	B	C	D	E
1	CMA	2006		2008	
2	Abbotsford-Mission, B.C.	164.3	=b2/b$36	170.7	
3	Barrie, Ont.	183.9		188.2	
4	Brantford, Ont.	135.4		136.6	
5	Calgary, Alta.	1,123.90		1,182.40	
6	Edmonton, Alta.	1,073.80		1,124.20	
7	Greater Sudbury, Ont.	164.2		164.8	
8	Guelph, Ont.	132.2		134.1	
9	Halifax, N.S.	384.8		394.6	
10	Hamilton, Ont.	719.9		731.5	
11	Kelowna, B.C.	167.1		180.1	
12	Kingston, Ont.	158		158.8	
13	Kitchener, Ont.	470.7		482	
14	London, Ont.	477.6		485.2	
15	Moncton, N.B.	129.5		132.2	
16	Montréal, Que.	3,685.00		3,750.50	
17	Oshawa, Ont.	344.2		356.6	
18	Ottawa-Gatineau, Ont.-Que.	1,169.00		1,198.70	
19	Peterborough, Ont.	120.5		120.8	
20	Québec, Que.	724.3		738.9	
21	Regina, Sask.	200.1		206.7	
22	Saguenay, Que.	152.5		153.3	
23	Saint John, N.B.	125		125.8	
24	Saskatoon, Sask.	240.5		250.4	
25	Sherbrooke, Que.	188.7		191.4	
26	St. Catharines-Niagara, Ont.	404.1		403.7	
27	St. John's, N.L.	183.4		185.7	
28	Thunder Bay, Ont.	127.1		124.6	
29	Toronto, Ont.	5,336.70		5,531.30	
30	Trois-Rivières, Que.	142.5		144.6	
31	Vancouver, B.C.	2,190.10		2,271.20	
32	Victoria, B.C.	339.8		348.2	
33	Windsor, Ont.	336.1		333.6	
34	Winnipeg, Man.	716.4		732.6	
35					
36		22211.3		22834	

When you press *<Enter>*, the answer appears:

	A	B	C	D	E
1	CMA	2006		2008	
2	Abbotsford-Mission, B.C.	164.3	0.00739714	170.7	
3	Barrie, Ont.	183.9		188.2	
4	Brantford, Ont.	135.4		136.6	
5	Calgary, Alta.	1,123.90		1,182.40	
6	Edmonton, Alta.	1,073.80		1,124.20	
7	Greater Sudbury, Ont.	164.2		164.8	
8	Guelph, Ont.	132.2		134.1	
9	Halifax, N.S.	384.8		394.6	
10	Hamilton, Ont.	719.9		731.5	
11	Kelowna, B.C.	167.1		180.1	
12	Kingston, Ont.	158		158.8	
13	Kitchener, Ont.	470.7		482	
14	London, Ont.	477.6		485.2	
15	Moncton, N.B.	129.5		132.2	
16	Montréal, Que.	3,685.00		3,750.50	
17	Oshawa, Ont.	344.2		356.6	
18	Ottawa-Gatineau, Ont.-Que.	1,169.00		1,198.70	
19	Peterborough, Ont.	120.5		120.8	
20	Québec, Que.	724.3		738.9	
21	Regina, Sask.	200.1		206.7	
22	Saguenay, Que.	152.5		153.3	
23	Saint John, N.B.	125		125.8	
24	Saskatoon, Sask.	240.5		250.4	
25	Sherbrooke, Que.	188.7		191.4	
26	St. Catharines-Niagara, Ont.	404.1		403.7	
27	St. John's, N.L.	183.4		185.7	
28	Thunder Bay, Ont.	127.1		124.6	
29	Toronto, Ont.	5,336.70		5,531.30	
30	Trois-Rivières, Que.	142.5		144.6	
31	Vancouver, B.C.	2,190.10		2,271.20	
32	Victoria, B.C.	339.8		348.2	
33	Windsor, Ont.	336.1		333.6	
34	Winnipeg, Man.	716.4		732.6	
35					
36		22211.3		22834	

Microsoft Excel - DD2_ApAimg8.xls — File Edit View Insert Format Tools Data Window Help — Arial 9.5 — C2 ▾ ƒx =B2/B$36 — Sheet1 / Sheet2 / Sheet3 / — Ready

Note, however, that the result is not displayed as a percentage. To correct this, we format the column as a percentage by left-clicking on the column header *C* to highlight the whole column, and then clicking on the 'percentage format' button on the toolbar. (If you don't see it, you may need to go to the View menu, choose 'toolbars', and pick 'formatting'.)

The result looks like this:

	A	B	C	D	E
1	CMA	2006		2008	
2	Abbotsford-Mission, B.C.	164.3	1%	170.7	
3	Barrie, Ont.	183.9		188.2	
4	Brantford, Ont.	135.4		136.6	
5	Calgary, Alta.	1,123.90		1,182.40	
6	Edmonton, Alta.	1,073.80		1,124.20	
7	Greater Sudbury, Ont.	164.2		164.8	
8	Guelph, Ont.	132.2		134.1	
9	Halifax, N.S.	384.8		394.6	
10	Hamilton, Ont.	719.9		731.5	
11	Kelowna, B.C.	167.1		180.1	
12	Kingston, Ont.	158		158.8	
13	Kitchener, Ont.	470.7		482	
14	London, Ont.	477.6		485.2	
15	Moncton, N.B.	129.5		132.2	
16	Montréal, Que.	3,685.00		3,750.50	
17	Oshawa, Ont.	344.2		356.6	
18	Ottawa-Gatineau, Ont.-Que.	1,169.00		1,198.70	
19	Peterborough, Ont.	120.5		120.8	
20	Québec, Que.	724.3		738.9	
21	Regina, Sask.	200.1		206.7	
22	Saguenay, Que.	152.5		153.3	
23	Saint John, N.B.	125		125.8	
24	Saskatoon, Sask.	240.5		250.4	
25	Sherbrooke, Que.	188.7		191.4	
26	St. Catharines-Niagara, Ont.	404.1		403.7	
27	St. John's, N.L.	183.4		185.7	
28	Thunder Bay, Ont.	127.1		124.6	
29	Toronto, Ont.	5,336.70		5,531.30	
30	Trois-Rivières, Que.	142.5		144.6	
31	Vancouver, B.C.	2,190.10		2,271.20	
32	Victoria, B.C.	339.8		348.2	
33	Windsor, Ont.	336.1		333.6	
34	Winnipeg, Man.	716.4		732.6	
35					
36		22211.3		22834	

Now, moving the mouse to the lower-left corner of cell *C2* until the little '+' appears, we drag down the column, still holding the left mouse button. When we release the button, Excel® will fill in the remaining percentages to the bottom:

	A	B	C	D	E
1	CMA	2006		2008	
2	Abbotsford-Mission, B.C.	164.3	1%	170.7	
3	Barrie, Ont.	183.9	1%	188.2	
4	Brantford, Ont.	135.4	1%	136.6	
5	Calgary, Alta.	1,123.90	5%	1,182.40	
6	Edmonton, Alta.	1,073.80	5%	1,124.20	
7	Greater Sudbury, Ont.	164.2	1%	164.8	
8	Guelph, Ont.	132.2	1%	134.1	
9	Halifax, N.S.	384.8	2%	394.6	
10	Hamilton, Ont.	719.9	3%	731.5	
11	Kelowna, B.C.	167.1	1%	180.1	
12	Kingston, Ont.	158	1%	158.8	
13	Kitchener, Ont.	470.7	2%	482	
14	London, Ont.	477.6	2%	485.2	
15	Moncton, N.B.	129.5	1%	132.2	
16	Montréal, Que.	3,685.00	17%	3,750.50	
17	Oshawa, Ont.	344.2	2%	356.6	
18	Ottawa-Gatineau, Ont.-Que.	1,169.00	5%	1,198.70	
19	Peterborough, Ont.	120.5	1%	120.8	
20	Québec, Que.	724.3	3%	738.9	
21	Regina, Sask.	200.1	1%	206.7	
22	Saguenay, Que.	152.5	1%	153.3	
23	Saint John, N.B.	125	1%	125.8	
24	Saskatoon, Sask.	240.5	1%	250.4	
25	Sherbrooke, Que.	188.7	1%	191.4	
26	St. Catharines-Niagara, Ont.	404.1	2%	403.7	
27	St. John's, N.L.	183.4	1%	185.7	
28	Thunder Bay, Ont.	127.1	1%	124.6	
29	Toronto, Ont.	5,336.70	24%	5,531.30	
30	Trois-Rivières, Que.	142.5	1%	144.6	
31	Vancouver, B.C.	2,190.10	10%	2,271.20	
32	Victoria, B.C.	339.8	2%	348.2	
33	Windsor, Ont.	336.1	2%	333.6	
34	Winnipeg, Man.	716.4	3%	732.6	
35					
36		22211.3		22834	

Cell reference: C2 fx =B2/B$36

Microsoft Excel - DD2_ApAimg11.xls

If you would like to see more decimal places, click on the 'add decimal places' button on the toolbar. The next step is to fill in the same percentages for 2008.

Doing this is simple. We cut and paste the formula by clicking on the cell containing the formula we want to copy, copying it using the keystroke combination <*ctrl*> C, then selecting the cell where we want to put the formula, and pasting it with the keystroke combination <*ctrl*> V. This is the result:

	A	B	C	D	E
1	CMA	2006		2008	
2	Abbotsford-Mission, B.C.	164.3	1%	170.7	1%
3	Barrie, Ont.	183.9	1%	188.2	
4	Brantford, Ont.	135.4	1%	136.6	
5	Calgary, Alta.	1,123.90	5%	1,182.40	
6	Edmonton, Alta.	1,073.80	5%	1,124.20	
7	Greater Sudbury, Ont.	164.2	1%	164.8	
8	Guelph, Ont.	132.2	1%	134.1	
9	Halifax, N.S.	384.8	2%	394.6	
10	Hamilton, Ont.	719.9	3%	731.5	
11	Kelowna, B.C.	167.1	1%	180.1	
12	Kingston, Ont.	158	1%	158.8	
13	Kitchener, Ont.	470.7	2%	482	
14	London, Ont.	477.6	2%	485.2	
15	Moncton, N.B.	129.5	1%	132.2	
16	Montréal, Que.	3,685.00	17%	3,750.50	
17	Oshawa, Ont.	344.2	2%	356.6	
18	Ottawa-Gatineau, Ont.-Que.	1,169.00	5%	1,198.70	
19	Peterborough, Ont.	120.5	1%	120.8	
20	Québec, Que.	724.3	3%	738.9	
21	Regina, Sask.	200.1	1%	206.7	
22	Saguenay, Que.	152.5	1%	153.3	
23	Saint John, N.B.	125	1%	125.8	
24	Saskatoon, Sask.	240.5	1%	250.4	
25	Sherbrooke, Que.	188.7	1%	191.4	
26	St. Catharines-Niagara, Ont.	404.1	2%	403.7	
27	St. John's, N.L.	183.4	1%	185.7	
28	Thunder Bay, Ont.	127.1	1%	124.6	
29	Toronto, Ont.	5,336.70	24%	5,531.30	
30	Trois-Rivières, Que.	142.5	1%	144.6	
31	Vancouver, B.C.	2,190.10	10%	2,271.20	
32	Victoria, B.C.	339.8	2%	348.2	
33	Windsor, Ont.	336.1	2%	333.6	
34	Winnipeg, Man.	716.4	3%	732.6	
35					
36		22211.3		22834	

Microsoft Excel - DD2_ApAimg12.xls

File Edit View Insert Format Tools Data Window Help

Arial — 9.5 — **B** *I* U

E2 — fx =D2/D$36

Sheet1 / Sheet2 / Sheet3 /

Ready

Now, using the same skills as before, we can fill that result to the bottom. The worksheet ends up looking like this:

	A	B	C	D	E
					E2 fx =D2/D$36
1	CMA	2006		2008	
2	Abbotsford-Mission, B.C.	164.3	1%	170.7	1%
3	Barrie, Ont.	183.9	1%	188.2	1%
4	Brantford, Ont.	135.4	1%	136.6	1%
5	Calgary, Alta.	1,123.90	5%	1,182.40	5%
6	Edmonton, Alta.	1,073.80	5%	1,124.20	5%
7	Greater Sudbury, Ont.	164.2	1%	164.8	1%
8	Guelph, Ont.	132.2	1%	134.1	1%
9	Halifax, N.S.	384.8	2%	394.6	2%
10	Hamilton, Ont.	719.9	3%	731.5	3%
11	Kelowna, B.C.	167.1	1%	180.1	1%
12	Kingston, Ont.	158	1%	158.8	1%
13	Kitchener, Ont.	470.7	2%	482	2%
14	London, Ont.	477.6	2%	485.2	2%
15	Moncton, N.B.	129.5	1%	132.2	1%
16	Montréal, Que.	3,685.00	17%	3,750.50	16%
17	Oshawa, Ont.	344.2	2%	356.6	2%
18	Ottawa-Gatineau, Ont.-Que.	1,169.00	5%	1,198.70	5%
19	Peterborough, Ont.	120.5	1%	120.8	1%
20	Québec, Que.	724.3	3%	738.9	3%
21	Regina, Sask.	200.1	1%	206.7	1%
22	Saguenay, Que.	152.5	1%	153.3	1%
23	Saint John, N.B.	125	1%	125.8	1%
24	Saskatoon, Sask.	240.5	1%	250.4	1%
25	Sherbrooke, Que.	188.7	1%	191.4	1%
26	St. Catharines-Niagara, Ont.	404.1	2%	403.7	2%
27	St. John's, N.L.	183.4	1%	185.7	1%
28	Thunder Bay, Ont.	127.1	1%	124.6	1%
29	Toronto, Ont.	5,336.70	24%	5,531.30	24%
30	Trois-Rivières, Que.	142.5	1%	144.6	1%
31	Vancouver, B.C.	2,190.10	10%	2,271.20	10%
32	Victoria, B.C.	339.8	2%	348.2	2%
33	Windsor, Ont.	336.1	2%	333.6	1%
34	Winnipeg, Man.	716.4	3%	732.6	3%
35					
36		22211.3		22834	

With just a few keystrokes, we have found out how each major metro centre has fared in terms of its share of the population of all major metro centres in 2006 and 2008.

Most other calculations in a spreadsheet follow this pattern. Do the first calculation, then fill or paste the formula into adjacent cells, rows, or columns.

One thing to be conscious of is how spreadsheets copy and fill formulas. The cardinal rule to remember is that as the copied formula moves across or down, the cells that it adds up (or multiplies, divides, etc.) move in lockstep.

So, the formula =SUM(A3:B3) written in cell C3 will become =SUM(A4:B4) if you copy or fill the formula to cell C4. This feature makes it easy to rapidly do the same calculation on multiple rows or columns. At times, however, you need to freeze the cell or cells on which a formula is applied. This is where the dollar sign comes in.

Use the '$' to lock or fix a cell used in a formula. If you place it before the 'C' in C18, then the formula will always refer to column C, while the row can move. If you place it before the '18', the reverse applies. If you lock both, the formula will act on cell C18, no matter where you copy it.

You will use this feature most often when you need to constantly divide by the same total. Typically, there are many subtotals to calculate, each one in a different cell. But there is only one total. This is why we used the dollar sign in our first percentage formula in the population table.

One other thing journalists will often want to calculate is a percentage change. This is a little more tricky than calculating a simple percentage, but still easy enough. You will have an 'old' number and then the new one that represents the changed value. The rule is as such: work out the difference between the old and the new value (always subtract the old from the new, even if the new value is smaller), then divide that difference by the old value. Now, format it as a percentage.

The next empty column is column F, so you enter the formula in cell F2.

Type in the formula =(D2-B2)/B2 as in this illustration:

	A	B	C	D	E	F
1	CMA	2006	2006%	2008	2008%	%CHG
2	Abbotsford-Mission, B.C.	164.3	1%	170.7	1%	=(D2-B2)/B2
3	Barrie, Ont.	183.9	1%	188.2	1%	
4	Brantford, Ont.	135.4	1%	136.6	1%	
5	Calgary, Alta.	1,123.90	5%	1,182.40	5%	
6	Edmonton, Alta.	1,073.80	5%	1,124.20	5%	
7	Greater Sudbury, Ont.	164.2	1%	164.8	1%	
8	Guelph, Ont.	132.2	1%	134.1	1%	
9	Halifax, N.S.	384.8	2%	394.6	2%	
10	Hamilton, Ont.	719.9	3%	731.5	3%	
11	Kelowna, B.C.	167.1	1%	180.1	1%	
12	Kingston, Ont.	158	1%	158.8	1%	
13	Kitchener, Ont.	470.7	2%	482	2%	
14	London, Ont.	477.6	2%	485.2	2%	
15	Moncton, N.B.	129.5	1%	132.2	1%	
16	Montréal, Que.	3,685.00	17%	3,750.50	16%	
17	Oshawa, Ont.	344.2	2%	356.6	2%	
18	Ottawa-Gatineau, Ont.-Que.	1,169.00	5%	1,198.70	5%	
19	Peterborough, Ont.	120.5	1%	120.8	1%	
20	Québec, Que.	724.3	3%	738.9	3%	
21	Regina, Sask.	200.1	1%	206.7	1%	
22	Saguenay, Que.	152.5	1%	153.3	1%	
23	Saint John, N.B.	125	1%	125.8	1%	
24	Saskatoon, Sask.	240.5	1%	250.4	1%	
25	Sherbrooke, Que.	188.7	1%	191.4	1%	
26	St. Catharines-Niagara, Ont.	404.1	2%	403.7	2%	
27	St. John's, N.L.	183.4	1%	185.7	1%	
28	Thunder Bay, Ont.	127.1	1%	124.6	1%	
29	Toronto, Ont.	5,336.70	24%	5,531.30	24%	
30	Trois-Rivières, Que.	142.5	1%	144.6	1%	
31	Vancouver, B.C.	2,190.10	10%	2,271.20	10%	
32	Victoria, B.C.	339.8	2%	348.2	2%	
33	Windsor, Ont.	336.1	2%	333.6	1%	
34	Winnipeg, Man.	716.4	3%	732.6	3%	
35						
36		22211.3		22834		

This subtracts the 2006 population from the 2008 population for Abbotsford-Mission, British Columbia (showing us the difference between the numbers), then divides the result by the 2006 population, yielding the percentage change. The first part of the formula is placed in parentheses to instruct Excel® to do that part of the calculation first.

Now, we fill the result down to the bottom of the column, as in the next image, remembering to format the result as a percentage:

	A	B	C	D	E	F
1	CMA	2006	2006%	2008	2008%	%CHG
2	Abbotsford-Mission, B.C.	164.3	1%	170.7	1%	4%
3	Barrie, Ont.	183.9	1%	188.2	1%	2%
4	Brantford, Ont.	135.4	1%	136.6	1%	1%
5	Calgary, Alta.	1,123.90	5%	1,182.40	5%	5%
6	Edmonton, Alta.	1,073.80	5%	1,124.20	5%	5%
7	Greater Sudbury, Ont.	164.2	1%	164.8	1%	0%
8	Guelph, Ont.	132.2	1%	134.1	1%	1%
9	Halifax, N.S.	384.8	2%	394.6	2%	3%
10	Hamilton, Ont.	719.9	3%	731.5	3%	2%
11	Kelowna, B.C.	167.1	1%	180.1	1%	8%
12	Kingston, Ont.	158	1%	158.8	1%	1%
13	Kitchener, Ont.	470.7	2%	482	2%	2%
14	London, Ont.	477.6	2%	485.2	2%	2%
15	Moncton, N.B.	129.5	1%	132.2	1%	2%
16	Montréal, Que.	3,685.00	17%	3,750.50	16%	2%
17	Oshawa, Ont.	344.2	2%	356.6	2%	4%
18	Ottawa-Gatineau, Ont.-Que.	1,169.00	5%	1,198.70	5%	3%
19	Peterborough, Ont.	120.5	1%	120.8	1%	0%
20	Québec, Que.	724.3	3%	738.9	3%	2%
21	Regina, Sask.	200.1	1%	206.7	1%	3%
22	Saguenay, Que.	152.5	1%	153.3	1%	1%
23	Saint John, N.B.	125	1%	125.8	1%	1%
24	Saskatoon, Sask.	240.5	1%	250.4	1%	4%
25	Sherbrooke, Que.	188.7	1%	191.4	1%	1%
26	St. Catharines-Niagara, Ont.	404.1	2%	403.7	2%	0%
27	St. John's, N.L.	183.4	1%	185.7	1%	1%
28	Thunder Bay, Ont.	127.1	1%	124.6	1%	-2%
29	Toronto, Ont.	5,336.70	24%	5,531.30	24%	4%
30	Trois-Rivières, Que.	142.5	1%	144.6	1%	1%
31	Vancouver, B.C.	2,190.10	10%	2,271.20	10%	4%
32	Victoria, B.C.	339.8	2%	348.2	2%	2%
33	Windsor, Ont.	336.1	2%	333.6	1%	-1%
34	Winnipeg, Man.	716.4	3%	732.6	3%	2%
35						
36		22211.3		22834		

You can now sort by the results to yield information for a story.

Sorting and filtering

Along with being wizards at calculations, spreadsheets are adept at sorting things out. So if you want to organize a column of numbers into a list running from largest to smallest, or smallest to largest, you can get the program to do it for you in a couple of easy steps. Doing this is very common, for example, when you want to know which government department spends the most money (and which the least), or who makes the biggest salary. Since it is such a useful operation for journalists, we will look at this one in a bit more detail here.

The key rule to observe in sorting spreadsheets is to ensure that all adjacent columns are sorted at the same time. Otherwise, they won't match up properly with each other and you will have a big mess. To ensure all rows are sorted together, it is crucial to ensure that the entire block being sorted is selected or highlighted. The only exception would be any totals at the bottom and any labels at the top that you want to remain as they are. In the following illustration, you can see how not to do it. Several columns have not been selected, and if we try to sort the worksheet, they won't be sorted with the others. Look carefully at what happens in this before-and-after sequence:

CMA	2006	2006%	2008	2008%	%CHG
Abbotsford-Mission, B.C.	164.3	1%	170.7	1%	4%
Barrie, Ont.	183.9	1%	188.2	1%	2%
Brantford, Ont.	135.4	1%	136.6	1%	1%
Calgary, Alta.	1,123.90	5%	1,182.40	5%	5%
Edmonton, Alta.	1,073.80	5%	1,124.20	5%	5%
Greater Sudbury, Ont.	164.2	1%	164.8	1%	0%
Guelph, Ont.	132.2	1%	134.1	1%	1%
Halifax, N.S.	384.8	2%	394.6	2%	3%
Hamilton, Ont.	719.9	3%	731.5	3%	2%
Kelowna, B.C.	167.1	1%	180.1	1%	8%
Kingston, Ont.	158	1%	158.8	1%	1%
Kitchener, Ont.	470.7	2%	482	2%	2%
London, Ont.	477.6	2%	485.2	2%	2%
Moncton, N.B.	129.5	1%	132.2	1%	2%
Montréal, Que.	3,685.00	17%	3,750.50	16%	2%
Oshawa, Ont.	344.2	2%	356.6	2%	4%
Ottawa-Gatineau, Ont.-Que.	1,169.00	5%	1,198.70	5%	3%
Peterborough, Ont.	120.5	1%	120.8	1%	0%
Québec, Que.	724.3	3%	738.9	3%	2%
Regina, Sask.	200.1	1%	206.7	1%	3%
Saguenay, Que.	152.5	1%	153.3	1%	1%
Saint John, N.B.	125	1%	125.8	1%	1%
Saskatoon, Sask.	240.5	1%	250.4	1%	4%
Sherbrooke, Que.	188.7	1%	191.4	1%	1%
St. Catharines-Niagara, Ont.	404.1	2%	403.7	2%	0%
St. John's, N.L.	183.4	1%	185.7	1%	1%
Thunder Bay, Ont.	127.1	1%	124.6	1%	-2%
Toronto, Ont.	5,336.70	24%	5,531.30	24%	4%
Trois-Rivières, Que.	142.5	1%	144.6	1%	1%
Vancouver, B.C.	2,190.10	10%	2,271.20	10%	4%
Victoria, B.C.	339.8	2%	348.2	2%	2%
Windsor, Ont.	336.1	2%	333.6	1%	-1%
Winnipeg, Man.	716.4	3%	732.6	3%	2%
	22211.3		22834		

The result when sorted on the 2008 population:

	A	B	C	D	E	F
1	CMA	2006	2006%	2008	2008%	%CHG
2	Abbotsford-Mission, B.C.	164.3	1%	5,531.30	24%	3267%
3	Barrie, Ont.	183.9	1%	3,750.50	16%	1939%
4	Brantford, Ont.	135.4	1%	2,271.20	10%	1577%
5	Calgary, Alta.	1,123.90	5%	1,198.70	5%	7%
6	Edmonton, Alta.	1,073.80	5%	1,182.40	5%	10%
7	Greater Sudbury, Ont.	164.2	1%	1,124.20	5%	585%
8	Guelph, Ont.	132.2	1%	738.9	3%	459%
9	Halifax, N.S.	384.8	2%	732.6	3%	90%
10	Hamilton, Ont.	719.9	3%	731.5	3%	2%
11	Kelowna, B.C.	167.1	1%	485.2	2%	190%
12	Kingston, Ont.	158	1%	482	2%	205%
13	Kitchener, Ont.	470.7	2%	403.7	2%	-14%
14	London, Ont.	477.6	2%	394.6	2%	-17%
15	Moncton, N.B.	129.5	1%	356.6	2%	175%
16	Montréal, Que.	3,685.00	17%	348.2	2%	-91%
17	Oshawa, Ont.	344.2	2%	333.6	1%	-3%
18	Ottawa-Gatineau, Ont.-Que.	1,169.00	5%	250.4	1%	-79%
19	Peterborough, Ont.	120.5	1%	206.7	1%	72%
20	Québec, Que.	724.3	3%	191.4	1%	-74%
21	Regina, Sask.	200.1	1%	188.2	1%	-6%
22	Saguenay, Que.	152.5	1%	185.7	1%	22%
23	Saint John, N.B.	125	1%	180.1	1%	44%
24	Saskatoon, Sask.	240.5	1%	170.7	1%	-29%
25	Sherbrooke, Que.	188.7	1%	164.8	1%	-13%
26	St. Catharines-Niagara, Ont.	404.1	2%	158.8	1%	-61%
27	St. John's, N.L.	183.4	1%	153.3	1%	-16%
28	Thunder Bay, Ont.	127.1	1%	144.6	1%	14%
29	Toronto, Ont.	5,336.70	24%	136.6	1%	-97%
30	Trois-Rivières, Que.	142.5	1%	134.1	1%	-6%
31	Vancouver, B.C.	2,190.10	10%	132.2	1%	-94%
32	Victoria, B.C.	339.8	2%	125.8	1%	-63%
33	Windsor, Ont.	336.1	2%	124.6	1%	-63%
34	Winnipeg, Man.	716.4	3%	120.8	1%	-83%
35						
36		22211.3		22834		

As you can see, it's a mixed-up mess. To make sure this doesn't happen, ensure all of the area to be sorted is selected. Luckily, Excel® makes this easy. First, we must select the *entire* area we want to sort, as shown here:

	A	B	C	D	E	F
1	CMA	2006	2006%	2008	2008%	%CHG
2	Abbotsford-Mission, B.C.	164.3	1%	170.7	1%	4%
3	Barrie, Ont.	183.9	1%	188.2	1%	2%
4	Brantford, Ont.	135.4	1%	136.6	1%	1%
5	Calgary, Alta.	1,123.90	5%	1,182.40	5%	5%
6	Edmonton, Alta.	1,073.80	5%	1,124.20	5%	5%
7	Greater Sudbury, Ont.	164.2	1%	164.8	1%	0%
8	Guelph, Ont.	132.2	1%	134.1	1%	1%
9	Halifax, N.S.	384.8	2%	394.6	2%	3%
10	Hamilton, Ont.	719.9	3%	731.5	3%	2%
11	Kelowna, B.C.	167.1	1%	180.1	1%	8%
12	Kingston, Ont.	158	1%	158.8	1%	1%
13	Kitchener, Ont.	470.7	2%	482	2%	2%
14	London, Ont.	477.6	2%	485.2	2%	2%
15	Moncton, N.B.	129.5	1%	132.2	1%	2%
16	Montréal, Que.	3,685.00	17%	3,750.50	16%	2%
17	Oshawa, Ont.	344.2	2%	356.6	2%	4%
18	Ottawa-Gatineau, Ont.-Que.	1,169.00	5%	1,198.70	5%	3%
19	Peterborough, Ont.	120.5	1%	120.8	1%	0%
20	Québec, Que.	724.3	3%	738.9	3%	2%
21	Regina, Sask.	200.1	1%	206.7	1%	3%
22	Saguenay, Que.	152.5	1%	153.3	1%	1%
23	Saint John, N.B.	125	1%	125.8	1%	1%
24	Saskatoon, Sask.	240.5	1%	250.4	1%	4%
25	Sherbrooke, Que.	188.7	1%	191.4	1%	1%
26	St. Catharines-Niagara, Ont.	404.1	2%	403.7	2%	0%
27	St. John's, N.L.	183.4	1%	185.7	1%	1%
28	Thunder Bay, Ont.	127.1	1%	124.6	1%	-2%
29	Toronto, Ont.	5,336.70	24%	5,531.30	24%	4%
30	Trois-Rivières, Que.	142.5	1%	144.6	1%	1%
31	Vancouver, B.C.	2,190.10	10%	2,271.20	10%	4%
32	Victoria, B.C.	339.8	2%	348.2	2%	2%
33	Windsor, Ont.	336.1	2%	333.6	1%	-1%
34	Winnipeg, Man.	716.4	3%	732.6	3%	2%
35						
36		22211.3		22834		

Be sure not to select any labels or 'total' rows. Now, in the Data menu, we would select 'sort':

	A	E			F	
1	CMA	200			%CHG	
2	Abbotsford-Mission, B.C.	1			4%	
3	Barrie, Ont.	1			2%	
4	Brantford, Ont.	1			1%	
5	Calgary, Alta.	1,12			5%	
6	Edmonton, Alta.	1,07			5%	
7	Greater Sudbury, Ont.	1			0%	
8	Guelph, Ont.	1			1%	
9	Halifax, N.S.	3			3%	
10	Hamilton, Ont.	7			2%	
11	Kelowna, B.C.	167.1	1%	180.1	1%	8%
12	Kingston, Ont.	158	1%	158.8	1%	1%
13	Kitchener, Ont.	470.7	2%	482	2%	2%
14	London, Ont.	477.6	2%	485.2	2%	2%
15	Moncton, N.B.	129.5	1%	132.2	1%	2%
16	Montréal, Que.	3,685.00	17%	3,750.50	16%	2%
17	Oshawa, Ont.	344.2	2%	356.6	2%	4%
18	Ottawa-Gatineau, Ont.-Que.	1,169.00	5%	1,198.70	5%	3%
19	Peterborough, Ont.	120.5	1%	120.8	1%	0%
20	Québec, Que.	724.3	3%	738.9	3%	2%
21	Regina, Sask.	200.1	1%	206.7	1%	3%
22	Saguenay, Que.	152.5	1%	153.3	1%	1%
23	Saint John, N.B.	125	1%	125.8	1%	1%
24	Saskatoon, Sask.	240.5	1%	250.4	1%	4%
25	Sherbrooke, Que.	188.7	1%	191.4	1%	1%
26	St. Catharines-Niagara, Ont.	404.1	2%	403.7	2%	0%
27	St. John's, N.L.	183.4	1%	185.7	1%	1%
28	Thunder Bay, Ont.	127.1	1%	124.6	1%	-2%
29	Toronto, Ont.	5,336.70	24%	5,531.30	24%	4%
30	Trois-Rivières, Que.	142.5	1%	144.6	1%	1%
31	Vancouver, B.C.	2,190.10	10%	2,271.20	10%	4%
32	Victoria, B.C.	339.8	2%	348.2	2%	2%
33	Windsor, Ont.	336.1	2%	333.6	1%	-1%
34	Winnipeg, Man.	716.4	3%	732.6	3%	2%
35						
36		22211.3		22834		

This will make the 'sort' dialogue box appear:

We can now sort as many as three columns, the first one taking precedence over the second, and so on. Choosing 'ascending' order will sort from A to Z and smallest to largest. 'Descending' order will do the opposite. In this case, we will sort by column *F* in descending order. (It is important to choose 'header row' if there is a row of labels across the top, and 'no header row' if there is not.) This will sort everything according to the change in metro population, from the largest change to the smallest.

There is an even simpler method, which the help files will suggest you use. You can choose a cell in the column you want to sort and click one of the 'quick sort' buttons on the toolbar. But when you do this, you are putting your fate entirely in the hands of a computer program's decision-making, and we have never trusted computers that much. We highly recommend sorting the old-fashioned, manual way.

In Appendix A, we have covered only the most basic features of Excel®. A brief glance at the software instructions will show you that there is much more spreadsheets can do, including rudimentary data analysis. Again, for a full guide, including details on how to analyze data, create pivot tables, and perform other advanced functions useful to journalists, see Vallance-Jones and McKie's *Computer-Assisted Reporting*.

Database Managers

Database managers are sophisticated computer programs used to manipulate, query, and organize electronic data.

The simplest database programs create **flat-file databases**, which are similar to spreadsheets in that they store data in rows and columns. Manipulation is usually limited to simple sorting and filtering.

Relational database managers do everything flat-file systems do, but also allow data to be stored in more than one table. As well as simple sorting and filtering, these programs employ sophisticated querying using a special language called SQL. SQL allows users to squeeze every last possible bit of raw and summary information out of the database.

Basic programs such as Microsoft Access® and Corel Paradox® are best used to work with smaller datasets. Server applications such as Microsoft SQL Server®, Oracle®, MySQL®, and PostgreSQL® work with databases of nearly any size. The latter two are open-source programs that are free to download and use. Any time you enter or retrieve information on a website, it is likely one of these sophisticated server databases is doing the hard work in the background.

We focus here on Access®, a commonly used desktop application, and one that, so long as the database has no more than a few hundred thousand records of average length, serves well. We are using the 2003 version for the illustrations because it is still widely used in academic and corporate environments. While most of the query operations are done in the same way in the most recent version, Access 2007®, users who want a more complete guide to the latter, and its ribbon-user interface, may wish to purchase Fred Vallance-Jones and David McKie's *Computer-Assisted Reporting: A Comprehensive Primer*, available from Oxford University Press.

Definitions

Microsoft Access® is a relational database management system (RDMS). It is specially designed to analyze and extract information contained in multi-column lists called 'tables'.

A **relational database** allows information to be stored in more than one table, saving both disk storage and memory space. The related information is linked by common ID codes.

In Access®, the term **database** refers to a kind of holding area that includes tables, queries, forms, and other Access® objects. The following illustration shows an Access® database with the 'tables' tab selected:

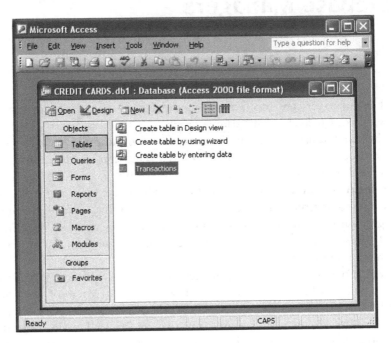

A **table** is where actual data is stored. It is made up of columns called *fields*, and rows called *records*.

A **record** contains all of the information about one instance of whatever is being recorded or tracked. For example, a record may contain all of the information about one government grant, one restaurant inspection, one police arrest, or one adverse drug reaction. A record is made up of fields.

A **field** contains one piece of the information recorded in a table. Sometimes, fields will be referred to as *data elements*. A field may contain a first or last name, a date, an address, a narrative description, an amount of currency, or just about any kind of information. Together, all of the fields in a record contain all of the information in that record.

A **query** is a question you ask of the database to extract information or summarize information from the database. Queries may be written in *structured query language* (SQL), but we will utilize a more user-friendly function in Access®, which writes the SQL for us. This interface is called the **query grid**.

Record length is the total length in bytes (1 byte = 1 character) of a record in a table. The record length multiplied by the number of records gives a rough idea of the size of the table (e.g., if the record length is 100, and there are 10,000 records, the data takes up roughly 1,000,000 bytes, which approximates to 1 megabyte).

A **record layout** is a list of all of the fields in a table or tables. The list will generally include the field name, its length, and its data type.

Different **data types** store different kinds of data. Some of the key data types are text, number, currency, date/time, memo (for very long text entries), and yes/no. You need to use the right data type. Text fields can store any characters, but you cannot do math with them (you can count them, however). Number fields can store numbers only, and allow for mathematical operations. Date/time fields are self-explanatory, as are currency fields (a specialized number type). Yes/no fields are used to define whether a certain variable is true or false (e.g., to record whether an event mentioned in another field, such as 'test_completed', occurred or not).

Basic Operations

The following is an illustration of a table in Microsoft Access®. It is a list of credit card transactions for the (fictional) city council of Ellersville, Alberta.

Toggles between 'design view' and 'datasheet view'

Sort in ascending or descending order

ID	LAST	FIRST	INITIAL	POSITION	DATE	TYPE	DESCRIPTION	CITY	AMOUNT
13	Elliott	John	R	Councillor	3/28/2006	Restaurant	Burgerama	Ellersville	$17.22
12	Elliott	John	R	Councillor	3/28/2006	Transportation	Zoom Taxi	Ellersville	$31.97
2	Elliott	John	R	Councillor	3/26/2006	Office Supplies	Office Galore	Ellersville	$79.88
4	Johnson	Ronald	D	Councillor	3/26/2006	Transportation	Busway Transport	Edmonton	$96.55
11	Robinson	Albert	C	Mayor	3/28/2006	Entertainment	Wild'N Wooly Casino	Las Vegas	$8,875.07
10	Robinson	Albert	C	Mayor	3/28/2006	Lodging	Wild'N Wooly Hotel	Las Vegas	$276.64
8	Robinson	Albert	C	Mayor	3/27/2006	Restaurant	Southern Desert Eats	Las Vegas	$377.99
7	Robinson	Albert	C	Mayor	3/27/2006	Entertainment	Wild'N Wooly Casino	Las Vegas	$2,709.00
6	Robinson	Albert	C	Mayor	3/27/2006	Transportation	Vegas Cabs	Las Vegas	$90.55
5	Robinson	Albert	C	Mayor	3/27/2006	Transportation	Canadawide Airlines	Toronto	$760.31
1	Robinson	Albert	C	Mayor	3/25/2006	Restaurant	Ray's Chinese Food	Ellersville	$105.28
9	Wilson	Jane		Councillor	3/27/2006	Office Supplies	Office Galore	Ellersville	$21.50
3	Wilson	Jane		Councillor	3/26/2006	Transportation	Zoom Taxi	Ellersville	$18.40

A record runs horizontally across the table

This table is not unlike the kind that a reporter might use either for a quick story produced close to the deadline, or for a more thorough investigation. It records the expenditures of public money by political figures, always a hot-button issue with readers and electronic-media consumers.

The next image shows what Microsoft calls the 'design view' of the same table, displaying the different data types. You can add, remove, and edit field entries in design view. You toggle between these views using the leftmost button on the Table Datasheet toolbar.

The simplest way to manipulate the information is to sort it. To do so, click on the field name so the entire field is selected, and then click on either the A to Z button on the toolbar, to sort in ascending order, or the Z to A button, to sort in descending order. In the following illustration, the table has been resorted on the name of the cardholder:

ID	LAST	FIRST	INITIAL	POSITION	DATE	TYPE	DESCRIPTION	CITY	AMOUNT
13	Elliott	John	R	Councillor	3/28/2006	Restaurant	Burgerama	Ellersville	$17.22
12	Elliott	John	R	Councillor	3/28/2006	Transportation	Zoom Taxi	Ellersville	$31.97
2	Elliott	John	R	Councillor	3/26/2006	Office Supplies	Office Galore	Ellersville	$79.88
4	Johnson	Ronald	D	Councillor	3/26/2006	Transportation	Busway Transport	Edmonton	$96.55
11	Robinson	Albert	C	Mayor	3/28/2006	Entertainment	Wild'N Wooly Casino	Las Vegas	$8,875.07
10	Robinson	Albert	C	Mayor	3/28/2006	Lodging	Wild'N Wooly Hotel	Las Vegas	$276.64
8	Robinson	Albert	C	Mayor	3/27/2006	Restaurant	Southern Desert Eats	Las Vegas	$377.99
7	Robinson	Albert	C	Mayor	3/27/2006	Entertainment	Wild'N Wooly Casino	Las Vegas	$2,709.00
6	Robinson	Albert	C	Mayor	3/27/2006	Transportation	Vegas Cabs	Las Vegas	$90.55
5	Robinson	Albert	C	Mayor	3/27/2006	Transportation	Canadawide Airlines	Toronto	$760.31
1	Robinson	Albert	C	Mayor	3/25/2006	Restaurant	Ray's Chinese Food	Ellersville	$105.28
9	Wilson	Jane		Councillor	3/27/2006	Office Supplies	Office Galore	Ellersville	$21.50
3	Wilson	Jane		Councillor	3/26/2006	Transportation	Zoom Taxi	Ellersville	$18.40
*	(ber)								$0.00

Record: 1 of 13

Datasheet View

Another simple way to manipulate data is to use the 'filter by selection' function. Select and highlight a word in one of the fields, as in this illustration:

ID	LAST	FIRST	INITIAL	POSITION	DATE	TYPE	DESCRIPTION	CITY	AMOUNT
13	Elliott	John	R	Councillor	3/28/2006	Restaurant	Burgerama	Ellersville	$17.22
12	Elliott	John	R	Councillor	3/28/2006	Transportation	Zoom Taxi	Ellersville	$31.97
2	Elliott	John	R	Councillor	3/26/2006	Office Supplies	Office Galore	Ellersville	$79.88
4	Johnson	Ronald	D	Councillor	3/26/2006	Transportation	Busway Transport	Edmonton	$96.55
11	Robinson	Albert	C	Mayor	3/28/2006	Entertainment	Wild'N Wooly Casino	Las Vegas	$8,875.07
10	Robinson	Albert	C	Mayor	3/28/2006	Lodging	Wild'N Wooly Hotel	Las Vegas	$276.64
8	Robinson	Albert	C	Mayor	3/27/2006	Restaurant	Southern Desert Eats	Las Vegas	$377.99
7	Robinson	Albert	C	Mayor	3/27/2006	Entertainment	Wild'N Wooly Casino	Las Vegas	$2,709.00
6	Robinson	Albert	C	Mayor	3/27/2006	Transportation	Vegas Cabs	Las Vegas	$90.55
5	Robinson	Albert	C	Mayor	3/27/2006	Transportation	Canadawide Airlines	Toronto	$760.31
1	Robinson	Albert	C	Mayor	3/25/2006	Restaurant	Ray's Chinese Food	Ellersville	$105.28
9	Wilson	Jane		Councillor	3/27/2006	Office Supplies	Office Galore	Ellersville	$21.50
3	Wilson	Jane		Councillor	3/26/2006	Transportation	Zoom Taxi	Ellersville	$18.40
*	(ber)								$0.00

Record: 12 of 13

Datasheet View

When you click on the toolbar button that looks like a funnel with a lightning bolt beside it, the table will be filtered to show only those records in the table that include the selected word in the selected field, as in the illustration on the next page:

	ID	LAST	FIRST	INITIAL	POSITION	DATE	TYPE	DESCRIPTION	CITY	AMOUNT
▶	9	Wilson	Jane		Councillor	3/27/2006	Office Supplies	Office Galore	Ellersville	$21.50
	3	Wilson	Jane		Councillor	3/26/2006	Transportation	Zoom Taxi	Ellersville	$18.40
✳	iber)									$0.00

Record: [◄] [◄] 1 [►] [►I] [►✳] of 2 (Filtered)

Datasheet View   FLTR

To remove the filter, click on the plain funnel on the toolbar.

Simple sorting and filtering, however, are relatively primitive functions. If you want to see the real power of a database manager, start working with queries. The following illustration shows the query grid with different parts illustrated.

Toggles between design and datasheet view

Table/fields window

Run query

'Totals' button

Query design grid

The simplest query duplicates the filter, showing only the records that meet certain criteria. There are several ways to start a query, but here we focus on a simple one: click on the query button while the table is open and pick 'design view', which brings up the query design grid.

To pick what fields you want to include, double-click on the selected fields in the small box in the upper left of the query grid. This will drop the fields into the grid.

To view only transactions for the mayor, we would type *"mayor"* (include the double quotation marks) into the criteria line below the 'position' field in the grid. If we would like to display the amount of each transaction in descending order, we can pick 'descending' from the list that appears when we click in the 'sort' line under the 'amount' field.

This illustration shows the query ready to run.

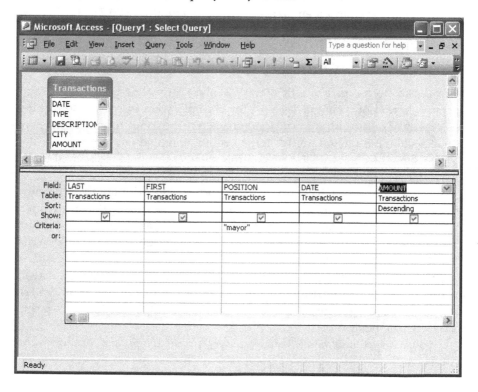

To run the query, click on the red exclamation point on the query toolbar. This is what the result looks like:

You can also use part of a field entry in the criteria line by using the 'like' operator. Instead of typing in *"mayor"*, for example, you can type in something like *"may*"*. The asterisk is a wild-card character that stands for any number of characters. You can use the asterisk at the beginning or end of a string.

The 'show' box below each field controls whether that field is displayed in the final result.

You can use standard mathematical operators in fields with number, currency, or date field types. You can limit results to amounts greater than 100, for example, by writing *100* in the criteria line under the 'amount' field. This would eliminate transactions of $100 or less. (To include $100 transactions, you would write *>=100*.)

You can write queries that limit results to a certain date by entering a date in the criteria line under the date field. For records between two dates, type *Between date1 and date2* in the criteria line. You can also use the >, >=, <, and <= operators with date fields

If you want to limit results based on a yes/no field, type 'yes' or 'no' in the criteria line.

Boolean operators

Database queries take advantage of Boolean logic, a system invented by British mathematician George Boole a century and a half ago. We won't go into the history or its more complex applications here, but the key thing to know is that Boolean logic uses the operators *AND, OR,* and *NOT.* You can use these operators to fine-tune your queries:

AND allows you to specify that more than one condition be true;

OR allows you to specify that one or another (or one of several) conditions be true;

NOT simply reverses the result, so that something must not be true to satisfy the criteria.

If we want to see all credit card transactions used by the mayor for entertainment, we would start a new query and bring all of the fields down into the query grid. Next, we would write "mayor" in the criteria line under the position field, and 'entertainment' under the detail line, as in the following illustration:

When Access® reads across the query grid, it assumes *AND* is the operator when the criteria line is filled in straight across in this way. This is the result:

The *OR* operator can be used in two different ways. You can write 'OR' between different terms under one field to get the query to return records that meet one of the terms. In our table of credit card transactions, we could write a query that would return transactions either for the mayor or Councillor Elliott by typing *"Robinson" OR "Elliott"* in the criteria line under the name field, as in this illustration:

You can also use the *OR* operator between more than one field, by putting the entries in the criteria lines on different levels, as in this example, which would find transactions either by the mayor, or for office supplies.

Summary queries

Access® is also adept at doing simple math, such as counting and adding. Click on the 'totals' button (which is a Greek sigma) on the query toolbar. This will make the 'totals' line appear, which is where you enter math instructions.

If we wanted to know how many records in the table relate to each councillor, we would start a new query and select the last, first, initial, and ID fields. The totals line automatically displays 'group by' under each field. If we changed the term under the ID field to 'count', the program would give us our answer. To sort the result from largest to smallest count, select 'descending order' in the sort line under the ID field. The query grid would look like this:

Running the query produces this result:

Remember that we are counting the rows in the table, each of which represents one transaction. The ID field is used to do the count because we know that the field contains no 'null' or empty values. If the field included null values, the result will be inaccurate because null fields are not counted by Access®. This quirk of the program can be a real pain.

When you group results in Access®, you are creating subtotals based on the entries in the field or fields. In this case, subtotals are created for each person. If we were to leave out the 'name' fields, and still run the count on the ID field only, the query would return the total number of records in the table.

You can also add things up in Access®. To add up the total amount spent by each person, we would start a new query and select the first, last, initial, and amount fields, click on the 'totals' button, then change the totals line under the amount field to 'sum'. To sort the result, we might choose descending order. The query would look like this:

This is the result:

We could also work out the average amount for each person, the maximum amount paid by each person, or the minimum amount, by choosing these entries instead of 'sum' in the 'group by' line.

To limit the calculation to certain records, we would use the 'where' operator in the totals line. We could limit the calculation to entertainment expenses exclusively by adding the 'type' field to the query (by double-clicking on the field name in the small box in the upper left), and entering 'entertainment' in the criteria line under the type field. (We would need to change the totals line under the new field to 'where'.) The query now includes only those records involving entertainment expenses, an area that looks promising journalistically.

This is what the query looks like when the results are limited to entertainment expenses:

And this is what the result looks like:

These are the basic types of queries used most often by journalists. They work equally well on much larger tables. Again, for full explanations of more advanced query types and how they relate to journalistic purposes, consult Vallance-Jones and McKie's *Computer-Assisted Reporting*.

Other Important Database Skills

Importing data

When you receive data from the government, perhaps after an arduous access-to-information battle, you will frequently be given a file in Excel® format or delimited text format, probably on a CD or DVD. You can import these directly into Access®.

If the field names are in the first line of the file, make sure you click the 'first row contains column headings' checkbox on the first screen of the *import wizard* (the interface that Access® gives you when you're importing data). On the penultimate screen, you are given the option of having Access® add a *primary key*, which is an automatically generated numbered list, added to the resulting table, assigning a unique number to each record, counting up from 1.

When importing 'delimited text', you need to specify what the delimiters are. These will usually be either commas or tabs; they act like column dividers in a file that doesn't have real columns. Access® can also import what are known as 'fixed-width text files', in which each field begins a specified number of characters in from the left. In practice, however, you will not run into such files very often.

You will notice that when you first click on 'get external data' in order to import material, you are also offered the opportunity to 'link' to a file. When you link, you don't create a copy of the data in your Access® database, but make a connection to the original file. This can be an advantage when the outside file will often be updated. Any updates will be reflected in the mirror-image file in your Access® database. When you import a file, you create a snapshot of the data as it was at the moment you imported it.

SQL

You will recall we mentioned that queries can be written directly in *structured query language*, or SQL, and that the query grid writes the SQL for you. If you want to see what the underlying SQL looks like—because i) you know SQL and would like to modify it, ii) you are curious, or iii) you enjoy visual torture—you can view it by clicking on the view button at the top left of the query-grid toolbar, and selecting 'SQL view'.

Be aware that Access® often adds unnecessary parentheses to its SQL, so it isn't as complicated as Access® makes it look. *Computer-Assisted Reporting: A Comprehensive Primer* includes a guide to using SQL in queries.

Finance Facts

Glossary of Key Financial Reporting Terms

analyst someone (usually employed by an institution such as a brokerage house) who analyzes the markets and certain companies in order to advise on whether they are good bets for investors.

assets anything of value that a company or an individual owns.

balance sheet the financial statement that shows the company's assets and liabilities at a set point in time, usually at the end of a quarter.

bankrupt a person or corporation who has made a voluntary assignment in bankruptcy or against whom a receiving order has been made.[1]

bankruptcy the state of being bankrupt or the fact of becoming bankrupt.[2]

book value (also **shareholders' equity**) the amount of money a shareholder would receive if the company was suddenly forced out of business, sold everything, and paid its investors the money.[3]

board of directors the people elected by the shareholders to review the company's strategy and operations. Reporters should not assume that boards are always looking out for the best interests of the company's investors.

bond a certificate of debt that is issued by a government or corporation in order to raise money, with a promise to pay the holder a specified sum (the principal plus interest) at a fixed time in the future. The main types are corporate bonds, municipal bonds, Treasury bonds, Treasury notes, Treasury bills (T-bills), and zero-coupon bonds.[4]

broker an individual or firm that acts as an intermediary between a buyer and seller, usually charging a commission. For securities and most other products, a licence is required in order to broker deals.[5]

cash flow the amount of cash the business is able to generate at any point in time. If a company's cash flow is strong, it has money to spend or give back to investors, which is a good indication that things are going well.

chief executive officer (CEO) the person in charge of the company, and the conduit between the board of directors and the company.

chief financial officer (CFO) the executive in charge of the company's finances.

commodity a physical substance such as a good, grain, or metal that may be traded for cash or another substance.

credit in one sense, *credit* is just another word for *debt*. Credit is given to customers when they are allowed to make a purchase with the promise to pay later, as with a consumer credit card. A bank gives credit when it lends money.[6]

creditor one to whom a debt is owed; in insolvency matters, a creditor is an individual having a claim provable under the *Bankruptcy and Insolvency Act*.[7]

current assets a balance sheet item that equals the sum of cash (and cash equivalents), accounts receivable, inventory, marketable securities, prepaid expenses, and other assets that could be converted to cash in less than one year. A company's creditors will often be interested in how much that company has in current assets, since these can easily be liquidated if the company goes bankrupt. In addition, current assets are important to most companies as a source of funds for day-to-day operations.[8]

current debt a balance sheet item that indicates the total of what the company owes and must pay within a year. In order to determine the company's real financial health, the reporter should compare the current debt to the current assets. The company is in trouble if it owes more money than it has to spend.

debtor one who owes money to another.[9]

depreciation the allocation of the cost of an asset over a period of time for accounting and tax purposes, or a decline in the value of a property due to general wear and tear or obsolescence.[10]

equity the difference between what a property is worth and what the owner owes against that property (e.g., the difference between the house value and the remaining mortgage or loan payments on a house).[11] On a balance sheet, the company's equity plus its liabilities equals its total assets.

earnings per share (EPS) it is equal to the net income divided by the number of outstanding shares.[12]

expense a cost of doing business; expenses include money spent on raw materials, marketing, salaries, and other items.

financial statements a set of four statements: (1) the balance sheet; (2) the income statement; (3) the statement of cash flows (the cash provided and used by operating, investing, and financing activities during the period); and (4) the statement of retained earnings (which shows the change in the 'retained earnings' account between the beginning and the end of the period).[13]

income statement a financial statement that shows how much money or revenue came in and how much money was paid out in expenses.[14]

involuntary bankruptcy a situation when creditors file a plan to force a debtor into bankruptcy-court protection. The debtor can go to court to contest.[15]

liability a debt that is recorded on the balance sheet. Current liabilities are debts payable within one year. Long-term liabilities are debts payable over a longer period.[16]

loss a reduction in the value of an investment, or a condition in which a company's expenses exceed its revenues. It is the opposite of profit.[17]

material news (or **material information**) an event that could affect the value of a share. A company is legally obliged to file information about such changes with the relevant securities regulator.

net income a company's total earnings after paying the costs of doing business, depreciation, interest, taxes, and other expenses. It is the same as net profit, and represents the proverbial *bottom line*. Do not confuse net income with operating income.[18]

Ontario Securities Commission (OSC) the largest Canadian securities commission. It is a self-funded Crown corporation, with a mandate to provide protection to investors from unfair, improper, or fraudulent practices and to foster fair and efficient capital markets in Ontario and confidence in their integrity.[19]

operating income the amount of money a company earns before deductions for interest payments and income taxes. It's also known as operating profit. Unlike the net income, it does not represent the bottom line.

price-to-earnings ratio a basic measure investors use to evaluate a company. To figure out the P–E ratio, divide the stock price by the earnings per share (EPS).[20]

private company a company that does not trade its shares on a public stock exchange. (Shares can be traded privately—for example, among a group of employees.)

public company a company whose shares are traded on a public stock exchange, and which is subject to the rules of securities regulators, such as the Securities and Exchange Commission (SEC) in the United States or the Ontario Securities Commission. Unlike private companies, a public company must disclose its financial information to the commission in question, which in turn makes it available to investors (the general public). The distinction between a public and a private company is an important one that a reporter should make before conducting research.

profit margin the number that many investors and business reporters use to measure a company's financial performance. To get the profit margin, you divide the net income by the revenue. Or, defined another way, it is net profit after taxes, divided by sales for a given 12-month period. The margin is expressed as a percentage.[21]

operating margin like profit margin, this is also a measure of a company's health. It divides operating costs by sales.[22]

preferred creditor a creditor who has been given priority under the *Bankruptcy and Insolvency Act* over other creditors in the distribution of dividends.[23]

retained earnings the portion of company profits that has not been paid out to shareholders. This retained portion becomes part of the company's equity.

return on equity (ROE) this is a way to measure a company with competitors in the same industry. To obtain the ROE, divide the net income by the shareholder's equity. Return on equity assesses how well a company uses shareholders' money.[24]

return on assets (ROA) another performance measure journalists can calculate when writing about a company's health is return on assets. To obtain the ROA, divide the company's net income plus its interest expense by the total assets. The ROA measures how much money was made for each dollar of assets. If the company is doing well, this ratio will increase over time.[25]

revenues the cash generated for a company by a product or a service during a specific time period.

secured creditor a person or company owed debt that is backed by collateral, such as a car loan or a home mortgage.[26] Secured creditors receive priority during the bankruptcy process.

security an investment instrument (or document) that offers evidence of a debt or equity. It is usually a stock (which is a form of equity) or bond (which relates to debt).

shareholder a holder of stock who has a claim on a part of a corporation's assets and earnings. In other words, a shareholder is an owner of a company. Ownership is determined by the number of shares a person owns relative to the number of outstanding shares (or the stock owned by other investors).[27] For example, if a company has a thousand shares of stock outstanding, and one person owns a hundred shares, he or she would own 10 per cent of the company's assets.

unsecured creditor a person or company owed debt, such as credit cards, medical bills, and utility bills, that are not backed by collateral. Unsecured creditors are among the last to get their money—if at all—during the bankruptcy process.[28]

stock a type of security that signifies ownership in a corporation and represents a claim on part of the outfit's assets and earnings. Stocks are the foundation of nearly every investment portfolio, and they have historically outperformed other investments over the long run. There are two main types of stock: *common* and *preferred*. Common stock usually entitles the owner to the right to vote at shareholder meetings and to receive dividends that the company has declared. Preferred stock generally does not garner voting rights, but has a higher claim on assets and earnings than the common shares. For example, owners of preferred stock receive dividends before common shareholders and have priority if the company goes bankrupt and is liquidated.

trustee in bankruptcy a person licensed by the superintendent of bankruptcy to administer a bankruptcy or proposal.[29]

Securities Regulators

Canada

Canada does not have a national securities regulator. Instead, we have provincial regulators. There is talk of replacing the provincial regulators with a national body. The Ontario Securities Commission (OSC) is by far the largest and tends to deal with the major Canadian companies (which is why we focus on the OSC in this book). The other Canadian regulators require much the same information as the OSC does. Websites for the major regulators are listed here:

- Alberta: *www.albertasecurities.com*
- British Columbia: *www.bcsc.bc.ca*
- Ontario: *www.osc.gov.on.ca*
- Quebec: *www.lautorite.qc.ca/index.fr.html*

The documents held by all these regulators can be searched using a special clearinghouse called SEDAR (*www.sedar.com*), which also contains links to profiles of each public company that trades stock in a given province.

United States

The national regulator is the Securities and Exchange Commission (SEC): *www. sec.gov.* The site has a limited search engine called Edgar. A more useful but expensive option is called Live Edgar.

State securities regulators can, and have, acted independently of the SEC, so it's worth checking their sites if you're conducting a serious investigation into a company that does business in the United States. See the website of the North American Securities Administrators Association, at *www.nasaa.org.*

Tips on Financial Statements

We paraphrase here some advice that was offered to delegates at the Investigative Reporters and Editors (IRE) Conference on 6 June 2003:

Cash is king

A company's real lifeblood is cash flow, not profit. Profit is simply the difference between revenue and expenses. Cash flow, found in the cash-flow statement, measures how effectively a company is managing its money so that it can expand, buy other businesses, or give back to shareholders. It's a bad sign when cash flow is decreasing. Best is what's called 'free cash flow', which is cash flow from operations minus property and equipment purchases.

Soft spots

The balance sheet, not the income statement, tells a better story about the company's overall financial condition. You can find out whether a company's debt is growing or whether it's having trouble collecting from its customers. If the debt is increasing, is the company earning enough money to pay it off?

It won't happen again (maybe)

Beware of costs labelled 'non-recurring' or 'unusual' or 'one-time'. Companies may be trying to disguise a systematic problem, and such charges could pop up again.

Breaking news

As we have already seen, the *Form 8-K*, which companies must file with the SEC in the United States, is the one to monitor because it may contain developments, such as the change of an auditor or the sale of a business that could affect the stock price.[30]

Quick Reference: What the Forms Tell You

You read about *Forms 8-K, 10-Q,* and *10-K* (and their Canadian equivalents), as well as proxy statements, in Chapter 9. The following list also refers to *Forms S-1, S-3, S-4, SC TO,* and *PRE 14-A (Proxy Statement),* which are other documents that companies are obliged to file with the Securities and Exchange Commission in the States.

Topic	Relevant form
Auditors and fees	*Proxy statements*
Auditor's resignation	*8-K (Publication of Material Change)*
Basic details of company's business	*10-K (Financial Statements, MD&A, the Annual Information Form)*
Bios and salaries of key employees	*PRE 14-A (proxy statement)*
Company's history	*S-1, S-3, 10-K*
Executive pay	*Proxy statement, 10-K*
Financial statements	*10-Q, 10-K, S-3, S-1*
Fiscal year	*10-K*
Former executives	*10-K (compare the most current one to the form from the previous year)*
Legal trouble	*10-Q, 10-K*
Management changes	*8-K*
Merger agreements	*8-K, Proxy statements, S-4, SC TO*
Products	*10-K*
Related party deals (back scratching)	*Proxy statements, 10-Q, 10-K[31]*
Severance for ousted executives	*Proxy statements, 10-Q (Interim Financial Statement), 10-K, 8-K*

Analysts as Journalistic Sources

Large Canadian and US companies are followed and monitored by analysts who work for brokerage houses, such as CIBC World Markets. In general terms, these brokerage houses buy stock for clients and manage their portfolios. It is the analyst's job to prepare reports for investors, who are clients of the brokerage house, on whether certain shares or bonds are worth buying. Most analysts who work at brokerage houses have beats such as transportation, or oil and gas. Analysts can tell you how well the industrial sector or even a specific company is doing. Depending on the analyst's viewpoint, the information may not be entirely balanced. So the reporter must be wary.

'You always have to be careful,' warns Christopher Waddell, a professor of journalism at Carleton University.

> Assume that people don't tell you something for nothing. They tell you something for a reason and you've got to figure out what the reason is. Subsequent to the Enrons and [other corporate scandals], there is now a much greater emphasis on disclosing when there are potential conflicts of interest between the analyst's employer and the company the analyst is talking about. And that also includes the analyst, too. You certainly find on an analyst's report a disclaimer page at the end, which will say that CIBC World Markets owns shares in this company, or acts as an investment advisor for this company. And the analyst may also own shares.[32]

Analysts also work for other institutions that invest money, such as the Ontario Teachers' Pension Plan. It is their job to examine the market, the economy, and the performance of certain companies to determine where the plan should be investing its money. However, Waddell points out that the analysts who tend to be quoted the most frequently in the mainstream media are those who work for the brokerage houses.

To get a sense of which analysts may be the best sources for balanced information, it is best to do what is done with any source: phone around and ask questions. It's worth asking some of a company's biggest investors, who are listed in its proxy filing. You can also contact a securities firm's public-relations department and acquire contact information for analysts, as well as information about the stocks or bonds they cover. Erik Schatzker of Bloomberg warns that 'many analysts have been prohibited from talking to reporters or have to get clearance from PR.'[33]

You can also check out debt-rating agencies, which evaluate the credit-worthiness of a company. Schatzker says that 'the reports they produce can be more sober and less cheerleading than what some equity analysts write. The subject matter is, however, complex and the language arcane.' The two biggest such agencies are Standard & Poor's (*www.standardandpoors.com*) and Moody's Investors Service (*www.moodys.com*).[34]

Online Resources for Business Investigations

First, we list sites that might help specifically with stories about legal problems a company is facing. We follow this with a section on more broadly useful online resources.

Legal

- SEC lawsuits

www.sec.gov/litigation/litreleases.shtml

This lists all the civil lawsuits brought by the Securities and Exchange Commission in US federal court. It also contains archived releases.

- Other US securities lawsuits (class actions)

http://securities.stanford.edu/companies.html

A US securities class-action clearing house. Click on the 'index filings' tab to begin your search.

- OSC lawsuits

www.osc.gov.on.ca/en/Proceedings_index.htm

Archived proceedings go back to 2000 (for prior information, you have to phone the Ontario Securities Commission).

- Disciplined persons list on the Canadian Securities Administrators website

www.securities-administrators.ca/disciplinedpersons.aspx

- Lexis

www.lexis.com

A searchable database of case law and congressional actions. Though costly, many news organizations have a corporate account.

- Pacer

http://pacer.psc.uscourts.gov

Pacer is a US courts service for electronic case and docket information from federal, appellate, state, and district courts, as well as bankruptcy courts. It is not as expensive as Lexis. Through his pursuit of companies that made drugs and other products, former New York attorney general (and more recently disgraced governor) Eliot Spitzer showed that investigations carried out at the US state level can be good sources of information about companies and executives.

- United States Department of Justice

www.justice.gov

According to its website, the department has become 'the world's largest law office and the central agency for enforcement of federal laws.'

- Bankruptcy court documents

www.uscourts.gov/bankruptcycourts.html

This is the general site. You may need to find out the particular 'circuit' where a case in question is located. If you know where a bankruptcy hearing might be taking place, you can follow the appropriate links. Incidentally, you could also visit *Bankruptcydata.com*, which mainly offers a service that costs money but can also be used as a handy reference site. Plug in the name of a company you suspect might be going bankrupt—this may produce information showing that documents do exist and where they are located.

- Courtlink

www.lexisnexis.com/courtlink/online

This is a Nexis product that charges a fee but offers some free services such as the latest news about companies.

- Findlaw

www.findlaw.com

This is a very useful free online service. The search engine allows you to hunt for information on US government sites, plus others. It also offers other services, such as a legal dictionary.

General business-related resources

- CLB Media Inc.

www.clbmedia.ca

A publisher of many trade magazines and other media services.

- More business magazines

http://allyoucanread.com

- Facsnet

www.facsnet.org

A good source of business journalism resources, such as glossaries and back-grounders.

- The McKinsey Quarterly

http://mckinseyquarterly.com

A business journal.

- Sources and experts

www.ibiblio.org/index.html

www.journalismnet.com/experts/

The latter site allows you to search just for Canadian experts; look for the link.

- The National Bureau of Economic Research

www.nber.org

A US-based non-profit research organization.

- National Institute for Computer-Assisted Reporting

www.nicar.org

- Commercial profiles (pay sites)
  - Dun & Bradstreet: *www.dnb.com/us*
  - Hoover's Online: *www.hoovers.com*

These are paid services that house profiles on thousands of public and private companies. They work more quickly than free search engines, providing information such as corporate histories to the number of employees, to sales estimates. You can get background information on key people such as the directors and CEO. Libraries often have accounts with these services. The information can also be obtained from media reports and other free sources, but these pay sites can be quicker and therefore more useful if you're on deadline.

- Basic free finance sites

http://finance.yahoo.com
www.siliconinvestor.com
http://ragingbull.quote.com

These offer, among other things, up-to-date financial news and stock quotes. Keep in mind, though, that free finance sites can be just as likely to send you off in the wrong direction, so they are not great to use on deadline unless you know exactly what you're looking for. It's better to familiarize yourself with them when you're not pressed for time.

Notes

Chapter 1

1 James L. Aucoin, *I.R.E.: Investigative Reporters & Editors, the Arizona Project, and the Evolution of American Investigative Journalism* (Evergreen, AL: Raging Cajun Books, 1997), 70, 99.

2 Tracey Tyler, 'Driving While Black: Driver stopped because of race, lawyer to tell top Ontario court' (*Toronto Star*, 24 October 1998), A8. Also: 'New Trial Ordered for man in police bias case. Appeal Court cites mistake by Judge' (*Toronto Star*, 5 May 1999), B1.

3 William Wray Carney, *In the News, The Practice of Media Relations in Canada* (Edmonton: University of Alberta Press, 2002), 56–7.

4 George Merlis, *How to Make the Most of Every Media Appearance* (New York: McGraw-Hill Ryerson, 2003), 13, 56–8.

5 Merlis, *How to Make . . .*, 57.

6 Jim Rankin et al., Race and Crime series (*Toronto Star*, 19–27 October 2002).

7 For the February 2010 follow-up story, see *www.thestar.com/specialsections/raceandcrime/article/761069--story-behind-the-numbers* (accessed 14 February 2010).

8 Cecil Rosner, interview with the authors.

9 Linday Kines, interview with the authors.

10 Cecil Rosner, interview with the authors.

11 Katherine Barber, ed., *The Canadian Oxford Dictionary* (Don Mills, ON: Oxford University Press, 2004).

12 Harvey Cashore, interview with the authors.

13 James S. Ettema and Theodore L. Glasser, *Custodians of Conscience: Investigative Journalism and Public Virtue* (New York: Columbia University Press, 1998), 3.

Chapter 2

1 Bob Woodward and Carl Bernstein, *All the President's Men* (New York: Simon and Schuster, 1974).

2 Fred Vallance-Jones, Car Fires series (*The Hamilton Spectator*, 19–21 February 2004).

3 Karl Karp and Cecil Rosner, *When Justice Fails, The David Milgaard Story* (Toronto: McClelland & Stewart, 1991 [revised, 1998]).

4 Robert Cribb, Dirty Dining series (*Toronto Star*, 19–22 February 2000).

5 Fred Vallance-Jones and Steve Buist, Smoke Screen series (*The Hamilton Spectator*, 18–23 September 2004).

6 Fred Vallance-Jones and George Stephenson, *The Secret War* (CBC Manitoba, 1996).

7 David McKie, Bob Carty, and Susanne Reber, *Faint Warning* (CBC Radio and Television, 2004).

8 Dean Tudor, *Finding Answers: The Essential Guide to Gathering Information in Canada* (Toronto: McClelland & Stewart, 1993), 119.

9 Robert I. Berkman, *Find It Fast: How to Uncover Expert Information on Any Subject—In Print or Online*, 4th ed. (New York: HarperPerennial, 1997), 286.

10 Steve Weinberg, *The Reporter's Handbook: An Investigator's Guide to Documents and Techniques*, 3rd ed. (New York: St Martin's Press, 1996), 4.

11 Fred Vallance-Jones and Steve Buist, 'Cheat took cash for fake test results' (*The Hamilton Spectator*, 18 September 2004), A1. Used with permission.

12 Canadian Association of Journalists, *Statement of Principles on Investigative Journalism* (available online at *www.caj.ca*).

13 Nick Russell, *Morals and the Media: Ethics in Canadian Journalism* (Vancouver: University of British Columbia Press, 1994), 97.

14 *Criminal Code of Canada*. R.S.C. 1985, c. C-46, s. 184(2)(a).

15 Michael Crawford, *The Journalist's Legal Guide*, 4th ed. (Toronto: Carswell, 2002), 122.

16 Crawford, *The Journalist's Legal Guide*, 118.

17 Robert Cribb and Christian Cotroneo, 'Toronto a hotbed for phone fraud—Telemarketers sell phony credit cards to US, Europe' (*Toronto Star*, 2 November 2002). Also: Robert Cribb and Dale Brazao, 'On the killing floor in Vaughan's illegal farm slaughterhouse' (*Toronto Star*, 16 December 2000).

Chapter 3

1 Jessica Mitford, *Poison Penmanship: The Gentle Art of Muckraking* (New York: Alfred A. Knopf, 1979), 5.

2 Julian Sher, 'A beginner's guide to the Internet: phobia, hype ... and help', *Media Magazine* 2.4 (Winter 1995), 7.

3 David Akin, interview with authors.

4 Steve Weinberg, *The Reporter's Handbook: An Investigator's Guide to Documents and Techniques*, 3rd ed. (New York: Bedford/St Martin's, sponsored by Investigative Reporters and Editors Inc., 1996), 17.

Chapter 4

1 Andrew McIntosh, 'New charges laid against two Chrétien supporters' (*National Post*, 7 December 2000).

2 Andrew McIntosh, 'Businessman who bought hotel from Chrétien given federal aid: $665,000 granted to Quebecer with criminal record' (*National Post*, 25 January 1999).

3 Andrew McIntosh, 'Into the rough: In 1988, Prime Minister Jean Chrétien bought into a golf course' (*National Post*, 23 January 1999).

4 Andrew McIntosh, 'PM lobbied for disputed loan: PMO's defence is that he was just doing what "MPs from every party do"' (*National Post*, 16 November 2000). Also: Robert Fife and Andrew McIntosh, '"It's the normal operation": PM defends intervention in federal loan to inn' (*National Post*, 17 November 2000). Also: Andrew McIntosh, 'New evidence on Grand-Mère loan' (*National Post*, 12 May 2003).

5 Andrew McIntosh, '$189,000 given to businessman with ties to PM: Quebecer received federal grants for inn bought

from Chrétien' (*National Post*, 2 February 1999).

6 See note 4.

7 Andrew McIntosh, 'Both Day and Clark accuse PM of conflict' (*National Post*, 2 March 2001). Also: Andrew McIntosh and Robert Fife, 'PM should stand down: Clark' (*National Post*, with files from Southam News, 24 March 2001).

8 Andrew McIntosh, 'Second developer given federal aid is focus of inquiry: $1.5M in federal money: Secured aid to build hotel after meeting the prime minister' (*National Post*, 20 March 1999). Also: Andrew McIntosh, 'Chrétien blasted in House for aiding "shady" hotelier: PM didn't know man is being probed in Belgium, aide says' (*National Post*, 23 March 1999).

9 Andrew McIntosh, 'The patronage machine: Three men with links to the prime minister have received millions in federal funding' (*National Post*, 19 June 1999).

10 See, for example, 'Tax Relief of All Canadians' (25 November 2004). Also: 'If Feds Will Not Reduce Taxes in the Upcoming Budget—It Should be Brought Down' (16 November 2004).

11 See, for example, 'Getting the most bang for our bucks; AFB technical paper calls for social reinvestment over tax cuts and debt repayment' (9 February 2005). Also: 'Surplus should be reinvested in people and communities' (7 February 2005).

12 Laurie Monsebraaten, Fred Vallance-Jones, and Phinjo Gombu, 'The fine art of giving' (*Toronto Star*, 24 May 2003).

13 Laurie Monsebraaten, interview with authors.

14 Office of the Auditor General of Canada, 'Chapters 3, 4, and 5—Government-Wide Audit of Sponsorship, Advertising, and Public Opinion Research' (Press release, 10 February 2004).

15 Robert Cribb, 'City audit shows big holes' (*Toronto Star*, 13 October 2001).

16 James Cowan, 'Liczyk says affair with consultant not city's business: Treasurer's former lover received $4.6-million in city contracts' (*National Post*, 9 November 2004). Also: James Rusk, 'It wasn't a

conflict to give ex-lover a contract, Liczyk testifies' (*The Globe and Mail*, 9 November 2004). Also: Linda Diebel, 'Questions about Liczyk grow' (*Toronto Star*, 12 November 2004).

17 Another helpful way of searching for federal government statistics is by subject. A private firm that specializes in online federal searches has created a useful research site at *www.gdsourcing.ca/indexa.htm*.

18 Kevin Donovan, 'Billions lost in charity scandal' (*Toronto Star*, 12 November 2002).

19 Andrew McIntosh, 'Unpaid aide to PM lobbied for additional $100,000 for hotel owner' (*National Post*, 15 May 1999). See also 'RCMP asked to probe activities of PM's aide' (*National Post*, 19 May 1999).

20 Andrew McIntosh, 'Businessman who bought hotel from Chrétien given federal aid: $665,000 granted to Quebecer with criminal record' (*National Post*, 25 January 1999).

21 Philip Mathias and Andrew McIntosh, 'Company with links to Chrétien awarded $6.3M contract from CIDA: Transelec Inc. donated $10,000 to PM's campaign' (*National Post*, 1 June 1999). Also: Andrew McIntosh, 'Quebec firm's CIDA project plagued by problems: audit' (*National Post*, 17 October 2000).

22 Jim Cairns, interview with the authors.

23 See *Regulated Health Professions Act*, 1991, S.O. 1991, c. 18, ss. 45 (1), (2), and (3). Also: Nova Scotia *Barristers' Society Regulations* (amended to 18 July 2003), available on the Internet at *www.nsbs.ns.ca/regs/CURRENTREGS.pdf*.

24 *Statutory Powers Procedure Act*, R.S.O. 1980, c. 484, s. 9 (1). Also: *Canadian Broadcasting Corp. v. Summerside (City)* [1999], 170 D.L.R. (4th) 731.

25 *Judges Act*, R.S.C. 1985, c. J-1, ss. 63 (5) and (6), 36 (1), and 37 (4).

26 *Judicature Act* (Alberta), R.S.A. 2000, c. J-2, ss. 34 (5), 36; *Courts of Justice Act* (Ontario), R.S.O. 1990, c. C.43, ss. 51.6 (7), (8), (9), and (10).

27 Robert Cribb, Rita Daly, and Laurie Monsebraaten, 'How system helps shield bad doctors' (*Toronto Star*, 5 May 2001).

Chapter 5

1 Paul Waldie, 'Aylmer owner had troubled history' (*The Globe and Mail*, 6 September 2003).

2 Steve Weinberg, *The Reporter's Handbook: An Investigator's Guide to Documents and Techniques*, 3rd ed. (New York: St Martin's Press, 1996), 268.

3 Stephen Overbury and Susanna Buenaventure, *How to Research Almost Anything: A Canadian Guide for Students, Consumers and Business* (Whitby, ON: McGraw-Hill Ryerson, 1998), 187.

4 Louis J. Rose, *How to Investigate Your Friends and Enemies* (St Louis: Albion Press, 1981), 27.

5 Josh Meyer, 'Court Records 101' (presentation to Investigative Reporters and Editors National Conference, Phoenix, Arizona, June 1997).

6 For a detailed description of the structure of the courts, see Dean Jobb, *Media Law for Canadian Journalists*, 2nd ed. (Toronto: Emond Montgomery Publications, 2010), Chapter 1.

7 The law governing access to the documents and hearings of courts and other bodies is examined in Jobb's *Media Law . . .*, Chapter 8.

8 Reference re: s. 12 (1) of the *Juvenile Delinquents Act* (Canada) (1983), (sub nom. *R. v. Southam Inc.*) 34 C.R. (3d) 27, 41 O.R. (2d) 113 (Ont. CA).

9 *Canadian Broadcasting Corp. v. New Brunswick (Attorney General)*, 3 S.C.R. 480.

10 *Nova Scotia (Attorney General) v. MacIntyre*, [1982] 1 S.C.R. 175 at 186–7.

11 Criminal Law Practice Direction (Consolidated) (British Columbia Supreme Court, 2 November 1998), available on the Internet at *www.courts.gov.bc.ca/sc/pdir/Pdir24.html*.

12 *Dagenais v. Canadian Broadcasting Corporation*, [1994] 3 S.C.R. 835.

13 This is the conclusion of the Report of the Publication Bans Committee, Criminal Law Section, Uniform Law Conference of Canada, November 1996. Available online at *www.ulcc.ca/en/poam2/*

index.cfm?sec=1996&sub=1996af#IIB1.
Publications bans and the impact of the
Dagenais ruling are explored in more
detail in Jobb, *Media Law for Canadian
Journalists*, Chapters 6 and 7.

14 *R. v. Mentuck*, [2001] 3 S.C.R. 442,
2001 SCC 76; *R. v. O.N.E.*, [2001] 3
S.C.R. 478, 2001 SCC 77.

15 *Sierra Club of Canada v. Canada (Minister
of Finance)*, [2002] 2 S.C.R. 522.

16 Michael Crawford, *The Journalist's Legal
Guide* (Toronto: Carswell, 2002), 38. If
the report as a whole is accurate, it will
be privileged despite the existence of a
few slight inaccuracies or omissions: see
Philip Lewis, ed., *Gatley on Libel and
Slander*, 8th ed. (London: Sweet &
Maxwell, 1981), 313. See also Dean
Jobb's *Media Law . . .*, Chapter 9.

17 An Ontario judge found that failing to
present a balanced report by omitting
key information and by 'deliberately'
failing to give the plaintiff a chance to
respond to criticism defeated a plea of
fair comment. *Leenen v. Canadian Broadcasting Corp.*, [2000] 48 O.R. (3d) 656,
upheld by the Ontario Court of Appeal,
12 June 2001, Docket no. C34272. For
a rundown of the cases illustrating these
points, see Crawford, *The Journalist's
Legal Guide*, 38, fn 64, 65.

18 *Hill v. Church of Scientology of Toronto*,
[1995] 2 S.C.R. 1130.

19 'Open Courts, Electronic Access to
Court Records, and Privacy' (discussion paper prepared on behalf of the
Judges Technology Advisory Committee for the Canadian Judicial Council,
May 2003), 22 (available on the Internet at *www.cjccm.gc.ca/english/publica-
tions/OpenCourts2EN.pdf*).

20 Dean Jobb, 'Courts struggle to balance
privacy and openness in giving access
to court files over the Internet', *The
Lawyers Weekly*, 18 July 2008. Available
on the Internet at *www.lawyersweekly.ca/
index.php?section=article&articleid=726*.

21 *Canadian Newspapers Co. v. Canada
(Attorney General)* (1986), (sub nom.
Canadian Newspapers Co. v. Canada) 53

C.R. (3d) 203, 29 C.C.C. (3d) 109 (Ont.
HC); *Canadian Newspapers Co. v. Canada
(Attorney General)* (1986), 28 C.C.C. (3d)
379 (Man. QB); *Girard v. Ouellet* (2001),
198 D.L.R. (4th) 58 (Que. CA).

22 Crawford. *The Journalist's Legal Guide*,
185. Also: *Martin's Annual Criminal Code,
2002* (Canada Law Book Inc., 2002),
801–2.

23 *Criminal Code.*, s. 487.3(2).

24 *Criminal Code.*, s. 487.3(4).

25 *Toronto Star Newspapers Ltd. v. Ontario*,
[2003] O.J.No. 4006. Also: Cristin
Schmitz, 'Appeal Court lays down rules
on sealing of search warrants' (*The Lawyers Weekly*, 31 October 2003).

26 Ownership and the return of exhibits
are discussed in *Halifax Herald Ltd v.
Nova Scotia (Attorney General)* (1992), 7
Admin. L.R. (2d) 46 (NSTD).

27 *Vickery v. Nova Scotia Supreme Court
(Prothonotary)*, [1991] 1 S.C.R. 671. Justice Peter Cory, who wrote a dissenting
judgment, argued that all court records
and exhibits are in the public domain
—even evidence ruled inadmissible—
unless there was an overriding interest
at stake. 'There should not be a priestly
cult of the law whereby lawyers and
judges exclusively determine those
items of the appeal record which can be
seen and heard by members of the public,' he wrote. Media law experts believe
the access rules set out in *Vickery* are
outdated, overly restrictive, and violate
the Charter's guarantee of freedom of
the press. See Dean Jobb, 'Access to
information: Law and reality miles
apart' (*The Lawyers Weekly*, 6 March
2009).

28 *R. v. Warren*, [1995] N.W.T.J. No. 9
(SC); *R. v. Thornton* [*Canadian Broadcast-
ing Corp. v. Nova Scotia (Supreme Court,
Prothonotary)*], [1999] N.S.J. No. 317
(SC).

29 *R. v. Dunlop*, ruling of the Manitoba
Court of Queen's Bench, 2 May 2001.
Available on the Internet at *www.adi-
dem.org/case/dunlop.html*; *R. v. Van Seters*
(1996), 31 O.R. (3d) 19 (Gen. Div.).

30 *Calgary Sun, a Division of Toronto Sun Publishing Corp. v. Alberta,* [1996] A.J. No. 536 (QB).

31 *R. v. Canadian Broadcasting Corporation,* 2008 CanLII 28062 (ON S.C.).

32 'Judge denies bid to view Virk autopsy photos' (*The Halifax Chronicle Herald,* 5 May 1999).

33 See, for instance, Prince Edward Island Supreme Court 'Practice Note 23: Transcripts and Tapes of Evidence', which directs that taped transcripts 'shall not, either in whole or in part, be used for broadcast, audio reproduction or re-taping.'

34 '500,000 cases on CanLII!' A press release issued 5 May 2008; available online at *www.canlii.org/en/blog/index. php?/archives/13-500,000-cases-on-Can LII!.html.*

35 *Corrections and Conditional Release Act,* S.C. 1992, c. 20,. s. 140 (4) and (5), s. 144 (1) and (2).

36 Robert Cribb, 'Sgro to resign: Affidavit says she promised aid in return for pizza' (*Toronto Star,* 14 January 2005).

37 *Lac d'Amiante du Québec Ltée v. 2858-0702 Québec Inc.,* 2001 SCC 51.

38 'Supreme Court Rules' (British Columbia), B.C. Reg. 221/90, rule 60(41); New Brunswick's *Judicature Act,* S.N.B., c. J-2, s. 11.3 (1); *Family Law Act* (Prince Edward Island), S.P.E.I., c. F-2.1, ss. 2 (4) and 41 (2); Newfoundland and Labrador's *Unified Family Court Act,* R.S.N.L. 1990, c. U-3, s. 11, and 'Rules of the Supreme Court', 1986 N.R. 52/97, rules 56A.03 and 56A.04 (1); 'Code of Civil Procedure' (Quebec), R.S.Q. c. C-25, ss. 13, 815.4, 827.5, and 827.6; Saskatchewan's 'Queen's Bench Rules', rules 587 (1) and (3).

39 'Provincial Court (*Child, Family and Community Service Act*) Rules' (British Columbia), B.C. Reg. 417/98, rule 8 (15); Nova Scotia's *Children and Family Services Act,* S.N.S. 1996, c. 3, s. 93 and 'Civil Procedure Rules', rule 69.16.

40 See, for instance, *Civil Code of Quebec,* S.Q. 1991, c. 64, s. 582, and Saskatchewan's legislation, *The Adoption Act* 1998, S.S. 1998, c. A-5.2, s. 20 (1).

41 *Courts of Justice Act* (Ontario), R.S.O. 1990, c. C.43, s. 137 (2); *The Court of Queen's Bench Act* (Manitoba), C.C.S.M., c. C280, s. 77 (1); Prince Edward Island's *Supreme Court Act,* S.P.E.I., c. S-10, s. 58 (2).

42 'Federal Court Rules', 1998, SOR/98-106, rules 151 (1) and (2).

43 *Sierra Club of Canada v. Canada (Minister of Finance),* [2002] 2 S.C.R. 522.

44 *Potash Corp. of Saskatchewan v. Barton,* [2002] S.J. No. 484. Also: John Jaffey, 'Nine years later, Saskatchewan court vacates sealing order' (*The Lawyers Weekly,* 11 October 2002).

45 *Criminal Code,* s. 486(3). The ban remains in force until rescinded or altered by a court with jurisdiction to do so. See *R. v. K.(V.)* (1991), 4 C.R. (4th) 338, 68 C.C.C. (3d) 18 (BCCA).

46 *Criminal Code,* s. 486(4.1).

47 *Criminal Code,* ss. 276.1(3), 276.2(1), and 276.3(1).

48 *Criminal Code,* ss. 278.4(2), 278.6(2), and 278.9(1).

49 *Criminal Code,* s. 517(1).

50 *Criminal Code,* s. 539(1).

51 *Criminal Code,* s. 542(2).

52 See, for example, *R. v. Wood* (1993), (sub nom. *R. v. Wood (No. 2)*) 124 N.S.R. (2d) 128 (NSSC).

53 *Southam Inc. v. R. (No. 2)* (1982), 70 C.C.C. (2d) 264 (Ont. HC).

54 *Canada Evidence Act,* R.S.C. c. C-5, ss. 31 (1), (1.1), (2), (3) and 37.21 (1).

55 *Canada Evidence Act,* R.S.C. c. C-5, ss. 37 (4.1), (5), and (6).

56 *Canada Evidence Act,* R.S.C. c. C-5, ss. 38.13 (1), (7), and (9), ss. 38.131 (1), (6), (8), (9), and (12).

57 *Criminal Code,* ss. 83.05 (6), 83.06(1), 83.13 (1), and 83.28(5).

58 *Vancouver Sun (Re),* [2004] 2 S.C.R. 332, 2004 SCC 43; In the Matter of an Application under s. 83.28 of the *Criminal Code,* 2003 BCSC 1172. Also: John Jaffey, 'Secrecy surrounds first test at SCC of anti-terrorism law' (*The Lawyers Weekly,* 15 August 2003). Also: Mark Bourrie, 'Supreme Court seals file in

secret witness case' (*Law Times*, 11 August 2003).

59 *Youth Criminal Justice Act*, ss. 110 (1) and (2), 117, and 119 (1)(s).

60 *Youth Criminal Justice Act*, s. 117; *R. v. A.A.B.*, 2006 NSPC 16.

61 *Youth Criminal Justice Act*, ss. 110 (1) and (2). In 2007, Nova Scotia media outlets successfully challenged a ruling that allowed a young man convicted of murdering a cab driver to have his identity shielded pending an appeal of his conviction. A judge ruled young offenders sentenced as adults are not entitled to have the ban on publishing their names extended, even though it's possible an appeal court may decide they should be sentenced under the *Youth Criminal Justice Act* and remain unidentified. See *R. v. G.D.S.*, 2007 NSCA 94 (CanLII).

62 *Youth Criminal Justice Act*, ss. 110 (3) and (6).

63 *Youth Criminal Justice Act*, ss. 111 (1), (2), and (3), s. 112.

64 *R. v. Sun Media Corporation*, 2001 ABPC 108 at paragraph 12.

65 *Courts of Justice Act*, R.S.O. 1990, c. C.43, ss. 135 (2) and (3); *Supreme Court Act*, S.P.E.I., c. S-10, ss. 57 (2) and (3); *The Court of Queen's Bench Act*, C.C.S.M., c. C280, ss. 76 (2) and (3).

66 *Dix v. Canada (A.G.)*, 2001 ABQB 838, at paragraphs 27 and 28.

67 *Nova Scotia (Attorney General) v. MacIntyre*, [1982] 1 S.C.R. 175, at 185.

68 *John Doe v. Canadian Broadcasting Corp.*, [1993] B.C.J. No. 1869, at paragraph 34 (SC).

69 Ontario's Criminal Injuries Compensation Board, to cite an example, can ban publication of evidence heard when it assesses applications from victims of crime for compensation. *Compensation for Victims of Crime Act*, R.S.O. 1990, c. C.24, s. 13.

70 *Extradition Act*, S.C. 1999, c. 18, s. 26.

71 *Immigration and Refugee Protection Act*, S.C. 2001, c. 27, s. 166.

72 *Immigration and Refugee Protection Act*, S.C. 2001, c. 27, ss. 77 and 78.

73 *Immigration and Refugee Protection Act*, S.C. 2001, c. 27, ss. 86 and 87.

74 *National Defence Act*, R.S.C. 1985, c. N-5, ss. 180 (1), (2), and 236 (2).

75 *Canadian Broadcasting Corp. v. Boland*, [1995] 1 F.C. 323 (TD).

76 Between the late 1970s and 1994, more than 20 inquiries and royal commissions conducted televised hearings. See Daniel J. Henry, 'Electronic Public Access to Court—An Idea Whose Time Has Come' (paper available online at *www.adidem.org/articles/DH1.html*).

77 *Judges Act*, R.S.C. 1985, c. J-1, ss. 63 (5) and (6), 36 (1), and 37 (4).

78 *Judicature Act* (Alberta), R.S.A. 2000, c. J-2, ss. 34 (5), 36; *Courts of Justice Act* (Ontario), R.S.O. 1990, c. C.43, ss. 51.6 (7), (8,) (9), and (10).

79 William Marsden, Rod MacDonell, and Andrew McIntosh, 'Short days for judges—long wait for justice: Municipal courts often deserted' (*Montreal Gazette*, 18 July 1992).

Chapter 6

1 Dean Jobb, '"Life was Cheap Then": The *King v. Farmer*', *Shades of Justice: Seven Nova Scotia Murder Cases* (Halifax: Nimbus Publishing, 1988), 95–114, 139–40.

2 Julian Sher, interview with the authors. Sher's book is *'Until You Are Dead': Steven Truscott's Long Ride into History* (Toronto: Knopf Canada, 2001).

3 W. Stewart Wallace, ed., *The Macmillan Dictionary of Canadian Biography*, 3rd ed. (Toronto: Macmillan Canada, 1973).

4 B.J. Grant, *Fit to Print: New Brunswick's Newspapers: 150 Years of the Comic, the Sad, the Odd and the Forgotten* (Fredericton, NB: Goose Lane Editions, 1987), 98.

5 Pierre Berton, 'Chapter 4: The Joy of Research', in *The Joy of Writing: A Guide for Writers, Disguised as a Literary Memoir* (Toronto: Doubleday Canada, 2003).

6 Julian Sher, interview with the authors, and *'Until You Are Dead'*, 165.

7 *Canadian Historical Review*, 85.2 (June 2004).

8 Sher, interview with the authors, 14 May 2009.

9 Paul MacNeill and Dean Jobb, 'Westray manager held key post at ill-fated Alberta mine' (*The Halifax Chronicle-Herald*, 7 August 1992), A1–2.

10 Stephen Kimber, interview with the authors. His book is *Sailors, Slackers and Blind Pigs: Halifax at War* (Toronto: Doubleday Canada, 2002).

11 Angus Baxter, *In Search of Your Canadian Roots: Tracing Your Family Tree in Canada*, 3rd ed. (Toronto: McClelland & Stewart, 1999).

Chapter 7

1 Cecil Rosner and Ross Rutherford, 'Dreamweaver', *Venture* (CBC Television, 13 December 1992).

2 Rosner and Rutherford.

3 Julian Sher, interview with the authors.

4 Carl Karp and Cecil Rosner. *When Justice Fails—The David Milgaard Story* (Toronto: McClelland & Stewart, 1991).

5 Robert Cribb and Lois Kalchman, 'From hockey dad to hockey mogul' (*Toronto Star*, 24 October 2004).

6 Patricia Orwen and Dale Brazao, 'The secret life of a deadbeat dad' (*Toronto Star*, 29 January 2000).

7 Cecil Rosner, interview with the authors.

8 Robert Cribb, 'Watchdog didn't stop "Butcher Bradley"' (*Toronto Star*, 5 May 2001). Also: Robert Cribb, '"Butcher" Bradley has retired to secluded cottage splendour' (*Toronto Star*, 20 May 2001).

9 Cribb, 'Watchdog didn't stop "Butcher Bradley"'.

10 Cribb, 'Watchdog didn't stop . . .'.

11 Cribb, 'Watchdog didn't stop . . .'.

12 Consent Order (Virginia Board of Medicine, 30 November 1999).

13 Robert Cribb, '"Butcher" Bradley has retired to secluded cottage splendour' (*Toronto Star*, 20 May 2001).

14 Orwen and Brazao, 'The secret life of a deadbeat dad'.

15 John Duncanson and Phinjo Gombu, 'The case of a missing ticket' (*Toronto Star*, 10 January 2004).

16 Jessica Leeder and Robert Cribb, 'Driving schools break rules' (*Toronto Star*, 18 September 2006), A1.

17 Leeder and Cribb, 'Driving schools break rules', A1.

18 Jessica Leeder and Robert Cribb, 'Road unworthy?' (*Toronto Star*, 18 September 2006), C1.

19 Leeder and Cribb, 'Road unworthy?', C1.

20 Steve Buist, 'Bankruptcy hasn't changed Martinos' luxurious lifestyle' (*The Hamilton Spectator*, 21 February 2004). Also: 'Province mum on Royal Crest forensic audit spending' (*The Hamilton Spectator*, 11 October 2005).

21 Steve Buist, interview with the authors.

22 Dale Brazao and Robert Cribb, 'The Royale treatment: Spa owner not in it for "headaches": Past charges no bar to new licence' (*Toronto Star*, 10 May 2005).

23 For a useful but dated overview of Canadian privacy law, see Gordon F. Proudfoot, *Privacy Law and the Media in Canada* (Ottawa: Canadian Bar Foundation, 1984).

24 The CBC's reporting handbook advises that intrusions into the private lives of individuals are warranted only when the person's private life spills over into his or her public life or when private matters become relevant to the discussion of a public issue. *CBC Journalistic Standards and Practices* (Canadian Broadcasting Corporation, 2001), 63.

25 See, for instance, Saskatchewan's *Privacy Act*, R.S.S. 1978, c. P-24, s. 3.

26 See, for example, British Columbia's *Privacy Act*, R.S.B.C. 1996, c. 373, s. 2 (3).

27 *Privacy Act*, Saskatchewan, s. 4 (1) (e).

28 *Personal Information Protection and Electronic Documents Act*, S.C. 2000, c. 5, s. 2.

29 *Silber and Value Industries Ltd. v. British Columbia Television Broadcasting System Ltd.* (1985) 69 B.C.L.R. 24 (SC).

30 *John Doe v. Canadian Broadcasting Corp.* (1993), 86 B.C.L.R. (2d) 202 (SC).

31 *Hollingsworth v. B.C.T.V.* (1996), 34 C.C.L.T. (2d) 95 (BCSC).

32 This point is made in Michael G. Crawford, *The Journalist's Legal Guide,* 4th ed. (Toronto: Carswell, 2002), 131–32.

33 *Charter of Human Rights and Freedoms,* S.Q.1975, c. 6, ss. 4, 5, and 9.

34 In addition, the judge considered the report exploitive and found the newspaper liable for the damage caused when other media outlets picked up the story. *Valiquette v. Gazette (The)* (1991), 8 C.C.L.T. (2d) 302 (Que. SC).

35 Ingrid Peritz and Colin Freeze,'Attempt to muzzle media fails' (*The Globe and Mail,* 30 June 2005).

36 *Aubry v. Editions Vice-Versa,* [1998] 1 S.C.R. 591.

37 *Haskett* v. *Trans Union of Canada Inc.,* [2001] OJ 4949.

38 *R. v. Patrick,* 2009 SCC 17.

39 *Nitsopoulos v. Wong,* 2008 CanLII 45407 (Ont. SC).

40 *MacDonnell v. Halifax Herald Ltd.,* 2009 NSSC 187.

41 See Dean Jobb, 'N.S. judge allows publication of minister's unguarded remarks' (*The Lawyers Weekly,* 26 June 2009). Also: Dean Jobb, 'Why press freedom trumped privacy rights' (*The Halifax Chronicle Herald,* 17 June 2009).

42 *Criminal Code,* R.S.C. 1985, c. C-46, ss. 322, 354.

43 This point is made in Proudfoot, *Privacy Law and the Media,* 46.

44 Sean Upton, 'The judge's decision was unequivocal' (*Ottawa Citizen,* 16 July 1990).

45 *R. v. Stewart,* [1988] 1 S.C.R. 963.

46 *Criminal Code,* s. 342.1. It is also an offence, under s. 430, to alter or destroy computer data or to block someone from accessing a computer system the person is authorized to use.

47 *Canadian Transportation Accident Investigation Safety Board Act,* S.C. 1989, c. 3, s. 24 (3); *Canadian Transportation Accident Investigation Safety Board v. Canadian Press,* 2000 CanLII 4353 (NSSC).

48 *Amherst (Town) v. Canadian Broadcasting Corp.* [1994] NSJ No. 291 (CA).

49 As discussed in Crawford, *The Journalist's Legal Guide,* 284–85.

50 *Criminal Code,* s. 372(3).

51 *Criminal Code,* s. 264.

52 Robert S. Bruser and Brian MacLeod Rogers, *Journalists and the Law: How to Get the Story Without Getting Sued or Put in Jail* (Ottawa: Canadian Bar Foundation, 1985), 14.

53 *Trespass to Property Act,* R.S.O. 1990, c. T.21, s. 1 (1).

54 *Criminal Code,* s. 177.

55 Rhéal Séquin, 'Security flaws at Hydro-Québec prompt countrywide checks' (*The Globe and Mail,* 18 February 2005).

56 *Criminal Code,* s. 184(2)(a).

57 Crawford, *The Journalist's Legal Guide,* 117.

58 The Supreme court of Canada has ruled this restriction does not violate the Charter right to freedom of the press. *CKOY Ltd. v. The Queen* (1978), 90 D.L.R. (3d) 1. An exception is made if the person phoned the station to participate in a program. See s. 3 (e) of the *Radio Regulations, 1986,* SOR 86-982.

59 *Criminal Code,* s. 183.

60 *R. v. Biasi* (No. 3) [1981], 66 C.C.C. (2d) 566 (BCSC).

61 *Criminal Code,* s. 193(1).

62 Stewart Bell, 'Wiretaps "integral part" of getting search warrants, media can report' (*National Post,* 14 August 1999).

63 The penalty for a conviction is up to two years in jail and an order to pay up to $5000 in damages to the victim of the invasion of privacy. See *Criminal Code,* ss. 193.1(1), 194.

64 The maximum punishment for anyone convicted of this offence is a $25,000 fine and a year in jail, while a corporation can be fined up to $75,000. R.S.C. 1985, c. R-2, ss. 9 (1.1) and (2).

65 *R. v. Gasper* [1976], W.W.D. 93 (Sask. Dist. Ct.).

Chapter 8

1 Lindsay Kines, interview with the authors.

2 Stewart Harral, *Keys to Successful Interviewing* (Norman, OK: University of Oklahoma Press, 1954), 36.

3 Eric Nalder, 'Loosening Lips' (seminar at Investigative Reporter and Editors Annual Conference, Atlanta, Georgia, June 2004).

4 Sally Adams and Wynford Hicks, *Interviewing for Journalists* (London: Routledge, 2001), 42.

5 John Sawatsky, *CAJ* interviewing seminar (Winnipeg, January 1999).

6 Sawatsky, *CAJ* interviewing seminar.

7 Sawatsky, *CAJ* interviewing seminar.

8 Nalder, 'Loosening Lips'.

9 Steve Buttry, *Getting the Most from Your Interviews*; available online at *www.journalism.org/resources/tools/reporting/interviewing/themost.asp*.

10 John Brady, *The Interviewer's Handbook: A Guerrilla Guide* (Waukesha, WI: Kalmbach Publishing, 2004), 135.

11 Buttry, *Getting the Most from Your Interviews*.

12 Adams and Hicks, *Interviewing for Journalists*, 35.

13 Nalder, 'Loosening Lips'.

14 Brady, *The Interviewer's Handbook*, 123.

15 See, for example, Brady and Sawatsky.

16 Joan Walters, interview with authors.

17 Ken Metzler, *Creative Interviewing: The Writer's Guide to Gathering Information by Asking Questions*, 3rd ed. (Upper Saddle River, NJ: Allyn and Bacon, 1996), 167.

18 Dean Jobb, *Media Law for Canadian Journalists* (Toronto: Emond Montgomery Publications, 2006), 311–12.

19 Bill C-426, introduced by Bloc Québécois MP and former journalist Serge Ménard, would have amended the *Canada Evidence Act* to give journalists the right to refuse to name a confidential source or to produce records that would identify one. This right would not be absolute—a judge could order disclosure if it was in the public interest to identify the source, if all other means of identifying the source had been exhausted, and after considering the impact on the source. Journalists would also have the right to withhold unpublished information unless it was deemed to be of vital importance and could not be obtained by other means. Also, the legislation would require a judge or justice of the peace to be satisfied, before issuing a warrant to search a journalist's materials or a media outlet, that the public interest in investigating and prosecuting an offence takes precedence over a journalist's right to gather and report information.

20 At least three have been jailed since 1900. In 1914, Nova Scotia's legislature jailed William McCurdy, news editor of the *Halifax Herald*, for 48 hours for refusing to identify the author of a letter to the editor that accused politicians of corruption. In 1969, when FLQ bombings in Quebec culminated in the October Crisis, Montreal's fire commissioner jailed a CBC Television reporter for seven days for refusing to name a man who claimed to be a bomber. In the third case, a camera operator with a television station in Hull, Quebec, spent 72 hours in jail in 1995 but later lost his job after acknowledging he had never promised to protect the source's identity. See William March, *Red Line: The Chronicle-Herald and The Mail-Star, 1875–1954* (Halifax: Chebucto Agencies Ltd., 1986), 119–22; Sidney N. Lederman, Patrick O'Kelly, and Margaret Grottenhaler, 'Confidentiality of News Sources', in Philip Anisman and Allen M. Linden, eds., *The Media, the Courts and the Charter* (Toronto: Carswell, 1986), 234; and André Picard, 'Journalist fired over false report: Hull camera operator served jail sentence for contempt of court in protecting source' (*The Globe and Mail*, 29 September 1995).

21 *R. v. National Post et al.* [2004] O.J. No. 178.

22 *R. v. National Post*, 2008 ONCA 139.

23 *R. v. National Post*, 2010 SCC 16.

24 For an analysis of what the ruling means for journalists, see Dean Jobb, 'The upside of the confidential sources ruling,' *J-Source* (available on the Internet: at www.j-source.ca/english_new/detail.php?id=5095).

25 *St Elizabeth Home Society v. City of Hamilton et al.*, ruling on show cause hearing 1 and 2 December 2004 (Ont. SC). For a discussion of the impact of this ruling, see Rebecca Caldwell, 'Media fear chill from ruling' (*The Globe and Mail*, 3 December 2004); and Dean Jobb, 'On the level: The case of the *Hamilton Spectator* reporter should teach us that it's important to spell out what kind of protection we can offer sources', *Media Magazine* (Winter 2005), 13, 20.

26 *St Elizabeth Home Society v. Hamilton (City)*, 2008 ONCA 182.

27 See *www.caj.ca/principles/principles-statement-investigative-2004.htm*.

28 See Jobb, *Media Law for Canadian Journalists*, 309–10.

29 See Andrew Mitrovica, 'Hear No Evil, Write No Lies' (*The Walrus*, December 2006/January 2007).

30 Nalder, 'Loosening Lips'.

31 Brady, *The Interviewer's Handbook*, 176–78.

32 Brady, *Interviewer's*, 176–78.

33 Brady, *Interviewer's*, 203.

Chapter 9

1 David Stewart Patterson, Canadian Association of Journalists panel discussion (April 1994).

2 Interview with Steve Buist, 11 August 2009.

3 Interview with Buist, 11 August 2009.

4 Interview with Buist, 11 August 2009.

5 Court File No. 31-OR-206980-T, Superior Court of Justice, Commercial list, *In the Matter of the Bankruptcy of The Royal Crest Lifecare Group Inc., First report of the trustee*, 10 November 2003.

6 See *www.ic.gc.ca/eic/site/bsf-osb.nsf/eng/home*.

7 Media outlets such as *The Globe and Mail* usually report on trends when the OSB reports its quarterly statistics on insolvencies, which are comprised of bankruptcies and proposals. For instance, on 12 August 2009, The *Globe's* Report on Business ran a piece on page B7 entitled 'Bankruptcies surge as job losses kick in'. The story was based on the statistics provided in the OSB's latest figures for that time period (*www.ic.gc.ca/eic/site/bsf-osb.nsf/eng/br02258.html*).

8 Interview with Buist, 11 August 2009.

9 Court File No. 31-OR-206980-T, Superior Court of Justice, Commercial list, *In the Matter of the Bankruptcy of The Royal Crest Lifecare Group Inc., First report of the trustee*, 10 November 2003.

10 Contained in a questionnaire Buist completed that asked specific questions about the stories.

11 Court File No. Comm. 32-134239, Comm. 32-134240, Superior Court of Justice—Ontario, *The Bankruptcy of Aldo Anthony Martino, The Bankruptcy of Giovanni (John) Martino*, 24, 25, 27 February 2004, 4.

12 David McKie, 'Advocates demand inquiry into Ontario's costly handling of Royal Crest nursing-home failure', 23 March 2009. See *www.cbc.ca/canada/story/2009/03/23/ontario-royal-crest-nursing-home.html*.

13 Books and Records of the Royal Crest LTC Facilities, April 2007, *Report to Legal Counsel for Her Majesty in Right of The Province of Ontario as Represented by Ontario Internal Audit*, Treasury Board Office, Ministry of Finance from Porter Hetu (Ontario) Inc.

14 Interview with authors, 18 March 2009. Scott James, the commander of the OPP health fraud investigation unit said in part, 'There were no grounds to commence an investigation. We did a thorough review. We didn't touch lightly on this. Taxpayers' dollars are involved.

I believe our full-blown investigation started in the early fall of '07 and over the next year, we were touching on various aspects. And we have other obligations that can sometimes impact on how quickly we can finish a review, but in this case, we were complete in the fall of 2008, reported our findings and closed the file.'

15 Because the Martino brothers conducted business in the United States, Buist broadened his search. In response to a question about the primary sources he used to conduct these searches, he listed the following: corporate and personal bankruptcy documents, US bankruptcy documents, US civil-court case documents through the US PACER system, Ontario Labour Relations Board documents, Ministry of Health documents related to long-term care facilities, land-title documents from a number of Ontario land-registry offices, US corporate-search documents, US property-search documents, Ontario corporate-search documents, Ontario vehicle-registry documents, Ontario personal-property-search documents (liens), Ontario civil-court-case documents.

16 See 'Advocates demand inquiry into Ontario's costly handling of Royal Crest nursing-home failure', 23 March 2009, at *www.cbc.ca/canada/story/2009/03/23/ontario-royal-crest-nursing-home.html*.

17 Conrad C. Fink, *Bottom Line Writing: Reporting the Sense of Dollars* (Ames, IA: Iowa State University Press, 2000), 140.

18 Leah Beth Ward, *What You Can Get from Public and Private Companies in Writing About Business: The New Columbia Knight-Bagehot Guide to Economics and Business Journalism* (New York: Columbia University Press, 2001), 199.

19 Leah Beth Ward, *What You Can Get from Public and Private Companies in Writing About Business: The New Columbia Knight-Bagehot Guide to Economics and Business Journalism* (New York: Columbia University Press, 2001), 197.

20 Chris Roush, *Show Me the Money: Writing Business and Economics Stories for Mass Communication* (New York: Lawrence Erlbaum Associates, 2004), 11.

21 On page 9 of his book, *Understanding Financial Statements*, Jay Taparia stresses the need to read financial statements thoroughly. 'It's absolutely critical for journalists to know the accounting rules underlying the financial statements,' he writes. 'I believe the financial statements provide only 20 percent of the story. You must read the footnotes to learn what accounting rules were applied and how the numbers were calculated. This will get you another 50 to 60 percent of the story. The remaining story comes from knowing what qualitative factors drove the company to generate revenue and profits.'

22 See *www.ic.gc.ca/eic/site/bsf-osb.nsf/eng/h_br01545.html*.

23 A bankruptcy judge under federal law has to be a superior court judge in a provincial court.

24 Interview between David Debenham and the authors, 14 August 2009.

25 See *www.ic.gc.ca/eic/site/bsf-osb.nsf/eng/br01467.html#N*.

26 Journalists can also conduct searches on the site for specific individuals or companies. Usually, there is an $8 fee. However, journalists can apply to the OSB for an exemption, which allows them to search for free. 'We consider that journalists contribute to supporting the integrity of the insolvency system by enabling the public to be well informed,' writes Ginette Trahan, the OSB's director general, Outreach Services, in an email correspondence. Once you are able to confirm that a company has received protection from creditors, or is bankrupt, you can start the real digging. When administering files that receive lots of publicity, many trustees under the BIA, or monitors under the CCAA, create special websites that contain documents related to the case.

27 Mary MacKay, 'A sign of wind energy

times: Prince Edward's Island Entegrity Wind Systems Inc. expands into new sales territory in the United States and Canada' (*The Guardian*, 30 March 2009), B8.

28 Teresa Wright, 'Wind turbine maker going into receivership: Province plans financial help for Entegrity Wind Systems' (*The Guardian*, 16 July 2009), A3.

29 Wayne Thibodeau, 'Wind firm turned down, *The Guardian* has learned' (accessed at *www.theguardian.pe.ca/index. cfm?sid=295171&sc=98* on 16 October 2009).

30 In the personal bankruptcy of John and Aldo Martino, the judge said from the evidence he reviewed, the brothers seemed more interested in lining their pockets than running a successful business. The document (Court File No.: Comm. 32-134239) can be found on CanLII (*http://canlii.org/en/index.php*) by using the search term 'Martino'.

31 'CanLII is a non-profit organization managed by the Federation of Law Societies of Canada. CanLII's goal is to make Canadian law accessible for free on the Internet.' You can find it at *http://canlii.org/en/databases.html*.

32 Interview between David Debenham and the authors, 14 August 2009.

33 Available online at *www.labour.gov.on.ca/ english/es/report_card/rc_2.html*.

34 Kevin Donovan, editor of investigations at the *Toronto Star*, wrote about his award-winning series, Give and Take, in the Canadian Journalists Association's *Media Magazine* special summer 2008 online awards edition (*www.caj.ca/ mediamag/CAR.htm*).

35 See *www.cra-arc.gc.ca/ebci/haip/srch/advanced searchresult-eng.action?n=&b=&q=&s=+ &d=&e=+&c=&v=+&o=&z=&g=+&t =+&y=+&p=1*.

36 You can find the Millennium Scholarship fund's publications at *www.millen niumscholarships.ca/en/research/AllPubli cations.asp*. For its annual report, go to 'About Us', and click on the reports section contained in the menu on the left-hand side (where you'll find the annual reports dating back to 1998).

37 David McKie, 'Bird strikes increasing at Canadian airports', CBC News, 14 May 2009. By law, airports are required to file what's called a *wildlife management plan* that spells out the steps the airport is taking to keep birds and wildlife away from planes. Neither Transport Canada nor the airport in question will advertise these plans, so you must demand them—either informally with a request to a media-relations person, or formally through an access-to-information request.

38 The following URLs lead to stories David McKie and Rob Cribb broadcast and wrote as part of their investigation into the crisis. The stories began during the federal election of October 2008 and continued for several months.
www.cbc.ca/consumer/story/2008/ 09/23/f-cfia.html
www.cbc.ca/consumer/story/2008/ 10/05/listeria-inspections.html
www.cbc.ca/consumer/story/2008/ 10/09/listeria-tests.html
www.cbc.ca/health/story/2008/10/09/ mccain.html
www.cbc.ca/canada/story/2008/10/21/ lawsuit-mapleleaf.html
www.cbc.ca/consumer/story/2008/ 10/27/listeria-nursinghome.html?ref=rss
www.cbc.ca/canada/story/2008/11/06/ listeria-regulations.html?ref=rss
www.cbc.ca/consumer/story/2008/ 11/07/mccain-memos.html
www.cbc.ca/consumer/story/2008/ 12/19/listeria-cfia.html
www.cbc.ca/canada/story/2009/01/20/ listeriosis-investigator.html?ref=rss
www.cbc.ca/canada/story/2009/01/23/ listeria-investigation.html?ref=rss
www.cbc.ca/canada/story/2009/02/05/ poultryvets-cfia.html?ref=rss
www.cbc.ca/canada/story/2009/03/25/ listeria-cfia.html
www.cbc.ca/consumer/story/2009/ 04/21/listeriosis-probe-cfia021. html?ref=rss

www.cbc.ca/canada/story/2009/04/23/ listeriosis-probe.html?ref=rss www.cbc.ca/canada/story/2009/04/30/ listeria-cfia-reports043009.html?ref=rss www.cbc.ca/canada/story/2009/06/10/ listeria-inspectors-maple-leaf.html?ref=rss

39 David McKie, 'Inspectors averaged 2 hours a day inside listeria-infected plant', CBC News (see *www.cbc.ca/can-ada/story/2009/06/10/listeria-inspectors-maple-leaf.html?ref=rss*).

40 It is usually a good idea to peruse the Health Canada and Food and Drug Administration websites in tandem, as in some cases, the FDA may have more information. For instance, every time a drug is approved by the FDA, the company that makes the drug and the FDA scientists who approved it have to appear before one of the agency's committees. Full transcripts of those hearings are available on the FDA website (*www.fda.gov/ohrms/ dockets/ac/acmenu. htm*). In the Relenza example, the committee that originally reviewed it was less than impressed with its efficacy.

Because drug companies are allowed to advertise their products directly to consumers in the United States—a practice that is illegal in Canada—their advertising practices are under constant, if not always rigorous, scrutiny. The FDA has an online database (*www.fda. gov/foi/warning.htm*) of warning letters. During the publicity surrounding anti-inflammatory drugs, these warning letters revealed that the companies had been told about misleading advertising, which came in handy for reporters doing stories in Canada.

41 David McKie, CBC Radio investigative report on Relenza (10 December 1999).

42 David McKie, 'Faint Warning' (CBC Radio, 18 February 2004; available online at *www.cbc.ca/news/adr/media.html*).

43 Roush, *Show Me the Money*, 173.

44 The agricultural union that represents federal meat inspectors with the Canadian Food Inspection Agency was instrumental in monitoring the CFIA's claims on issues such as staffing and adherence to inspection regulations. The union's skepticism about the agency's inability to hire enough inspectors in the lead-up to the listeriosis crisis was echoed in the majority report of a parliamentary committee that studied the issue. And an investigator appointed by Prime Minister Stephen Harper also recommended that extra attention needed to be paid to the staffing issue.

45 Julie Ireton, *The National* (CBC Television, 16 November 2004; available online at *www.cbc.ca/ story/business/ national/2004/11/16/nortel_041116. html*).

46 Teresa Wright, 'Number of Islanders filing for bankruptcy takes dramatic rise: Numbers up by almost 37 per cent in a year' (*The Guardian*, 27 January 2009), A1. During an interview on 23 July 2009, Wright talked about the importance of reporters working in smaller markets such as Charlottetown to find ways to localize important stories about the economy. 'Things that are happening to people elsewhere could have implications locally. And if the question that you ask when reading a story about finances or a national story is "How would that affect your location and my hometown?" then it's important to at least check into it. And in this case, personal bankruptcies did rise on PEI. So, looking at those numbers was a good thing to do because it took something big and showed how it was affecting my readers.'

47 Heather Landy, 'Executives Took, but the Directors Gave' (*The New York Times*, 4 April 2009).

48 The salaries of Ontario's highest-paid public bureaucrats (*www.fin.gov.on.ca/ en/publications/salarydisclosure/2010*) can be downloaded into a spreadsheet like Microsoft's Excel or the database manager, Access. For information on how to perform such tasks, please refer to Chapter 11 of this book for some

of the basics on computer-assisted reporting. For a more detailed explanation of how to analyze Ontario's salary databases using Excel, you can consult Chapters 3 and 4 of *Computer-Assisted Reporting, A Comprehensive Primer*, co-authored by Fred Vallance-Jones and David McKie.

49 It's much more valuable to examine a percentage change than a dollar change. A percentage change can tell you more about how the company is really doing than a raw number, and thus avoid company spin. This is why it's important to do some of the math yourself. If you're unclear about what kinds of ratios to use, talk to an expert such as a business professor.

50 Jay Taparia, *Understanding Financial Statements: A Journalist's Guide* (Portland, OR: Marion Street Press, 2004), 9.

Chapter 10

1 Daniel Leblanc and Campbell Clark, 'Ottawa can't find $550,000 report' (*The Globe and Mail*, 11 March 2002).

2 Leblanc and Clark, 'Ottawa can't find . . .'.

3 *Dagg v. Canada (Minister of Finance)*, [1997] 2 S.C.R., 403.

4 John Reid, 'Annual Report, Information Commissioner 2000–2001' (June 2001).

5 Reid, 'Annual Report' (June 2001).

6 Robert Marleau, Office of the Information Commissioner of Canada, 2008–09 Annual Report, 'Message from the Commissioner'.

7 Denis Desautels, 'Reflections on a decade of serving Parliament' (Office of the Auditor General, February 2001).

8 Desautels, 'Reflections' (Office of the Auditor General, February 2001).

9 Reid, 'Annual Report'. Also: Kathryn May and Glen McGregor, 'Martin's office attempted to influence government contracts' (*Ottawa Citizen*, 23 April 2004). Also: Elizabeth Thompson, 'Guité implicates Martin's office: Sponsorship probe' (*Montreal Gazette*, 23 April 2004).

10 Luke Simcoe. 'Gomery perceives threat to society' (*The StarPhoenix*, 17 April 2009), A4.

11 Alasdair Roberts, interview with the authors.

12 Reid, 'Annual Report' (June 2001).

13 Stanley Tromp, *Fallen Behind: Canada's Access to Information Act in the World Context* (*www3.telus.net/index100/report*), September 2008, 12.

14 Karen Kleiss and Charles Rusnell, 'Critics attack Klein's $3.5-million-a-year air fleet as wasteful' (*Edmonton Journal*, 2 March 2005), A1.

15 Darcy Henton, 'Government deliberately withheld flight logs, adjudicator rules', (*Edmonton Journal*, 27 June 2007), A2.

16 Henton, 'Government deliberately . . .' (*Edmonton Journal*, 27 June 2007), A2.

17 See, for example, the Information and Privacy Commissioner/Ontario, *Order P-1190 and PO-2271*.

18 Information and Privacy Commissioner/Ontario, *Order PO-2271*.

19 Kevin Donovan and Moira Welsh, 'Nursing home records declared to be free' (*Toronto Star*, 27 October 2004).

20 Donovan and Welsh, 'Nursing home records . . .' (*Toronto Star*, 27 October 2004).

21 Donovan and Welsh, 'Nursing home records . . .'.

22 Office of the Information Commissioner of Canada, Case Summary; Canadian Newspaper Association complaint. See www.oic-ci.gc.ca/findings/CNA2008-e.asp.

23 Information Commissioner, Case Summary; Canadian Newspaper Association complaint.

24 Glen McGregor, 'Minister's past expenses raise eyebrows', (*Ottawa Citizen*, 3 April 2009), A3.

25 Joel Kom and Kim Guttormson, 'Taxpayers bought $1863 office chair', (*Calgary Herald*, 11 July 2009), A1.

26 Jim Rankin, Scott Simmie, John Duncanson, Michelle Shephard, and Jennifer Quinn, 'Singled out—*Star* analysis

of police crime data shows justice is different for blacks and whites' (*Toronto Star*, 19 October 2002).

27 Nicolaas van Rijn, 'Ruling favours *Star*; Highest court kills $2.7B class-action libel suit Toronto Police Association's third straight loss' (*Toronto Star*, 28 January 2005).

28 Jim Bronskill, 'Courts bullied; Ottawa seeks remedy' (*Southam News*, 30 December 2000).

29 Jim Bronskill, 'Hundreds of foreign women, girls forced into Canadian sex trade: RCMP report' (*Canadian Press*, 6 December 2004).

30 Jim Bronskill, 'Incoherent jumble of watch-lists could doom anti-terror measures: Report' (*Canadian Press*, 23 January 2005).

31 See, for example, Jack Aubry, 'Government warned in 2002 to give up trying to recoup lost sponsorship funds' (*Ottawa Citizen*, 28 February 2005). Also: Dean Beeby, 'System failing growing numbers of mentally ill convicts, report says' (*Canadian Press*, 27 February 2005); 'Polygamy study partly driven by concern over same-sex legislation: document' (*Canadian Press*, 27 February 2005); 'Tax agency violated government's own rules, audit reveals' (*Canadian Press*, 15 February 2005); David Pugliese, 'Defence papers suggest Canada already involved' (*CanWest News Service*, 25 February 2005).

32 Martin Mittelstaedt, 'Note shows Tories knew of Ipperwash claim' (*The Globe and Mail*, 6 December 1996).

33 Peter Edwards and Harold Levy, 'Ipperwash memo ignored by minister' (*Toronto Star*, 24 July 2000).

34 Edwards and Levy, 'Ipperwash memo . . .'.

35 Ann Rees, 'Tories used bogus delay tactics' (*Toronto Star*, 21 September 2003).

36 Michael Tutton, 'Staff shortages created patient risk in N.S. hospitals' (Canadian Press, 21 June 2009).

37 'eHealth contracts worth $5 million apparently not put to tender, CBC reports' (Canadian Press, 27 May 2009).

38 Tanya Talaga, 'Taxpayers nickel-and-dimed' (*Toronto Star*, 3 June 2009), A3.

39 Tanya Talaga, 'eHealth executive ejected' (*Toronto Star*, 8 June, 2009), A1.

40 Sarah Schmidt, 'UBC rigs class size to boost rank: documents' (*CanWest News Service*, 31 January 2004).

41 Sarah Schmidt, interview with authors.

42 Schmidt, 'UBC rigs class size . . .'.

43 Sarah Schmidt, 'UBC releases letter on university rankings race: Memo written by official calls the university's ratings campaign a "sham"' (*CanWest News Service*, 9 November 2004).

44 Catherine Rolfsen and Mary Frances Hill, '$571,788 severance paid to city manager' (*The Vancouver Sun*, 20 March 2009), A6.

45 Suzanne Wilton, 'East Village firings cost $1M' (*Calgary Herald*, 10 October 2004).

46 Suzanne Wilton, interview with authors.

47 Lisa Priest, 'Health care likely focus for Manley' (*The Globe and Mail*, 15 Feburary 2003).

48 Stanley Tromp, 'Lottery CEO fired one day after poll', (*The Globe and Mail*, 16 October 2007), S1.

49 Chad Skelton, 'Secret tests reveal cattle feed contaminated by animal parts' (*The Vancouver Sun*, 14 December 2004).

50 Chad Skelton, interview with the authors.

51 Robert Cribb, 'Meat inspections lasted less than 2 hours a day' (*Toronto Star*, 11 June 2009), A11.

52 Moira Welsh, 'Shocking neglect of elderly' (*Toronto Star*, 6 December 2003).

53 Moira Welsh, interview with the authors.

54 Dean Beeby, 'Chrétien led bid to reform pot laws' (*Canadian Press*, 22 September 2002).

55 Reid, 'Annual Report'.

56 Press release. 'Commissioner Cavoukian draws the government a blueprint for action on access and privacy' (Office of the Information and Privacy Commissioner/Ontario, 15 June 2004).

57 See Canadian Association of Journalists press releases (*www.caj.ca*) on Code of Silence Award.

58 Canadian Association of Journalists, 'Health Canada wins 4th annual Code of Silence Award' (9 May 2004).

Chapter 11

1 For a more complete list of stories that have used CAR, go to *www.carincanada. ca/Stories.htm*.

2 Adrian Humphreys, *Media Magazine*, 6 (1), 25.

3 Margaret H. DeFleur, *Computer-Assisted Investigative Reporting: Development and Methodology* (New York: Lawrence Erlbaum Associates, 1997), 99.

4 Peter Cheney, Taxi, Special supplement: CAJ Award Winners (*Media Magazine*, Summer 1999), 11.

5 Peter Cheney's account at the 1998 CAJ convention.

6 Peter Cheney, interview with the authors.

7 Cheney, Taxi (*Media Magazine*, Summer 1999), 11.

8 Cheney, interview with the authors.

9 Philip Meyer, interview with authors.

Chapter 12

1 James B. Stewart, *Follow the Story: How to Write Successful Nonfiction* (Touchstone Books, 1998), 72.

2 Roy Peter Clark, 'Writer's Toolbox: A Work in Progress' (available online at *www.poynter.org*).

3 Anne V. Hull, 'Metal to Bone' (*St Petersburg Times*, 2 May 1993).

4 Clark, 'Writer's Toolbox'.

5 Don Gibb, 'Quotes should be real, engaging and meaningful' (*Media Magazine*, Winter 2005), 8.

6 David Stewart-Patterson, 'Economics for the numerically challenged' (Canadian Association of Journalists panel discussion, April 1994).

7 Bob Carty, 'Overdosed: The Drugging of Canadian Seniors' (*The Sunday Edition*, CBC Radio, 10 April 2005;

available online at *www.cbc.ca/news/ background/seniorsdrugs*).

8 Carty, 'Overdosed . . .'.

9 Don Gibb, 'The warm body syndrome' (*Media Magazine*, Fall 2004), 6.

10 For a more detailed examination of defamation law and its impact on journalism, including online journalism, see Dean Jobb, *Media Law for Canadian Journalists*, 2nd ed. (Toronto: Emond Montgomery Publications, 2010), Chapters 9 and 12.

11 Quoted in Robert Martin, 'Ontario paper's coverage shows why we need law of libel' (*The Lawyers Weekly*, 27 March 1992), 12.

12 Michael Crawford, *The Journalist's Legal Guide*, 3rd ed. (Toronto: Carswell, 1996), 18.

13 Robert Martin, *Media Law* (Toronto: Irwin Law, 1997), 122.

14 Raymond E. Brown, *The Law of Defamation in Canada*, 2nd ed. (Toronto: Carswell, 1994), 298–99.

15 Crawford, *Journalist's Legal Guide*, 18–19.

16 *Montague (Township) v. Page*, 2006 CanLII 2192 (Ont. SC).

17 For more on the *Star* investigation and the ensuing lawsuit, see David Akin, 'Race Matters' (*Media Magazine*, Fall 2002); available online at *www.caj.ca/ mediamag/fall2002/race.html*.

18 *A.U.P.E. v. Edmonton Sun* [1986], A.J. No. 1147 (QB).

19 *Booth et al. v. BCTV* [1983], 139 D.L.R. (3d) 88 (BCCA).

20 The leading US case is *The New York Times Co. v. Sullivan* [1964], 376 U.S. 254.

21 *Hill v. Church of Scientology of Toronto*, [1995] 2 S.C.R. 1130.

22 P.J. O'Rourke, *Give War a Chance: Eyewitness Accounts of Mankind's Struggle against Tyranny, Injustice and Alcohol-Free Beer* (Atlantic Monthly Press, 1992), 125.

23 *Hodgson v. Canadian Newspapers Co.* [1998], 39 O.R. (3d) 235 (Gen. Div.) at 252–3.

24 'Calling B.C. alderman a "son of a bitch" isn't libel, but adding "sick" is libel' (*The Lawyers Weekly*, 27 March 1992), 12. The article reports on the ruling in *Ralston v. Fomich*. See also the Canadian Press report of the ruling in *The Press and the Courts. 11.2* (Canadian Newspaper Association), 8.

25 *Gouzenko v. Harris* [1976], 13 O.R. (2d) 730 (HC).

26 Martin, *Media Law*, 126.

27 Crawford, *Journalist's Legal Guide*, 27.

28 *Grant v. Torstar Corp.*, [2009] SCC 61; *Quan v. Cusson*, [2009] SCC 62.

29 *Grant v. Torstar Corp.*

30 See *Reynolds v. Times Newspapers Ltd.*, [2001] 2 A.C. 127, and *Jameel v. Wall Street Journal Europe Sprl*, [2007] 1 A.C. 359.

31 *Grant v. Torstar Corporation*, 2008 ONCA 796; *Cusson v. Quan*, 2007 ONCA 771.

32 Joseph Dean, *Hatred, Ridicule, or Contempt: A Book of Libel Cases* (Penguin Books, 1964), 16.

33 Crawford, *Journalist's Legal Guide*, 34. In 2002 Nova Scotia's Court of Appeal overturned a libel verdict against two lawyers over comments made at a press conference. The fact the comments were made at a press conference, however, was not the deciding factor—the court ruled the statements were protected by privilege because the lawyers had a duty to publicize allegations of racist behaviour by police. See *Campbell v. Jones*, 2002 NSCA 128.

34 Brown, *The Law of Defamation in Canada*, vol. 2: 14–62 to 14–66.

35 *Fletcher-Gordon v. Southam Inc. et al.* [1997], 33 B.C.L.R. (3d) 118 (SC).

36 In a 1999 ruling an Ontario judge noted the media's ability to use the privilege defence 'may be expanding,' particularly when journalists can establish a 'social or moral duty' to report. See *Myers v. Canadian Broadcasting Corp.* [1999], 47 C.C.L.T. (2d) 272 (SCJ), citing *Grenier v. Southam Inc.* [1997], O.J. No. 2193 (C.A.), *Silva v. Toronto Star Newspapers Ltd.* [1998], 167 D.L.R.

(4th) 554, and *Moises v. Canadian Newspaper Co.* [1996], 30 C.C.L.T. (2d) 145 (BCCA). In *Camporese v. Parton* [1983], 150 D.L.R. (3d) 208 (BCSC), a columnist reported that a company might be distributing tainted canned goods. While the information turned out to be false, a judge ruled the warning of possible food poisoning was issued in the public interest and dismissed the company's libel suit.

37 This evolution of the law is noted in *Jameel v. Wall Street Journal Europe Sprl*.

38 *Pearlman v. Canadian Broadcasting Corp.* [1982], Man. L.R. (2d), 1 (Man. QB).

39 *WIC Radio Ltd. v. Simpson*, 2008 SCC 40.

40 See also *Holt v. Sun Publishing Co.* [1979], 100 D.L.R. (3d) 447 (BCCA).

41 This criteria was earlier established in *Chernesky v. Armadale Publishers* [1979], 90 D.L.R. (3d) 321 (SCC).

42 Stephanie Nolen, 'Fiddler was just playing with Halifax newspaper' (*The Globe and Mail*, 29 January 2000), A3.

43 An Ontario judge found that failing to present a balanced report by omitting key information and by 'deliberately' failing to give the plaintiff a chance to respond to criticism defeated a plea of fair comment. *Leenen v. Canadian Broadcasting Corp.* [2000], 48 O.R. (3d) 656, upheld by the Ontario Court of Appeal, 12 June 2001, Docket no. C34272.

44 *Munro v. Toronto Sun Publishing Corp.* [1982], 39 O.R., (2d) 100 (HC).

45 *Leenen v. Canadian Broadcasting Corp.* See note 42.

46 See note 43.

47 See note 42.

Appendix C

1 See *www.ic.gc.ca/eic/site/bsf-osb.nsf/eng/br01467.html#B*.

2 See *www.ic.gc.ca/eic/site/bsf-osb.nsf/eng/br01467.html#B*.

3 See *www.investorwords.com/1245/current_assets.html*.

4 See *www.investorwords.com/1416/depreciation.html*.

5 Chris Roush, *Show Me the Money: Writing Business and Economics for Mass Communication* (New York: Lawrence Erlbaum Associates, 2004), 105.

6 See *www.investorwords.com/2896/loss.html*.

7 See *www.ic.gc.ca/eic/site/bsf-osb.nsf/eng/br01467.html#C*.

8 See *www.investorwords.com/1245/current_assets.html*.

9 See *www.ic.gc.ca/eic/site/bsf-osb.nsf/eng/br01467.html#D*.

10 See *www.investorwords.com/1416/depreciation.html*.

11 Roush, *Show Me the Money*, 105.

12 Jay Taparia, *Understanding Financial Statements: A Journalist's Guide* (Portland, OR: Marion Street Press, Inc, 2004), 25.

13 Roush, *Show Me the Money*, 105.

14 Roush, *Show Me the Money*, 105.

15 Roush, *Show Me the Money*, 324.

16 Roush, *Show Me the Money*, 105.

17 See *www.investorwords.com/2896/loss.html*.

18 See *www.investorwords.com/1245/current_assets.html*.

19 See *www.osc.gov.on.ca/Contact/ct_index.jsp#publicrecords*.

20 Roush, *Show Me the Money*, 90.

21 Roush, *Show Me the Money*, 90. Also, see *www.investorwords.com/3885/profit_margin.html*.

22 Roush, *Show Me the Money*, 90.

23 See *www.ic.gc.ca/eic/site/bsf-osb.nsf/eng/br01467.html#P*.

24 Roush, *Show Me the Money*, 90–91.

25 Taparia, *Understanding Financial Statements*, 78.

26 Roush, *Show Me the Money*, 324.

27 See *www.investopedia.com/terms/o/outstandingshares.asp*.

28 Roush, *Show Me the Money*, 324.

29 See *www.ic.gc.ca/eic/site/bsf-osb.nsf/eng/br01467.html#T*.

30 William Baker, David Dietz, and Jonathan Weil., 'Interpreting Corporate Reports'(Tipsheet at the Investigative Reporters and Editors Conference, Washington, DC, 6 June 2003).

31 Bloomberg, 'Finding and Breaking News from SEC Filings', IRE tipsheet.

32 Christopher Waddell, interview with the authors.

33 Erik Schatzker, 'Backgrounding US Businesses' (seminar at CAJ/IRE workshop in Montreal entitled 'Crossing the 49th', 4 October 2003).

34 Erik Schatzker, 'Backgrounding US Businesses' (4 October 2003).

Index